JOHANNIC BAPTISM

" I STAND to whatever God has said; what men infer from it is merely human and weighs with me just nothing. As a Christian I think I can, in my poor way, defend what God has said; what man has inferred from it man may defend if he can; I am not responsible."

WAYLAND.

" THE meaning of a Greek word, of which he had been ignorant till then, suddenly cleared up his theological ideas. What consolation and what joy did he not feel, when he saw, for instance, that the Greek word μετάνοια, which, according to the Latin Church, signifies a *penance*, a satisfaction required by the Church, a human expiation, really meant in Greek, a *transformation* or *conversion* of the heart. A thick mist was suddenly rolled away from his eyes."

LIFE OF LUTHER.

" A DOCTRINE of grace may dwell in the right understanding of a single preposition."

LILLIE.

JOHANNIC BAPTISM

BAΠTIZΩ

AN INQUIRY INTO THE
MEANING OF THE WORD
AS DETERMINED BY THE USAGE OF
THE HOLY SCRIPTURES

BY

James W. Dale

NEW INTRODUCTION
BY
Robert H. Countess

Bolchazy-Carducci Publishers
P&R Publishing Company
Loewe Belfort Projects, Inc.

Cover design
Cynthia Henderson

Reprint of
1898 Edition, Philadelphia
Presbyterian Board of Publication and Sabbath-School Work

© Copyright 1993
Robert H. Countess, Introduction

Published by:

BOLCHAZY-CARDUCCI   P&R
PUBLISHERS   PUBLISHING
1000 Brown Street   P.O. Box 817
Wauconda, IL 60084   Phillipsburg, NJ 08865

ISBN 0-86516-259-X   ISBN 0-87552-232-7

LOEWE BELFORT
PROJECTS, INC.
120 Sagewood Circle
Toney, AL 35773

Printed in the United States of America

Library of Congress Cataloging-in-Publication Data

Dale, James W. (James Wilkinson), 1812-1881.
    [Inquiry into the usage of [baptizō] and the nature of Johannic
baptism, as exhibited in the Holy Scriptures]
    Johannic baptism : [baptizō] : an inquiry into the meaning of the
word as determined by the usage of the Holy Scriptures / by James W.
Dale : new introduction by Robert H. Countess.
       p. cm.
    Originally published: An inquiry into the usage of [baptizō] and the
nature of Johannic baptism, as exhibited in the Holy Scriptures.
Philadelphia : Presbyterian Board of Publication and Sabbath-School
Work, 1898. With new introd.
    Includes bibliographical references and indexes.
    ISBN 0-86516-259-X — ISBN 0-87552-232-7
    1. Baptism. 2. Baptism—Biblical teaching. 3. Baptizein (The
Greek word) 4. John, the Baptist, Saint. 5. Bible. N.T.—Criticism,
interpretation, etc. I. Title.
BV811.D33 1993
234'.161'09015—dc20   93-25479

INTRODUCTION

Robert H. Countess

JOHANNIC BAPTISM heralds the opportunity for serious students and casual readers to confront New Testament usage firsthand of the famous duo *bapto* and *baptizo*.

The reprints of *Classic Baptism* (1989) and *Judaic Baptism* (1991) may have, at first glance, appeared to be of interest to specialists in Ancient Greek and thus to have little direct bearing on New Testament study. However, the present volume should dispel such thinking as it will demonstrate that they were necessary precursors in building-block fashion.

Based upon *usage* only, we confront the question, How did John the Baptist/Baptizer apply water when he baptized multitudes and, at length, Jesus Christ with water? Dr. Dale's answer is found at the end of this volume, similarly as I found, when an algebra student, the answers to the problems at the end of the textbook. He concludes:

> The manner of using the water in John's ritual baptism is not stated by any word. The word *baptizo,* as used in Scripture, has no more control over or connection with the manner of using this water, than a broken arm has control over or connection with the movement of the solar system.
>
> Dipping or mersing "into water" is phraseology utterly unknown to John's baptism. (p. 417)

I must urge readers of this volume to refer back to my Introduction in *Classic Baptism* (pp. 3-15) for an overview to this five-volume series, especially the two illustrations I

(v)

sketched, Figures One and Two. Understanding this material is a must, for without it the reader may wander in a
bewildering maze needlessly.

It does bear repeating, however, that Dale did not try to
solve the problem of baptizing infants. (He in fact did baptize
them.) He also did not cast aspersions on those who apply the
water of ceremonial baptism in specific ways: dipping, pouring, sprinkling. What he did attack was the *dogmatism* of
anyone who insisted that ceremonial baptism *had* to be
performed by the application of water in a certain manner.

Johannic Baptism will further concretize his conclusions.

Students must learn anew that Dale's results will fly in
the face of dictionary entries, even that of the *Theological
Dictionary of the New Testament* (1:529ff.). And students
may learn the valuable lesson that dictionaries are guides,
not dogmatic authorities. *Usage* is always the key to understanding a word.

In short, Dale's twenty-year examination of usage of
baptizo in contexts led him to state succinctly that

WHATEVER IS CAPABLE OF THOROUGHLY CHANGING THE CHARACTER,
STATE, OR CONDITION OF ANY OBJECT, IS CAPABLE OF BAPTIZING THAT
OBJECT: AND BY SUCH CHANGE OF CHARACTER, STATE, OR CONDITION
DOES, IN FACT, BAPTIZE IT. (*Classic Baptism,* p. 354)

Again, special appreciation goes to Bryce Craig and Lou
Bolchazy for their collaborative support of this reprint project.
Their effort makes possible a transforming experience like
that of Martin Luther when he realized that the Greek word
metanoia was quite differently *used* by the New Testament
authors from the churchly Latin *penance,* the latter connot-
ing human expiation for sins. For Luther, discovering that
metanoia conveyed *in context* a transformation of the human
heart when confronted by the grace of God in Christ's atoning work, was like a thick mist rolling away from his eyes.

Readers of *Johannic Baptism* may also learn that the
dogmatism of "the theorists" cannot stand the hard scrutiny
of the canons of *usage.*

JOHANNIC BAPTISM.

1.

BAPTIST CRITICISMS.

2.

VARIOUS VIEWS OF JOHN'S BAPTISM.

3.

JOHN'S KNOWLEDGE OF $\beta\alpha\pi\tau i\zeta\omega$.

4.

JOHN'S COMMISSION.

5.

PLACES OF BAPTISM.

6.

BAPTISM OF THE LORD JESUS.

7.

SUMMARY.

New Testament usage of βαπτιστὴς, βάπτισμα, and βαπτίζω; New Testament usage of ἐν and εἰς; Their discriminating usage in baptism; Agreement and difference as compared with Classic and Jewish usage; A dipping is not a baptism; A dipping into water is not John's baptism; There is no exemplification of physical baptism in the New Testament; The word βάπτισμα originates in the New Testament; New

DIVERSE BAPTISMS.

PASSAGES OF SCRIPTURE EXAMINED.

PASSAGES OF SCRIPTURE REFERRED TO.

AUTHORS QUOTED OR REFERRED TO

Alford,
Alex. Aphrod.,
Ambrose,
Æsop,
Alcibiades,
Arrian,
Augustin,
Arnold, Prof. A. N.,
Alciphron,
Apocrypha,
Achil. Tat.,
Akiba Rabbi,
Barclay,
Basil,
Beecher,
Bengel,
Beza,
Booth,
Calvin,
Campbell, of **Bethany,**
Campbell, of **Aberdeen,**
Clem. Alex.,
Coleman,
Cox,
Conant,
Carson,
Cod. Sin.,
Cyprian,
Cyril,
Dagg,
De Wette,
Douay,
Didymus,
Ebrard,
Ellicott,
Epiphanius,
Ernesti,

Eupolis,
Eustathius,
Fairbairn,
Firmilian,
Fuller,
Gale,
Godwin,
Grotius,
Gregory,
Hodge,
Heliodorus,
Hippolytus,
Halley,
Hall,
Hackett,
Hilary,
Heracleon,
Harrison,
Ingham,
Irenæus,
Jelf,
Jerome,
Jewett,
Josephus,
John of Dam.,
Kuinöl,
Kühner,
Kalisch, Rabbi **Isidor,**
Lange,
Lexicons,
Lexicographers,
Le Nourry, Alex. D.,
Lightfoot,
Lucian,
Matthies,
Maimonides,
Martyr, Justin,

JOHANNIC BAPTISM.

INTRODUCTORY EXAMINATION

OF CRITICISMS AND OF SOME THINGS ADJACENT.

JOHANNIC BAPTISM now claims our attention. But before entering upon the direct consideration of this subject, there are some things suggested by friends of the theory in their notices of the Inquiry, as thus far prosecuted, which claim attention. Passing by the elegant sneer and the supercilious contempt (which has now become so much a part of the theory that it is looked for as a matter of course), and cheerfully confessing that this shower of expletives falls more worthily on myself than upon those who have gone before me, I proceed to matters more important to the merits of the subject. Very earnest complaint has been made that nothing has been said about Lexicons; undoubting confidence has been expressed in the worth of Talmudic traditions; and the judgment of a worthy Russian councillor has been offered as the conclusion of the whole matter.

It is most true, that in this Inquiry but little has been said about Lexicons, and but little reference has been made to the authority of the wise and the good. And this has been said to be the result of ignorance. Perhaps it was so. But happily for the relief of one so ignorant there comes from the wisest and the best the acknowledgment that higher than they, and rightful claimant to supreme homage from all, is the Usage of language. To this appeal has been made. The language of Plato and of Plutarch, of Josephus and of Philo has been quoted as expository of their understanding of the use and meaning of words. My office has been a very humble one; that, simply, of quotation, of comparison, and of

2

analysis. If quotation has not been made correctly, if comparison has not been made fairly, if analysis has not been
made thoroughly, the facts still remain out of which error
may be rebuked and truth may be vindicated. The hardest
blow which a wrongdoer can receive is from *the proof* that
he has done wrong. The whip whose thongs are made up
of charges of "ignorance," and "idiocy," and "pedantry,"
and "imposture," and "impudence," and "insolence," may,
perchance, hurt the smiter quite as badly as the smitten.

But while Lexicon and Talmudic tradition may be fairly
omitted when determining the meaning of a word by the
highest authority, still some notice may be given to these
sources of information when relied upon by others, and
thrust prominently forward by them into notice. This will,
now, be done in connection with a brief glance at some
notices, from Baptist sources, of this Inquiry as already
developed.

AMERICAN CHRISTIAN REVIEW.

"Mr. Dale, the author of Judaic Baptism, is a clear and
vigorous writer, courteous and respectful to those who differ
from him, and discusses the question of the action of baptism
with some degree of candor and ability.

"He argues that it is not a specific word, and therefore
has no clearly defined modal signification. In the estimation
of Mr. Dale, *baptizo* does not express action, but rather condition. He says, 'It utterly rejects modal act as its meaning.' 'It shows, in the most absolute manner, the meaning
to be a condition effected by an unexpressed act.'

"If he will pardon us, we feel like expressing the opinion,
that the argument throughout, whether intended or not, is
an effort to obscure the plain and simple meaning of a positive ordinance of Christ, and to darken counsel by a show
of learning and by a multitude of words without knowledge. We have not examined it sufficiently for an elaborate
review."

The first paragraph is quoted to deal fairly with the theory.
The debit and the credit side of the account should be fairly

posted. Whatever of relative value should be given to "clearness," "vigor," "respectful," "candor," "ability," as over against "idiocy," "trickery," "insolence," "sophistry," and "ignorance," I leave to be settled, without appeal, by those who thus differ about the "Inquiry," and yet differ no more as to this, than they differ as to the meaning of the word in dispute.

The second paragraph is quoted in order to show that the representation given of the theory, namely, that it declares βαπτίζω to express *a specific act* to be done, and not a specific condition to be effected by any competent act, is accepted as a correct statement. It is not easy to secure this confession. It is simply impossible to get any one to stand by it when it is made. Even the honest and courageous Carson shrinks from meeting the issues. And the bold and confident Campbell, of Bethany, dare not follow the confession to its logical end. Whether Dr. Conant, who has brought so much labor and learning to bear upon this word, makes such admission as to its character, it would, perhaps, be venturesome to say, since he has said so much on both sides; but there is no peril in saying that he has made no attempt to maintain it. But whatever else may be said about it, this is true; that just here is the pulsating point in the life of this controversy, and hence must the theory draw its legitimate life-development, or here, under the piercing sword of truth, perish.

The third paragraph shows what has characterized every notice of this Inquiry from Baptist sources, namely, *an indisposition to meet the issue in hand.* Classic Baptism presented a distinct and well-defined issue. In its discussion there was no reference to "the ordinance of Christ." Was this sharply defined issue, free from entanglement, met? There was no attempt to do it. Some, in wonder, exclaimed, "Why he has not so much as stated what he thinks Christian baptism to be!" And others said, "We will wait and see how this ends." In Judaic Baptism there was also presented an issue having equally clear boundaries separating it from "the ordinance of Christ," affording a field to deter-

mine the usage of this word by Jewish uninspired writers
without once touching the distracting element of "the ordinance." Has there been any attempt made to rebut the
evidence sustaining the usage claimed for this word by these
writers? There has been none. At least none better than
that of the "American Christian Review," a lament over
"an effort to obscure the plain and simple meaning of a
positive ordinance of Christ," about which ordinance not
one word was said!

RELIGIOUS HERALD.

"We have neither time, space, nor inclination to review
Judaic Baptism.

"We had hoped that the Doctor would stick to his first
definition of *baptizo*. It was interesting and instructive to
observe the precision with which *merse* (or immerse as we
use it) answered to *baptizo* through all its variations in Greek
literature.

"We are really desirous to know to what conclusion Dr.
Dale proposes to conduct us."

The Religious Herald concluded a long review of Classic
Baptism by saying, "We can only promise that should life,
and strength, and opportunity be allowed us, and should we
be able to procure the forthcoming volumes, we will give
them a candid notice. Here, for the present, we take respectful leave of Mr. Dale."

Willing to submit the results of our inquiry to any fair
criticism, and especially pleased to have the intelligent judgment of those holding different views, this proposal of the
Herald to review Judaic Baptism, "should life, and strength,
and opportunity allow, and a book be procurable," was met
by forwarding an early copy of that work. But somehow
or other there was no review. The reason assigned was,
not that a copy was not procurable; its reception was acknowledged. It was not that "life, or strength, or opportunity" had proved treacherous; but "time, and space, and
inclination" were lacking. How this latter trio happened
to take the place of the former triplet I cannot say. The

case, however, is mainly remarkable only as being ditto to a number of other cases. Copies of Judaic Baptism were sent to leading Baptist periodicals, but if one of them (except the Religious Herald) has done so much as to acknowledge the reception of a copy, it is more than has come to my knowledge. Every one must select their own line of policy. And if this be the policy of the friends of the theory, no one has a right to interfere with it. And the discourtesy of interfering with it even in appearance, by sending a copy of the present volume will, probably, not be committed.

There is as much fairness, perhaps, as could be expected from one not feeling his cause to be strong in truth, in the statement, that Judaic Baptism abandons the definition given of $\beta\alpha\pi\tau\acute{\iota}\zeta\omega$ in Classic Baptism. The Herald had before it (in the book which it reviewed through nine columns), on p. 135, the following definition formally stated: " I would define $\beta\alpha\pi\tau\acute{\iota}\zeta\omega$ to mean primarily, 1. To INTUSPOSE;" which general statement of the thought is illustrated by *five* more specifically defining terms, and one by appropriation. " 2. To INFLUENCE CONTROLLINGLY:" Which general thought is illustrated, also, by *five* other terms defined specifically, as, also, an appropriation growing out of this secondary sense. It is farther stated, that *to stupefy, to bewilder, to pollute, to purify,* &c., are correct defining terms of the Greek word. Was it in view of this definition that the Herald said, that *merse—immerse* was the defining term "through all variations in Greek literature?" Is it said, that "merse" is used in all the translations where $\beta\alpha\pi\tau\acute{\iota}\zeta\omega$ occurs? That is most true; but it is also most expressly stated (p. 132), that this word entirely fails to express the thought of the Greek word in primary use where *influence* is to be developed; that it fails to express it in *secondary* use; and that it fails to express it in absolute use. But as it expresses the idea of $\beta\alpha\pi\tau\acute{\iota}\zeta\omega$, to some extent, in its primary use (and no word in the English language does it throughout), it was used in all translations to *represent*, not to *define*, the Greek word.

I would not make this statement if it were not that others also had, for some cause, found it more agreeable to substitute their own statement in this matter for that given in Classic Baptism.

As to the "conclusion to which Mr. Dale proposes to conduct the Herald," I would say, Mr. Dale knows nothing about the road or the end except as marked by the footprints of the word. His business is to track the word. He has not "proposed to conduct" the Herald through Classic or Jewish paths. Βαπτίζω has been the conductor. I propose again to place myself under the same sure guidance, having no "conclusion" of my own, and if the Herald will bear me company, we will together find such conclusion as John's use of the word shall conduct us to.

CHRISTIAN STANDARD.

The Christian Standard contains a review of Classic Baptism extending through several numbers and covering some dozen columns. The goodnaturedness of the writer shows that he would not willingly harm any one, and disarms any one of all wish to harm him. The errors of the review are so many, so varied, and so patent, as to preclude all discussion. The review reminds one of the profound skill of those engineers whom Napoleon encountered in his Egyptian campaign, who planted their cannon so as to be immovable, and which the Great Captain made worthless by changing the line of his approach. The likeness, however, is not without a difference. Those guns were shotted, and originally pointed against the enemy; but the guns of the review have their muzzles toward the earth, toward the sky, toward the right of Classic Baptism, toward the left of Classic Baptism, and when the fusillade is over, the enemy is found in front, smiling at the engineering wit, and admiring the pyrotechnics of unshotted guns.

NATIONAL BAPTIST.

In an article headed "Dr. Dale and the Jewish Rabbi," the National Baptist remarks: "We only wish to say that a modern Jewish Rabbi has been studying the subject of baptism, and he reaches a very different conclusion from Dr. Dale. Rabbi Isidor Kalisch, of New York, writes to the Christian Union that all Christians are astray on the form of baptism. 'Baptism has been for thousands of years a sign of admittance to Judaism. It was adopted as an initiatory rite at the beginning of the Christian religion. All Christian sects perform it now in a very different manner from its original and proper form.' 'It appears from the ancient traditions, handed down to us in the Talmud, that proselytes, male and female, were baptized *in a nude state*, and by *a submersion of the whole body in water*. All agreed, in ancient times, that *immersion of the whole body* (not the clothes) in water was necessary for a new member of the Jewish or Christian religion. There was *no sprinkling of water*, as can be seen by a description of the baptism which was performed by John. Yes, the Greek expression *baptisma*, used in the New Testament, shows clearly that *submersion of the whole body in water* is required. It is certain that this ceremony was scrupulously done in the Jewish style. A real baptizing, or bathing of the body, and not of the clothes, ought to take place, and hence male should be baptized by male, and female by female. *This is now customary among the Jews, and has been from time immemorial.*'

"We commend that last sentence to Dr. Dale. It is almost too bad that a man, who has probably not seen his book, should thus summarily upset its very foundation, and unqualifiedly deny its chief assertion. We are not disposed to make any rash promises, but we shall not accept the premises and conclusions of Judaic Baptism until its author has satisfactorily answered Rabbi Kalisch."

If the National Baptist is to become a proselyte to the very worthy Rabbi Isidor Kalisch, and henceforth be *addictus jurare* to whatever this new "master" may teach, it might be well to take a second look before leaping into the dark.

Has the National Baptist accepted that last sentence commended to Dr. Dale, to wit, "This, baptizing men and wo-

men naked, is now customary among the Jews, and has been
from time immemorial?" Is the error too "naked" to win
acceptance? Then why "commend to Dr. Dale?" Was it
the "submersion" without the nakedness? But I find no
rule in "Starkie on Evidence" which allows a party to sift
the evidence of his own witness on the stand and take only
what suits him, and reject what don't suit him. Besides,
your witness says, "the submersion," in itself, is worthless;
that submersion with the clothing on is only a baptism "of
the clothes," and not "of the body," and therefore is not
worth a straw. Is it by this teaching of the "magister" that
the National Baptist "swears?" But John the Baptist and
the Apostles surely baptized in the same way—"men and
women in a nude state." Is this, too, a part of the new faith
of the National Baptist? Did John baptize only men? If
so, who was his illustrious coadjutrix that baptized the
women? It has, heretofore, been found to be an infinite
embarrassment for the theory to dispose of men and women
coming out of the river with their clothing soaked with
water; has this learned Rabbi been introduced to solve the
difficulty? And is the solution this? Their clothes were
not wet at all; for men and women to be baptized with their
clothes on is to baptize *the clothes*, not the body; "they were
baptized in a nude state, male by male and female by female."
And who can deny that this meets the difficulty in the most
absolute manner? A way has been found, through the traditions of the Talmud, by which men and women may be
dipped in the Jordan without moistening a thread of their
clothing. Let no one hereafter say—"Wet clothes!" But
the Rabbi says, "It is certain that this ceremony was scrupulously done in the Jewish style, by the Apostles" as well
as by John. With the permission of the National Baptist,
I would like to inquire of this witness, What female (inasmuch as Paul did not "lead about a sister") baptized Lydia?
And while the witness is on the stand, another question:
Rabbi Kalisch, do you think that there were likely to be any
children in the household of Lydia, or of the Jailor, or of
Stephanas, and if so, what was to be done with such children

of proselyted parents? " Children are generally an appendage to households, and they were baptized with their parents." But is not the baptism of children " a rag from the lady that dresses in purple?" In other words, Did you not " borrow this practice from the Romish church?" " Oh, no; this has been our practice from time immemorial; ' for thousands of years' before the church of Rome existed we baptized little children." Well, that will answer on that point, unless the National Baptist should enter a plea against the credibility of its own witness. But we are not in the habit of regarding Talmudic traditions as the best authority for either faith or practice. I would like, however, to ask of the National Baptist (which has introduced a witness testifying that the baptism of John was a waif picked up as it was floating by on the stream of Jewish tradition), what answer it would give to that old question, " The baptism of John, was it from heaven or of men?" This question bothered the Jews when it was first asked. It may not bother this Jewish Rabbi, now, for he is not (as were his ancestors) " afraid of the people;" but it might be supposed that the Christian National Baptist would hesitate to say that John's baptism was not " from heaven," but emerged out of the turbid flood of Talmudism.

But, Rabbi, our editorial friend, who has brought you into the witness-box, says, that, without seeing Judaic Baptism, you have " upset its very foundation, and unqualifiedly denied its chief assertion." Is this so? Judaic Baptism " asserts" that the end of Judaic Baptisms was ceremonial purification. Do you deny this " unqualifiedly," or in any other way? " Certainly not; that has been settled with us for ' thousands of years.' " Judaic Baptism also " asserts," that ceremonial purification is effected, indifferently and equally, by various acts. Do you " unqualifiedly" deny this? " I unqualifiedly affirm it." Judaic Baptism " asserts" that βαπτίζω is used in the narration of these purifications in which diverse acts are employed, and makes this (proved to be true), the foundation for the farther " assertion," that this Greek word cannot be used to express a definite act, and must be

used to express the common result of these diverse acts,
namely, ceremonial purification. Now, have you upset
("without seeing the book"), or do you claim the power to
"upset this foundation?" "Well, the way in which you
state the case puts another aspect on the matter. When my
Baptist friend, here, called me to his help, he told me that
you gave no meaning to '*baptize*,' and that it might be 'sig-
nificant or nonsensical,' 'anything or nothing,' or might just
as well, or a little better, have been left 'blank.' And I told
him that Jewish *practice* in the baptism of proselytes was by
submersion in a nude state. But, now that I have seen your
book, I perceive that you have said nothing about proselyte
baptism, and made no denial of Jewish *practice* in receiving
proselytes." No; I have done neither; and for the very
simple reason that up to the time of John, in following
βαπτίζω to know its meaning from usage, I have never met
with it as used by a Jew in connection with any proselyte
baptism. But I would take it as a very special favor if you
would point out a few of such cases that I might examine
them. "There are no such cases." Well, any time during
John's ministry. "There are none. The subject is not
mentioned by Philo or Josephus, or by the Targums of
Onkelos or Jonathan. But it is mentioned in the Jerusalem
Talmud, written in the latter part of the third century, and
by the Babylonian Talmud, written in the fifth century, and
by Pseudo-Jonathan, who wrote in the seventh or eighth
century, and by Maimonides, in the twelfth century. But
we have no doubt at all, *from our traditions*, that proselyte
baptism was practiced a thousand years before John was
born." Have you been able to satisfy the learned world of
the truth of such tradition? "Not exactly." Is there any
agreement among learned men, outside of the traditionists,
as to the existence of proselyte baptism in the time of John?
"I must confess that there is not." I hope, then, you will
hold me excusable for not mentioning among Jewish baptisms, of written record, that proselyte baptism which, if it
has a traditional life before John, has left behind no written
monument to testify of its existence. My business is to learn

the meaning of βαπτίζω from its use in the writings of those who understood the Greek language. I cannot cite as contemporaneous *writings* the most venerable traditions which crop out centuries after, even though they claim to go back so far that "the memory of man runneth not to the contrary."

However, as our friend of "the National" thinks that you can upset the foundations of things without even seeing them, by your knowledge of this word, and as I am quite willing for error to be upset, and myself with it, so far as I rest upon it, please give us your views of this much-debated βαπτίζω. "I do not know that I have much to say about βαπτίζω." Indeed! and why not? "I am a Jewish Rabbi. Jews don't write in Greek. The Talmud, Babylonian and Jerusalem, the Targums of Onkelos, Jonathan, Pseudo-Jonathan, and Joseph the Blind, as well as Mishna, are all written in another language." Well, this is not a little surprising. Our Baptist friend has brought you, the very learned Rabbi Isidor Kalisch, forward to upset the foundation of a Greek word (established by the usage of Greek writers through more than a half thousand years) by means of a lever whose long arm is weighted by centuries of Talmudic traditions, and whose fulcral point is a Hebrew root! Is not this novel? But Jew or Greek, tradition or record, let us learn. What is this Hebrew word, and by what alchemy does it become transmuted into Greek? Will you, Rabbi, instruct us on these points? "When we speak of *baptizing* proselytes we use, in Hebrew, the word טָבַל. Some might say that we borrowed this word ('baptize'), in this application, from Christians or from John, while we would claim its use before Christianity or John, and from time immemorial, and as a translation of the Hebrew word." A discussion of your right of proprietorship in this word since John's baptism might involve us in all the intricacies of the *sub lite* question, What is the origin of proselyte baptism? therefore, passing this by, please inform us by what right, at or before John's time, you make טָבַל represent βαπτίζω. ."The New Testament and the Apocrypha, both, show that

βαπτίζω was used to express Jewish purifications at and lor g
before the time of John." This is certain. Now, make it
as certain by contemporaneous writing, that these purifyings,
baptizings, were called *tabalings*, and in what sense such
designation was used. "I do not know that I have the
materials for doing the one or the other." Have you the
materials for determining, in any way, the meaning during
this period of this Hebrew word and its relation to the
Greek word? "Yes; the Septuagint, a translation by Jews
of the Hebrew Scriptures into Greek, made before John and
current in his day, furnishes such material. The word occurs in the Hebrew Bible some eighteen times. It is found
once (1 Chron. 26 : 11) in composition as a proper name,
signifying, as some (Gesenius) suppose, 'Whom Jehovah
has *purified*.' In Ezekiel 23 : 15 it is applied, in a derivative,
to a head-dress, with the meaning *dyed*. In Genesis 37 : 31
it is translated (μολύνω) *to smear*, *to stain*. In all other passages
it is translated by βάπτω, except in II Kings 5 : 14, where it
is translated by βαπτίζω." It appears, then, that out of eighteen cases of usage, it is untranslated once (Ταβλαὶ), in a
proper name, having as supposed the significance, *washed*,
cleansed, purified; once translated *dyed* (παραβαπτά); once translated *stained*, and in all other cases translated by βάπτω, with
one exception, where βαπτίζω appears; that is to say, it is
translated by βάπτω fifteen times out of eighteen. Now, can
you tell me in what sense the Hebrew word is used these
fifteen times, and can you give any reason why there should
be an exception to the otherwise uniform translation in the
two instances you have mentioned? "There is little or no
question from any quarter as to the meaning of the Hebrew
word and as to the meaning to be attached to its translation
by the Septuagint in these fifteen passages. There is common consent that the meaning of both words is *to dip*. The
translation (μολύνω) in Genesis 37 : 31 may be accounted for
by supposing that the Hebrew word, like the Greek, meant
to dye, to stain, as well as *to dip*, or that the translators chose
to express *the effect* of the dipping rather than *the act* itself.
And it may be that the other exceptional case (II Kings

5 : 14) should be explained in the same way. It is possible that the Hebrew word may have obtained, as some (Gesenius, De Wette, Stuart, and others) suppose, the secondary meaning, *to wash, to cleanse, to purify.* The Chaldee Targum uses the same word (טְבַל, *to wash, to cleanse*—Godwin) to express the command, 'Go *wash*' (רְחַץ), and the execution of the command (טְבַל). It may also weigh with some, in assigning a meaning to the word in this passage, that it is not the performance of an act that is involved or commanded, but a purification by a miraculous healing. In view of all the facts, it is possible that the translators may have attributed a secondary meaning to the word in this passage, as in Genesis 37 : 31, and expressed that meaning by βαπτίζω; or if they supposed a definite act to have been performed (which was not in the command), they have preferred to express in their translation the effect secured and not the act done. Whether Joseph's coat was 'dipped' or not, the Septuagint was right in saying that it was *stained;* and whether Naaman dipped himself or not, the Septuagint was right in saying that he was *purified* from his leprosy." Then these Jewish translators represent the meaning of the Hebrew word to be, 1. To dip, 2. To dye, 3. Possibly, to *cleanse,* which they express in Greek by βάπτω; while there is no sufficient evidence to show that in the single instance in which they use βαπτίζω that they designed to express *the act* of dipping. Are there any other translations of the Hebrew Scriptures into Greek that bear upon this question? "Aquila translates the word in Job 9 : 31, '*baptize* in corruption.' Symmachus translates the kindred word (טָבַע) in Psalm 69 : 3, '*baptized* in boundless depths.' An unknown writer also translates the same word, as Symmachus, by *baptize.* And the Septuagint, translating Isaiah 21 : 4, *terror terrifies* me, not verbally but *ad sensum,* substitutes 'iniquity *baptizes.*' In none of these cases is there expressed the specific act of *dipping* which belongs to βάπτω." Two things then, Rabbi, appear to be very clear from your statements : 1. The Jewish translators of the Hebrew Scriptures understood טְבַל to

express the specific act *to dip*, and therefore employed βάπτω (which in Greek has the same specific meaning) as its trans-lation. 2. They refused to translate by βαπτίζω, because it did not mean *to dip*, but employed it where no definite act was to be expressed, but a state or condition. Will you now tell me whether any of the personal washings or purifications enjoined upon the Jews by the divine law were ever expressed by טָבַל? "They were not." Will you tell me what is the word which you find in Jewish Greek writings to express ceremonial purifications for one or more centuries before John's time, and reaching to his time; was it βάπτω or βαπτίζω? "It was βαπτίζω, and never βάπτω." Do you mean to say that that word, βάπτω, which the Jewish Bible translators use as the representative of טָבַל (while they steadily refuse to represent it by βαπτίζω), is never employed in ceremonial purifications, while βαπτίζω always is? "Such is the fact." Then you confess that your tabal-baptizing is not derived from the written law of Moses, and is by the authority of Jewish translators of the Hebrew Scriptures declared to be an unlawful conjunction of terms, except as the Hebrew word may have laid aside its primary significa-tion of a specific act? "That would seem to be a fair con-clusion. But remember that Talmudic traditions are, with us, of supreme authority." I do not propose to meddle with your traditions. Hand them over to our friend of "the National." And give him a friendly caution against "bap-tizing clothes;" as also against forgetting that whatever may be the character of the Talmudic טָבַל, that word in the He-brew Old Testament is not quite the same as the βαπτίζω of the Greek New Testament. And now, Rabbi, if "the Na-tional" does not wish your presence any farther, we will, with thanks for your information, and admiration of the manner in which you "upset the foundations," respectfully bid adieu. What says the National Baptist?

The National Baptist says, "The cross-examination of wit-nesses is a nuisance. Talmudic traditions are as good as gospel when for the theory. They are as worthless as old

wives' fables when against it. The Rabbi has no right to
say that our baptism is worth nothing because we baptize
'clothes.' He has no right to say that the children of proselytes should be baptized with their parents. He has no right
to say that טָבַל is not βαπτίζω. He can go. He had better
never have come."

VOCABULARY—THEOLOGICAL SEMINARY TANG.

In a second article the National Baptist deals so largely in
the vocabulary, and in that theological seminary "tang,"
heretofore noticed, that we could almost believe that the pen
which wrote this second article was dipped into this same
theological seminary ink-bottle. It reads thus: "And now
for the *redoubtable* Dr. Dale. Our *honest* opinion of Dr. Dale's
books is that, besides being *a reproach to American letters*, they
are *a direct insult* to Presbyterian scholarship. He *openly
snubs* every eminent Presbyterian writer on the subject of
baptism, from John Calvin to Alexander Hodge." " Others
show *some honesty and principle*" (Dr. Dale shows none).
" Dr. Dale is a *mere sophist and trickster.*" " He is shut up
to solitary seclusion; all the thinking world is outside. We
have no wish to disturb his *repose and egotism*, and leave his
books to the *ridicule and oblivion* which await them."

"Honest" opinions are always valuable. They show
truthfully the mind and heart of the utterer of them, even
if they do not show truthfully the merits or demerits of the
subject embraced in them. When the National Baptist says
this is our " honest" opinion, does it mean to say that the
opinion heretofore expressed of " Dr. Dale and his volumes"
was *not* "honest?" That there is some difference between
this " honest opinion" and that "free to say" opinion, the
following citations from an earlier number of the National
Baptist will show: "Dr. Dale has spent a great deal of time
and labor, *and no small ability*, in investigating the subject,
and in some respects, to say the least, is *entitled to speak with
confidence* on the subject." " To observe what impression he
has made on *some of the first scholars* of the country is to find

evidence that the work is *worthy of careful attention.* For Dr. Jonathan Edwards says, ' It is the most complete, unanswerable, and amiable treatise the Church possesses on this point.' Dr. Thomas H. Skinner says, ' I marvel at the labor and ability shown in your masterly discussion.' Dr. Plummer says, ' Mr. Dale proves that Baptist argument has no weaker point than philology.' While similar testimony is given by Dr. Hodge, Dr. Lyman Coleman, Dr. Henry B. Smith, and many others prominent in different pœdobaptist denominations." " The *deliberateness and fulness* of the investigation *challenge our admiration.*" " We are free to say that Mr. Dale's labors *cannot prove worthless or unimportant.* He *has established a difference* between βάπτω and βαπτίζω. He has, also, brought clearly out what our own examination had before proved, that *the word* (βαπτίζω) *does not,* of itself, *involve the lifting out of the fluid of that which is put in.*"

Which, now, is the " honest opinion," this or that? Is it *that* which speaks contemptuously of " the redoubtable Dr. Dale," or *this,* which speaks of " the author of no small ability?" Is it *that* which adjudges the volumes to be " a reproach to American letters," or *this,* which declares them to be the " admiration " of the editor? Is it *that* which proclaims them to be " an insult to Presbyterian scholarship," or *this,* which announces their profound " impression on some of the first scholars of the country?" Is it *that* which declares that these volumes " snub every eminent Presbyterian from Calvin to Hodge," or *this,* which recounts the words of praise uttered by " Edwards and Skinner, Plummer and Hodge, Coleman and Smith, and many others?" Is it *that* which announces the labors of Dr. Dale to be those of " a sophist and a trickster," " without honesty or principle," " without thought and without sense," of one who dwells in abandoned " solitude," a lonely " egotist," and whom " ridicule and oblivion " are eager to swallow up; or *this,* which says, " the labors of Mr. Dale cannot prove worthless or unimportant; " he has " established a difference" where Carson of Ireland, and the Campbells (of Scotland, and of Virginia), and a host of others, declared no difference to exist; and " he has brought clearly out" (what is vital to this controversy), "that βαπτίζω does not lift out of the fluid that which it puts in."

These are the match horses in the National Baptist " turn out." Whether the very worthy editor will undertake to mate them by proving the white horse to be black, or the black horse to be white, or will choose rather henceforward to drive on with a parti-colored team, I cannot say. And I do not know that the question, "Whether *that* be *this*, or *this* be *that?*" need trouble any one beyond the holder of the reins.

Mem.—" A system of artificial memory" would not be a bad addendum to the editorial sanctum of some folks.

WATCHMAN AND REFLECTOR.

In contrast with " that" opinion, and in harmony with " this" opinion of the National Baptist, is the following language, full of characteristic manliness and self-respect, by the Watchman and Reflector. " Dr. Dale is already well known as the author of ' Classic Baptism.' The thorough discussion of the subject of baptism demanded an inquiry into the usage and nature of the rite among the Jews. Dr. Dale, in the above volume, enters into an investigation of this part of the subject. It is not our purpose at this time to criticize the author's work. We can say, however, from the little reading which we have been able to give to the book, that the author shows a large acquaintance with his subject. His investigations have been wide, and he discusses the various points with a candor and good nature which are worthy of praise. Differing as we do from his conclusions, we can yet respect the ability and commend the spirit which characterize Dr. Dale's argument."

When the friends of the theory cease to depend on "the vocabulary" for support, and write after the style of this extract, they will lose nothing in the estimation of their readers.

CHRISTIAN QUARTERLY ("CAMPBELLITE" BAPTIST).

In the January number, 1871, of the Quarterly of the Christian or Disciples Church (popularly known by the name of Alexander Campbell) there is a review of Classic Baptism occupying forty-four pages. If this review had but grasped the merits of the case as clearly, and discussed their issues as fairly, as it has passed over the ground minutely, there would be little left to be desired. But I regret to say that this extended review has carried us but little forward. The positions of Classic Baptism are not even confronted, much less answered. The errors of the review are so numerous and so elementary that it would be as unprofitable as it is discouraging to attempt to point them out.

A fair specimen of the logic, rhetoric, imagination, assumption, assertion, and extravagant error of this review (which is but illustrative of the theory in general) may be found in the following passage, taken from pp. 83, 84 of the review. "The whole object of 'Classic Baptism' is to lay down in the end, by inference or in some other way, premises from which he can infer that sprinkling and pouring are Baptism."

This grim spectre (imagined to stand at the end of this Inquiry and evoked by the fears of the Reviewer) seems to frighten him from his propriety, and induce the assembling of all approved instruments of torture, ready to crush bones and to dislocate joints whenever any threatening demonstration may be made against "dip, and nothing but dip." The Reviewer thus proceeds: "He even infers from a garbled quotation that an *immersion* was once effected by a sprinkling. . . . But we admit no such conclusion. The passages which he quotes contain no grounds for such inference. Here they are: 'Disgorging the sea-water which he had swallowed during his immersion;' and, 'The boat received the shower which the animal spouted aloft, and the adventurous Triptolemus had a full share of the immersion.' Was Triptolemus immersed? Does a 'share' of anything amount to the whole of it? It is not said that he was immersed.

The very reverse is affirmed. He only received a share of
' the imn.ersion.' We may ask what immersion is here referred to? For *the* immersion must mean some special immersion. What immersion is that? But one immersion is
mentioned to which an allusion can be made. That immersion is the immersion of the animal which 'spouted aloft'
' the sea-water which he had swallowed during his immersion.' It is a share of this immersion that Sir Walter Scott
referred to. The animal imbibed a large quantity of water
during his immersion, which he threw aloft, and Triptolemus was covered with it; and this is called 'a share,' 'a full
share of the immersion.' . . . The Doctor is entirely too superficial; and if the partisans who have extolled such criticisms do not become ashamed of their own eulogies, it must
be owing to their theologies, not to their scholarship."

Seldom has a criticism furnished richer elements for good-
natured merriment than does the above. In the first place
the writer never saw, *in situ*, the passages quoted, and was
profoundly ignorant of their connection. And yet he not
only ventures to elaborate a criticism on each of the two
passages (making a context for that unknown one written by
Sir Walter), but in doing so joins together two passages
which have no more affiliation, connection, relation, or even
propinquity, than fire and water, or the zenith and the nadir.
In this venture of the Reviewer the "garbled extract" is a
pure myth, the affirmation being made under a profound
ignorance of the real character of the passage; the immersion of "the animal" is equally mythic, no such statement
having been made by Sir Walter; the profound exegesis
which makes Triptolemus share in the "immersion of the
animal" will be found valuable when it proves adequate to
reverse the adage *ex nihilo nihil fit;* as there is nothing of the
animal immersion, the full share of nothing cannot be much.
The animal of the Reviewer (which imbibes a quantity of
water in his immersion, and spouts it aloft, sending down a
shower of brine into the boat, and giving Triptolemus "a
full share") *is the Pirate Cleveland,* who floats, insensible,
ashore from his wrecked vessel. This more than half-

drowned sailor (who by the help of a brandy stimulus " disgorges the sea-water which he had swallowed during his immersion") is converted by the Reviewer into a whale gambolling in the deep, imbibing its brine, and generously sharing its deep-sea immersion with Triptolemus, the Udaler, and the harpooning boat's crew generally! This is a choice specimen of the *ad nauseam* imaginative immersions of the theory. Their grossness does not always admit of the same patent exposure as in the present case, but their absurdity is none the less real to every sober mind.

This mirth-inducing error is in nowise due to the manner in which the two passages are quoted in Classic Baptism. They are not quoted as illustrative of the same point. They are not placed even in juxtaposition. The first (the ship-wreck of the Pirate) is on p. 200, and the second (the shower immersion) is on p. 209. It does not give the shadow of a vinculum uniting them together as referring to the same transaction. Their being brought together and made to expound one transaction can only be explained by that spirit of audacity which leads the gambler of the turf to shut his eyes and select a racer on which he stakes his all " against the field." The Reviewer has seen proper to pick up two widely-separated quotations, and blindly wager his reliability against infinite odds, that these two passages refer to the same transaction. He has lost. The most audacious exposition cannot convert a drowned sailor into a spouting whale!

The amusement furnished by this *faux pas* is good reason for allowing it to go scot free from any severe philippic. It would not have been noticed except that (in all its extravagance) it is a substantially fair example of the reckless interpretations of the theory.

BAPTIST QUARTERLY.

In the Baptist Quarterly for January, 1870, there is an article by Professor Albert N. Arnold, of the Baptist Theological Seminary, Chicago, on Baptism and the Greek Church. In this article he casts a glance of sneering pity at " the volumes of Dr. Dale," but passes them by as too leprous to be touched. But reference is made to this article, not because of what is said or unsaid of these volumes, but because of some things adjacent. Among which things is the following testimony (Appendix to The Old and the New, or The Changes of Thirty Years in the East, by Rev. Wm. Goodell).

" Rev. E. Riggs thus describes a Greek baptism which he witnessed in Smyrna in April, 1851 :

" The priest, taking the infant, perfectly naked " (aid and comfort to Rabbi Kalisch), " in his hands, and holding it over the font, said, ' The servant of the Lord, Iphigenia, is baptized (placing it in the water, which reached up to its neck, and thrice taking up water with his right hand, and pouring upon the child's head) in the name of the Father (then lifting the child up, and again placing it in the water, and repeating the affusion as before), and of the Son (same movement repeated), and of the Holy Ghost, now and ever, even for ever and ever : Amen.' I have witnessed this ceremony a number of times, and in no instance was the whole body of the person baptized, immersed in the water. In many instances the size of the font would not have admitted it.

" Rev. Mr. Wood, for many years a missionary at Constantinople, and now one of the Secretaries of the A. B. C. F. M., adds his testimony, that the practice is the same in the Armenian Church, and he cites the testimony of Dr. Perkins, in an article contributed to ' Coleman's Ancient Christianity Exemplified' (p. 574), in which Dr. Perkins thus describes the way of baptism among the Nestorians : ' The children are set into a vessel of tepid water, which extends up to the neck, and held there by a deacon, while the priest takes up water with both hands (not the right hand only), and suffuses it over the head, repeating the name of one person of the Trinity each time.'

" The Armenian clergy, it is added, base their practice of baptism by affusion on the fact, received among the traditions " (over against Rabbi Kalisch's traditions) " of their church, that the Saviour was thus baptized. In all

their pictures of the scene of the baptism, Christ is represented as standing in the Jordan, and the Baptist as pouring water from his hand upon his head. Jews, who sometimes enter the Armenian Church, are baptized in the same
manner.

"The Armenian Church (it is further stated) acknowledges
the validity of baptism by sprinkling, and receives, without
rebaptizing them, Romanists and Protestants who seek admission into its communion with no other baptism. The
Greeks rebaptize, but the writers must be mistaken who
represent the ground of this to be a view of immersion as
essential to baptism. Regarding all other bodies of Christians as in heresy and schism, they arrogate valid ordinances
and salvation to their own church exclusively, and would no
sooner receive one baptized by immersion, without rebaptizing him, than they would one whose baptism was by
sprinkling. Their own baptism, if it ever is, very extensively to say the least, is not an immersion."

What, now, does Professor Arnold say of these baptisms
of the Armenian, Nestorian, and Greek churches? Hear
him: "There is no baptism without immersion; but they
are not punctilious about the totality of the immersion. Affusion comes in only to supply the defect and complete the
immersion." Is not this a marvellous utterance from a
friend of the theory? He does not dare reject these baptisms of the Eastern churches, and yet there is not in one
of them a baptism according to the theory. But "the totality
of the immersion" has suddenly become "a punctilio!"
And "the defect" in the immersion is remedied, hear all ye
friends of the theory, by "affusion!!" We are told that in
the bottom of the Dead Sea there is a sudden break down
from "thirteen feet to thirteen hundred feet." But this
sudden fall of a thousand feet is a trifle to this *bathic* break
down of the theory in the hands of Professor Arnold. But
it is a shame to strike a foe when fallen without the proffer of
generous quarter; how much more, then, a kindly opponent
like Professor Arnold. He has fallen as heavily as one of
his weight (and I am sure he is not one of the "light weights,"

intellectually or morally) can fall. We, therefore, extend to him our hand and assist him to rise, that he may do battle on another field of his selection.

ALEXANDER DE STOURDZA.

Alexander de Stourdza takes the place with Professor Arnold which Rabbi Isidor Kalisch took with the National Baptist. Whether the former will prove a more valuable ally than the latter remains to be seen. The challenge under which the Professor proposes to do battle is this: "The verb βαπτίζω, *immergo*, has but one meaning. *It signifies literally and perpetually*, TO PLUNGE." This is the language of de Stourdza which, when the Professor adopts as his own, is accompanied with this plaintive lament, "It is a pity that this Greek scholar should be left without the light of Dr. Dale's volumes." Having no hope that the light from these volumes can reach to the Professor's height, I will seek to throw light upon this thesis from some other sources which he may hold in higher estimation.

And, first, I presume the Professor will pay due respect to light proceeding from himself. Let me, then, ask of him, Do you, Professor Arnold, believe that "βαπτίζω has but one meaning, and that that meaning is, literally and perpetually, *to plunge?*" To be more specific, Do you believe that when the sea-coast is baptized by the tide coming over it, that the sea-shore is "plunged" into the water? "Well, of course, I know that it is not; but de Stourdza says that it is, and who am I that I should oppose Stourdza?" Do you believe that when, in the overflowings of the Nile, its banks, and the plants in the Egyptian fields, and their land-animals are baptized, that banks, and plants, and animals are taken up and "plunged" into the water? "Why, of course, I know that they are not; but de Stourdza says that they are, and what can I say, but say what Stourdza says?" Do you believe that the soldiers, who were baptized by marching all day through the water to their waists, were "plunged" into the water by anybody or anything? "Why ask such

a question? I know as well as any one that they were not;
but so long as de Stourdza says that they were, what can I
do?" Do you believe that the altar on Mount Carmel, baptized by water poured upon it, was "plunged" into the
water? "Why persist in asking such questions? Any one,
though more stupid than Baal's worshippers, must know
that it was not; but Stourdza! Stourdza!" Do you believe
that souls, at the gates of Paradise, baptized by the waving
of a flaming sword in the hands of the Great Baptist, are
"plunged?" "I must positively decline listening to any
more such questions. What will de Stourdza say?" I will
ask no more questions. It is quite plain that there is light
in you, but the deep de Stourdza shadow turns it into darkness. There may, however, be some of your friends possessed of courage to express, as well as hold, an opinion
which may not exactly square with that of the Russo-Greek
Councillor. What does your friend Gale say? Dr. Gale,
do you believe in "one meaning, literally and perpetually,
to plunge?" "I have tried as hard as any man to carry
through 'one meaning,' but, as you know, I have my mis-
givings; we may have, at last, to fall back on something
beyond act of any kind; it may be that it is *condition* and
not act which is expressed." And what is your opinion, Dr.
Cox? "I believe that any man made very wet by the drop-
pings of the night dew falling on him is baptized thereby."
Dr. Fuller, what is your faith on this point? "I give up
plunge, and nothing but plunge. If water is poured over a
man long enough, he will need no plunging to baptize him."
Dr. Carson, what do you say? "I have very little to say for
'plunge, literally and perpetually,' but I am ready to stake
all on 'dip, and nothing but dip, through all Greek literature.'" And what does "the Professor of the Baptist Theological Seminary, Rochester, New York," say? "Brethren!
my advice is, get rid of senseless dipping." Will Dr. Conant
give us light upon this issue? "I have translated βαπτίζω
and its derivatives, in the Bible and out of the Bible, nearly
five hundred times, and *seventeen* times (against opposing
hundreds) I have translated it *plunge.* That is all the aid

and comfort which I can give to Stourdza-ism." Will the
venerable Booth give us his judgment on this question?
" My judgment is on record long ago. An opponent of mine
once translated βαπτίζω, ' literally and perpetually, to plunge,'
and I said, in reply, that he did so ' to make our sentiments
and practice ridiculous.' De Stourdza may mean very well
by his literally and perpetually plunging, but this only leads
me the more earnestly to cry, Save me from my friends!"
So much for de Stourdza's "plunge."

" It is a pity that this Greek scholar should be left without
the light of Dr. Dale's volumes," or, in its absence, let me
add, without the light of this voluminous testimony of Professor Arnold's friends.

The simple truth is, that there is not a thoughtful and
well-read man on earth who believes this doctrine of de
Stourdza. And there is no risk in saying that neither Professor Arnold, nor de Stourdza himself, believes what their
language affirms. I will not say (as the Baptist Quarterly
says of Dr. Dale and his volumes) it is " *an attempt to impose
upon* the unlearned and the half learned," for I have never
learned that the correction of error required the maligning
of character. I do not believe that these worthy men have
made " an attempt to impose " error for truth upon any one.
Their best defence must be in the apologetic abandonment
of their position, saying, " We did not really mean what, in
words, we said." This plea has already been entered for
Dr. Carson and his disproved " dip, and nothing but dip."
It must be re-entered for the patently erroneous " plunge,
and nothing but plunge" of Arnold and de Stourdza.
Neither Jewish Rabbi nor Greek Councillor can save the
theory.

" SEE ALL THE LEXICONS."

" See all the lexicons," says Professor Arnold, to prove
that βαπτίζω means *to plunge*, a strictly definite act. And
another writer in this Baptist Quarterly says, " Mr. Dale
dces not assail us with Stephens and Scapula." And a third
writer, speaking of lexicons, says, " It is not creditable to

our religious journalism that such works as Mr. Dale's Classic Baptism should find countenance or favor in any quarter."

My desire in examining into the meaning of this Greek word has been to place the inquiry on an ultimate basis, and to collect material for a final and irreversible judgment. My judgment has not been presented as final or irreversible for any one, not even for myself. Disprove my evidence and you change my judgment. The materials on which that judgment is based are uncovered for the inspection and the independent judgment of every one as well as for myself. If in my judgment I have, as charged, played the fool and shamed idiocy, then, even "the unlearned and the half learned" will not be likely to be harmed by my "attempt to impose upon them." But if the judgment reached is so clearly indicated that even "a mere country pastor" may be considered as competent to see it, and if that judgment be sustained by the independent judgment of all outside of the theory, then that judgment will be final and irreversible, and the friends of the theory will, sooner or later, confess it to be so. Heretofore in this inquiry reliance has been placed on usage, and nothing has been said about lexicons, because it is a matter of universal admission that manifold imperfections attend upon general lexicography, and its conclusions are without authority except as they may give a true interpretation of usage. But inasmuch as appeal is now made from usage to lexicography, and the theory claims that every lexicon is a pillar of support to its doctrine, it may be well to turn aside for a while and inquire into the facts of the case.

But before we "see all the lexicons," let us clearly understand what it is that we are expected to see in them. Let there be no confounding of this with that. If it is one thing and but one thing, then let it not be diverse things and nothing but diverse things. The theory boasts of its one meaning and of its denial of any second meaning. If this were not, as Professor Stuart declares it to be, "an adventurous position," but one founded in fact, then it would be the simplest thing in the world for the theory to announce that one meaning, plant itself squarely upon it, and indicate its truth by pointing out fact after fact. This has never been done. This has never, really, been attempted to be done. When Carson gives the one meaning in the sharpest possible definition, there is not enough of attempt to carry the definition into the facts of usage to dignify it by entitling it a failure. And when Arnold-Stourdza gives the one meaning in another character, and by a definition matching well that of Carson in sharpness, Booth replies, that its application to the facts of usage "makes our sentiments and practice ridiculous." This utter failure through two centuries to present the one meaning in a tangible shape and to verify it by laying it alongside of the universal facts of usage, is, itself, proof that the claim cannot be true, and that the claim for lexical support must be equally untrue. But while there has been no general attempt to give embodiment to the meaning in one word, and when the attempt has been made it has awakened dissent and resulted in failure, still there has been an almost universal assent to the position, that βαπτίζω makes demand for an act, to be done, in contradistinction from a result or a condition consequent upon the doing of an act; and farther, that this act demanded to be done is properly described as specific in its nature, definite in its character, and modal in its form. This word is said to maintain its meaning unchanged in ideal as well as in physical relations. And any secondary meaning is peremptorily denied.

What we are called upon, then, to "see in all the lexicons" is, 1. A definite act; 2. A ——— where a secondary meaning should have been.

This statement is, perhaps, sufficiently substantiated by what has been said in the general treatment of the subject, but inasmuch as special appeal has been made to the lexicons, and this meaning of the theory (act in opposition to condition), is the alpha and the omega determinative of the whole subject, it will be desirable to have distinctly before us authoritative evidence of the teaching of the theory on this point. For this purpose the following quotations are made from representative writers.

Dr. Gale, London, 1711, *p.* 93. " We cannot believe that it is so doubtful, in Scripture, as many pretend, whether *dipping only* be baptism. I'll begin with the words βάπτω and βαπτίζω, for they are synonymous."

This is doubly plain. Gale not only says that the definite act " dipping" is, and " only" is, baptism, but he says that βαπτίζω is synonymous with the *definite act* verb βάπτω. He, then, beyond all question, regarded βαπτίζω as a verb demanding the performance of *a definite act.*

Booth, London, 1792, *p.* 265. " The verb baptize, in this dispute, denotes an *action* required by the divine law. And the simple question is, What *is* that *action?* Is it immersion, or pouring, or sprinkling? Not what is the principal *end* or *design* of that *action?* Be the action itself, and the design of it, whatever they may, they certainly are different things, and must be so considered."

Booth could not state the point more sharply : " Baptize *denotes an* ACTION required by the divine law." The error in using " immersion," as " pouring and sprinkling," to ex press the act of the verb should be noted as of constant oc currence in this class of writers. *Pouring* expresses the act in the verb " to pour;" and *sprinkling* expresses the doing of the act in the verb " to sprinkle;" but " immersion" does not express the doing of the act in the verb *to immerse.* " Immersion" is the result of the act of immersing.

P. 279. " That many tyrants and fools have given laws to secular kingdoms, and have even presumed to legislate for Jesus Christ himself, is a fact; that some of their laws have been marked with tyrannic subtilty, and others with egregious folly, is also a fact; but that any of them were ever so crafty as to contrive a law which by a *single* SPECIFIC *enacting term* equally required *three different* acts of obedience, and yet were so complaisant as to feel themselves perfectly satisfied with having *any one* of those acts performed, I do not believe." *P.* 280. " Βαπτίζω is a *specific* term. The English expression *dip* is a *specific* term." *P.* 286.

We may question the propriety of making "tyrant and fool" the alternative title of the Divine lawgiver under any possible contingency; but he must be more than "a tyrant," and less than "a fool," who would doubt that Booth means to say, that βαπτίζω expresses *a specific act*.

Cox, London, 1824, *p.* 46. "The idea of *dipping* is *in every instance* conveyed; and no less so by all the current uses of the terms (βάπτω and βαπτίζω) in question. A person may indeed be immersed by pouring, but immersion is the being plunged into water or (the being) overwhelmed by it. Were the water to ascend from the earth, it would still be baptism, were the person wholly covered by it."

Nothing could be more explicit or more harmonious with the theory than the first sentence; nothing could exhibit "confusion worse confounded" beyond the remainder of the quotation. Observe the confusion in the use of "immersed" and "immersion." In the case of the first the usage is proper; "immersed" expresses *a condition*, the result of the act of *pouring;* but "immersion," instead of being used as the *condition* resultant from the act in "being plunged," "being overwhelmed," is exhibited as only another form of those acts.

Observe, again, the absurdity of representing βαπτίζω as "*to dip* in every instance," and then representing as fulfilled in its demand by the diverse specific acts of *plunging, pouring,* and *rising up!* Was it such a case that Booth had in view when he said, that "to use a *single* SPECIFIC *term* equally requiring *three different* acts of obedience, was beyond the craft of the most consummate tyrants and fools?"

Observe, further, that Cox, while affirming a specific act (dipping) "in every instance," abandons all *act* as expressed by the word and substitutes for it CONDITION. The *act* of plunging is of no moment, it may be there or it may not be there; the *act* of pouring is of no moment, it, too, may be there or may not be there; the *act* of rising up of gushing waters, is of no moment, it, likewise, may be there or may not be there; but that which is of moment, and cannot be wanting, is the covered *condition!* Now, can fatuity go be-

yond the affirmation, that βαπτίζω makes demand for the performance of a specific act, and yet is squarely met by a *condition*, the result of any one of a score of diverse acts, or by
the conjoint operation of any half dozen of them? But it is
precisely this absurdity, more or less baldly presented, which
meets us everywhere in the writings of the upholders of the
theory.

Morell, Edinburgh, 1848, *p.* 167. " That the word βαπτίζω
uniformly signifies *to dip*, I will not venture to assert or undertake to prove. I believe that the word does mean *to dip*,
and this is its *most usual* meaning. But it appears quite evident, that the word also bears the sense of *covering by super-
fusion*. This is admitted by Dr. Cox. Thus far we surrender the question of immersion in company with Dr. Cox."

Morell is evidently a cultivated as well as an ingenuous
man. How it escaped him that the same word could not
possibly express the diverse specific acts of *dipping* and *super-
fusing*, I cannot understand. The error, however, which
resorts to attributing to one word two diverse specific acts,
rather than abandon the theory of a specific act altogether,
shows how ingrained in the minds of the Old World and the
New is the conception of βαπτίζω as expressing *a definite act*.

Stovel, London, 1846, *p.* 470. " On *the act* of Christian baptism. The student of the Holy Scriptures may determine
for himself the nature of *the act* which Christ the Lord *hath
enjoined under the name of baptism.*" *P.* 486. "It is impossible
to dip by *pouring*, or to pour by *sprinkling;* and since there is
but one baptism, it must be *one* or the *other* of these *acts;* it
cannot be *either* or *all.* Βαπτίζω is the same with βάπτω, only
with a causal force."

The statement that verb and substantive alike express
definite act could not be more absolute.

Ingham, London, 1865, *p.* 47. " That βαπτίζω is *synonymous
with the primary meaning of* βάπτω appears to the writer to
have the most abundant confirmation from the instances
where it occurs, admitting that βάπτω may more exclusively
retain the idea of putting anything *into* another, whilst
βαπτίζω means to immerse, not only when the object is put

into the element, but, as in occasional instances on record, when the element is brought upon and around the object. The primary meaning of βάπτω is *to dip*."

Here, again, we meet the affirmation of a specific act and the absurd admission of a second meaning the direct contrary of the first. We, also, see the same wretched use of "immerse" to hide the nakedness of *a specific act*.

President Wayland, Principles and Practice of Baptists, p. 89. "We immerse the whole body in water." *P.* 91. "Few things are more impressive than *the act* of Christian baptism. *The act* may be an offence to the world, but it is glorious in the sight of God, of angels in heaven, and of saints on earth."

Dr. Wayland appears to use "immerse" as expressive of "the act" in baptizing which, among Baptists, is by *dipping* the upper part of the body. In so doing he adds his honored name to the long list of those who maintain that God has enjoined a *specific act* to be done in baptizing.

Professor Curtis, On Communion, p. 71. "Those who rightly receive baptism are assured by a *formal act* that they actually *are* 'heirs of God, joint heirs with Christ.' Baptism is *the act* of consecration. What sight on earth so beautiful as to see the young and lovely *descending into* the waters of baptism."

Professor Curtis, not writing formally on the subject of baptism, is not so explicit as to "the act" as others. His language, however, "a formal act," "the act," "descending into," must be accredited to the theoretical *specific act*.

Professor Jewett, Baptism, p. 13. "*Βάπτω* has two meanings, *to dip, to dye;* βαπτίζω, in the whole history of the Greek language, has but one meaning. It signifies *to dip* (or immerse), and *never has any other meaning*. Either βάπτω or βαπτίζω may signify *to dip* generally."

Professor Jewett stands straight up for "specific act," "one meaning through all Greek literature," as, also, for the perversion of "immerse" in being made to perform the role of *dip* in executing a specific act.

Professor Dagg, Church Order, p. 33. "If βάπτω signifies *to immerse,* βαπτίζω signifies *to cause to be immersed.* This makes

the words nearly or quite synonymous. Βάπτω more frequently denotes slight or temporary immersion than βαπτίζω.
Hence *dip*, which properly denotes slight or temporary immersion, is more frequently its appropriate rendering.   In
nearly half the examples in which βαπτίζω occurs, in the
literal sense, it signifies the immersion which attends
drowning or the sinking of ships." *P.* 35. "The propriety
and force of the metaphorical allusions cannot be understood
if the word does not signify to immerse."

Professor Dagg, in these statements, mingles truth and
error, with truth more predominant than in the case of any
writer yet noticed.   It is an error to translate βάπτω *to immerse.*   This is evident from the declaration that this word
"denotes slight or temporary immersion;" but "immerse"
does *never* "*denote* slight or temporary immersion;" it, therefore, cannot be the translation of βάπτω.   But why does Dr.
Dagg translate, here, "immerse," when he says, it means
dip, and when, in a formal statement of the passages in
which βάπτω occurs, he translates it "*to dip*" in every instance?   The reason is the same as that which leads all
Baptist writers to murder "immerse" in order to save the
life of "dip."   Dr. Dagg wished to introduce into βαπτίζω a
meaning to meet the facts of usage, which the theory had no
power to give him.   He wanted to get into βαπτίζω a widely
different meaning from that of βάπτω, while the theory says,
they are "nearly or quite synonymous."   He, in obedience to
theory, makes the former differ from the latter only as causative.   If, now, βάπτω is allowed to retain the meaning "to dip,"
then βαπτίζω must be made to mean "to cause *to dip;*" but the
trouble is, that this meaning *will not meet the facts of usage.*
Instead, now, of accepting the obvious truth, that βαπτίζω
differs essentially in nature from βάπτω, the Professor robs
this word of its *dip*, and substitutes for it *immerse*.   And,
thus, having overlaid dip by immerse, he is enabled, by
causation, to extract it for the benefit of βαπτίζω.   There is
no end to the twistings and turnings which grow out of essential error substituted for central truth.

Professor Dagg uses "immersion" properly when he distınguishes it from the *acts* of drowning and sinking, making it a *condition* resultant from those acts. He is, also, right in bringing into bold relief the "*slight* and *temporary*" immersion (dipping) of βάπτω, which necessitates withdrawal, and the unlimited *depth*, *duration*, and *action* of the immersion of βαπτίζω, which excludes withdrawal, as of the meaning of this word. It is only remarkable that Dr. Dagg should have failed to perceive that a word of such characteristics must express *condition* and not a specific act. Professor Dagg is emphatically right when he says, "the propriety and force of the metaphorical allusions cannot be understood if the word does not signify *immerse*," always provided, that the abuse of "immerse" to the sense of *dip* is here abandoned. If "immerse" in this statement be used as when it is said, "βάπτω *to immerse* (dip), βαπτίζω to cause to immerse (*to cause to dip*"), then every particle of truth has evaporated out of it. The breadth of a sunbeam may as well be taken to swathe a continent as the feebleness of "dip" be used to interpret the power of influence which everywhere pervades the secondary use of βαπτίζω. And, herein, we find one of the clearest and most beautiful of the many evidences proving that the theory is wrong to the very heart. That which it declares (dip) to be the exclusive meaning of the word through all Greek literature has not the shadow of fitness, Dr. Dagg being judge, to meet one-half of the cases of the usage of the word.

Dr. Fuller, Baptism, p. 13. "The act of baptism. And just so βάπτω *to dip*, βαπτίζω *to make one dip*, that is, to immerse." *P.* 25. "Βαπτίζω signifies *to immerse*, and has no other meaning." *P.* 29. "The fourth case is produced to show that βαπτίζω does not always denote *the act of plunging*. My position is that βαπτίζω means to immerse. It matters not how the immersion is effected." (*P.* 31.) "Suppose a man should lie in the baptistery while it is filling. The pouring of the water would not be the immersion, but an immersion would take place if he remained long enough. In the case of Elijah, the twelve barrels of water were first poured, and the trenches all around filled, and it is *the effect* of

4

this, it is the being thus drenched, surrounded, and steeped, which Origen figuratively calls a baptism."

Dr. Fuller here, again, treats us to the ever recurring masquerade of dip and immerse. "Just so βάπτω to dip; βαπτίζω *to make one dip*, that is *to immerse*" (!) "*Βαπτίζω* signifies to immerse, *to make one dip*, and has no other meaning." Dr. Fuller has written a book of several hundred pages, and has used the word immerse scores of times; if he has used it in a solitary instance in the meaning "to make one *dip*" (and it "has no other meaning"), I have not met with the case. How the specific act *dip* (slight and temporary) is to be converted by figure into "the effect" of pouring—"drenching, surrounding, steeping"—I leave the imaginator to settle with his friend Dr. Dagg.

The pinching necessity of this case which constrained Dr. Fuller to accept of "effect" as expository of βαπτίζω, in contradiction of the theory, and in disregard of the expostulations of Carson, should have revealed the true character of this word as making demand not for the doing of an *act*, whether to dip, to plunge, to sink, to pour, or what not, but for an end to be secured, an effect, a condition, the result of any competent act or acts.

Dr. Conant, BAPTIZEIN, pp. 59–67, 103–107. Dr. Conant, in common with those whose views have already been presented, says, that the word is severely limited to one meaning. (iii.) "The translation expresses its true and only import." "From the earliest age of Greek literature down to its close (a period of about two thousand years), not an example has been found in which the word has any other meaning." "Showing its unvarying signification through all this time." "This unvarying sense of the word." "The constant usage of Greek writers, and the only recognized meaning of the word." "The word BAPTIZEIN, during the whole existence of the Greek as a spoken language, had a perfectly defined and unvarying import."

The character of a word, used for two thousand years in one unvarying meaning, ought not to be doubtful. Dr. Conant expresses no doubt upon the subject. He, again, agrees with his friends in classifying it with those verbs which definitely express *an act to be done*, and not *a definite result to be effected* by an unexpressed act. These are his statements: " *This act* is always expressed in the literal application of the word, and is the basis of its metaphorical uses." " The literal *act* of immersion as the means of cleansing." " The word is used of the most familiar *acts*." " With the preposition *into* expressing fully *the act of passing* from one element into another." " *The act* it expresses took place." " A Greek could be at no loss to know *what was done*, or what was *required to be done*." " The other *acts* with which it is compared." " The Greek word expresses nothing more than *the act* of immersion." " This *act* is performed on the assenting believer." " *The act* expressed by the same word." " *The act designated* by the word in all these cases is the same." " *The act* associates with itself obligations." " *The act* which it described retained its primary meaning." " *The act* which it describes was chosen for its adaptation." " The same closely marked *corporeal act* as is expressed by the Greek word."

When Dr. Conant says, that βαπτίζω " always *expresses this act*," " *expresses the act* that took place," " *expresses* nothing more than *the act*," " *designates the act*," " *describes the act*," there is nothing more certain than that he is in error. The Greek word is devoid of all power to inform us as to the form or character of " the act" by which any baptism is effected. It cannot inform us whether a baptism is effected by one act or by two acts. If Thales, the wisest of " the Seven," were alive again, he could not answer the question, " What is *the* act which βαπτίζω expresses?" How much less could " *any* Greek know what was done or what was required to be done." If the offer were made to Dr. Conant to pay for the next edition of his BAPTIZEIN in case he should answer this question, the question must remain unanswered. There is no such thing as " *the* act" expressed by βαπτίζω in contradistinction from an untold number of other and diverse acts by which the demand of the word may be as well and

as truly met. That this is true will be seen by farther statements made by Dr. Conant. If this word expresses an act
done daily through two thousand years, then, since nothing
is so sharply limited, so unvarying, so universal, and so
easily to be expressed, there ought to be a *fac simile* for
every such act in Greece in every land under the sun, and
its enunciation ought to be met with in every spoken tongue.
Has Dr. Conant furnished us with the counterpart of this act
and its expression in the English language? This is the
answer: "BAPTIZEIN means, to immerse, immerge, submerge, to dip, to plunge, to imbathe, to whelm." And is
this to be received as verifying the declaration that βαπτίζω
" designates," " describes," " expresses *the* act" of baptism?
There are but two words out of the seven which express a
definite act (dip and plunge), and these two acts are essentially diverse in their character, so that if βαπτίζω expresses
either, it cannot express the other. And, beside, we have
seen Dr. Conant's friends repudiating both; the venerable
Booth declaring that "plunge makes our practice and sentiments ridiculous;" and "the Professor of the Baptist Theological Seminary, Rochester, New York," exclaiming, "Baptist brethren! Christian baptism is no mere literal and senseless *dipping*." Just in so far as these seven defining terms
fail to express " one unvarying act," they fail to express
" *this* act," *the* act which, we are told, βαπτίζω " *always* designates, describes, and expresses."

But Dr. Conant acknowledges that these seven words do
not express any one, common, form of act. By an analysis
he groups their differences into two classes: 1. Such as move
the object, "*putting into*" the element; 2. Such as move the
element, " putting under" the element. These two classes
cannot be reduced any farther, retaining act as the distinguishing basis of the classification. They may, however, be
reduced to one class by the abandonment of *the act*, in which
they differ, and the acceptance of *the result*, in which they
agree. Whether the object be moved so as to *put into* the
element, or whether the element be moved so as to *put under*
the object, "put into" and "put under" meet together in

put within. The differences in act are merged in a common result, and this result becomes the characteristic expression of the verb. It is *this* (result) and not " this " (act) which βαπτίζω " designates," " describes," and " expresses."

It is obvious that this *put within* (*intus-pono*) brings us face to face with the " intus position " declared by Classic Bap tism to be the characteristic demand of the word.

Additional proof of the correctness of this conclusion is found in the word, selected from these seven, as the representative word. That word is *immerse.* " The word *immerse*, as well as its synonyms *immerge, submerge, dip, plunge, imbathe, whelm,* expresses *the full import* of the Greek word BAPTI-ZEIN." " The rendering given to this word, in this revision (*immerse*), is its *true* and *only meaning*, as proved by the unanimous testimony of Greek writers, both Pagan and Christian." " The word *immerse* has been selected for use in this Revision as *most nearly* resembling the original word in the extent of its application."

If " immerse " be the " *true* and *only* meaning " of βαπτίζω, then the other six words have no right to appear as its translation, for they differ both from " immerse " and from each other. As they, thus, have no right to appear, so there can be no possible necessity, when there is a word which expresses " the true and only meaning." But, again, if " immerse " only comes " most nearly " to the meaning of the Greek word, it is quite unwarranted to say that " it is *proved* to be its *true* and *only* meaning." If the exposition by Dr. Conant of the word in question, namely, " it expresses the act," be correct, then he was shut up to the choice, out of the seven, either of *dip* or *plunge*, for these are the only terms which express the definite, executive act. Therefore it was that Stourdza makes " plunge " the literal and perpetual act. And, therefore, Carson makes " dip " the only act expressed through all Greek literature. Dr. Conant should, in obedience to the theory, have followed their example and chosen the one or the other. But he does not do this. He selects another word—" immerse." And each, alike, claims that his word " expresses the *true* and *only* meaning through two thousand years!" Now is there a living man who will say that these words are equivalent terms, so that it is a matter of indifference in assigning a radical, critical definition to a word from which usage through twenty centuries is to be evolved, whether such definition be expressed by DIP, or by PLUNGE, or by IMMERSE? If no such person can be found, then dipping, or plunging, or immersing, or all three, must be rejected. But "Baptist brethren" have already been warned against *dip* and *plunge* as "senseless" and "ridiculous;" there remains, therefore, for us only to consider "immerse." The word *immerse* does not express *movement* out of one thing into another thing, but only the *within* result reached. Therefore the demand of the word is fully met though the baptized object remain as fixed as the shore of the sea or as the fields of Egypt. If the mountain will not come to Mohammed, Mohammed must go to the mountain. Objection has been already entered against using a word (im-merse) derived from the compound *im-mergo* to express, critically, βαπτίζω. The Latin devolves upon one preposition the double duty of expressing motion *into* a place, and rest *in* a place. On this ground, apparently, and in contradiction of English usage, occasion has been taken to use im-merse as directly expressing *movement into;* and not only so, but, also, to use it, as convenience required, in its legitimate meaning as expressive, simply, of withinness of position. This double usage vitiates all the writings of the friends of the theory. Dr. Conant says, it means "passing into," and in proof appeals to the construction with εἰς. But the proof is not, hereby, furnished. The preposition does indeed prove that there is a "passing into," but it does not prove that such *passing into* is expressed by βαπτίζω. "The ship was immersed into the lowest depths of the sea." The preposition, here, proves that there is a *passing into* the depths from the surface; but it does not prove that such "passing into" is expressed by "immersed," any more than in, "the ball was buried *into* the palmetto wood," the preposition proves that the passing into is expressed by "buried."

There is such a thing as the act of dipping, the act of

plunging, the act of sinking, the act of falling, the act of walking, as distinctive severally from all other acts, but there is no such thing as the act of immersion as distinctive from all other acts. There is no such thing as the act of dyeing, soaking, steeping, imbuing, immersing, as distinctive, severally, from all other acts. These terms express results equally reached by diversity of acts and processes.

But Dr. Conant does not confine himself to the use of this word as expressive of movement; he employs it, also, as expressive of rest. Thus he says, " The ground-idea expressed by this word is *to put into or put under water*, so as entirely *to immerse or submerge*." Here it is impossible for " immerse," " submerge," to express movement; they can only express the result of the movement *put into, put under*, namely, *a covered condition*. It is the capability of " im-merse" for this unlawful double use (without the same naked exposure of the wrong), which qualifies it to take the place of *dip* and *plunge*, without its friends feeling constrained to say that it makes their theory " senseless" and " ridiculous."

That the true character of *immerse* has been given is made certain by what Dr. Conant says of the " ground-idea" of the word.

" The ground-idea expressed by this word is *to put into or under*" (the act), " so as entirely to immerse or submerge" (the covered condition). " This ground-idea is expressed by the terms (synonymous *in this ground element*) *to immerse, immerge, submerge, to dip, to plunge, to imbathe, to whelm*." " The object immersed or sub-*merged*" (covered condition) " is represented as being plunged, or as sinking" (the act) " into the ingulfing" (covering) " fluid; or the immersing" (covering) " element overflows" (the act), " and thus ingulfs" (covers) " the object." " A sense founded on the idea of total *submergence*." " Whenever the idea of total *submergence*" (covering) " was to be expressed, this was the first word which presented itself." " All agreeing in the *essential* idea of *submergence*" (covering). " By constant usage expressed entire *submersion*" (covering). In all these statements *act* is most expressly excluded from the characteristic of the word and *condition* is substituted. And it is this "con dition," and not "act," which is made the basis of meta phorical use. "The *ground-idea* is preserved in the several metaphorical uses of the word." "The idea of a total *sub mergence*" (covering) "lies at the basis of these metaphorical uses." "A sense founded on the idea of total *submergence*" (covering), "as in floods of sorrow." "During the whole existence of the Greek as a spoken language, it meant *to put into or under*" (act), "so that the object was wholly *covered* by the inclosing element" (resultant condition). "By analogy, it expressed the *coming into a new state of life or experience*" (change of mental or moral condition), "in which one was as it were inclosed or swallowed up, so that temporarily or wholly he belonged unto it."

This metaphorical or secondary use of βαπτίζω can by no possibility be traced to any act by which the resultant con dition is induced, but is traceable solely to condition, with out any regard to the inducing act. That is to say, it springs out of the ground-idea of the word, which is a resultant con dition, and therefore the word *cannot express* "act," and *must express* "condition." Words which express act have their secondary use founded in the characteristics of such act. Thus, "I *plunged* into dissipation," is grounded in the literal characteristics of plunge—rapidity and violence. "I *dipped* into the dissipation of the city," is grounded on the literal characteristics of "dip"—limitation in force and entrance. "Tempted, I *fell* into dissipation," is grounded on the literal characteristics of "fall"—suddenness. "I *glided* into dissi pation," is grounded on the literal characteristics of "glide" —gentle, insensible movement. "I became *immersed* in dis sipation," is grounded in no literal characteristics of *plunge*, or *dip*, or *fall*, or *glide*, or of any other *act* expressed in lan guage. In the phrases, "*soaked* with rum," "*steeped* with love," "*imbued* with truth," "*infected* with vice," there is no grounding in act, for there is no characterizing act in "soak," "steep," "imbue," "infect." These words represent, liter ally, resultant condition of unexpressed act, and in their secondary use they express the characteristics of condition

and not of action. Now, if we could say, "immersed *with*
rum, *with* love, *with* truth, *with* vice" (which we cannot
under the sanction of usage), we would express not the characteristics of an act, but a condition characterized by the influence of "rum," "love," "truth," "vice." Now, this
failure in "immerse" to enter into such usage makes it
utterly break down as to its capacity to represent βαπτίζω.
For such usage is emphatically the usage of the Greek word.
Its characteristic duty is to give the fullest development to
the distinguishing quality of its adjunct. For this duty the
literal ground-idea of the word pre-eminently qualifies it,—
namely, a condition of complete envelopment. An object,
which is in a condition of envelopment within a fluid or
other related substance, is in a position best qualified to develop, exhaustively, the characteristic quality of the investing medium. That this is true, from the nature of the case,
is obvious. That this office is, in fact, performed by βαπτίζω,
is shown by additional statements of Dr. Conant.

He says, "By analogy, it expressed the *coming into a new
state of life or experience*, in which one was as it were inclosed
and swallowed up, so that, temporarily or permanently, he
belonged wholly to it." A remarkable deduction from *a
dipping !*

"Coming" is italicized. Is it meant to indicate that
βαπτίζω has anything to do with the manner of transition
from one state into another? whether by plunging, dipping,
sinking, falling, running, walking, or "coming" in any other
conceivable way? If so, nothing could be more groundless.
"Baptized into any state of life or experience" indicates a
complete change of condition characterized by the nature
of such state or experience whatever it may be; as to the
manner of "coming" into such state or experience the language says nothing. To be "inclosed and swallowed up *as
it were*" is a nonentity by self-declaration. As a reality it
must, without a miracle, involve misery and death as much
as Jonah's being "inclosed and swallowed up" in the whale's
belly. The Greek word, in secondary use, has nothing to
do with "inclosure and swallowing up," except as allusively

to that condition of things in physical relations by which
influence is fully developed. And this is the only use which
is made by Dr. Conant of such "as it were" condition; for
he declares that the only reality expressed is, that a man
"baptized into a new state of life" thenceforward "*belongs
wholly* to such state," that is to say, is brought under its *controlling influence*. If this is not the doctrine of Classic Baptism, then I do not know how to express it. Again, it is
said, "one was baptized in (there is no authority for 'in,'
it should be *by*) wine, when his faculties were *totally over-
borne* and *prostrated* by it." Here "controlling" influence is
directly acknowledged without the "inclosure and swallowing up," which has no existence, in such usage, but in a diseased imagination. So, also, "one was baptized with soph-
istries, when his mind was wholly confounded by them."
Here, again, we have the unequivocal acknowledgment that
βαπτίζω, in such usage, expresses controlling influence characterized by the nature of the adjunct. And this receives
distinct, general enunciation in the words immediately following,—"the relation in which it (βαπτίζω) was used associated with it, for the time being, the ideas peculiar to that
relation." What is this but the controlling assimilative influence of Classic Baptism, and the developed "qualitas,"
"vis," "δύναμις," of Judaic Baptism?

It has been my endeavor to give a faithful exhibition of
the teachings of Dr. Conant as to the meaning of this word.
I do not believe that a comparative study of all those teachings can furnish any other results. When the error as to
βαπτίζω expressing *act* is corrected, from Dr. Conant's own
teachings, and the ground-thought of *condition* (intusposition)
is substituted for "act," and when the farther consequent
correction is made, namely, the rejection of *act* as the basis
of interpreting metaphor, and condition as the source of influence, is substituted for it, then the teachings of Dr. Conant will overturn the theory and establish the results of
Classic and Judaic Baptism. Verbally Dr. Conant says, that
both Stourdza and Carson are right, βαπτίζω had but one

meaning for two thousand years, which meaning was an *act* equally well expressed by the diverse " plunge" and " dip;" in reality he proves, most indubitably, that βαπτίζω never did express an *act* whether of "plunge" or "dip," but a condition resultant from an unexpressed act.

President Alexander Campbell, Baptism, p. 148. " I would rather say, βαπτίζω is a word of *specific action.*" " There is no need of any other proof that βαπτίζω signifies a specific act. If then βαπτίζω once mean *dip*, it never can mean any other acts unless those actions are identically the same. It means *to dip* by consent of the whole world, and being a specific word, it never can have but one meaning."

The President of Bethany, like all others, under the iron stringency of theory brings out specific act as the meaning, and *dip* as its representative, only to sink it out of sight in *immerse* just as soon as he comes to the exposition of historical baptisms. It is as great a folly to take *plunge, dip,* and *immerse* as ground-thoughts, and to expect that their language development would be the same, as to take wheat, oats, and barley for seed, and expect each, in harvest, to bear the same grain as each other one.

Alexander Campbell, although outside of the regular Baptist ranks, stands squarely with them on the theoretic platform, *one meaning, and that meaning a specific act.*

There are evidently two features of uniformity among all these writers: 1. They all say one thing; 2. They all work out another thing.

We are, now, prepared to " see all the lexicons," to learn whether lexicographers indorse the one thing that is said, or the other thing that is done.

LEXICONS.

"All the lexicons" cannot be produced; but if any one should think the number insufficient, there is full liberty to add indefinitely to the list.

SCAPULA: mergo seu immergo, item submergo, item abluo, lavo.

STEPHENS: mergo seu immergo, ut quæ tingendi aut ablu-
eṇdi gratia aqua immergimus.

BASILEÆ: immergo.

BUDÆUS: immergo, mergo: pessundo, demergo, submergo,
intingo unguento, medicor, imbuo, colore inficio, inficio.

STOCKIUS: lavo, baptizo: proprie; est immergere ac intin-
gere in aquam; est lavare, abluere (tropice). Per
Synechdochen, designat totum Johannis ministerium,
miraculosam Sanctus S. effusionem.

PASSOW: βάπτω et βαπτίζω: mergo, immergo, tingo—quod sit
immergendo; differt a δύναι quod est profundum petere
et penitus submergi.

SUICER: mergo, immergo, submergo, aqua obruo; abluo,
lavo.

SCHLEUSNER: 1. Proprie; immergo ac intingo, in aquam immergo. 2. lavo, abluo (quia hand raro aliquid immergi
ac intingi solet ut lavetur).

SCHŒTGEN: mergo, immergo, abluo, lavo, largiter profundo.

DAMM: βαπτίζω et βάπτω: descendere facio, immergo, intingo.

HEDERICUS: (1) mergo, immergo, aqua obruo, (2) abluo,
lavo, (3) baptizo significatu sacro.

WAHL: a βάπτω, mergo; sæpius mergo in N. T. 1. immergo.
2. pro νίπτω lavo.

ROBERTSON'S SCHREVELII: mergo, lavo.

BRETSCHNEIDER: lavo, abluo—immergo in aquas; submergo.

PASSOW, *Leipzig*, 1831: oft und wiederholt eintauchen, un-
tertauchen, daher benitzen, anfeuchten, begiessen,
übertr, ὅτι βεβαπτίσμενοι, betrunkene, die sich begoessen
haben, *vino madidi*.

PARKHURST: from βάπτω to dip; to dip, immerse, or plunge
in water; Mid. and Pass., to wash oneself, be washed,
wash; to baptize, to wash in or with water in token of
purification from sin and from spiritual pollution; to
baptize as with cloud and sea; baptized (not *unto*, as our
English version has it, but) *into* Moses, *i. e.*, into the
Covenant, &c.; into Christ, &c.; Figurative of the Holy
Spirit, &c.

ROBINSON: to dip in, to sink, to immerse; to wash, to lave,

to cleanse by washing; to baptize, to administer the rite of baptism.

LIDDELL AND SCOTT: to dip in or under water; of ships, to sink them; metaphorically of the crowds who flocked into Jerusalem at the time of the siege. Pass., to bathe; metaphorically, soaked in wine; over head and ears in debt; a boy drowned in questions. II. To draw water, wine, &c.; III. To baptize.

DONEGAN: to immerse repeatedly into a liquid; to submerge, to soak thoroughly, to saturate; metonymically, to drench with wine; to dip in a vessel and draw.

SOPHOCLES: (βάπτω) to dip, to immerse; to sink, to be drowned as the effect of sinking, to sink. Tropically, to afflict, to soak in liquor, intoxicated; oppressed by debt; sunk in ignorance. 2. Mid., to perform ablution, to bathe. II. Bathed in tears, to plunge a knife. 4. Baptizo, mergo, mergito, tingo, or tinguo, to baptize.

A glance at these definitions will show how well grounded was Dr. Carson's acknowledgment, that "all the lexicographers" were against him as to his notion that βαπτίζω had no secondary meaning. This is the general doctrine of the theorists, and as a like error was once held by them respecting βάπτω, which was a perpetually occurring vice vitiating the interpretation of that word, and must do so in the case of every other word, I will give Dr. Carson's statement in his own language, italics, and capitals. "BAPTO, the root, I have shown to possess two meanings, and two only, to *dip* and to *dye*. BAPTIZO, I have asserted has but one signification. It has been formed on the primary meaning of the root, and has never admitted the secondary. Now, both these things have been mistaken by writers on both sides of this controversy. It has been generally taken for granted that the two words are equally applicable to baptism; and that they both equally signify to *dye*. Both of them are supposed in a secondary sense to signify to *wash* or *moisten*. I do not admit this with respect to either. I have already proved this with respect to BAPTO; the proof is equally

strong with respect to BAPTIZO.   My position is, THAT IT
ALWAYS SIGNIFIES TO DIP; NEVER EXPRESSING ANYTHING BUT
MODE.   Now, as I have all the lexicographers and commentators against me in this opinion, it will be necessary to say
a word or two with respect to the authority of lexicons.
Many may be startled at the idea of refusing to submit to
the unanimous authority of lexicons, as an instance of the
boldest skepticism.   Are lexicons, it may be said, of no
authority? Now, I admit that lexicons are an authority, but
they are not *an ultimate authority*. Lexicographers have been
guided by their own judgment in examining the various passages in which a word occurs; and it is still competent for
every man to have recourse to the same sources. *The meaning of a word must be determined by an actual inspection of the
passages in which it occurs, as often as any one chooses to dispute
the judgment of the lexicographer.*"

Dr. Carson and friends, thus, confess themselves to be at
war with " all lexicographers " as to βαπτίζω having a secondary meaning.   But this confession extends its influence
beyond the simple fact of error as to secondary meaning.
Every secondary meaning is inseparably connected with the
primary meaning by a natural and obvious bond.   Now, the
theory insists upon it, that the primary meaning is an act
characterized by mode and nothing but mode, and that such
act forms the basis of all metaphorical usage.   But is there
anything like modality of act in the secondary meaning of
this word?   There is none whatever.   Lexicographers give
" wash," and " cleanse," by more than twenty varying or
repeated defining terms, as the secondary meaning of this
verb; and in washing or cleansing, there is no modal act,
whether of dip, plunge, sink, or anything else.   So with regard to other secondary meanings—" intingo unguento, inficio colore, largiter profundo, imbuo, inficio, medicor, benitzen, anfeuchten, begiessen, betrinken, to afflict, to oppress,
to drown, to saturate "—these are the farthest possible removed from modal act as their basis.   We then conclude,
that the lexicographers not only differed from the theorists
as to a secondary meaning, but that the nature of tne

secondary meanings assigned by them to the word prove that they differed from the theorists entirely as to the nature of the primary meaning. Whether this conclusion be correct or not we shall be better able to determine by looking, directly, at the primary meanings assigned. And in doing so, we find that lexicographers furnish us with *mergo*, and its compounds, together with "immerse," and its equivalents (in which there is no modal act), more than thirty times; while the modal act in *tingo*, "dip," is represented only some half dozen times; "sink," three times; and "plunge," scarcely at all. This rare use of words of specific act to define this term (in a throng of words utterly devoid of modality in the act) is conclusive proof, that those who used them did not mean to use them in their modality, but for other considerations pertaining to them. None knew better than these lexicographers, that the same word could neither express two diverse acts, nor a modal act and a result of that or any other act as its primary meaning. They could not, therefore, have used several diverse acts to express the meaning of the same word. The point in which these and other diverse acts meet together is in the change of condition characterized by complete envelopment, which change of condition, and not act, they express, mainly, by "mergo." There is no evidence, worthy of consideration, to be deduced from the lexicons to prove, that they who made them supposed for a moment that βαπτίζω expressed act, specific or general. The evidence is all one way, proving that it expressed result effected by unexpressed act.

But several words may express condition, and have envelopment as a common characteristic of that condition, and still have a diverse language development. This is true of βυθίζω, and βαπτίζω. In many cases of primary use either of these words might be indifferently employed. But while there are few cases in which the former is used in which the latter might not be substituted for it, the converse is by no means true; βαπτίζω has a vastly greater and more diverse range of usage than βυθίζω. And while the latter is limited to the expression of **destructive** influences, the former has no

such limitation; but is adapted to express the development
of any influence which is penetrating, pervading, and assimilating in its character.   There could be no greater mistake
than to suppose that this word carried simply, or carried
always, with it the idea of envelopment.   *Βυθίζω* is translated
"*to throw* into, *to sink* into the deep." Does the word express
the modal acts *to throw, to sink?* Farther illustration may be
found in *immerse* and *steep*.   Both of these words are characterized by an enveloping element, but their usage differs as
widely as possible.   The former is never used to express a
development of the quality of the encompassing medium;
the latter is constantly so used.   And to perform this same
duty is a leading characteristic of *βαπτίζω*, which "immerse"
is just as incompetent to fulfil as it would be to perform the
functions of "steep."

   That the lexicographers understood that the function of
βαπτίζω was to express that controlling influence which so
naturally belongs to an encompassing medium is evident
from their secondary meanings, which could only originate
in such a source. To what else could be due such meanings
as "to cleanse religiously," "to imbue," "to infect," "to
medicate," "to saturate," "to afflict," "to oppress," "to
bewilder," "to intoxicate?" From what "specific act"
could such meanings spring?   What "specific act" is revealed as present and running through these meanings as
their unifying bond?

   The lexicons and the theory are not at one.

   But Dr. Carson says, "This word has been formed on the
primary meaning of the root, and has never admitted the
secondary.   My position is that it always signifies dip;
never expressing anything but mode." For this statement
there is not the shadow of support, as seen by the facts of
usage and the defining terms of lexicographers.   The reverse statement would be far nearer the truth, if indeed it
be not the absolute truth.   There is no evidence that *βαπτίζω*
does ever give expression to dip in its specific character.
There is no evidence that it expresses modal act of any kind.
There is no conclusive evidence that "this word has been

formed on the primary meaning of the root." There is, I think, conclusive evidence to the contrary. It is incredible that a second word should be created which was to be the simple *ditto* of one already existing. The whole history of the word declares that what was *a priori* incredible has, in reality, no existence. The attributes of a dipping—feebleness and evanescence—nowhere attach themselves to the usage of this word. On the other hand, the general characteristics of the secondary meaning of the root appear in the boldest relief through all the history of the word. I say the general characteristics, for, of course, it can have nothing to do with the specialty of βάπτω *second* in the direction of *dyeing, staining, coloring,* &c. But this being laid aside, we have an object placed within an enveloping medium, by an unexpressed act, without limitation of time as to its continuance, for the purpose of developing the quality of the encompassing element by its penetrating, pervading, and assimilating the object to itself alike in βαπτίζω and in βάπτω second. 2. And as in the case of βάπτω *second*, we have, in progressive usage, the encompassing feature of the influential agency laid aside and qualities of like characteristics developed, in any way, harmonious with their nature; so is it with βαπτίζω. Βαπτίζω is an extension of βάπτω *second* (its preoccupied dye-tub excluded), with all its rights and privileges as to freedom of act and rejection of envelopment, and advancing to give full development to characteristic qualities, powers, and influences over appropriate objects.

Few, I think, can look at the usage of βάπτω *first*, and βάπτω *second*, and doubt where the immediate relationship of βαπτίζω is to be found. This view harmonizes with that of Grammarians who derive βαπτίζω from βάπτος, a derivative from βάπτω *second*. The Hindoo theory, which rests the world on the back of a tortoise, is as just as that which rests the usage of βαπτίζω on *dip*. Whether Professor Arnold still thinks that there is an elephantine power in "plunge, literal and universal," to uphold the theory, when that of the tortoise fails, I do not know.

WANT OF GENERALIZATION.

The definitions of this word as given by the lexicons are too individual and isolated. They are often very alien from each other in some outstanding features, and do not present an obvious radical unity. There is a want of generalization which would group the various cases together under some common characteristic. This is necessary when the same word is defined by *mergo, im-mergo, sub-mergo, de-mergo, pessundo, aqua obruo, descendere facio, plunge, sink, dip.* Dr. Carson attempts to effect such generalization by swallowing up all other terms in "dip." He might as well attempt to put the millions of London into one room, eight by ten. His own friends begin to feel the folly of this and shrink back from a "senseless dipping." Professor Arnold would remedy this error by substituting "plunge." But "the venerable Booth" says that this is only exchanging that which is "senseless" for something which is "ridiculous." Dr. Conant proposes to remedy the difficulty through "immerse," used in a double sense, now as expressive of act (*put into*), and now of condition (*put under*), using the one or the other as the exigency of the case may demand. But this is only a fruitless attempt to substitute the *impossible* for what his friends have condemned as "senseless" and "ridiculous." I submit, with cheerful deference, to all who are disposed to examine the facts of the case, whether the true and only element of unity in such defining terms is not found in inness of condition—*mersion.* If this be true, then they should be grouped together under such ground-thought.

But there is another class of defining terms, such as "intingo unguento, medicor, imbuo, colore inficio, inficio" (Budæus); "benitzen, anfeuchten, begiessen, betrinken" (Passow, Franz); "flocking crowds, soaked in wine, over head and ears in debt, drowned in questions" (Liddell and Scott); "soak thoroughly, drench with wine, saturate" (Donegan); "to be drowned (as effect), to afflict, to soak in liquor, to intoxicate, to oppress, to sink in ignorance" (Sophocles); which require another generalization. These are all cases which indicate not an act to be done, but an end to be accomplished, an influence or quality to have its highest development.

Nothing is more obvious than that a condition of mersion is calculated to influence the object in such mersion, in the completest degree, by such quality as may belong to the investing element. Hence proceeds the secondary meaning of controlling influence effected in other ways than by mersion. Some of the lexicographers tell us expressly, that it is on this feature that they ground their secondary meaning. Thus Schleusner says, " Lavo, abluo, quod hand raro aliquid immergi ac intingi solet ut lavetur;" and Stephens, in like manner, says, "Ut quæ tingendi aut abluendi, gratia aqua immergimus." While washing or ablution may be secured by putting a thing into water, it is, also, true that it may be and commonly was effected otherwise; and in religious washings and ablutions was almost universally effected in other ways. It is also true, that this secondary meaning of " washing," " cleansing" (so universally ascribed by lexicographers to this word), applies to religious purifications. I do not know of a single instance in Classic, Jewish, or Christian writings in which βαπτίζω is used to denote a physical cleansing. It is expressly stated in some of the lexicons, that it was religious washings which they had in view. Thus Hedericus says, " baptizo, significatu sacro;" and Parkhurst says, " To wash in or with water *in token of* purification from sin and spiritual pollution."

The various defining terms, now under consideration, have no possible connection with the modality of act either in " dip" or in " plunge." That they do unite together under influence, characterized by thoroughness and assimilation, will, I think, be the judgment of all outside of the theory. And under this ground-thought they should be classified.

The appropriation of βαπτίζω, by Classic writers, to express the influence of wine when drunk, is so frequent and so absolute, that it fairly claims the right and power to express that influence directly; and, in like manner, this same word is so frequently and absolutely used, both by Jewish and Christian writers, in religious rites, that it, no less justly, claims the right and power to express, directly, the purifying influence (ceremonially or symbolly) of such rites.

The conclusion, then, to which we are brought, after "seeing all the lexicons," is this: We may and, in my judgment, must define substantially thus: I. *ΒΑΠΤΙΖΩ*, TO MERSE: (To effect the intusposition of an object within a closely investing element, by any competent act or acts, for an indefinite time.)

II. TO BAPTIZE: (To effect a mersive (complete and assimilative) influence, thoroughly changing the condition (whether physical, mental, or moral), without limitation in the act, in the time of continuance, or in the character of the influence.)

III. (1) To INTOXICATE; (2) To PURIFY, ceremonially or symbolly.

How much this decision, of the lexicons, differs from that to which we were conducted, by usage, in Classic and Judaic Baptism, I leave for others to determine. It may be assumed, however, that the theorists will no longer say that we fled from the lexicons to usage because "all the lexicographers were against us." And if any should feel that the gratification of their desire "to be assailed by Scapula and Stephens" has brought big rocks into uncomfortable proximity to their "position," they must not complain of those who have obligingly met their earnest request.

BAPTIST QUARTERLY—"UNLEARNED AND HALF LEARNED."

"J. T. C.," in another article of the Baptist Quarterly, says: "It is not creditable to our religious journalism that such works as Mr. Dale's Classic Baptism should find countenance or favor in any quarter. Such a caricature of philological discussion has any but a healthy influence on the field of scientific inquiry, and tends only to embitter denominational strife. We feel assured that the scholarship of the country silently condemns, as it sometimes does audibly,

such attempts to impose on the unlearned and the half learned."
It appears to be singularly difficult for "J. T. C." and his
friends to harmonize in their estimate of the demerits of
" Mr. Dale's works."

A Baptist theological professor, and a particular friend of
"J. T. C.," thus writes in this same Baptist Quarterly:
" Men eminent in the pulpit and the lecture-room have been
unable adequately to express their admiration of the extraordinary skill and learning which Mr. Dale has brought to
his task, and their delight at the accession to their ranks of
this new and potent ally. Mr. Dale must not be deceived
by this multitudinous din of applause."

The National Baptist mentions the names of some of those
" unlearned and half learned men imposed upon by Classic
Baptism." They are " Jonathan Edwards, President of
Washington and Jefferson College, Pennsylvania; Thomas
H. Skinner, Professor of Union Theological Seminary, New
York; William S. Plummer, Professor of Columbia Theo-
logical Seminary, South Carolina; Charles Hodge, Professor
of Princeton Theological Seminary, New Jersey; Lyman
Coleman, Professor of La Fayette College; and many
others;" among which "many others," the National Baptist
might have enumerated Bishop Stevens, of Pennsylvania;
Bishop Coxe, of New York; Bishop Clarke, of Rhode
Island; Bishop Cummins, of Kentucky; Bishop Lee, of
Delaware; Bishop Simpson, M. E., of Pennsylvania; Bishop
Scott, M. E., of Delaware; and scores of like "unlearned
and half learned men," just the people (?) to be imposed
upon by "a caricature of philological discussion."

And those weeklies, monthlies, and quarterlies, East,
West, North, and South, which have brought "discredit"
upon our religious journalism by showing "countenance
and favor" to Mr. Dale's works, will please take warning,
and hereafter forever hold their peace, or speak in that
vocabulary which proves membership in "the scholarship
of the country" by crying, "trickster," "thimblerigger,"
" caricaturist," "impostor," and "ignoramus."

To these remarks on things adjacent to the special point of our investigation I will only add that I am well convinced that " J. T. C." can write on this subject something better than " a philological caricature."   And should it please him so to do, he will find that (however incompetent the present writer may be) there are four thousand " mere country pastors " in the Presbyterian church, who, coming dusty and bronzed from the prairie and the mountain, from the crossroad and the log cabin, from the coal mine and the gold digging, are fully competent " to read, mark, and inwardly digest" anything which he may write, without danger of being imposed upon by " unlearned or half learned " lucubrations, or, even, by theories learnedly sustained against the laws of language and the teachings of the word of God.

JOHANNIC BAPTISM

CONSIDERED IN ITS NATURE AND AS ILLUSTRATIVE OF THE
USAGE OF

ΒΑΠΤΙΖΩ.

Various Views.

JOHANNIC BAPTISM belongs exclusively to the Holy Scriptures. In connection with this baptism we meet for the first time with the Greek word *βαπτίζω* as employed by inspired men. And the related words, *βαπτιστής* and *βάπτισμα*, we meet, chronologically, for the first time in any writings. This fact is of the highest importance. It is an assertion by inspired writers of the highest sovereignty, within the realm and laws of language, to use, to modify, or to form words according to the exigencies created by the utterance of inspired truth. No thoughtful man will claim for inspired men an arbitrary authority over the usage or meaning of words. And no wise man will attempt to fetter these writers to a sterile usage of words and meanings antedating the fruitful thoughts of inspiration. With the most unbounded confidence in the *ipsissima verba* of inspiration as well-chosen words, having a precise meaning which may be learned by the use of proper helps without and within the Scriptures, in the docile looking for light unto their only wise Author, I will endeavor, thus, to learn the scriptural meaning and usage of that word which is the special end of this inquiry.

John's baptism on its first announcement awakened inquiry as to its origin—" Was it from heaven or of men?" and, also, as to its nature—" What baptism dost thou baptize?" But it was not until more than a thousand years after his ministry had been completed, that any one thought it worth while to ask—" In what mode did John use water in ritual baptism ?" There is every reason to believe that we can find satisfactory answers to the evidently important and scriptural inquiries as to the authority and nature of John's baptism; and if the inquiry respecting the manner in which he used the symbol water be either important or scriptural, we shall, no doubt, also, find its solution. Should we, however, be disappointed in this, we may bear such disappointment with equanimity on the ground, that it was rejected from record by inspiration, and that God's people never felt the need of making inquiry about it for the space of a thousand and a half thousand years.

Opinion as to the nature and power of John's baptism has been diverse. This diversity, however, has not arisen, so much, under an independent examination of the terms and circumstances of the baptism, as under the demands of a previously conceived religious system.

Early Christian writers agreed, very generally, in saying, that John's baptism was, in its nature, superior to Jewish baptism, but, no less, inferior to Christian baptism. Their sentiment is well expressed by Chrysostom in the following passage: " The baptism of John was, indeed, far superior to the Jewish but inferior to ours; it was a kind of bridge between the two baptisms leading from that to this." More particularly they believed, that John's baptism was destitute of the Holy Spirit and of power to remit sins. If this language be interpreted according to its terms it is obvious, that " baptism" can by no possibility refer to " the mode and nothing but the mode" of using the water. According to the theory, Jewish baptism, and John's baptism, and Christian baptism, were pure and identical forms; but according to these early Greek writers they were characterized not by uniformity but by diversity. Doubtless this may all be rectified by the introduction of " figure" (that servant of all work to the theory) by which one thing is made to take the place of some other thing; but it has been shown, that words expressive of definite action or of condition, do come to express, directly, the effects resultant from such action or condition; and, in particular, it has been shown, that this is true of βαπτίζω. Until this is disproved these early writings must be allowed to stand as unfigured utterances when they declare, that baptism Judaically administered differed from baptism Johannically administered; and baptism Johannically administered differed from baptism Christianly administered; and baptism Christianly administered differed from both the others. They speak of ashes, blood, and water as possessed of diverse powers in their ritual use, and therefore effecting diverse conditions on the part of those to whom they are ritually applied. These diverse conditions they designate as *Jewish* baptism, *John's* baptism, *Christian* baptism. And I do not see but that it must so stand, inasmuch as the authority to revise and correct their writings has not been bequeathed to any after generation.

The Roman Catholic Church adopts, unreservedly, these views of the early Christian writers. The Tractarians share, with as little reserve, in the same sentiments. The Reformers, generally, did not adopt these views, or, at least, not without both modifications and differences. Calvin says: "This is the peculiarity of Baptism, that it is said to be an outward representation of repentance for the forgiveness of sins. Now, as the meaning, and power, and nature, of that baptism are the same as ours, if we judge of the figure by its true import, it is incorrect to say, that the baptism of John is different from the baptism of Christ. It ought not to have any weight with us that an opinion has long and extensively prevailed that John's baptism differs from ours. We must learn to form our judgment from the matter as it stands, and not from the mistaken opinions of men." Lightfoot says, " The baptism of John and the baptism of the Apostles was one and the same."

Among more modern writers subordinate differences are revealed. Dr. Halley says: " To be baptized, then, was to be initiated as a disciple or learner of the new doctrine—the speedy coming of Christ. Of this baptism of John we have, I think, sufficient evidence for determining two particulars,

the one that it was indiscriminately administered to all ap-
plicants, the other that it effected no change, moral or
spiritual, upon their minds. The baptism of John and of
the disciples during our Lord's personal ministry were
really Christian baptisms." Dr. Miller, on the other hand,
says: "John's baptism was not Christian baptism." Professor Wilson (Royal College, Belfast) says: "The baptism
of repentance for the remission of sins, whether administered by John, or the disciples of Jesus, uniformly appears
in the character of a rite, which foes and followers equally
comprehended."

Baptist writers, generally, identify the baptism of John
with the baptism of Christianity. Thus Stovel says: "The
baptized person was committed to all the intents and purposes of the kingdom of heaven. This dealing with individuals, and setting them apart for the kingdom of Christ,
because of their personal faith and repentance, commenced
with John, it formed the peculiarity of his ministration."
Dr. Carson, as usual, is very positive and very explicit; he
says: "What is baptism in one case is baptism in another.
Whatever difference there may be, in any other respect, between the baptism of John and the baptism of Christ, *there
could be no difference in the mode.*" Inasmuch as this writer
believes that baptism is essentially mode and its conception
is exhausted in its mode, there could not possibly be any
difference between these two baptisms, or any other conceivable number of baptisms from any quarter. But the
early Christian writers declare, with one voice, that these
baptisms were diverse. The conceptions, then, of baptism
entertained, respectively, by these writers and by Dr. Carson must have been radically different. To attempt to unify
these statements by saying, that the Patrists did not refer to
the mode when they said that one of these baptisms differed
from the other, is to make them say, on the principles of the
theory, that John's baptism (mode) differed from Christian
baptism (mode), yet John's mode (baptism) was the same
as the Christian mode (baptism). Robert Hall thinks that
there is a contrast rather than an agreement between the two

baptisms—"The baptism instituted by our Lord is in Scripture distinguished from that of the Forerunner by the superior effects with which it was accompanied, so that instead of being confounded they are contrasted in the Sacred Writings."

The diversity exhibited in some of these statements is more apparent than real. The writers have not the same thing in view. The baptism of John (I mean baptism properly and scripturally speaking, not a modal use of water) agreed, in certain respects, with Christian baptism (again rejecting all reference to a modal use of water), while in certain other respects it differed from it. It is proper to say, that the two baptisms, while distinguished by distinctive characteristics, were in perfect harmony with each other. It is not proper to say, that they are the same baptism in all respects. Nor are they so far the same that they could be interchanged. Christian baptism is complementary of John's baptism.

The phraseology, "Baptism of John," implies a distinctive difference between this baptism and other baptisms, and especially between this baptism and Jewish baptism, with which it was brought into contact and contrast. It could not be brought into comparison with Christian baptism, for that baptism had not yet received development. The discriminating difference between this and other baptisms must be sought in one or the other of the only two elements entering into the expressive phrase—"John's baptism." It must be found in *John* personally or in the *baptism*. That there is room for discriminating between John as a preacher of baptism and the administrator of the ritual ordinance of baptism, and Christ or the Holy Spirit, the divine executors of baptism, is most obvious. This amazing difference is most pointedly stated by John himself. While he places the baptism preached by him in immediate contact with Christ and of its proper nature preparative for and essential to welcoming him at his coming, he does at the same time separate the ritual use of water (grounded on this baptism preached), both as to its nature and power by a limitless distance from

Christ and his kingdom. But the phrase under consideration as used in Scripture, never raises the question as to the
measure of power invested, personally, in John, or the Jewish administrator, as causative of the difference in their respective baptisms. No solution of the question as to the
differential nature of John's baptism is to be found in the
powers of the administrator. The difference must be found
in the baptism. But if in the baptism, yet, not in the act
by which the baptism is effected. It is in proof that the
form of act by which a baptism is effected is a matter of infinite indifference. The Jews used, indifferently, the varied
action of sprinkling, pouring, washing, in effecting their
baptism; and John might use any one of these or any other
act, and it could not be a discriminating mark of his baptism,
for there is no such element entering into the essence of
baptism. The Jews used, indifferently, ashes, blood, fire,
water, in effecting their baptism; and John might have used
some one of these or some other thing in his baptism, and
the specialty of his baptism have not been, thereby, determined. The instrumental means may determine the character of a baptism, but does not do so necessarily. As a
matter of fact the Jew used water in his baptism, and John,
likewise, used water in his baptism; still, their baptisms
were not the same. The Jew may have administered his
baptism to men, women, and children, beds, pots, and cups;
and John may have baptized only men or pots; and this
would not have determined the peculiarity of his baptism.
The subjects of baptism do not, by any necessity, control
the baptism. Although they may, by their nature, limit the
application of the baptism. Beds, pots, and cups were, in
their nature, well adapted to be objects of Jewish baptism;
but that same nature excluded them, in the most absolute
manner, from John's baptism.

Bengel, speaking of the distinguishing character of John's
baptism, says: " At the baptism of repentance men confessed their sins, at the baptism of Christ they confessed
Christ." Olshausen, most wisely, disjoins and yet conjoins
preaching baptism and ritual baptism: " It would readily

occur to him *to represent by a symbolical rite the repentance which he preached.* The Divine Spirit, who quickened him, was his guide in this institution as in all that he did; he was sent to baptize with water. The baptism of John cannot be identical with the sacrament of Baptism, which was not ordained till after the resurrection. It was a washing of repentance, but not a washing of regeneration."

THE ESSENCE OF BAPTISM.

The absolute exclusion of "pots, cups, and couches," "legs, breasts, and shoulders" of sacrificial victims from "John's baptism" turns, wholly, on the nature of that baptism. John made demand for repentance. The utensils of domestic life and the elements of temple service could make no response to this demand. The baptism was not for, and could not, possibly, be received by such things.

And, here, arises the question—Are baptisms distinguishable not by the form of act by which they are effected, not by the subjects receiving the administration, not by the elements used in the service, not by a physical envelopment or otherwise, but by a distinctive character, whether attained by uniformity or diversity in any or all of these particulars? And does this distinguishing character constitute the very baptism, so that as it is present or absent, the baptism has, or has not an existence? We answer these questions in the affirmative, and say, that the phrase "John's baptism" neither expresses modal action, nor fluid envelopment, but a peculiar character or condition, separating it, in nature, especially from Jewish baptisms, and, in general, from all other baptisms endlessly diverse in character.

It may be proper to introduce, here, some remarks as illustrative and sustaining these positions. That a baptism is expressive of the condition of an object brought into a state of physical envelopment by any competent act, for an indefinitely prolonged period of time, or which is brought under the power of some controlling influence without actual or suggested envelopment, is a truth which has been established, in the opinion of competent judges, by an amount of evidence seldom brought to the vindication of any philological question.

It follows, therefore, that when a baptism is spoken of (the character of which is not unquestionably determined), it is an open question, whether it belongs to the class of baptisms distinguished by physical envelopment, or to that class which rejects physical envelopment and presents only a mental or moral condition, the result of some controlling and assimilating influence. And, consequently, when Dr. Carson says, in reference to the baptism of John and the baptism of Christ—"What was baptism in one case is baptism in another, there could be no difference in the mode"—he makes the most unwarrantable assumptions: 1. That the mere use of the word baptism in any number or variety of cases establishes, in all, an identity of character; 2. That that identity is exhibited in mode; and 3. That that mode is a dipping. The language of Scripture—"the baptism of John," "the baptism of Moses," "the baptism of Christ"— involves of necessity discriminating difference. If, now, this discriminating difference be not exhausted in the difference of persons—John, Moses, Christ—then it must be in the baptism; but if in the baptism, then baptism cannot be modal act or modal envelopment, for such things do not allow of any discriminating differences. If to escape this conclusion it should be said, that "baptism" may include more than *baptism*, it may take in appendages, and in these the difference may be found. I answer: these appendages are essential to the baptism or they are not; if they are essential, then they are the baptism; if they are not essential, then they cannot expound the differences of baptisms. If it should be said, that a Hottentot differs from an Esquimaux, would we be satisfied that this statement was met by showing that the one was dressed in a cotton strip and the other in furs; that the one was housed in an open kraal and the other within walls of solid ice; that the one lived on fruits and the other on train oil? All these things may be true, and they may truly expound the differences in clothing, in housing, and in eating; but do they expound the differential characteristics which distinguish a Hottentot from a Laplander? The theory claims a difference for its baptism as compared with the baptism of the rest of the Christian world. Would it be judged satisfactory to expound this difference as consisting in the wearing in one case a water-proof suit and in the other case ordinary apparel? Would anything be considered satisfactory but what related to the essence of baptism? If not, then, when the Scriptures teach a difference between the baptism of Moses, and the baptism of John, and the baptism of Christ, we, in like manner, must insist that the differences shall be found in the essentials and not in the accidents of these baptisms. The necessity which is, here, laid upon the theory for departing from the simple and explicit statement of the Scriptures, is a necessity which is found to be evermore recurring in its history, and is the most conclusive evidence that it is not in harmony with the word of God.

ILLUSTRATION FROM CLASSIC BAPTISMS.

In farther elucidation and vindication of this position, I would refer to the illustrative Classic Baptisms of Thebe, Ishmael, and Satyrus. Were these baptisms identical or diverse in character? Inasmuch as the term "baptism" is applied equally to each, they must have a common element establishing a generic unity. And as they are distinguished from each other as the baptism of *Thebe*, the baptism of *Ishmael*, and the baptism of *Satyrus*, we look for differences which shall resolve baptism as a genus into its species. Carson says, that baptism is a simple, ultimate, unresolvable element; that baptism is baptism; that mode is mode; that the meaning of the word is mode, and that this meaning was never changed. If this be true, then, this mode will be found in all these baptisms, and such mode will constitute the baptism. And, as matter of fact, there is mode in each baptism; I was about to say, that it was found in the common handing of the wine, but in this there may be diversity;

I, then, fell back on the common drinking of the wine, but, here, there is no absolute assurance against diversity, and rest was found only in the common act of swallowing. This, I believe, is severely modal, a simple, ultimate, unresolvable act, and which, according to the theory, must constitute the baptism. The only embarrassment in the case is to show that the modal act of swallowing is neither more nor less than the modal act of dipping, whose presence or absence we are told makes or mars a baptism.

If this can be done the theory is safe so far as the baptisms of Thebe, of Ishmael, and of Satyrus are concerned.

If any should be so doubtful of the success of such an attempt as to be unwilling to wait its issue, I will endeavor to indicate some other common element in which these baptisms agree, and which constitutes the justification in applying a common name to cases which present specific differences.

Historically the baptism of Thebe was by wine, which she furnished profusely to her husband. The simple drinking of wine will not effect a baptism, nor can the drinking of any quantity effect a dipping or an envelopment; but profuse drinking will so develop the power of wine as to bring the mental faculties and the physical powers under its control. This thorough change of condition (the passing out of a condition of sobriety into a condition of ebriety) is a baptized condition. It is so, generically, because it is a condition effected by some controlling and assimilating influence; and it is so, specifically, to wit, the baptism of *Thebe*, because it is a specific influence effecting a specific condition. The wine-drinking causative of this baptism, and the drunken condition caused by this wine-drinking, are alike inseparable from this Thebe baptism. The one cannot be without the other. If the peculiarity which marks the influence of the agency is known, then the peculiarity which characterizes the condition is equally known.

The baptism of Ishmael was by wine like that of Thebe, and yet was not specifically the same. It was a baptism be-yond that baptism. It was a development of the power of drunkenness effecting a still farther and peculiar controlling influence over mind and body, introducing them into a condition of "insensibility and sleep." Now, no one needs to be told, that there is an amazing difference between the condition of a man bewildered in mind and staggering in walk, and a man lying under the table insensible and asleep. Wine enters into both conditions as the ruling power; in the one case it is the immediate influence, in the other case it is the proximate influence; both conditions are properly called baptisms, because they both have the characteristic of condition resultant from some controlling influence; and they are specifically diverse baptisms, because the specific controlling influence of wine over a sober man is diverse from the specific controlling influence of drunkenness over an intoxicated man. This specific difference is stated, with a fulness and a clearness beyond which language cannot go, when we are told, that "Ishmael baptized Gedaliah by drunkenness into insensibility and sleep." The statement that Ishmael "baptized" Gedaliah conveys no specific information; while the statement that "he baptized him *into insensibility*" has a sharpness which will cut its way irresistibly through all barriers of modal act, or water envelopment, that ever were or that ever can be constructed.

The baptism of Satyrus exhibits the element of wine, but not as the controlling power effecting the baptism. There was, also, in it "insensibility and sleep," and yet not of the same specific character with that which is effected by overpowering drunkenness. There was not enough of wine drunk to cause ebriety, consequently that was not the baptism; if there was no ebriety, then there was no baptism from this cause.

But there was a baptism of Satyrus. What was it? It was a thoroughly changed condition resultant from the controlling influence of an *opiate drug* swallowed by being mingled in a cup of wine. In these facts we find justification for applying the generic term baptism to this transaction, because there is a condition resultant from a controlling influence which has left its characteristic enstamped upon the subject of its power; while they, also, vindicate the discrimination of this baptism as the baptism of *Satyrus*, from the baptism of *Thebe*, and the baptism of *Ishmael*, because, specifically, it ranks with neither of these baptisms.

These facts show in the most indubitable manner, that where the same fluid element is present, and the same formal act is executed, the resultant *baptism* (not something else, some appendage or accident, but the very baptism) may be essentially diverse. This diversity will, ordinarily, be designated with clearness by the simple statement of the power effecting the baptism, because the baptism receives its characteristic from the characteristic of this controlling influence; but if this baptizing power is capable of producing diverse conditions, immediately or remotely, then a specific designation may be required in addition to the influence itself. Thus, the remoter wine baptism of Ishmael is saved from being confounded with the immediate wine baptism of Thebe by the superadded statement, that it was remotely by wine and immediately "by drunkenness into insensibility and sleep."

Can anything be more unwise or more alien from outjutting facts, than the attempt to repudiate the distinctive character of these baptisms by the round assertion, that "baptism in one case is baptism in another, there could be no difference in the mode?"

"THESE BAPTISMS ARE FIGURATIVE."

An attempt is made to get rid of these baptisms and bury them (if not "without benefit of clergy," yet beyond the reach of the clergy), in some bottomless abyss, by affirming that these baptisms are "figurative." If by this term is meant that these are not actual and most real baptisms, the statement could not be more deeply stamped with error. Is not the condition of a drunken man, of a sleeping man, of a drugged man, a most substantial reality? If it is meant to say, that these baptisms are not physical baptisms, then, again, I reply, the error, still, is as profound as in the other case. Is not drunkenness a physical condition? Does it not affect the intellect only as it affects the physical organs through which it operates? Is not this, also, true of sleep? And is it not, equally, true of drugged stupor? Is not wine a real, substantial fluid? Is not opium a real existence whose solidity may be seen, and felt, and weighed in the balances? Do fluids and solids produce purely metaphysical, ideal, unreal, nonentical conditions?

Is it meant to say, that these baptisms are not "dipping" baptisms? Then, the response may be given with a smile: Certainly if they are, appearances must be deceitful, for they have any other appearance! Is it meant that there is no physical envelopment? I would not like to undertake to prove that there is, but I would like, very much, to see such ·attempt made on the part of those who affirm that "baptism in one case is baptism in another; there can be no difference in the mode." And this more than Herculean task they must enter upon and perfect, or else confess (to the undoing of their theory), that the Greeks called conditions, without physical envelopment, baptisms.

Finally: Is it meant, that although there is no physical envelopment, yet there is an imaginary envelopment? The theory luxuriates in the realms of imagination. We need not care, so far as any practical end of this inquiry is concerned, to disturb its enjoyment there. But so far as mental science, or rhetorical exposition, or language development are concerned, it may be worth while to enter a denial and call for proof. And, first, I would ask: Of what is this fiction envelopment to be constituted? With what, for example, is Thebe's husband to be enveloped in order to his baptism? With vinous influence? something that would make drunk come? Then there must be physical embodiment of this influence, and the imagination has constructed a physical envelopment as truly as if the object were placed at earth's centre, and it were wrapped about with al. continents and oceans. Besides, the imagination not only makes bankrupt all her powers in such vain endeavor, but plays the lunatic in assuming it, for we have this vinous influence already operating in and through the man, with his full stomach as its interior base. Why, then, this "fifth wheel to the wagon?" A like issue is reached in attempting to eliminate from the baptisms of Ishmael and of Satyrus the act and the form of development assigned to them by the Greeks, and substituting for them acts most impracticable and forms most irrational. But, secondly, I would ask: If the imagination could construct a nonentity dipping or a nonentity envelopment, how could diverse results spring out of envelopment, one and simple? Whence the diverse baptisms: 1. Of Thebe—drunkenness; 2. Of Ishmael—insensibility and sleep; 3. Of Satyrus—drugged stupor? Is a remedy sought for this by impregnating these several nonentity envelopments with various energizing powers qualifying them for the needed end? Then, all hail! to the theory which abandons dipping-envelopment as a reed on which she has leaned but to pierce her hand, and, at length, accepts of controlling influences as executors of baptism and marking their diversity by enstamping upon them their several characteristics.

It is most obvious, that in these baptisms, and in all kindred baptisms, there is a declaration of controlling power exerted by a given influence over its object. This is made in the most direct and simple manner in the case of Thebe's baptism—ὄινω δὲ πολλῷ 'Αλεξανδρον βαπτίσασα; here, it is not wine as a fluid dipped into, made to envelop in any way, sprinkled upon or poured out, which effects the baptism, but as a fluid which may be drunk, and which when drunk (and not in any other way) develops a peculiar power controlling the physical system and the mental operations. As long as words shall have meaning, and common sense shall reign in their interpretation, these Greek words will declare wine to be the baptizing power, and the resultant condition the baptism, whose distinctive character is determined by that of wine, the baptizing power.

The phraseology expressive of Ishmael's baptism (as limited to the baptizing power) is not so self-asserting as to the distinctive character of the baptism as is that of

Thebe. It is evident that the phrase βεβαπτισμένον ὑπὸ μέθης will never be of so common occurrence as the phrase βεβαπτισμένον οἴνῳ. The possible conditions within the competency of drunkenness to effect are also various. Unless frequent usage, therefore, should identify it with some one condition in particular, there must be more or less ambiguity in the phrase "baptized by drunkenness." Where the greatest perspicuity is desired all ambiguity is removed in the most absolute measure by the addition of a verbal element. This is done by Josephus, in the present case, by saying, βεβαπτισμένον ὑπὸ μέθης εἰς ἀναισθησίαν καὶ ὕπνον. It is impossible for language to express a definite baptism more definitely than is done by these words. The form of the phraseology carries us back to the primary use of βαπτίζω, where we see an object passing into some permeable element (never more to emerge so far as this Greek word is concerned), and therefore brought completely under the influence of such element. It is impossible for Thebe's husband to enter, actually, "*into* insensibility and sleep," and it would be labor lost if we could, imaginatively, give him such a local habitation, for withinness without influence would be nothing and worse than nothing, while to hunt up controlling influence through such left-handed method would, if found, be only to find what was already legitimately in possession by the allusion, stamped in the phraseology, to the primary use.

While, therefore, in the great majority of cases it may be sufficiently clear what was the character of the baptism by a statement limited to the baptizing power, the addition of the element into which the baptism, by verbal figure, takes place, gives a precision to the statement beyond which language cannot go. After Josephus had once made the full statement βεβαπτισμένον ὑπὸ μέθης εἰς ἀναισθησίαν καὶ ὕπνον, there was no farther necessity for its repetition when the context clearly showed that he referred to this baptism. It would be abundantly sufficient for him to say, βεβαπτισμένον ὑπὸ μέθης, or simply βεβαπτισμένον. The ellipsis would, readily, and must necessarily, be supplied.

In the baptism of Satyrus the statement is, τῷ αὐτῷ φαρμάχῳ
χαταβαπτίσας. The context making explicit declaration of the
peculiar power of the drug, namely, *sleep producing*, the
phrase (limited to the baptizing power)—"baptizing by the
same drug"—has an explicitness, as to the nature of the baptism effected, which does not admit of increase by the addition of any other words.

The baptism of Thebe, then, expresses not a distinction in
any accidents which may have been associated with the baptism, but a distinction in the baptism itself. It was a *drunken*
baptism. The same is true of the baptism of Ishmael. It
was a *stupidly insensible* baptism. And so of the baptism of
Satyrus. It was a *drugged stupor* baptism. It is irrational
and impracticable to convert these distinctions into accidents.

In like manner, among scores of kindred baptisms, we
have the baptism of Otho, which was a baptism by *debt;* and
the baptism of the Sophists, which was a baptism by *questions;* and the baptism of Demosthenes, which was a baptism
by *contentious words*. So, also, we have baptism by *grief,* by
taxes, by *diseases*, &c., &c., without number. Now, can any
one, not born in lunacy and grown gray amid its phantasies,
affirm, that all these baptisms are one and the same in nature?
Is not the adjunct term introduced for the very purpose of
precluding any such error, and for making affirmation of
diversity? Unity of genus there is; diversity of species
there must be. And this same affirmation is made again
and again, most expressly, by the Patristic writers. If I ask
for a definition of a *watch* spring, of a *coach* spring, of a *water*
spring, shall I be told that there is no difference, that a spring
is a spring? There is, indeed, a generic common thought
running through these phrases, but the adjunct terms, *watch*
spring, *coach* spring, *water* spring, do make and are designed
to make an essential difference in the idea of "spring" itself.
Are the differences expressed by *woman's* dress, *man's* dress
court dress, to be nullified and swept out of sight by the utterance of the wise saw—"what is dress in one case must be
dress in another, there can be no difference in dress?" If
one longs for a Pentecost baptism, shall he be furnished with

a huge beaker of wine and be told—"Here it is, drink and be drunken, for Plato and Plutarch declare that drunkenness is baptism, and what is baptism in one case must be baptism in another?"

We return, then, to the baptism of Moses, and the baptism of John, and the baptism of Christ, with the fullest evidence that these adjunct terms, Moses, John, Christ, do, by their natural force, qualify and give a determinate, distinguishing character to the baptisms with which they are respectively associated. In what these distinguishing characteristics consist these phrases give no information. They reveal the fact of a diversity; the nature of the diversity must be sought elsewhere. Any one who will make investigation to this end will not labor in a barren field. The teaching of Scripture is as explicit as language will allow. If it were said, that the philosophies of Greece gave their disciples a baptism into Platonism, a baptism into Stoicism, and a baptism into Epicureanism, would any one in the wide world imagine, that he was giving proof of singular perspicacity in proclaiming these baptisms to be "one and the same baptism, for baptism in one case must be baptism in another case; there can be no difference in the mode?" Could any one possibly understand otherwise than that these baptisms were diverse baptisms; that the disciples of the Academy were baptized into, brought under the full influence of, the loftiest and the purest teachings of uninspired wisdom; that the disciples of the Porch were baptized into, brought under the full influence of, a cold fatalism; that those who gathered around the feet of Epicurus were baptized into, brought under the full influence of, a centralized selfishness? And is this unity without the most essential diversity?

In like manner the baptism of Moses is, as we have seen, a baptism into ceremonial purification, while the baptism of John is, as we shall see, a baptism into repentance for sin, and the baptism of Christ is a more glorious baptism into all the fruits of the incarnation—legal obedience, penal suffering, atoning death, triumphant resurrection, glorious ascension, gracious mediation, intercession, and High priest-

hood of the Lamb of God.   Do these baptisms sound like
one and the same baptism ?

In reference to that other and infinitely diverse question
agitated in these latter days, namely, " What was the manner in which John used water in his ritual baptism?" I have
only to say, Our inquiry will lead us to examine every case
in which βαπτίζω and its related words occur, and if they
should throw any light upon this very profound question
whose terms are suggestive of such momentous issues (indeed, almost mounting up to the high level of the schism-
causing question—" Does Christianity require that our coat
should be fastened with buttons or by hooks and eyes?"), we
shall have the fullest opportunity to benefit by such light;
but if we should find that they throw no light upon this
question (which some think so pregnant with high and holy
issues as to challenge their hallowed zeal in gulfing the
church of God deep as the cities of the plain, and islanding
the body and blood of Jesus amid impassable waters), we
must be content to remain in ignorance whether it be due
to its profundity, or to its atomistic character that the light
of revelation has not been suffered to fall upon it.   Only,
I would beg leave to indulge the hope, that any who may
take the trouble to follow this inquiry will believe that some
other end has been had in view than a solution of the question—" How did John use water in ritual baptism?"   If
after having preached the gospel for more than a quarter
of a century, I have not felt called upon to preach but once,
formally, in answer to such question, it can hardly be supposed, that I am now so oppressed by its immensity as to
enter upon the task of writing three or four volumes to resolve its mysteries.   I hope that something higher than this
may be accomplished; but, if among other results, they who
in answering this question feel constrained (by a faithfulness
to duty outvying the Roman father giving his children over
unto death) to drive brother and sister from their Father's
house and their elder Brother's table with a scourge whose
cords are made up of charges of " dishonesty and not lack

of knowledge," may be relieved from this soul pressure by
finding that the Holy Ghost has not committed this painful
task to them as custodians of the great truth of revelation
embodied in the manner in which water was used in ritual
baptism, I shall be very happy.

Dr. Halley, in his work on "The Sacraments," says, in
reference to Baptism, "Let us agree to find out the truth,
adhering closely to Scripture, seeking all aid in its correct
interpretation, assuming nothing without proof, and carefully
endeavoring to detect the cause of the error, on which ever
side it be, the πρῶτον ψεῦδος, which, lurking in the breast of
the one party or the other, in this, as in almost every controversy, vitiates all the subsequent reasoning, and, ever
present in the dispute, colors, with a false light, the arguments adduced on each side of the question; concealing
the weakness of some, and imputing a fictitious value to
others. Let us reach, if it be possible, the *arx causæ* of this
dispute, and then it surely cannot be difficult for an unprejudiced mind to ascertain the truth." The justness and the
efficiency of such a method of investigation must be obvious
to all. It has been my endeavor, thus far, to assume nothing, to prove every position, and to adhere, sternly, to the
letter of the text. I will, still, endeavor to do so. And,
more especially, in passing over the ground of revelation
will I lean, in the most absolute dependence, on the *ipsissima
verba* of the Holy Spirit. In revelation I know nothing save
as taught by God. Nor do I claim to be an expounder of
"things difficult and hard to be understood." I have neither
right nor wish to assume the character of a teacher of my
brethren. My pretension is this, no more—To have followed
the golden thread of truth, slowly, steadily, simply, absolutely, through intricacy, winding, and bewilderment, until
brought into a broad place. Of this I make report. Those
who examine and believe that they see the golden filament
stretching unbroken, unwrested, all along the way, will approve and accept; others will condemn and reject. Accepted
or rejected, no man is "made a judge over us." The only
wise God is the adorable and awful arbiter of truth.

It should be the especial endeavor of all, in this perplexed inquiry, "to adhere closely to Scripture, to seek all aid in its correct interpretation, and *to assume nothing without proof.*" As bearing upon this last particular it may be noted, that "the theory" turns upon this double pivot: 1. Βαπτίζω expresses unalterable modal action; 2. Βαπτίζω is so grammatically connected with water in the Scripture as to expound and require its modal use in ritual baptism. Now, I would ask, Whether these two points have ever been proved? and, farther, whether there has ever been an attempt to prove them? If any such attempt has ever been made, I have never heard of it. Dr. Carson says, the Greek word means "dip and nothing but dip through all Greek literature, expressing mode and nothing but mode." But he has not taken the first step toward proof. His own examples of usage not only show that his assumption is erroneous, but that it is an error of the extremest character. No point in philology has been or can be proved with more absolute evidence than that βαπτίζω does not express modal action. This first assumption of the theory, then, disappears forever from all controversy. With the evanishment of the first assumption, the second, also, largely if not wholly, passes away as a shadow. Whatever remains will receive due consideration as occasion may demand.

In entering upon an examination of the details of usage, I would remind the friends of the theory of the words of President Wayland—"I stand to whatever God has said; what men infer from it is merely human and weighs with me just nothing. As a Christian I think I can, in my poor way, defend what God has said; what man has inferred from it, man may defend if he can; I am not responsible." All others I would remind of those words of John Calvin, stamped on the ploughshare of the Reformation, "It ought not to have any weight with us that an opinion has long and extensively prevailed. We must learn to form our judgment from the matter as it stands, and not from the mistaken opinions of men." These are noble sentiments of noble men. Let it be our nobility to carry them into practice.

JOHN'S KNOWLEDGE OF *ΒΑΠΤΙΖΩ.*

CURRENT JEWISH BAPTISMS.

JOHN'S knowledge as to the essential meaning and breadth of usage of *βαπτίζω* must, obviously, enter, as an important element, into any satisfactory determination of his own usage of that word in connection with his baptism. What sources of information, on these points, were available to him? The Septuagint translation of the Hebrew Scriptures, in which this Greek word appears, had been made more than two centuries before John's ministry began. The apocryphal Jewish Greek writings which, also, use this word, were in existence for nearly as long a time. Jewish ritual purifications to which this word was applied, and had been applied for more than a hundred years, were in full and daily observance all through the ministry of John. Josephus, writing in Greek, immediately upon the close of John's ministry, employs this, and related words, in historical reference to his ministry and baptism.

These facts make it obvious, that the word could not enter as a novelty into John's vocabulary. They, also, teach us, that if the word had received any coloring, before it reached John, what was the medium through which it had passed, and from which such coloring must have been received.

As to the extent of usage shown by these writings in the employment of this word, I would observe, 1. There is no conclusive evidence that the Septuagint uses this word, in any case, in its simple, primary, physical sense. The same is true with regard to the apocryphal writings. The only instances in which it is so employed by Josephus contemplates the destruction of life. This is its legitimate and ordinary classical use. Such use excludes, of necessity, a dipping from the meaning of this word. A dipping kills nobody. As a consequence from this, and what we would assume without any definite information, there is no conclusive evidence that the word is used in any of these writings, in a single instance, to express a designed momentary envelopment or the modal act of dipping. There is, however, conclusive evidence to show, that the Septuagint, the Apocrypha, and Josephus, do, all, use this word to express condition resultant from controlling influence. There is, also, conclusive evidence furnished by these writings of the perfect adaptability of the word to express, by appropriation, any specific condition resultant from controlling influence, and the very highest probability from these writings (certainty from others), that it was, in fact, so used.

Having already examined the usage of this word as shown by the Septuagint and the Apocrypha, we shall, now, proceed to examine the use of this word in connection with those Jewish baptisms which antedated and were current with the whole course of John's ministry. The importance of doing this is twofold: 1. As showing John's knowledge; 2. As showing the necessity, if these baptisms differed, for having some evident, unmistakable mark of discrimination separating contemporaneous baptisms.

CEREMONIAL PURIFICATION.

BAPTISM FROM THE MARKET.

MARK 7 : 4.

"And when they saw some of his disciples eat bread with defiled, that is to say with unwashen, hands, they found fault. For the Pharisees and all the Jews, except they wash their hands oft, eat not, holding the tradition of the elders.

"And except they baptize themselves from the market, they eat not."

" Καὶ ἀπὸ ἀγορᾶς ἐὰν μὴ βαπτίσωνται, οὐκ ἐσθίουσι."

The Text.

The Codex Sinaiticus has ῥαντίσωνται instead of βαπτίσωνται. Whether this be accepted as the better reading or not, it shows that the copyist saw no difficulty in a baptism being effected by sprinkling. For in whatsoever way the water may have been used, on this occasion, it was used to effect a baptism. So, in the hand washing, which Campbell and others say was by "pouring a little water on them," the purpose was to effect a baptism. This is evident from the general custom of the Jews and the language used to expound it, as, also, from the spirit and phraseology of this particular passage. The word required to be supplied in connection with ἄλλα πολλά ἐστιν ἅ is βαπτίσματα. And it is obvious that βαπτισμοὺς so reflects back upon the purification of the hands, and the purification from the market, as to bring them into the same class of baptisms. This seems to be Campbell's view, who, in explaining why he translates βαπτισμοὺς baptisms, and βαπτίσωνται dip (their hands) says: 1. "That the appellation baptisms, here given to such washings, fully answers the purpose;" and 2. "That the way I have rendered that word (dip) shows better the contrast between it and νίψωνται so manifestly intended by the evangelist." He seems to think that although he has represented the hands as purified by pouring water upon them in one case and by dipping them into water in another case, they are sufficiently designated as baptisms, by using that term to denote the purification of pots, cups, and couches, since that designation embraced them all. However this may be, it is in proof that baptisms were, indifferently, effected by sprinkling, by pouring, and by washing more or less of the person.

The text of the Codex Sinaiticus teaches that the baptism was by sprinkling; the received text teaches that the purification was complete, saying nothing of the manner in which it was effected.

Translation.

The common version introduces the clause—*When they*

come "from the market." Codex D. has the addition ἐὰν ἔλθωσιν, which Meyer, De Wette, and others regard as a good interpretation. Bloomfield would supply ἔλθοντες, or γενόμενοι, or ὄντες. Sirach 31 : 30 βαπτιζόμενος ἀπὸ νεκροῦ, "*i. e.*, after returning *a mortuo curando*," is cited in support of this view. Krebs objects to this interpretation as needing confirmation. He, together with Kuinöel, Olshausen, Lange, and others, would make the reference to provisions brought from the market and washed before eaten. Winer does not regard this as satisfactory, because to do this would be required by the fitness of things and not by a mere precept of Phariseeism. It is evident that no interpretation has been suggested which commends itself to universal acceptance. It may, therefore, be allowable to suggest an interpretation which lies close at hand and is grounded in the very phraseology —"except they baptize—thoroughly purify themselves *from the market.*" This intimate relation of the Greek verb and the preposition ἀπὸ does not, now, meet us for the first time. We have had βαπτιζόμενος ἀπὸ νεκροῦ, *baptized from the dead* (Sir. 31 : 30), and βαπτιζόμενος ἀπὸ τῆς κοίτης, *baptized from the bed* (Clem. Alex., I, 1184), and βαπτίσθητε ἀπὸ ὀργῆς, *baptize from anger*, Justin M. In all of these cases the same principle of interpretation must rule. Few would translate—"they baptize themselves returning from the dead, or the things brought from the dead;" nor, "they baptize themselves returning from the bed, or the things brought from the bed." It is evident that pollution has been received "from the bed," "from the dead," and "from the market," and that the object of the baptism is to remove this pollution from themselves, and thus themselves "from the market," "from the bed," and "from the dead," causative of the pollution. The correctness of this interpretation receives support from the parallel phrase ἐρραντισμένοι ἀπὸ συνειδήσεως πονηρᾶς (Heb. 10 : 22), in which the other modes of interpretation have no fitness, but which is readily expounded in the way suggested. This latter phrase reminds us of the text of the Codex Sin., ἀπὸ ἀγορᾶς ῥαντίσωνται; the form by which the purification was effected representing the purification itself. And this phraseology was of such frequent recurrence amid Jewish purifications, that it seems to have lost its elliptic character and became directly interpretative. Winer (p. 622, Thayer's Ed.) says, μετανοεῖν ἀπὸ τῆς κακίας (Acts 8 : 22) originates in like manner with Mark 7 : 4 in a constructio pregnans, though by us it is scarcely felt. This acceptance by the mind of such phrases as conveying thought directly often requires that the verb which is retained shall accept the meaning of the verb which is suppressed. Thus Professor Stuart (Heb. 10 : 22) says, the construction ἐῤῥαντισμένοι ἀπὸ shows that the participle is to be taken in a secondary or metaphorical sense, i. e., *purified from, cleansed from.* So Ebrard, "'Ἀπὸ depends on the idea of ' cleansing' which is implied in the (pregnant) ῥαντίζειν," which he translates *cleansed.* And Ernesti translates, "Animis a conscientiâ peccate puris purgatis." In like manner, "*baptized from* the market" indicates, by the construction, by that construction persisted in through one or more centuries, by its necessary daily recurrence, that βαπτίζω has attained a secondary meaning, and that the phrase must mean, "*thoroughly purified from* the market." So, Professor Godwin appeals to this construction as evidence that the verb has secured a new meaning. The meaning *to purify ceremonially* has been, already, shown to belong to βαπτίζω as used in Jewish rites, by a score of facts in which any other meaning was out of the question. This position is, now, fortified still farther by a grammatical form whose legitimate interpretation under the laws of language demand that that same meaning be assigned to the word.

Between the washing of the hands with " a quarter of a logus, an egg full and a half, about twenty-seven drachms," and the baptism from the market, there is made a distinction. It probably consisted in a less thorough and a more thorough purification. But the *quo modo* in neither case is stated. The word βαπτίζω always denotes completeness of condition, however the influence may be brought to bear for its accomplishment.

Interpretation.—Carson.

Dr. Carson says of this passage, "It ought to have been translated—'Except they dip themselves, they eat not.' But as respects my argument I care not whether βαπτίσωνται here refers to the hands or the whole body; it is perfectly sufficient for me if it here admits the usual meaning.

"I bring passages without number to prove that the word *must* have the meaning for which I contend. No passage could be a valid objection against my conclusion, except one in which it *cannot have* that signification.

"If another signification is found, I will not insist that immersion *must* of *course* be the signification here. In such a case as this the meaning must be settled by additional evidence. When a word has two or more meanings actually in proof, which of them may, in any passage, be the true meaning is a question; but if no secondary meaning is in proof, there can be no question on the subject. *Now, there is not in all Greek literature a single instance ever alleged in which the word* MUST *have a secondary meaning.*

"I admit that βάπτω has a secondary meaning, because such secondary meaning is in proof, and instances may be alleged in which its primary meaning is utterly impossible. When applied, for instance, to the lake, the immersion of a lake in the blood of a frog, is beyond the bounds of possibility. Show me anything like this with respect to βαπτίζω, and I will grant a secondary meaning; and as soon as a secondary meaning is ascertained on sufficient grounds, I do not demand, in every instance, a proof of impossibility of primary meaning before the secondary is alleged.

"I *assume* nothing but self-evident truth. I never used a *shift* in all the controversy that I ever wrote. Does it require a shift to prove in all the cases referred to immersion was possible? The proof that immersion was used in the cases referred to is that the word has the meaning and no other."

Untenable Positions.

1. "It ought to have been translated, except they dip

themselves. I bring passages without number to prove that the word must have this meaning."

Dr. Carson has not adduced one passage which proves that βαπτίζω means *to dip*. He has, in fact, made no attempt to prove'it. To make an assertion and then to quote passages without showing their relevancy to the point at issue is neither proof nor worthy to be called an attempt at proof. As a matter of fact the passages quoted do, many of them, most expressly contradict and most absolutely disprove the point which they are brought to sustain. They not only show, that the action of dipping is not present in the baptism, but that the baptism is effected by other action which is utterly irreconcilable with such action. In other cases in which the action of dipping was present, or might be conceived to be, there is no attempt to identify βαπτίζω with such action. To attach *dipping* to βαπτίζω, as its distinctive meaning, is to reach an issue by the most absolute and unwarrantable assumption, not only unsupported by facts, but contradicted by them.

When Dr. Carson says, "I care not whether the hands or the whole body is dipped," it might be added,—"and for good reason, seeing that neither hand *dipping*, nor body *dipping* is baptism." All classic usage enters a protest against confounding a dipping and a baptism. A dipping (under the theory which insists on a definite act, mode and nothing but mode) can never be converted into a baptism. And yet under a true view of this word (which has nothing to do with a form of action, but makes demand for condition) a dipping of the hands may effect a Judaic baptism of the entire body. In such case the verb does not expound, nor has it the least concern with the act performed, but contemplates, exclusively, the resultant condition, which is not a ceremonial purification of the hands, merely, but of the entire person. This is on the same principle that the maidservant (C. B., p. 309) is said to have been baptized by a glass of wine. Neither her whole body, nor her hands, nor yet the tips of her fingers were dipped into the wine; she drank it, and, although it touched but a small part of her person, it baptized her completely, changed her condition. The condition of the Jew was ceremonially changed, his person entirely baptized, by dipping his hands into pure water. Whether the action was dipping or drinking, pouring or sprinkling, is a matter of infinite indifference to the baptism. The Greek word never, under any circumstances, defines the form of act which may be employed in effecting a baptism.

2. " *There is not in all Greek literature a single instance ever alleged in which the word* MUST *have a secondary meaning.*"

The italics and capitals are as I find them. In reply to this position it may be stated, that the primary meaning of βαπτίζω makes demand for intusposition within a solid, semisolid, or a fluid, without limitation of act, time, or influence. Such a condition, as is obvious, must result in exercising the fullest measure of influence which the enveloping element is capable of exerting over the enveloped object. As a result from this, the word is naturally, I might say unavoidably, used, where no envelopment is or can be, to express, directly, controlling influence generically, as, also, by appropriation, specific influences. Of this secondary usage Greek literature furnishes not merely "a single instance," but multitudinous examples. Some of which it may be well to adduce.

(1.) Water poured into wine is said to baptize Bacchus. The god of wine is, here, introduced as exercising the power of making drunk through wine-drinking. While he is represented as despoiled of this power by means of the influence of water poured into wine. Bacchus is brought under restraint by the greater power of water. The nature of wine to intoxicate is brought under the influence of water, and being assimilated to that controlling influence is made like it unintoxicating. This in-pouring of water and its resultant controlling influence "MUST" be set down to secondary use.

(2.) A drunken man is said to be a baptized man (C. B., p. 317). A man is not made drunk by being *dipped*. No Greek could ever so blunder as to attribute, by imagination, a thoroughly drunken condition to a *dipping!* A physical dipping into a full wine cask never was and never will be an image of drunkenness, so long as the imagination shall remain sober. To merse a man, to place him for an indefinite period, within a wine cask, in order to exhibit an image of drunkenness, would indicate to all sober men that the imagination of such persons was already under the influence of the tipsy God. The Classic use of this word to express the condition of drunkenness "MUST" result from secondary use.

(3.) A man who drinks at the fountain of Silenus becomes a baptized man (C. B., p. 307). Until there shall be traced an identity between the definite action in drinking and the definite action in dipping, we must abandon this as illustrative of the primary meaning of the theory, and accept the condition effected by a controlling influence as a conclusive "MUST" be for a secondary usage.

(4.) Cities, and all Asia, are represented as baptized by sleep, by the running away of bakers, by defeat in battle, &c. (C. B., p. 284). Does sleep, no baking, or defeat, *dip* its victims into anything? Is not the imagined dipping of a city, or a continent, or even of an Asia *Minor*, a freak of imagination whose originality belongs, by exclusive right, to the theory? So long as sleep, an empty oven, and a lost battle shall exercise controlling influence over their objects, in disregard of definite act, we "MUST" adhere to a secondary use.

(5.) A person bewildered with questions is said to be baptized (C. B., p. 334). Until this baptism can be accomplished by *dipping* into a pool, or river, or bag full of perplexing questions, we must be content to accept the baptism of sophistically propounded questions as a proof that there "MUST" be a secondary usage.

Without extending this list of Classic baptisms in which there cannot be a dipping and must be a secondary use, I add a few of like character from Judaic Baptism. (1.) Baptism by ashes sprinkled (p. 100). Dipping is excluded and controlling influence is a necessity. (2.) Baptism by the troubled waters of Bethesda (p. 164). As the baptizing power of these waters did not depend on their allowing an

object to be *dipped* into them, but upon their power of influence to heal the diseased, a dipping is excluded and a
secondary use is established. (3.) Baptism by a coal of fire
(p. 239). Isaiah could not be dipped into a coal of fire, nor
could a coal of fire dip him into anything else. Definite
action is excluded from the word and controlling influence
marks the secondary use. (4.) Baptism of sins by a flaming
sword (p. 236). A flaming sword cannot dip, nor can sins
be dipped. He who baptizes by the flaming sword (the
Lord Jesus Christ) does exercise a controlling influence
whereby sins are cleansed. And, again, dipping is excluded
and influence is established. (5.) Baptism by pouring water
on the altar (p. 328). If the action of pouring is not the
action of dipping, then this baptism was not by dipping;
and if there be a purifying influence proceeding from the
ritual use of water extending over the altar and its sacrifice,
preparing it for the burning attestation of Jehovah to his
deity, then there must be a secondary meaning entering into
the use of this word.

The number of these baptisms might be greatly extended.
But as one, only, was asked for, ten may suffice. There is
dipping in none. There is controlling influence in all. The
primary meaning of the theory has no standing-place. The
secondary meaning is a necessity—an absolute " MUST."

3. " Βάπτω has a secondary meaning. The immersion of
a lake in the blood of a frog is impossible. Show me anything like this with respect to βαπτίζω, and I will grant a
secondary meaning." Dr. Carson can see no evidence in
favor of his opponent's position and no evidence against his
own. The difficulty of dipping a lake into a few drops of
blood is all owing to a sudden dearth of imagination. The
theory has performed this very same feat many a time. All
that is needful is, to treat the syntax as of no authority and
substitute a local for an instrumental dative, next call on
catachresis to plead guilty to the use of the act of dropping
instead of the act of dipping, and then summon hyperbole
to expand the blood-drops so as to receive the avalanche
of waters, and all will be done. Literality will disappear,

secondary meaning will vanish, while the beauty of figure and the power of imagination will be in the ascendant. And to all this the theory attaches her seal with the legend—" Can any child fail to understand this?"

It is by rhetorical appliances like these that βαπτίζω has been cheated out of a secondary meaning. And under the same heroic treatment no word in any language could ever attain to a secondary meaning.

But Dr. Carson thinks that no use of βαπτίζω can parallel this case which proves so indisputably a secondary meaning for βάπτω. How much easier is it to dip Lake Myrrha into a piece of wood thrown into it, than it is to dip this Homeric lake into a frog's blood? How much easier is the feat of dipping a city into runaway bakers? Or, to dip an altar into poured on water? Or, to dip Asia into anything you please? But such trifles as altars, cities, lakes, and young continents can be dipped in a trice when a secondary meaning is to be denied, at all cost, to βαπτίζω; while a denial of a secondary meaning to βάπτω, under similar circumstances, is hooted at.

Yet, as surely as βάπτω loses its modal act under the coloring influence of blood dropped into the lake, so surely does βαπτίζω lose its intusposition under the purifying influence of water poured upon the altar.

4. "I never used a shift in controversy. The word has this meaning (dip) and no other." I believe, most absolutely, in Dr. Carson's honesty of intention. And, yet, I believe, that there never was a book written which does more completely turn, in its argumentation, on a shifting of words, than does this book—" Carson on Baptism."

He sets out with the unqualified position—"the word means dip and nothing but dip through all Greek literature" —and when the word is used to express the condition of the coast under the flux and reflux of the tides, this condition is converted into modal action by shifting from fact to figure, and from prose to poetry, and rhetoricizing " covered and bare" (not included in the use of the word at all) into the in and out of a dipping. And when the altar is baptized by pouring water upon it, the modal act of pouring is converted into the modal act of dipping, in the same shiftily style, as was the modal act of flowing. When vessels lie baptized at the bottom of the sea, the most dazzling proof of the in and out of dip is furnished by shifting to *immerse*, in which word such action never had and never will have place. Thus "without a shift" (!) the univocalism of βαπτίζω is established. This error of univocalism, both of fact and of kind, is the exclusive dependence of Dr. Carson in his interpretation of the passage before us.

HAND-WASHING BAPTISM.

Ambrose.—Hand-washing.

Ambrose presents this comment: "Ut manus non lavarent, cum panem manducarent; quoniam, *Qui lotus est totus, non habet necesse ut manus lavet* (John 13 : 10). Laverat eos Jesus, lavacrum aliud non quærebant; uno enim Christus baptismate omnia solvit baptismata"—The Jews in following the tradition of men, neglect that of God; the disciples in giving precedence to that of God, neglected that of men, so that they would not wash their hands when they ate bread: Since "he who is completely washed has no need that he should wash his hands." "Jesus had washed them, they sought no other baptism; for Christ by one baptism resolves all baptisms" (II, 1789).

This passage recognizes, most explicitly, hand-washing as a baptism. The argument is, The disciples having received the one perfect baptism of Christ did not need that lower purification effected by hand-washing baptism. And they needed, just as little, any other among the "omnia baptismata."

Justin Martyr addresses the same argument to the Jews: "This baptism is the only one able to cleanse . . . of what use is that baptism which cleanses the flesh and the body only? Baptize the soul and the body is pure" (504). Ambrose uses almost the same words: "Ergo mysterio intendebant discipuli, non sui munditiam corporis, sed animæ requirentes. Hoc reprehendebant Judæi; sed argute redarguntur a Domino, quod inania observent, profutura despiciant. The disciples understood the mystery to require, not the cleansing of the body, but of the soul. The Jews objected to this; but the Lord wisely rebuked them, because they observe profitless (baptisms) and reject the profitable."

The only rational interpretation of these baptisms is that which refers them to diverse conditions of purification—of the body, ceremonially, and of the soul, spiritually.

Clement of Alexandria.

Clement of Alexandria (I, 1352) speaks of hand-washing as a baptism, εἰκὼν τοῦ βαπτίσματος. He refers to hand-washing by Telemachus—" Τηλέμαχος δε, χείρας νιψάμενος "—and adds,—" Ἔθος τοῦτο Ἰουδαίων, ὡς καὶ τὸ πολλάκις ἐπὶ κοίτῃ βαπτίζεσθαι—This (hand-washing baptism) was a custom of the Jews, so as even to be baptized frequently upon the couch." When we consider the severe absolutism assumed by the friends of dipping, it is truly wonderful how continually the facts and phraseology of usage seize hold of "the theory" and shake it to pieces. And when they make shift to rebuild, it is only *agere actum*, to reconstruct out of a renewed ruin a yet frailer tenement.

At the baptism of Judith effort was made to change "at" (ἐπί) the fountain into "in" the fountain; here, effort is made to change the baptism "on" (ἐπί) the couch into baptism "*after* the *bed.*" Neither the preposition nor the place suits the theory. A guest reclining on a dining couch is as poor a subject for dipping, as the altar crowning Carmel. It is true that water can be poured over the altar, and was poured in fact, which pouring Origen says baptized the altar; and it is also true, that water can be poured over the hands of a guest on his couch, and was in fact so poured, which pouring Ambrose and Clement declare baptized the guest; but if all this be admitted, what becomes of the theory? Poetry and rhetoric will no doubt furnish a sovereign panacea.

Alexander D. Le Nourry, a commentator on Clement

(II, 9 : 1), says, "Nostri porro sacri baptismatis imaginem non solum apud Judæos, sed etiam gentiles fuisse Clemens noster ostendit. Et apud gentiles quidem in eo, quod de Penelope et Telemacho cecinit Homerus Odyss. *A'* et *Δ'*. Apud Judæos autem, quia mos eorum erat, ut sæpe in lecto tingerentur. Sed scite Clemens monet hæc plane imperfecta fuisse baptismata quandoquidem non lavacro, sed animo mundi purique esse debemus—Moreover that the image of our sacred baptism existed not only among the Jews but also among the heathen, our Clement shows. Among the heathen as shown by what Homer sang of Penelope and Telemachus, Odyss. *A'* and *Δ'*. But among the Jews, because it was their custom to be frequently cleansed on the couch. But Clement justly admonishes that these baptisms were evidently imperfect, because we ought to be clean and pure by the mind and not by washing."

According to this interpreter of Clement, hand-washings were baptisms, and they were administered (even by *tingo*, " tingerentur") " on the couch."

Mode of Hand-washing.

Wetstein (Matt. 20), speaking of the quantity of water used and the mode of applying it in hand-washing, says : " Rabbi Akiba was cast into prison, and Rabbi Joshua Garsites ministered unto him. And they brought him, daily, water for washing and drinking. Now it happened on one occasion that the jailor found him and said, ' You have a large quantity of water to-day; is it to perforate the walls of your prison ?' Then he poured one-half of it out and left the remainder. Rabbi Akiba was told what had been done, yet he said, ' Pour the water on my hands.' An eggful and a half is the quantity fixed for washing the hands of one person." Lightfoot says a *log* was six eggshells full, and a quarter of a log was sufficient to wash the hands of one or two persons, a half of a log for three or four persons, and a whole log for five, ten, or one hundred persons. *W.* 447.

PROTRACTED USAGE.

Two hundred years, more or less, intervene between the baptisms in Sirach 31 : 30, Judith 12 : 7, and this baptism in Mark 7 : 4. They were all of the same general character, designed to change a condition of ceremonial defilement into a condition of ceremonial purity. At the beginning of these two centuries and at their close, we find the same word (βαπτίζω), never expressing form of action, always expressing completeness of condition, used to express the thorough change of condition effected by this Jewish rite. There is the most positive evidence that materials varying in nature and applied by varying forms of action were employed in these rites, and yet one word is found living through all changes. Is there any unity pervading these diversities? There is a unity of ceremonial condition effected, indifferently, by ashes, blood, or water, by washing, pouring, sprinkling; and that uniform condition is uniformly characterized by βαπτίζω, which word does never express form of action, but does always express condition, and by long appropriation expresses the specific condition of ceremonial purification. During these centuries of baptism there is no conclusive evidence of a single man, woman, or child having ever been dipped into water in order to this ceremonial purification. And if there were evidence that any such fact had ever occurred, it could not be laid at the door of βαπτίζω, for it has no such meaning. To change the meaning of this word from a demand for intusposition unlimited in time, to a *dipping*, an act of momentary continuance, is to revolutionize the word in the most radical manner. Dr. Conant says, that the metaphorical meaning of βαπτίζω is the same as its literal meaning. When or where does such meaning point to a *dipping* origin? To dip is to perform a transient act, ordinarily if not universally, issuing in a feeble and limited result. For this reason the word is adapted, in metaphor, to express a result characterized by feebleness and limitation. And this is its invariable usage. A writer who wished to express a mental or moral impression which was in its char-

acter pervading, persistent, and profound, and should employ
dip for that purpose, would not act less absurdly than the
man who should throw a feather into the scales to counter-
balance a ton weight. On the other hand the intusposition of an object within an enveloping solid, semi-solid, or
fluid, for an unlimited time, must be exhaustive of the influence of such enveloping material over the inclosed object.
If, therefore, it is desired to express beyond the range of
physics a condition which is exhaustive of influence, full,
pervading, controlling, the word which is expressive of such
intusposition is the word fitted to the task.   And that word
which is so used by the Greeks, century after century, is
βαπτίζω. This distinction of conception is in the fitness of
things and is most radical. It is the elemental distinction
between βάπτω and βαπτίζω. It is invariably observed by all
Classic, Jewish, and Christian writers. There is not the
shadow of a difference, as to this radical element, among inspired and uninspired writings.

In the Classic fable of Mars, Vulcan, and Neptune, Mars
(iron) is represented as having his condition changed by
being brought under the power of Vulcan (fire); but Mars
(iron, now heated) is released from this new condition and
restored to his original condition of coldness through the
intervention of Neptune (water). Iron is brought under the
influence of fire, but hot iron is brought under the influence
of cold water—βαπτίζεται ὕδατι. It is not the mersing quality
of water which is here involved, but its cold-producing
quality. The whole fable turns on influence, overmastering
influence, and this is expressed by the form of the Greek.*

In like manner the Jew who came in contact with " a
bone," " a heathen camp," or " the market," had his condition changed from ceremonial purity to ceremonial impurity.
And in this condition he remained (as Mars under the power

---

* In like manner (in the absence of all semblance of dipping or covering)
Cyril of Alexandria speaks of the baptism (changed condition) of water by
fire and the Holy Spirit—" As water in a caldron, set to the fire, receives
the force of the fire, so, the water of baptism by the Spirit is raised to a
divine and ineffable virtue."—*Lightfoot,* v. 37.

of Vulcan) until released from it by the ritual use of ashes
or pure water (as Mars was released by Neptune). To make
βαπτίζω express in such cases a "dipping" involves the twofold radical error, 1. Of engrafting into the word the idea
of modal action, which is entirely foreign to its nature, and
2. Of making its condition essentially evanescent, which is
outright murder.

Such usage could not but be eminently instructive to John
as to the meaning and power of this word which he was
called upon to use so freely in his ministry.

BAPTIZINGS OF DOMESTIC UTENSILS AND DINNER COUCHES.

MARK 7 : 4.

"And there are many other things which they have received
to hold, the baptizings of cups, and pots, and brazen vessels,
and couches."

"*Καὶ ἄλλα πολλά ἐστιν ἃ παρέλαβον κρατεῖν βαπτισμοὺς ποτηρίων καὶ
ξεστῶν καὶ χαλκίων καὶ κλινῶν.*"

Mode of Purification.

It will be admitted, that these various articles were in a
condition of ceremonial impurity. It will, also, be admitted,
that the end sought by the tradition of the elders was to
change this condition into one of ceremonial purity. And
it will be, farther, admitted, that the power to effect this
change of condition belonged to water, ritually used, independently of its physically cleansing power.

These things being admitted, it follows, 1. That the demand made by this rite for its objects was not a physical
mersion. 2. It was not a physical cleansing. 3. It was for
ceremonial purity. 4. The power of water to make ceremonially pure being independent of the quantity used, and
of the manner of use, quantity and manner cannot enter into
the rite unless by express statement. 5. Inasmuch as βαπτίζω
affixes no limit to the form of action by which its demand

is accomplished, and as little to the time of continuance of the condition effected by it, and there being no other limiting word, it follows that if these "cups, and pots, and brazen vessels, and couches" are put into the water by this word, no provision is made for taking them out, which is an incredible, not to say absurd, use of language. 6. To effect a thorough change of condition, not physical but ceremonial, exhausts the requirement of the rite; and to effect such condition, without limitation in the form of the action and without limitation in the time of its continuance, exhausts the demands of βαπτίζω. It is, therefore, perfectly adapted to meet the demands of the rite, not through any change in its character effected for the occasion, but because of its own essential nature.

Does any one ask, " May not these cups, and pots, and brazen vessels have been baptized by dipping them into water?" The answer is unhesitatingly given—Undoubtedly they may have been, and, although we have no certain knowledge on the subject, quite possibly, were so in fact. But why ask this question? Is it with a view to the conclusion, " Then, dipping is baptism?" To draw such a conclusion from these premises would be as erroneous as to conclude that an axe is a chip, because an axe makes chips. The dipping of a "cup" into pure water may effect a certain kind of baptism, to wit, that of ceremonial purification. And it does so for the same reason that sprinkling or pouring water upon the "cup" will effect the same baptism. The power to effect the baptism is in the nature of water, and the manner in which the water is applied has no more to do with the result than the nourishing quality of food depends upon its being taken by means of a knife, or a fork, or a spoon. There are some baptisms which cannot be effected by a dipping. A drunken baptism, a drowning baptism, a foundered ship baptism, cannot be effected by a dipping. Very few can be; into none does it enter except as an accident. The capability of dipping to effect a baptism is limited to secondary baptisms of a special character.

The essential difference between βάπτω and βαπτίζω cannot

be too deeply impressed upon the mind. The distinction is neither fictitious nor nominal, but most radical and incapable, except destructively, of being confounded.

The secondary usage of these words not only reveals but magnifies their differences. The dipping of an object into a fluid will, ordinarily, produce but a trivial effect; but if the fluid be impregnated with some coloring substance, then the object dipped into it becomes materially affected by it. From this result the word secured a new meaning. But other forms of action besides dipping produce a coloring effect; so, form of action is eliminated from βάπτω and it is employed to denote a result (dyeing, coloring) without any regard to the modal process by which such result may have been attained. Βαπτίζω has never been applied to dyeing. But it is much more naturally and directly related to this secondary use of βάπτω (by which a result is expressed without restriction as to the form of action by which it is secured and without limitation as to the time of its continuance) than it is related to its primary use, where there is the sharpest limitation both as to form and time. In the secondary use of βαπτίζω there is not, as in the case of βάπτω, an abandonment of formal action and limited time, for these things never entered into its primary use; but a simple elimination of physical intusposition as essentially entering into the exercise of controlling influence, and extending the application of the word so as to include all cases of pervading, controlling, and assimilating influence by whatsoever process they might be accomplished. As an object may be *bapted* (though undipped), *colored*, by having berry-juice dropped, sprinkled, poured upon it, so, an object (cups, pots) may be *baptized* (not mersed), *thoroughly changed as to ceremonial condition*, by having pure water dropped, sprinkled, or poured upon it. Unless the usage of βαπτίζω be traced to the secondary use of βάπτω, the words must be regarded as the representatives of mental conceptions which are the extreme opposites. While if the point of contact be in this secondary use, then modal action is, of necessity, excluded, unless it has ceased to be true that *ex nihilo nihil fit*.

Whether, then, these cup, pot, and brazen vessel baptisms were effected by dipping, by pouring, or by sprinkling, βαπτίζω says nothing of, and cares nothing for, the modal act. The word makes demand for and is satisfied with a change of condition from ceremonial impurity to ceremonial purity.

Baptism of Couches.

The baptism of "couches" is separated from that of "cups, pots, and brazen vessels," because while it is quite possible or even highly probable that these small articles would be baptized (purified) by dipping, it is, also, quite improbable, not to say quite impossible, that "couches" (large enough for three persons to recline upon) would be taken up and dipped into water, or would, by any process, be entirely enveloped in water in order to their ceremonial purification. An argument in proof of *dip* as the meaning of βαπτίζω is derived by Dr. Carson from the size of the objects said to be baptized. He says that the word is not applied to a house or to any object so large that it cannot be taken up and dipped. As, not unfrequently, Dr. Carson is, here, in error, and the real facts of the case turn the argument, heavily, against him. The altar on Mount Carmel may not have been as big as "a house," but it was too big for Dr. Carson to attempt to pick up and dip, and so he was content to allow it to be baptized by water poured over it. Some ships that lie baptized in the ocean are quite as large as some "houses," and yet Dr. Carson has witnessed their baptism many a time in Classic story without any arm being strong enough to lift them up and give them a dipping. The sea-coast is as unmanageable in any attempt to lift it up and dip it into the ocean as would be "a house," and yet Dr. Carson confesses that the coasts of his island home are baptized daily. The city of Jotapata, and the city of Jerusalem, contained not merely one house, or one score of houses, but hundreds and thousands, and yet, somehow or other, they were baptized. "All Asia" embraced not merely houses and cities, but kingdoms, and yet "all Asia" was baptized! How utterly devoid of foundation is the statement that no objects but such as can be lifted are said to be baptized, this reference to facts will show. The friends of the theory involve themselves in the most inextricable embarrassments by confounding dippings with baptisms. Greek writers never employ βάπτω (*dip*) to denote these or any other baptisms.

Of these couch baptisms Dr. Carson (p. 71) says, "It would, indeed, be a very inconvenient thing. It would be a foolish thing. Such religious practice was, indeed, absurd." And yet (p. 367) he says, this dipping of couches "is not only possible, but of easy performance. Couches may be immersed (dipped) without any difficulty; and if the Holy Spirit reports truly, couches were immersed (dipped) as they are said to have been baptized." And (p. 453) he farther says, "In fact, to allege that the couches were not immersed (dipped), is not to decide on the authority of the word used, but in opposition to this authority; to give the lie to the Holy Spirit. Inspiration employs a word to designate the purification of the couches which never signifies anything but *immerse* (dip). If they were not immersed (dipped) the historian is a false witness."

Such language may seem to the theorists to indicate high courage, intense conviction, and assured truth. To sober-minded persons it will be indicative of immeasurable self-esteem and a reckless forgetfulness of that reverence which is due to the never-erring Deity. No man, under any circumstances, has a right to make falsehood in the Deity the alternative to the truth or error of his convictions. To do so exhibits the most condemnable forgetfulness of that ignorance and liability to error which separates, by an infinity, man from God. Dr. Gale was as fully satisfied that βάπτω never signifies anything but "dip" (rejecting the signification *to dye*), as that Dr. Carson was convinced that "βαπτίζω signifies through all Greek literature to dip and nothing but dip." Suppose, now, that Gale in interpreting Revelation 19 : 13, βεβαμμένον ἅιματι, had said, "If the Holy Spirit reports truly the garment was '*dipped* in blood,' as it is said to be βεβαμμένον. To allege that the garment was not *dipped* in blood, is ' to give the lie to the Holy Spirit.' If the garment was not *dipped* in blood the inspired historian 'is a false witness.' " This, once, was the ground occupied by all who, now, stand on the theory. The explosion of this erroneous univocalism of βάπτω, long refused at the hands of others, was at length accepted at the hands of Carson. And he and they gathered their forces to make a final stand for "dip and nothing but dip" under the auspices of βαπτίζω. If Dr. Carson, standing by the grave of his friend Gale, had read— " this garment was *dipped* in blood or 'the Holy Spirit has not reported truly' "—would not the statement have been most painful to him in view of the better knowledge to which he and his friends have attained? Would he not have been grieved at heart to think that his friend had ever been guilty of the presumptuous folly of saying, that a garment, βεβαμμένον αἵματι, must be "*dipped*" in blood or John, inspired of the Holy Ghost, does not tell the truth, for "βάπτω means dip and nothing but dip?" He now sees that Gale's univocalism was all wrong, and that John was no "false witness," and that the Holy Spirit did report truly, although the garment, βεβαμμένον αἵματι, was not "dipped in," but *dyed by* blood.

Dr. Fuller says, that he is abundantly convinced that βαπτίζω does not mean "dip and nothing but dip." If he should visit the grave of Carson at Tubbermore, would not he, in turn, feel sincere sorrow that his honored friend had, with regard to this word, fallen into a similar error with Gale in attributing to it a modal univocalism? That he had ever allowed himself to say, "if the Holy Spirit reports truly, the couches were immersed (dipped), as they are said to have been baptized." Dr. Fuller, now, sees that couches might be said to be "baptized," though not *dipped*, and "the Holy Spirit report truly," as Carson saw, that a garment might be *baptized by* blood, although not *dipped in* blood.

The editor of Lange (Professor Shedd) remarks on this baptism of couches: "That these couches were immersed in every instance of ceremonial washing, can be thought probable, or even possible, only by those who are under the necessity of holding that this Greek word not only means to dip or plunge, originally, but, unlike every other word, transferred to a religious use, is always used in that exclusive and invariable sense, without modification or exception; to those who have no purpose to attain by such a paradox, the place before us will afford if not conclusive evidence, at least a strong presumption, that beds (to say no more) might be baptized without immersion."

But all difficulties in the way of such baptisms must go down before the theory. Dr. Carson provides for dipping these couches by taking them to pieces and carrying them forth to the water. With no less thoughtfulness he made provision by a cattle trough for Judith's dipping at the fountain. Why he did not take the altar to pieces and carry it down to the Mediterranean and dip it by stone, I do not know. If the pouring of "four pitchers of water" over a couch would not suffice for its baptism, although it might answer for the baptism of an altar, yet would not the out-pouring of "twelve barrels" meet the case? However this baptism may be settled, whether dipped by Carson, or made "very wet" by Fuller, we must decline the offered inter-vention of a bed-screw to get them to the dipping.

Βαπτισμοὺς.

We meet in this passage the form βαπτισμοὺς for the first time. By its form the idea of action, the process for effect-ing the baptism, is preserved. It might more definitely be translated *baptizings, purifyings*, thus distinguishing it from the form βάπτισμα, denotive of the accomplished result. The plural form may have arisen either from a diversity of species under the same generic defilement and purification, or from a diversity in the forms of purifying as suggested by the diversity in the objects, as in the case of cups, and couches, and persons, or from the necessarily very repetitious char-acter of the ceremonial.

BAPTISM BEFORE MEALS.

LUKE 11 : 37, 38.

" And as he spake a certain Pharisee besought him to dine with him; and he went in and sat down to meat.

" And when the Pharisee saw it, he marvelled that he was not first baptized before dinner."

" Ὁ δὲ Φαρισαῖος ἰδὼν ἐθαύμασεν ὅτι οὐ πρῶτον ἐβαπτίσθη πρὸ τοῦ ἀρίστου."

The Theory in Difficulties.

The friends of the theory must have their equanimity not a little tried by meeting with baptism after baptism in which there is no plain, nor probable, nor possible " dipping." If there were a few rare cases of such baptisms, overshadowed by a multitude of manifest dipping baptisms, such exceptional cases might be made light of; but when score after score of baptisms pass in review without satisfactory evidence of dipping in a single case, what shall be said of the axiom—" No dipping no baptism ? "

Dr. Carson admits, that Noah was not, in fact, dipped into the flood, but he points to him down in the hold of the floating ark, and declares that therein is a clear case of *quasi* " dipping." As the millions of Israel march through the divided sea, he admits, that there is no actual dipping, but he declares that he can construct a baptistery out of water walls and cloud roof, which will assuredly give the marching hosts a *quasi* dipping. He admits, that Elijah was not dipped as he crossed the river to mount the chariot which was to bear him to the skies; but he declares that the going down and the coming up is certainly a *quasi* dipping. Israel in crossing the Jordan under Joshua are admitted not to have received an actual dipping; but, then, to cross the dried channel of a river he declares to be, most plainly, a *quasi* dipping. Carmel's altar it is admitted was not dipped; but, then, it is declared, with all the force of interrogation, " Who cannot but see, that four pitchers of water thrice poured is a most

admirable *quasi* dipping?" And so this "*quasi* dipping"
runs through the long list of baptisms in which actual dipping never makes an appearance. Difficulties, thick and
sharp as a thorn hedge, meet the theory at every turn,
mocking every attempt to prove "dipping is baptism and
baptism is dipping."

When the *modus operandi* of a baptism is distinctly stated,
and there is no dipping in it, the cry of "figure" is raised,
and all difficulties are hidden in a cloud of imaginings.
When no *modus* is stated, and yet the case bristles with difficulties protesting against a dipping, then appeal is made to
"the word." The appeal of the theory is not to facts, but
to an illy regulated imagination and to a fundamentally
mistaken conception of the nature of the word.

The baptism under consideration must be added to the
long list of those that have gone before in which no shadow
of evidence for a dipping could be traced. Our blessed Lord
was, in this world, without a home of his own under whose
roof he might lay his head, and within whose walls he might
take his meals. On this occasion being, at mealtime, near
the house of a Pharisee, he is invited by him to dine. The
invitation is accepted. He enters the house and takes his
place at the table, without making any use of water for
ceremonial purification before eating. The Pharisee is surprised that he has not first been baptized (purified). The
facts of this case point to certain well-assured conclusions:
1. The Pharisee must have expected the anticipated baptism
to take place in his own house; (1) because if in any other
house, he could not have known whether it had or had not
been observed; (2) because there was no opportunity for its
observance, after the invitation, except in his own house.
2. Provision must have been made in the Pharisee's house
for this baptism; otherwise he could not have marvelled at
the neglect. 3. The baptism must have been of such a
nature as to be open to the inspection of others; else the
Pharisee could not have "seen" the omission. 4. The
master of the house must have partaken of this baptism
subsequent to the invitation, and after leaving the throng

of the highway; and if so, then it must have been a baptism which could be effected without retirement, for which the narrative makes no provision. 5. There were many others at this dinner. There is no evidence that any other failed to observe the baptism, but the Saviour. There is no reason to believe that this Pharisee would have permitted any other to have sat with him at the table with "unclean hands." The Pharisees (Mark 7 : 1) are not represented as eating with the "unbaptized disciples." The implication is, that they stood aloof and found fault. But if all the Pharisees and lawyers sitting at that table were baptized after coming from the highway and the crowd, before they sat down to eat, then the baptism must have been of such a nature as could have been effected by a large number, in a private house, on a suddenly arising emergency.

In connection with these facts, stated or of necessary inference, must, also, be taken the following truths: 1. There is no satisfactory evidence that the Pharisees were in the habit of dipping themselves in water before dinner. 2. There is no satisfactory evidence showing, that guests were in the habit of dipping themselves in water, at the house of their host, before dinner. 3. There is no satisfactory evidence to show, that the Saviour was expected to do what was not equally expected to be done by others. If, therefore, he was expected to dip himself in water, all others would be expected to dip themselves in water. 4. There is no satisfactory evidence to show, that any facilities for dipping into water were provided on this occasion. 5. There is no satisfactory evidence to show, that βαπτίζω is here used in its primary meaning, and if it was, no two leading Baptist writers agree as to what that meaning is. 6. There is the most satisfactory evidence to show, that βαπτίζω does not mean *to dip*, and that such a meaning is diametrically opposed to the force of the word. 7. There is satisfactory evidence (John 2 : 6) to show, that provision was made in Jewish houses for the purification of guests in other ways than by dipping their persons into water, or by covering the entire body with water in any way whatever. 8. There is

satisfactory evidence that such provision was made in the
house of this Pharisee, and one score or one hundred could
have made use of such provision, "according to the custom
of the Jews," in passing from the highway to the dinner-
table.   9. There is satisfactory evidence to show, that the
washing of the hands, whether effected by pouring water
upon them or by washing them in water, was called, not a
baptism of *the hands*, merely, but a baptism of *the entire person*.   The testimony of Clement and Ambrose to this effect
has, already, been given; see, also, that of Theophylact (in
loc.), who describes the purification expected (which of necessity extended over the entire person) as a hand-washing.

Interpretation.

The facts of this case are so patent and so inimical to a
dipping of the body into water, that commentators (even
when accepting, erroneously, *to dip* as the primary meaning
of the word) have, almost unanimously, refused to recognize
a dipping of the body as entering into this transaction.

Campbell, of Aberdeen, who contends very unqualifiedly
for *dip* as the meaning of $\beta\alpha\pi\tau\acute{\iota}\zeta\omega$, and who translates in Mark
7 : 4 by "*dip* (their hands)," in this passage translates, "the
Pharisee was surprised to observe that he used *no washing*
before dinner."   Such language can neither point to an exclusive dipping of the body, nor of the hands.   Bengel says,
"He sat down to meat forthwith, *without having washed.*"
Calvin says, "The Jews had added many other *washings*
to those prescribed by law, and more especially, that no
person should partake of food till he *had been washed* with
the water of purification," and refers to the hand-washing
in Mark 7 : 3, and the purifyings in John 2 : 6.   Olshausen
makes the baptism a hand-washing—"He observed that
Jesus ate *without having washed his hands.*"   So, Rosenmüller,
"Pharisaeus autem admiratus est, quod non ante cœnam
manus abluisset. 'E$\beta\alpha\pi\tau\iota\sigma\theta\eta$, *i. e.*, $\grave{\varepsilon}\nu\acute{\iota}\psi\alpha\tau o$ $\tau\grave{\alpha}\varsigma$ $\chi\varepsilon\tilde{\iota}\rho\alpha\varsigma$."   This
hand-washing Rosenmüller understands to be a washing-
purification, not of the hands, merely, but of the entire
person, a complete baptism.   He adds, "*Illotis* ex Iudaico

dogmate omnis cibus erat immundus." Grotius, in like
manner, regards ἐβαπτίσθη as used for ἐνιψάτο τὰς χεῖρας.
Bloomfield thinks, that "βαπτίζεσθαι has the same sense as
λούεσθαι and χερνίπτειν, *washing* and *hand-washing*, and agrees
with Beza, Pole, and Pococke, that it was so used as to comprehend the one as well as the other."

Carson.

How do these facts, which so strongly impress the learned
and the good, affect Dr. Carson? Does it lead him to question the correctness of his "demonstration" that this word
means "dip and nothing but dip through all Greek literature?" By no means. He puts his back against "the
word," and shutting his eyes against everything else but the
"demonstration" (of which his friends are getting heartily
tired), he declares, in language which few would venture to
use,—"They expected that Christ would have immersed
(dipped) before eating. To deny this is to give the lie to
the inspired narrator. The word used by the Holy Spirit
signifies immersion (dipping) and immersion (dipping)
only" (p. 450).

It might have been supposed that Dr. Carson would have
been satisfied with challenging the worth of all human learning which did not accept his *dictum*, without making issue
with divine inspiration; but it seems otherwise. To send
philosophers and archangels to school for "peeping" against
his demonstration is but an appetizing morceau to an insa-
tiable self-confidence. He gambles with the Deity as his
stake, crying,—"I win, or God is not true!" So the theory
works itself out in one direction.

The Absolute Use of Βαπτίζω.

We have met with the constant and unhesitating absolute
use of βαπτίζω in connection with Jewish purifications. Such
usage claims our special attention. Such phraseology does
not express a complete idea except to those who by familiar
use are able to supply what is lacking, or who apprehend a

meaning, through appropriation, not originally inherent in the words.

No complete idea is expressed by—"he marvelled that he was not first baptized;" whether "baptized" be represented by *mersed* or *dipped*. But the friends of the theory would supplement by adding—"dipped IN WATER." But here we would inquire where the "water" comes from? We have such expressions as "diverse baptisms," "baptisms of cups and couches," "baptize from the market," "baptize from the dead," "baptize at a fountain," but in none of them does "water" appear by verbal statement. Is it replied, that although "water" is not expressly stated, and *blood*, and *ashes*, and *fire*, did enter into some baptisms, still, there is abundant evidence that into these baptisms before eating, water, and not blood, nor ashes, nor fire, entered as the element used, as shown by the baptism of Judith at a fountain, by "the *water* pots" at Cana, and by other historical evidence. This is satisfactory so far as the presence of this element is concerned. It has a clear right to appear in the rite. We would, now, ask for authority for the manner of its introduction. Can any case of Jewish ceremonial baptism be pointed out in which it is, by express statement, declared that a person or a thing was "baptized *into* water?" As no such statement is known to us, we shall take the liberty of assuming that none exists, until evidence to the contrary is adduced; and this the more especially because it is expressly stated, that Judith was baptized *at* the fountain and not *in* it, and whatever baptisms took place in Cana, "after the manner of the purifying of the Jews," they, too, must have been *at* the water pots and not *in* them.

Is it said, that the "into" is provided for by "dip;" one cannot be dipped without being dipped *in*. The reasoning is, in itself, quite unexceptionable. If "dip" has the right of presence, his attendant "into" has an equal right. But we deny the right of dip to the fellowship which he seeks. We pronounce him to be an impostor, who, under a title to which he had no just claim, has thrust himself into relations to which, on his own merits, he could never attain. And until he shall bring better credentials than he yet has done, we must unceremoniously strip him of his borrowed habiliments and dismiss him from Jewish baptisms together with his prepositional satellite.

Are the friends of the theory willing to accept the exposed imposture (not by any means of themselves, but) of *dip*, and manfully take *merse* in its stead? They may do so, with the joyous conviction that "*in* water" will wait on this word as faithfully as on the discarded impostor. Let us see: 1. Βαπτίζω is used abundantly in cases where it is followed by the prepositions *with* and *by*, expressed or implied in the nude dative. This is so where the baptism is effected by fluids (ὄινῳ, ὕδατι, C. B., p. 317). Βάπτω is, also, used with a nude dative, but in such case the change of form betokens a change of meaning, and "dip *in*" becomes metamorphosed into "dyed *by*." Who shall forbid βαπτίζω from announcing, by like change of syntax, a no less fundamental change of meaning? Certainly these facts do utterly preclude the assumption, that this and like baptisms were *in* water and not *by* water. Any passage declaring, that men and women were, in Jewish baptisms, to be *baptized in* water, and not *by* water, has never been adduced; and such assumption is not only intolerable in view of the facts stated, but, also, 2. Because the essential force of the word does not allow such use of water to be made in religious rites. To baptize a human being in water would, by the force of its terms, convey to the mind of a Classic Greek the idea of death by drowning. Æsop, Alcibiades, Heliodorus, Lucian, Plutarch, Themistius, all, drown by βαπτίζω (C. B., p. 266). It is inadmissible, therefore, to suppose (there is no such statement to be found), that these Jews were baptized *in* water. Is it said, "There was no design to drown these persons, therefore the natural force of this word cannot apply." I answer: If *merse* has so far changed as to be transformed into *dip*, the change is as great as if *alpha* were changed into *omega*, in which case the univocalism of the theory perishes. That this is no exaggerated representation of the difference between *merse* and *dip* will be seen by the following quotations:

"Immersed
Deep in the flood, found, when he sought it not,
The death he had deserved, and *died* alone."

"Dead
By cold submersion, razor, rope, or lead."

What is there, here, which produces death but mersion *in water?* Is there one iota added to the proper force of the terms? If in these passages you substitute *dipping* for mersion, will any one be hurt? Is not one of the grand distinctions between "mersion in water" and "dipping in water," that the former will drown (will always drown unless some foreign influence interfere to prevent this result), while dipping in water will not drown? Is it not, then, one of the most extraordinary assumptions that ever was made, to assume, without support by a single statement, that the baptism was in water, and, then, to escape a drowning, to make the farther extraordinary assumption, that *merse* has been changed into *dip*, βαπτίζω into βάπτω!

We say, that this absolute use (persisted in through centuries in a rite of daily recurrence) is proof, that the word had received a coloring from its surroundings, and did, directly, express the purifying character of the rite. The Pharisee "marvelled that he was not first *purified*" before he took his place at the table.

By a similar process words are continually securing new meanings. Thus (Winer, p. 593), "διάγειν absorbs τὸν βίον, with which it had been associated in familiar phrase, and, alone, expresses *to live*. So, διατρίβειν, absorbing τὸν χρόνον, expresses *to sojourn*. And in a similar manner προσφέρειν secures the meaning *to sacrifice*, and προσκυνειν *to worship*."

Ellipsis.

This is not a case of mere ellipsis, but a case in which the power to express directly a new meaning has been attained. Winer (p. 581) says, "Ellipsis consists in the omission of a word the meaning of which must be supplied in thought in order to complete the sentence," and quotes *Herm.* p. 153:

"Ellipseos propria est ratio grammatica, quæ posita est in eo, ut oratio, etiamsi aliquid omissum sit, integra esse censeatur, quia id quod omissum est, necessario tamen intelligi debeat, ut quo non intellecto sententia nulla futura sit." The usage before us has clearly passed beyond this form. It comes rather under the subsequent statements: "The ellipsis in all these expressions has been sanctioned by long usage, and for that very reason is plain, especially in particular contexts, to all familiar with the language." "On the other hand, a number of transitive verbs have, in a similar way, rid themselves in the course of time of the case of the noun with which they formed a current phrase, and are *now used all alone to express the same meaning*" (pp. 592, 593). This acquired meaning is established in Judaic Baptism by most abundant and direct evidence.

Parallel Classical Usage.

Between Plato and Plutarch there was an interval of five centuries. During all that time there was an absolute use of βαπτίζω, with a special application. Thus Plato says, "I am one of those *baptized;*" and Plutarch, half a thousand years afterward, says, "not yet *baptized;*" no adjunct expository word being used. The word is evidently self-expounding. A meaning has been secured from long use in uniform relations, and, then, those relations no longer needing verbal expression, are dropped. This use, among the Classics, is developed in connection with wine-drinking, a custom as universal, as frequently recurring, and as abiding through centuries, as was the Jewish custom of water purifications. In the one case the word represents an intoxicating influence, and in the other a purifying influence. But wine has other qualities than that by which it effects a condition of intoxication, and when these other, rarer, baptisms are referred to, it is necessary to introduce an appropriate adjunct. Thus, when a wine baptism, not intoxicating but destructive of life, is spoken of, the word is not used absolutely, but with explanatory terms, thus: "Why do many wine drinkers die? Because the quantity of the wine baptizes *the physical and the vital power and warmth"* (*Alex. Aphrod. Medical Problems, I,* 17). In ordinary wine baptism it is the power to regulate mental and physical action which is baptized. Josephus, in like manner, when he would speak of a wine baptism other than that which is ordinary, introduces appropriate adjunct terms, as—" baptized *into insensibility and sleep.*" But Philo, when he would speak of that wine baptism to which the word was appropriated, uses it, like the Classics, without any adjunct—" before they are completely *baptized.*" Water, like wine, is capable of effecting a variety of baptisms. When the Classics would express that baptism of water which is effected by its cold-producing quality, they use water with the instrumental dative—" hot iron is baptized *by water.*" When they speak of that water baptism which is destructive of life, they represent the victim as baptized *in water.* Thus the man-hater Timon murders his victim by baptizing him *in water.* And the no less man-hating Herod murders his rival by baptizing him *in water.* But when the Jews would speak of that water baptism which results from the purifying quality of this element, they then use the word without adjunct, as a self-expressive term— " he marvelled that he was not first *baptized*"—purified ceremonially.

Evidence the most manifold and from all quarters (from language development, from appropriation, from change of syntax, from the impossibility of a primary, physical use) proves most indubitably, that as this Greek word indicates a complete change of condition by mersion, so it no less indicates any analogous change of condition though not effected by mersion. Βαπτίζω marks the change of condition of an impure object passing into a condition of purity by sprinkling or pouring, without any regard whatever to a mersion, just as βάπτω marks the change of color in an object on which berry-juice is sprinkled or poured, without any regard whatever to a dipping. The proof of the former is as varied, as clear, and as direct, as is the proof of the latter. Βάπτω does not mean to sprinkle; yet white linen sprinkled with blood is *bapted by* blood; not because of the sprinkling (the action might have been that of dropping, or pouring), but because blood, however applied to white linen, *changes its color*. Βαπτίζω does not mean to sprinkle; yet a ceremonially impure object sprinkled with pure water is baptized by water (not because of the sprinkling, the action might have been in any other form, but), because pure water, in whatever form it is applied to a ceremonially impure object, has a power to *change the condition* of that object. If sprinkled blood did not *change the* COLOR of its object, its work could not be represented by βάπτω; and if sprinkled water did not *change the* CONDITION of its object, there would be no demand for the service of βαπτίζω.

What, now, does the theory say to all this? Does it sternly point to a great cloud of witnesses in the shape of unquestionable water *dippings* (exponential of βαπτίζω) in Jewish purifications? Not to a great cloud, certainly, and just as certainly, not to a solitary case. But instead of such hard argument we have the cry—"The word! the word! any child can understand that it means 'dip and nothing but dip through all Greek literature,' and if the archangel Gabriel dares to doubt, we will send him to school; and if what we thus affirm be not true, then the word of God is ——!"

This ironism of the theory lasts until some waxiness is needed for its aid, and, then, the plastic fingers of poetry and rhetoric mould it with the greatest facility imaginable into any needed form. Thus, baptism by *pouring* (on Carmel) becomes one of the most intelligible things in nature, and squares, to a hair, with "dip and nothing but dip." But, when we enter a plea for this Carmel baptism by pouring in behalf of ungainly couches, or for the person of our divine Lord in the house of the Pharisee, we are curtly told, that there must be a *dipping*, the word makes absolute demand for it; that baptism by pouring is no baptism, any more than pouring is dipping; and if the couches and the Lord Jesus were not dipped into water, then, the inspired writer is a "false witness!" So, the theory arrogantly dashes itself against the throne of "the faithful and true Witness." Which shall be broken?

We have, now, passed in review the last of the Jewish baptisms recorded in the New Testament as practiced before, and during, and after, the ministry of John. The facts of this last case show, 1. That the Lord Jesus Christ was expected to be baptized in passing from the wayside to the dinner table; 2. We have shown the means by which this could be done, through "the water pots" furnished for guests "after the manner of purifying of the Jews;" 3. We have shown, the manner in which these purifyings were effected, by water poured upon the hands, purifying the entire person; 4. We have shown, that these purifyings were called baptisms; and 5. We have shown, that such use of words was in harmony with the Classic usage of this same word, with that of the related word βάπτω, and with the general laws of language development. Matthew and Mark speak of the process of this baptism. Luke speaks of the changed condition resultant from this process. The disciples were expected "to wash their hands" before dinner in order to their baptism. Their Master was expected " to be baptized" before eating, that is, to go through the process of hand-washing. The two statements are complementary of each other. As John was born, and lived, and died, amidst these daily Jewish baptisms, he had the fullest opportunity, in this direction, for knowing the meaning and usage of βαπτίζω.

JOSEPHUS AND JOHN'S BAPTISM.

" *Βαπτισμῷ συνιέναι οὕτω γὰρ τὴν βάπτισιν ἀποδεκτὴν αὐτῷ φανεῖσθαι, μὴ ἐπὶ τινῶν ἁμαρτάδων παραιτήσει χρωμένων, ἀλλ' ἐφ' ἁγνείᾳ τοῦ σώματος, ἅτε δὴ καὶ τῆς ψυχῆς δικαιοσύνῃ προεκκεκαθαρμένης.*"

" For Herod slew him (John the Baptist), a good man, exhorting the Jews to cultivate virtue and observing uprightness toward one another and piety toward God, to come for baptizing (purification); for thus the baptizing (purification) would appear acceptable to him, not using it for the remission of sins,

but for purity of the body, provided that the soul has been previously purged by righteousness."—JOSEPHUS, *Jew. Ant.* xviii,
6, 2.

"Quippe hunc Herodes obtruncaverat, cum esset vir bonus,
Judæosque ad virtutis studium excitaret, præcipiens ut juste
quidem inter se, erga Deum autem pie agentes, ad lavacrum
accederent. Tunc enim demum acceptum, Deo fore lavacrum
aiebat, cum eo non ad expiationem criminum uterentur, sed ad
corporis munditiem, ut mentibus jam ante per justitiam expur-
gatis, corporis quoque adderent puritatem."—VALESIUS, *in Eusebius*, ii, 116.

Twofold Baptism = 1. Of the Soul; 2. Of the Body (Symbol).

This reference to John's baptism by Josephus is valuable,
1. As showing the usage of the Greek words under consideration by Jews, and 2. As showing the Jewish understanding of the teaching of John and the nature of his baptism, both of the soul and of the body. There is, I think,
internal evidence in the passage, that the knowledge of John
and of his baptism was obtained by Josephus not from the
Scriptures, but from the current popular understanding.
He does not use the same form of word for baptism as that
employed by John. Nor does he use the same grammatical
form which John uses to give definiteness to his baptism.
He does, however, describe with great accuracy the impression as to these things which the preaching of John must
have made upon the minds of his hearers.

The points noticeable in this extract are: 1. The use of
βαπτισμῷ and βάπτισιν for baptism. They are not found in Classic writers, nor are they used by John. 2. The absolute use
of these words; there is no explanatory adjunct appended.
Water is not mentioned, and, of course, no dipping into it.
3. The explanation of the baptisms; John's water baptism
(baptism of the body) is not described as a Jewish baptism.
That baptism was for the removal of ceremonial impurity
contracted by touching a dead body, &c. But the ground
of John's baptism of the body is made to rest on an en-

tirely different basis, namely, *to bring it into harmony with the previous baptism of the soul by righteousness.* In such case, the baptism of the body can only be regarded as a reflection of the baptism of the soul. The water which purifies the body is a symbol of the righteousness which purifies the soul. 4. He speaks of the soul as baptized. A soul which is thoroughly purged from sin has completely changed its condition. This change, we are told, is effected " by righteousness "—instrumental dative. Analogous changes in the condition of the soul, Classic writers say, is a baptism effected by love, by hate, by wrath, &c., instrumental datives. If this baptism of the soul is "*by* righteousness," and the baptism of the body is a symbol of this, we are shut up to the conclusion, that the body is baptized, also, *by* water and not *in* water. Thus Josephus is exhibited in the most perfect harmony with all kindred baptisms and with the true force of the word. 5. If we had, merely, been informed, that the soul was baptized—thoroughly purged—by righteousness, it would be language strictly modelled after the most common classic form, and is but little lacking of the highest precision; but, as heretofore stated, the addition of a verbal element to the baptism gives absolute precision. Thus Josephus, on another occasion, not content with the mere statement " baptized by drunkenness," gives the last degree of definiteness of which language is capable, by adding—" into insensibility and sleep." He does not, here, give formally the verbal element of baptism, but he does substantially by declaring, that the baptism of the body is not for the remission of sins, with the evident teaching, that " the baptism of the soul is, by righteousness, *into the remission of sins.*"

And this leads to the statement of the last important feature of this extract: 6. The orthodoxy of its doctrine of baptism. The soul is to be first baptized—*thoroughly changed as to its moral condition*—which is not effected by water, but " by righteousness," and, then, the body is to be baptized by water, which does not take away sin, but which does bring the body into a *condition of symbol purity*, harmonious with the new condition of the soul purified by righteousness.

An analogous twofold baptism (of the soul and of the body) is spoken of both by the Jew Philo, and by the Classic Plutarch. Philo (Jud. Bap., p. 84), in general terms, says, "I know some who when they become slightly intoxicated (intellect baptized) before they become thoroughly drunk (corporeally baptized)." Plutarch speaks more definitely (C. B., p. 338): "Of those slightly intoxicated only the intellect is disturbed; but the body is yet able to serve its impulses, being not yet mersed (baptized)." Wine, then, effects a twofold baptism: 1. Of the intellect, in the earlier stages of intoxication, when it can no longer, justly, perform its functions; 2. Of the body, in the later stages of intoxication, when it can no longer, adequately, perform its functions. This twofold baptism is ruinous to the notion of "a dipping," unless poetry and rhetoric can discover some method by which the intellect can be dipped first, and the body be dipped afterward. It is obvious, that both Philo and Plutarch use baptism to express a change of condition in the intellect and in the body, effected by the intoxicating principle in wine which obtains the ascendency earlier over the intellect than over the body. These baptisms, of course, are wholly different in nature from those of which Josephus speaks; but they agree in their double character (of the spiritual and of the physical man), and in that the baptism of the spiritual nature precedes that of the physical nature. The agency inducing such baptisms, the mode by which it is used, the order of their origination, their coexistence, their continuance, their agreements, and their differences, are all worthy of attention.

This testimony of Josephus as to *the nature* of John's baptism (alas! that he too, like all others, failed to see, and therefore failed to say a word about that momentous question, "How did John use the water?") is of great interest as an independent testimony, and of great value because of its explicit statement and accurate representation.

No one can reflect upon the facts: 1. That Jewish Greek writings, speaking of baptisms, were in existence for two centuries before John's ministry. 2. That these baptisms were in daily observance all through his ministry and his life. 3. The perfect knowledge of these Greek words shown by Jewish Greek writers closely his contemporaries—without feeling that abundant facilities for attaining to a correct knowledge of the true power and varied usage of βαπτίζω were perfectly accessible to John.   And no thoughtful person will, I am sure, regard it as a matter of little importance to have these things very distinctly before us as preparatory to the direct inquiry—" What usage of βαπτίζω is shown by the writings descriptive of John's ministry?"

NEW TERMS INTRODUCED.

ΒΑΠΤΙΣΤΗΣ.

MATTHEW 3:1.

"John the Baptist came preaching in the wilderness."

'Ιωάννης ὁ βαπτιστὴς.

THE Forerunner of the Messiah is termed ὁ βαπτιστὴς. Although many others baptized, yet to none is this title ever applied but to John. There must be a special reason for this. The reason, no doubt, is embodied, more or less distinctly, in the word. What, then, is the meaning of this word? becomes a question both of special and general interest in its bearing on our inquiry. The means for a satisfactory answer to this question are not so abundant as in the case of many other words. Classic Greek writings do not furnish, so far as I am aware, a single instance of its use. Inspired writings, in like manner, furnish no example of the use of this word except as applied to John. Patristic writings are almost as destitute of the use of this word except in this single personal application. There is one exception, and, I believe, but one exception to this fact. That one is remarkable and valuable, and will claim our attention in seeking an answer to this question.

Among the sources of information available for determining the meaning of any word are, 1. Etymology. 2. Usage. 3. The special features of the passage in which it occurs. 4. The time and circumstances in which it originates. From some or all of these sources we may look for valuable aid in determining the meaning of the word under consideration.

1. *Etymology* is the natural source for primary appeal in determining the meaning of any word. It is a source of information which can never be wisely neglected. But what-

(130)

ever may be the result of such appeal, we can never, safely, rest in it as a finality. Hermeneutical writers unite in saying, that words, under long or hard usage, may have every feature which would identify them with their etymological parentage entirely obliterated. This is comparatively rare. But cases of words whose meanings depart widely and essentially from that of the etymon are quite common, and the tracing back of the dim waymarks left by the wanderer until, with growing clearness, they bring us to the original point of departure, is one of the most interesting features in the study of language.

We know, by universal consent of grammarians, that the structure of this word indicates a person who is an executor of the demand of the verb whence it is derived, unless something has intervened to modify or thoroughly change that meaning.

Dr. Carson says, " The Greek verb means *to dip* and nothing but dip;" and the Baptist Confession of Faith says, " Baptizing is *dipping* and dipping is baptizing;" Dr. Gale says, "The primary meaning is simply *to dip;* Christ by commanding to baptize has commanded *to dip* only." The venerable Booth says, " The primary sense of the term is *to dip.*" Dr. Cox says, " The idea of *dipping* is in every instance" (C. B., pp. 30–40). According to these statements there is no alternative for this derivative; it must mean "the Dipper."

But to assign to $\beta\alpha\pi\tau\acute{\iota}\zeta\omega$ the same meaning as $\beta\acute{\alpha}\pi\tau\omega$, " neither more nor less," is a self-evident error. Language never, thus, repeats itself. Facts make the most absolute disproof of any such meaning. And, besides, Baptist baptism is only an *e gratia* dipping. The theory requires that the object shall be " so small that it can be lifted up" and dipped in all its entirety; but this cannot be done with men and women; hence, the plan of walking into the water " to a convenient depth," and dipping so much of the body as may remain above the water. The disproof of this meaning is so overwhelming that it is abandoned in the Baptist Quarterly for January, 1869.

Professor A. N. Arnold, D.D., of the Baptist Theological
Seminary, Chicago, quotes, with unreserved approbation,
the statement—" *Βαπτίζω* has only one meaning. It signifies
literally and perpetually *to plunge*." This estimable Professor
forgets, that the theory has, already, been on trial under the
auspices of this " only " meaning, and that when placed in
the critical vice it groaned out in agony—" This is very
unfair; *plunge* gives a ridiculous air to our sentiments and
practice." Has Professor Arnold found a remedy for the
" ridiculous " plunging which so troubled " the venerable
Booth ?" Unless this is so, the friends of the theory will
not insist, that this derivative must mean *the Plunger*. But
as the theory is accustomed to seesaw from one " only meaning" to another " only meaning," as exigencies demand, we
break up this second etymological definition by the statement, that facts show that Booth was right in saying, " It is
ridiculous to make *plunge* the ' always and perpetual ' representative of *βαπτίζω*."

Dr. Conant says : " *BAIITIZEIN : To immerse, immerge, submerge, to dip, to plunge, to imbathe, to whelm*." The derivative, then, must be, " the Immerser, the Immerger, the
Submerger, the Dipper, the Plunger, the Imbather, the
Whelmer."

As Dr. Conant does not avow any purpose to revolutionize
the definitions of all preceding Baptist writers, we must understand this language as expressing some definite act as
the vital meaning of this word.

If Dr. Conant will abandon this idea (as I presume he
will), and fall back on *result* in " immersion," then, it is obvious, that there is made the greatest possible revolution in
the conception of the word. If Baptist reasoning in the past
will answer for this new basis, then that reasoning must,
surely, have been of the most remarkable character. Would
they claim, that their reasoning and interpretation under
the position that *βάπτω* had but one meaning, would answer
equally well after the acknowledgment, that they were entirely mistaken; that it had a secondary and entirely diverse
meaning? But what, under such change of base, would be

the force of this derivative—"the Immerser," "the Submerger?" It points out one who effects a certain condition characterized by complete envelopment, without self-limitation as to time of continuance any more than of the act of its accomplishment. What self-limitation (as to time of continuance in the condition induced) is there in the title "the Submerger," "the Immerser?" Would not the making of "the Submerger" to destroy the submersion, at the same time, annihilate the character of "the Submerger?" A man who puts in and takes out of a liquid may be entitled a *Bobber*, a *Dabbler*, a *Dipper*, but he cannot be called a "Submerger," an "Immerser." Limited continuance is involved in the former words; unlimited continuance is involved in the latter words. But while unlimited continuance is demanded to the excluding of momentary inness and outness, there is not demand for absolute permanence of continuance. This may be or may not be. It will always be if left to the force of the word, "the Submerger," "the Immerser." A foreign influence must intervene to destroy the condition induced. One and the same party cannot, in the same transaction, act in the double rôle of Submerger and Emerger. It is indeed true that a Submerger by hurriedly putting on the character of an Emerger may save the life of one whom he has submerged; but it is only at the expense of philological suicide. Timon played the part of a "Submerger" and murdered his victim; Alcibiades would play the part of a "Submerger" to murder his victim; Herod's assassins played the part of "Submergers" and murdered Aristobulus; and as with these, so with all other Greeks, they knew nothing of an *Emerger* entering into the office of a "Submerger," or being consistent with it. If, then, "Immerser," or "Submerger" be insisted on as the representative of this derivative, etymology will never reach forth a hand to rescue its victims from perishing under the waters.

If, then, ὁ βαπτιστής be made "the Dipper," etymology enters her absolute protest against any such abuse of her name. And if it be made "the Immerser," "the Submerger," Christianity enters her equally absolute protest against putting men and women under water, in her name, by a word which has drowned hosts of heathen Greeks.

Such is the issue of the etymology of the theory.

OUR etymology connects this derivative with a verb which makes demand, 1. For change of condition by intusposition within an enveloping element, solid, as the human body; semi-solid, as a marsh; fluid, as water, blood, &c. 2. A change of condition by any controlling and assimilating influence without intusposition. 3. A specific change of condition; (1.) To intoxicate; (2.) To purify. Ὁ βαπτιστής, therefore, might represent, a "man-hater," murderer of men by drowning; one who excels in the exercise of a controlling influence, whether of contentious words (such as Demosthenes speaks of), or any other kindred influence; one who is preeminent in making drunkards; or, one who is remarkable as a Purifier. As a matter of fact it is limited to the latter designation.

Etymology cannot be relied upon as the sole and ultimate arbiter in determining the meaning of words. "There are many cases in which, though the descent of a word may be clearly traced, we should err egregiously if we were to fix its meaning from that of the primitive or root. I know nothing in which modern critics are more frequently misled than in their reasonings from etymology." (Campbell, Prelim. Diss.)

2. *Usage* is of higher authority than etymology. The meaning assigned to a word by use may or may not be traceable to the root idea. "The three words, κωμικος in Greek, *paganus* in Latin, and *villain* in English, though evidently so conformable in etymology that they all ought to denote the same thing, namely, *villager*, have, for many ages, both lost that signification, and acquired others in which they do not in the least resemble one another. If the use in these languages should ever come to be very little known, and the history of the nations nearly lost, we may form a guess at the absurdities in explaining those terms into which men would be misled by etymology." "In settling the meaning of words we must have respect chiefly to the *usus loquendi*, the current sense, or established usage at the time,—to this

more than to their etymology" (Campbell-Fairbairn). The usage in regard to the word in question is, as already stated, very limited. It is not found in Classic Greek, nor is it employed in the New Testament in circumstances or in grammatical relations which are necessarily determinative of the meaning. It occurs in Arrian (C. B., p. 347) in a compound form, παραβαπτισται, a hundred and fifty years after John's ministry. In this case the meaning is obscure. The ablest scholars cannot agree as to the meaning. The theme of the passage is *character;* and it is highly probable, that the word refers to character as induced by controlling influence, and not to the performance of any physical act.

The corresponding word, βάπτης, derived from βάπτω, is still more limited in its usage. It is found only in Classic writings, and there only in a single relation, namely, as a title given to a certain class of persons (C. B., p. 165). Scholars differ as to the probable relation of this derivative, whether to *dip* or to *dye.* It is quite possible, that the immediate reference is neither to dipping nor dyeing, but to the more advanced meaning of stained, polluted, infamous, character. The verb is freely used in this aspect: "The soul is *imbued* by the thoughts"—"*imbued* by integrity"—"lest you *be imbued* by Cæsarism"—"*imbued* the Muse"—"adopt the character of one *imbued*" (C. B., p. 143). The οἱ βάπται of Eupolis, the priests of Cotytto, were, probably, neither "the Dippers," nor "the Dyers," but "the Imbuers" of their disciples with the pollutions entering into the rites of a deified courtesan. There is, certainly, nothing in this related verb, or its derivative, which would bind down ὁ βαπτιστὴς to the meaning—"the Dipper."

There is but a single instance, so far as I am aware, in which this word is ever applied to any other person than John, and in that case it is applied to John's Lord. The passage is as follows: "Veniet ergo Baptista Magnus, sic enim eum nomino quomodo nominavit Gabriel dicens, 'Hic erit Magnus' (Luc. 1: 32)—Then shall come the Great Baptizer (for so I call him, as Gabriel called him, saying, 'He shall be Great,' Luke 1: 32), he shall see many stand-

ing before the entrance of Paradise, he will wave the sword
turning every way, and will say to those on the right hand,
not having great sins,—'Enter ye who are of good courage,
who fear not the fire.'" *Ambrose*, II, 1227. Here the meaning—"Great Dipper," "Great Immerser," "Great Submerger," "Great Plunger"—is out of all question: 1. Because Christ never did *dip, immerse, submerge,* or *plunge* any
one. 2. Because the act attributed to him, as expository of
his title and executory of his functions—"waving a flaming
sword"—is inconsistent with and wholly excludes any such
meaning. The passage is, in a remarkable degree, self-ex-
plaining. The meaning which it demands, and the only
meaning which it allows is, "*the Great Purifier.*" This interpretation is fortified, beyond appeal, by the parallel passage
in Origen (III, 704), who in expounding the passages, "I
came not to send peace upon earth but a sword"—"I came
to send fire upon the earth," says: "Igitur defert utrumque
Salvator, gladium et ignem, et BAPTIZAT QUÆ non protuerunt
Spiritus Sancti purificatione purgari—Therefore the Saviour
brings both, *sword* and *fire,* and BAPTIZES THOSE SINS WHICH
could not be purged by the purification of the Holy Spirit."
This passage shuts up, in the most absolute manner, the interpretation of the verb to the meaning—*to purify.* We are
furnished, therefore, with passages in which both the verb
and the derivative signify *to purify,* and *the Purifier.* And if
we are governed by the authority of Ambrose and Origen
(and there is no opposing authority), ὁ βαπτιστής must mean
"the Purifier." The full sanction of language development
to such meaning is evidenced by a parallel appropriation.

Parallel Appropriation—Merger.

On asking a classical scholar, What is the meaning of
Merger? he gave an answer based on the primary physical
usage of *mergo.* The answer was wrong. It was, however,
the only intelligent answer which could be given without
the knowledge of a modifying usage. With such usage he
was unfamiliar. The Law appropriates "Merger," while
the Gospel appropriates ὁ βαπτιστής.

I will now present in illustration of the case in hand, the feature which characterizes all the passages in which this word appears in its absolute use, distinguishing, as a title, the bearer of it from all others.

3. The phrase "John the Baptist" ought to be and was an intelligible phrase. Whether "John the Dipper" was an intelligible phrase or not, it cannot, etymologically, represent the Scripture terms for the unanswerable reason, that the root does not mean *to dip*. "John the Immerser," "the Submerger," cannot, rationally, be the interpreting phrase, for the root requires that the entire object shall be "immersed," "submerged," and gives no more recognition to the dipping of a part, than the dipping of the whole. Again, and again, do the Classics give us instances of persons in the water from their ankles to their necks, not one of whom is said to be baptized except with some limiting term. In many such cases where the head has been submerged and the parties drowned, they are unqualifiedly pronounced baptized. In some of such cases death has been escaped not under favor of the word, nor through any grace of the baptizer, but in spite of both. There is no case of any person in the water, more or less, and the rest of the person being designedly put under the water for a moment and taken out, being called a baptized person. There is no evidence, that the force of the word would allow of any such usage as explicative of its primary meaning. And, according to the theory, the word has no other meaning. To introduce momentariness into the root of this word is to expel its only rightful occupant. To declare, that submerged men and women must, in a moment, be taken from under the water to save life, is only to declare, that they were never put under the water by $\beta\alpha\pi\tau\dot{\iota}\zeta\omega$, or that that word has undergone a revolution as to its meaning. Let it be proved, that John the Baptizer ever put men and women under the water in answer to the demand of $\beta\alpha\pi\tau\dot{\iota}\zeta\omega$, and we will listen to a plea for saving their lives, and, also, for changing John's title. Until such proof shall be adduced we must abide in the faith, that John, $\dot{o}$ $\beta\alpha\pi\tau\iota\sigma\tau\dot{\eta}\varsigma$, knew too well the force of both

the primary and secondary meanings of this Greek word
ever to enter upon any such task.

But what is the ground or the fitness for the title "John
the Dipper," "the Immerser," "the Submerger?" Were
there not a thousand others who engaged in the acts of dipping, immersing, submerging? Is it replied, that his action
was in connection with a religious service? And does not
the theory declare, that ten thousand such acts were every
day performed through all Jewry in the fulfilment of religious
service? Is it farther said, In the one case the parties dipped, immersed, submerged themselves, while in the other
the action was performed by somebody else? This may be
a distinction, but its breadth is so nearly equal to that of a
razor's edge, that to build a theory upon it will involve im-
minent peril of its being cut in twain. We prefer the breadth
and depth of the title which marks the Forerunner out as
the sole executor of a peculiar work, and proclaims him as
standing alone among his fellows, practicing ceremonial
purification of the body, as emphatically "the Purifier," the
proclaimer of a higher purification than that ceremonialism
which characterized the religion of his day.

4. The time and circumstances under which a word originates may render valuable aid in determining its meaning.

The time at which ὁ βαπτιστής makes its appearance is indubitably certain. It springs out of John's ministry. It is
never met with, previously, in either Classic or Jewish
writings. At the opening of his ministry it is assigned to
him as a distinguishing title, and is so appropriated throughout that ministry.

The circumstances which make the soil in which this word
is rooted, and out of which it springs, are just as well known.
John, from first to last, was encompassed with religious rites
observed for the purpose of securing ceremonial purity.
These rites had both a divine and human original. The
purifying agencies were made up of water, blood, ashes, and
fire. The Greek word βαπτίζω and the verbal βαπτισμός are
employed in connection with these rites, but without evidence, in a single instance, of primary use. The unmodified

primary force of the word could not be applied to living persons. There is absolute proof, that objects not enveloped by water, blood, ashes, or fire, are said to be baptized—ceremonially purified. In the midst of this condition of things John appears and preaches another and higher purification, that of the soul not of the body, real not ceremonial, by repentance not by water. In connection with this purification preached and as illustrative of its character, pure water was employed as a symbol shadowing forth the purification of the soul by repentance. A more perfect groundwork for the title—"the Purifier"—could not be laid.

There is but little room for doubt as to the persons who first gave this title. It certainly had no family origin. There is no evidence for a divine origin. It is not usual for such titles to arise among disciples. Quaker, Methodist, Puritan, Christian, were titles which originated with outsiders. They were not intended to be titles of honor. There is no honor in the title "the Immerser," "the Submerger;" there may be none designed in "the Purifier." John could not claim it in any self-ennobling sense, for he ever magnified "the Coming One" as "the Great Baptizer;" his disciples would not give it to him, for their very discipleship bound them to look for a Mightier One. The title originated, beyond reasonable doubt, among Jews who were not John's disciples. There is as little just room to doubt, that it originated before John had immersed, submerged, dipped, sprinkled, or in any other way applied water to a single individual. It must have been so: 1. Because there was no foundation amid Jewish water purifyings for grounding a distinguishing title on the modal use of the water. 2. Because John necessarily preached his purification of the soul before he administered its water symbol. In doing this he must, of necessity, contrast the purification of the soul and the body, the real and the ritual; and must treat as comparatively worthless all Jewish ceremonial purifications.

All this is clearly embraced in the account of John's preaching which is given by Josephus. And it is just here, and just for this reason, that the title ὁ βαπτιστής, *the* Purifier, is given to John by Jews whose purifications he rejects, and calls them to receive one which is true, real, and spiritual, in their stead. This is a simple, adequate, and only satisfactory origin of the title. And in accordance with this John is introduced to us as ὁ βαπτιστής, before his foot or hand has touched the water for the administration of symbol baptism.

Whether, then, we look to etymology, which refuses to expound this word in a primary sense, or to the time and circumstances of its origin, which furnish such explicit testimony, or to the usage of Ambrose and Origen, or to parallel appropriation, we are shut up to the conclusion, that John bears the title ὁ βαπτιστής not as "the Dipper," "the Immerser," or "the Submerger," but as *the Purifier;* yet, under no claim of his own, but given to him, probably, by undiscipled or discipled Jews whose purifying rites he rejected, by teaching a higher spiritual purification demanded by the Coming One.

This view is sustained by Matthies (Exp. Bapt., § 4): "Nam ita Joannes nominatur, quia novam ei dat significationem, et quia maxime solum baptismum præ ceteris tractat, id quod etiam Bengelius annotavit—For John is so called, because he gives *a new meaning* to the word, and because he treats, especially, of baptism, beyond others." And Professor Godwin (Notes on Mark 7 : 4), referring to the peculiarity of βαπτιστής and βάπτισμα, says, "The nouns for 'Baptizer' and 'Baptism' are not found in Classic Greek, and seem to have been formed from the verb *in its restricted* (Jewish and Scriptural) *usage.*"

MATTHEW 21 : 25.

"The Baptism of John, whence was it? from heaven or of men?"

Τὸ βάπτισμα Ἰωάννου.

ΒΑΠΤΙΣΜΑ.

ΒΑΠΤΙΣΜΑ is another derivative not found in Classic Greek, yet formed in entire accordance with the laws of the language. Jewish Greek writings, antecedent to John's ministry, are, also, destitute of cases illustrative of the usage and meaning of this derivative. We meet with it first in the preaching of John; thence it passes into the language of Christianity, but never enters, I believe, into merely secular or physical relations.

Substantives, derived from verbs, ending in μa, are used to express the *effect, result, product, state*, induced by the verb. In this view all grammarians concur. "Substantives with the ending μa denote *the effect* or *result* of the transitive action of the verb" (*Kühner*). "Nouns formed from verbs to denote *the effect* or *object* of the action, have μa added to the root of the verb" (*Crosby*). "The ending μa denotes *the effect* of a verb" (*Sophocles*). "Nouns ending in μa, derived from verbs, express *the effect* of the transitive notion of the verb" (*Jelf*). "The most numerous formations, however, are those in μa and $\sigma\iota\varsigma$, the former mostly confined to the New Testament, yet always conformed to Greek analogy, as $\beta\acute{a}\pi\tau\iota\sigma\mu a$, &c., mostly in the sense of *product* or *state*" (*Winer*).

It is, then, clear, that we are to look for the meaning of this word in the direction of an accomplished *result* or *state*. Our field of observation is, also, limited to the Scriptures, and writings which grow out of them, as such writings bound its use. Such an inquiry is suggestive of the thought—Some verbs do not issue in producing by their action an effect, result, product, or state, which finds a verbal embodiment. Whether this is a consequence of the nature of the action of the verb, or because of failure in demand for any such embodiment of thought, the fact claims attention. On the other hand, there are verbs which do, pre-eminently, issue in effecting a resultant state or condition. The course of this inquiry has shown, that these peculiarities are illustrated in the verbs $\beta\acute{a}\pi\tau\omega$ and $\beta a\pi\tau\acute{\iota}\zeta\omega$. The former verb, as $\beta\acute{a}\pi\tau\omega$ *to dip*, has no derivative in μa expressive of *result* or *state* produced by the action of the verb. Indeed, it is impossible, from the nature of the case, that a dipping, a momentary passing in and out of a fluid, could issue in a *state* within that fluid. Such a derivative could only express, 1. A con-

sequent superficial wetness, or, 2. A superficial result of any
kind. The English language presents the same facts. We
have no formation (*diption*) to express "result or state." The
verb is one of modal action, feeble in power, and momentary
in continuance, and its derivatives express this action with
consequent peculiarities of feeble and limited influence. The
case is very different with βάπτω *to dye*. This stem of the
verb has undergone a radical change in throwing off limitation in act and time, and in making demand for a result or
condition characterized by *color*. In such a verb we would
look for a derivative expressing " the effect, product, state "
produced by the action of the verb. We are not disappointed; βαμμα declares the result of the action of the verb
in effecting a dyed, colored, stained condition.

The differences between βάπτω *to dip*, and βάπτω *to dye*, are
not more or greater, are not so many or so great, as between
βάπτω *to dip*, and βαπτίζω *to merse*. The community between
βάπτω TO DYE, and βαπτίζω TO MERSE, is extended and profound. No change of nature would be requisite to fit the
one to perform the office of the other. It is the high sovereignty of Use, only, which has limited the action of the one
verb to the production of a colored condition, with its outgrowth, and has committed to the other the broader field
of controlling condition with and by envelopment together
with its outgrowth, not specifically but generically.

Since whatever form of act may be employed to meet the
behests of βαπτίζω it does not demand form of action, but
condition (1. Condition of envelopment, 2. Completeness of
influential condition without envelopment), it follows, that
βάπτισμα must be expressive of the one or the other of these
conditions. There is no necessity for its being limited to
the expression of physical condition or, indeed, of its referring to such condition at all. We have seen, that βαμμα has
no relation to the primary use of βάπτω, *dipping;* and it may
be, that βάπτισμα has just as little relation to the primary use
of βαπτίζω.

This clear possibility becomes a strong probability in view
of the facts : 1. That there is no clear evidence of a physical

βάπτισμα being referred to at any time in the New Testament. 2. There is clear evidence of the use of the word when a physical βάπτισμα is not referred to. 3. It is applied to living persons, who must perish in a physical βάπτισμα unmodified, and the theory repudiates all modification. 4. The exigencies of language demand the disjunction and extension of the conceptions which are involved in a physical envelopment. This is manifest from the English use of *merge* and *immerse*. These words, having the same original, occupy entirely different spheres in our language. No good writer uses *merge* in physical relations. The import of these words in English use is so utterly diverse that it is impossible to interchange them. Try the following: "It provides for *merging* our Presbyteries into the Synods." Was provision made for *immersing* the Presbyteries? "The States are united, not *merged*." Would the same idea be expressed by saying, "The States are united, not *immersed?*" "The carriage road *merges* into the bridle path." Is this convertible into—"The carriage road *immerses* into the bridle path?" "An ordinance to *merge* the department of the market houses into that of the city property," would sound a little odd if converted into "an ordinance to *immerse*" the one into another. On this use is grounded the law term, "a merger," which metamorphosed into "an immerser" would, certainly, make the court-room stare. The Greek intellect needed all these modifications of thought. They are wrapped up in βαπτίζω, and were, thence, substantially, evolved by the most normal development of its resources.

It is as utterly incongruous to substitute the primary use of βαπτίζω for the secondary, as to substitute *immerse* for *merge*, or *dip* for *dye*. 5. It is admitted, that in the βάπτισμα resultant from βαπτίζω, there is no self-termination. And it is, also, admitted, that if John's disciples were put into a water βάπτισμα without deliverance (for which the Scriptures make no shadow of provision), they must perish. To fill up this *lacuna* of inspiration the theory offers its services. There are, certainly, formidable difficulties in the way of giving βάπτισμα a physical interpretation.

If, on the other hand, it be considered as related to the secondary use of βαπτίζω, from which physical envelopment has been thrown off, and therefore expressive of completeness of condition to be determined, definitely, by its adjuncts, then we can dispense with the labors of the theory in supplementing the Scriptures; for no one ever put into this βάπτισμα will ever need or desire to be taken out! It will not destroy life, but give life. And, here, arises a possible explanation of John's use of βάπτισμα (the *state* unlimited in duration except through the counteraction of some higher power) rather than the βαπτισμός or βάπτισιν of the Jews, which expressed the act of the verb and not the state resultant from the act. Jewish baptizings were continually liable to be annulled. The acts of baptizing (ceremonial cleansing) needed evermore to be repeated. There was a fitness, therefore, in using the class of words which they did, making the act to stand out prominently; while the baptism of John, making demand for a condition of the soul (a *state* of complete repentance, never to be abrogated), could have used no better term than one making demand for a state which had no self-limitation, and which no power, as against God, could ever annul. This βάπτισμα would outlast that of the ship of Josephus, which has been these eighteen hundred years embosomed (baptized) in the depths of the Adriatic.

Having, now, met with four words—βάπτισιν, βαπτισμός, βαπτιστής, and βάπτισμα—used by Jewish writers, inspired and uninspired, in religious rites, none of which appear in Classic Greek, it seems remarkable, that we should be called upon to repudiate inspiration as a competent witness for the meaning not only of the words which it uses, but of the words which it originates, and accept the testimony of heathen writers as to the meaning of words which they never used in any relations, much less in the observance of religious rites.

It would seem, that if the inspired writers had sufficient knowledge of Greek to construct these different forms of words to meet new exigencies, they had sufficient knowledge to indicate, by the usage of those words, what were the meanings which they attached to them. We make this remark, not because of need of any other aid than that which Classic usage and language development fairly give, but because it is simple common sense. John had the most thorough knowledge of the essential power and large capabilities of βαπτίζω, and was fully competent to wield them for any special service demanded by his new ministry.

WHAT BAPTISM?

JOHN 1 : 25.

"What (baptism), then, dost thou baptize?"

Τί οὖν βαπτίζεις.

The translation of this passage, which gives to τί its usual pronominal force, affords a more facile and harmonious interpretation than that which gives to it an adverbial character.

The translation "*Why* dost thou baptize?" is grounded, mainly, in the idea, that the Jews believed that the Messiah and his adjutors would baptize and no others. The evidence that the Jews held such an opinion is rather inferential than of direct statement. Olshausen says, "The Pharisees evidently considered baptism as nothing unbecoming to the Messiah or Elias. But it cannot be demonstrated from this passage, that the Jews believed that the Messiah or his forerunner would baptize. At any rate it could not be regarded as a prerogative belonging *only* to the Messiah to baptize the Jews, because in that case John would not have adopted it.'" Origen thinks, that they should not have expected Elias to baptize, because he did not baptize the sacrifice and altar, but committed that work to others. But just as certainly as the Jews believed that the Messiah and Elias would baptize, just as certainly did they believe that their baptism was to have a peculiar character. As Olshausen further remarks: "The words only signify that the baptism of Israelites, by these individuals, was not inappropriate, since they would not merely—like ordinary prophets—strengthen the existing theocratic life, but would found a new, higher constitution."

When John had denied that he was the Messiah, and, also (according to their understanding), that he was Elias, or that Prophet, he did make claim, in answer to their farther inquiry, "Who art thou?" that he was a Messenger divinely appointed to prepare the way of the Lord. The fact that in the fulfilment of his office he preached a baptism which was incorporated in a ritual ordinance was patent to all. "*Why* he baptized" is sufficiently explained by his claim to be a divinely appointed messenger. The baptizing is necessarily involved in his divinely appointed ministry. No answer could go beyond this. To make the inquiry was, therefore, out of place. But it being settled, that his mission was divine, and that baptizing was included in that mission, there remained the question of prime importance, "*What* baptism dost thou baptize?" This would specifically determine the character of his ministry. Nothing is more indefinite than *a* baptism; while nothing is more definite than a defined baptism. The theory, indeed, does say, "All baptisms are water *dippings*," and John's dipping must, of necessity, be the same as any other dipping. But this is a doctrine of these last days. The universal testimony of the ages is,— "Multa genera baptismatum"—and the Jews, in particular, were familiar with "βαπτισμοῖς διαφόροις." Nothing, therefore, could be more to the purpose than the question—"*What* baptism dost thou baptize?" What is its nature?

Or, inasmuch as it is in proof, that the Jews in religious rites employed βαπτίζω in the appropriated sense *to purify*, the phraseology might be modified while the substance remains the same, thus: "What (defilement) dost thou purify?" Is it an actual removal of ceremonial defilement, or of spiritual defilement? or, is it only a symbol purification? What is its character? To such inquiry John's answer is perfectly apposite—"I baptize with *water*. My baptism has no other power than that which belongs to simple water, and is therefore merely symbol in its character." In this language there is no semblance of an answer to the question, "*Why* dost thou baptize?"

Versions.

Modern versions, generally, translate the passage adverbially, but the translation by Jerome retains the pronoun— "*Quid* ergo baptizas?" And in the 21 v. he translates "*Quid* ergo?" And in the 22 v. "*Quid* dicis?" And in the 39 v. "*Quid* quæritis?"

There should, clearly, be the same translation in these four passages, of the same chapter, unless some adequate and well-established reason can be given for making an exception. The translators, probably, felt a difficulty in connecting "What" with "baptize," and so framed another relation for this verb. There is, however, no just ground for embarrassment, as is conclusively shown by the use of the phrase βαπτίζειν βάπτισμα. Baptisms are of endless variety; and this very passage brings the fact into bold relief. Origen (IV, 252) takes this view of the passage. In answer to an objection made by Heracleon, that John's reply was not apposite to the question addressed to him, he uses this language: "But we say that the answer meets the very letter. For to the inquiry: Τί οὖν βαπτίζεις; τί ἄλλο ἐχρῆν εἰπεῖν, ἤ τε τὸ ἴδιον παραστῆναι βάπτισμα σωματικώτερον τυγχάνον. Ἐγω, γὰρ, φησὶν, βαπτίζω ἐν ὕδατι. What else was necessary to say, beyond the showing that his own baptism was corporal? For, he says, 'I baptize with water.'" And, to enforce this interpretation, he quotes the parallel passages in Matthew, Mark, and Luke, where the nature of his baptism, "with water," is contrasted with the nature of Christ's baptism, "with the Holy Ghost." It may be added, that in quoting Mark, as well as Luke, he gives ὕδατι without the preposition, as does the Codex Sinaiticus, and the Vulgate translation. Origen, then, understands the question as did Jerome—" *What kind* of baptism dost thou baptize?" And, he says, The answer which expounds his baptism as that of simple water affecting merely the body (a mere symbol baptism), meets the question exhaustively. Chrysostom (II, 367), after quoting the passage—"I, indeed, baptize you with water, but he shall baptize you with the Holy Ghost and fire"—adds, " Δηλονότι ὁυτος ὁυχ ἐβαπτίζε Πνεύματι—Plainly he did not baptize *by the Spirit*" (without the preposition). He then asks the question : " Τὶ δὲ ἐστιν, 'Εν Πνεύματι ἁγίῳ χαὶ πυρί—But *what* is baptism by the Holy Ghost and fire?" And he answers his question by referring to " the cloven tongues, like fire, which appeared to the Apostles and sat upon each of them." It is very manifest, that Chrysostom felt no embarrassment in using τί as a pronoun in connection with baptism. This is shown, still farther, when he asks, immediately after, " Ποῖον οὖν ἐβαπτίσατο ; Οὔτε τὸ 'Ιουδαϊχον, οὔτε τὸ ἡμέτερον, ἀλλὰ τὸ 'Ιωάννου—What baptism was he baptized with? Not with Judaic baptism, not with our baptism, but with John's baptism." Here we have an exhibition, in part, of that variety in baptism which was in the mind of the Jews when they asked John, " *What* baptism, then, dost thou baptize?"

Ambrose (II, 1581), quoting John's language—"Ego vos aqua baptizo"—says, "Aqua enim corpus abluitur, spiritu animæ delicta mundantur . . . aliud fuit baptisma pænitentiæ, aliud gratiæ est—For the body is purified by water, the sins of the soul are cleansed by Spirit . . . baptism of repentance was one kind, baptism of grace was another kind.

Such language sustains, unmistakably, the translation— " *What* baptism dost thou baptize?" Matthies (Baptismatis Expositio, § 4) takes the same view of the passage. After quoting Bengel's judgment, that this question did not relate to the meaning of baptism, but to the distinguishing character of that of John—"non nisi ad sui baptismi essentiam" —he says, " Cui sententiæ nos quidem non repugnamus . . . illis non externum baptizandi ritum curæ fuisse, sed internam potius hujus baptismi vim—We do not oppose this opinion, but think that it may be sustained yet more strongly, if we examine more closely both the question of the Pharisees and the answer of John. But it is evident from the question of the Pharisees, that they did not refer to the outward rite of baptizing, but rather to the inner power of this baptism, since they do not ask of John: 'What

is it to baptize,' or ' What is baptism,' but they, rather, ask,
' What, then, dost thou baptize?' (εἰς τι κ. τ. λ.—quo tandem
nititur baptismus tuus?—*into what* dost thou baptize—to
what end does thy baptism tend?") . . . "If baptism was
well understood, then the answer, 'I baptize with water,'
has a proper thought, for the words ἐν ὕδατι have great force,
and contain the answer, which is: *'aqua (purgationis*, i. e.,
pœnitentiæ symbolum) mei baptismi est essentia'—water (of purification, i. e., the symbol of repentance) is the essence of my
baptism." These statements are eminently satisfactory.

But the true view of this passage is very clearly settled by
Acts 19 : 3 : "Εἰς τί οὖν ἐβαπτίσθητε; ὃι δὲ εἶπον, Εἰς τὸ Ἰωάννου
βάπτισμα—*Into what* (baptism), then, were ye baptized? And
they said, *Into* JOHN'S BAPTISM." This question of Paul reveals
the same truth as the question of the Pharisees, to wit, *Variety
in the* NATURE *of baptisms.* And when a baptism is announced
we feel, that we know nothing of its essence until we receive
an answer to the query—τί εστι; And when persons tell us,
that they have been baptized, we are left in the dark as to
all valuable knowledge, without an answer to this question—
Εἰς τί ἐβαπτίσθητε; As Paul knew well what was the *nature*
of John's baptism, the answer, "We were baptized into
John's baptism," gave him all the information he desired.
And in like manner the answer of John himself, that his
baptism was effected by simple water, having no other than
a symbol power, gave to the Pharisees all the information
they sought by the inquiry τί οὖν βαπτίζεις; But the question
of the Pharisees, Τί βαπτίζεις; and the question of Paul, Εἰς τί
βαπτίζεις; are by no means identical in every respect. Had
Ishmael been asked Τί βαπτίζεις; he would have answered,
Ἐγω βαπτίζω οἰνῳ—I baptize with wine. But had he been
asked, Εἰς τί βαπτίζεις; his reply would have been, Εἰς ὀναισθησίαν
καὶ ὕπνον. In the former case, the general character of the
baptism is revealed by the statement of the *instrumental
means;* in the latter case, the most specific information possible is given, by stating *the element* (actual or verbal) *into
which* the baptism takes place. We should here note the
clear and all-essential distinction between a baptism *by* wine

(ἐν οἴνῳ Hebraistically, οἴνῳ Classically) and baptism *into* wine
(εἰς οἶνον). The former baptism is *by* wine-drinking issuing
in a baptism *into a condition of drunkenness or stupor;* the
latter baptism is *by* some unstated act *into wine* as a physical
envelopment, issuing in death, as in the case of the Duke
of Clarence and his butt of Malmsey wine; and as in the
case of Cupid, except his godship had saved his life (C. B.,
p. 245). The confounding of such distinction (as does the
theory) is hermeneutically monstrous. In perfect parallelism
(as to phraseology and twofold character) with this wine baptism, is water baptism, ἐν ὕδατι (according to the Hebrews,
Matthew and John; ὕδατι, according to the more Classical
Mark and Luke), *by* water, as a symbol instrument, setting
forth a baptism *into—what,* is not *here* stated, but which we
shall, hereafter, find most expressly mentioned, and baptism
into WATER, εἰς ὕδωρ, which phraseology (issuing in death by
the simple force of its terms) is no more known to the
Scriptures than is torrid heat amid polar snows.

When the answer of John is considered we must feel, that
there is nothing there which meets the question " *Why* dost
thou baptize?" but that it does, distinctly, meet the inquiry, *What* is the character of that baptism which thou dost
baptize? John contents himself with saying here, that his
baptism makes no claim to any power to effect any essential
change in the condition of those who receive it (whether of
a ceremonial or of a spiritual character), but is possessed,
merely, of that symbol character obviously belonging to pure
water used in religious service. Nothing could be more
natural or necessary at the outset of a ministry preaching
the development of a new order of things, and illustrating
that preaching by a religious rite, than the inquiry—"What
is the precise nature and value of this rite?"

If the interpretation, now given, of this passage be correct,
it has an obviously important bearing upon our inquiry. But
all the materials furnished by the Scriptures for solving the
question—"What is John's baptism?"—are not found in
these brief words as recorded by the Apostle. We will,
therefore, take a step onward from this firm footing which

has been already secured. And this will naturally bring us to consider that baptism of Christ with which, as to essential power, this of John is contrasted, but with which it is in the most intimate alliance as its forecasted symbol shadow.

BAPTISM OF THE MIGHTIER ONE.

WHAT WAS IT?

MATTHEW 3 : 11.

" He that cometh after me is mightier than I, whose shoes I am not worthy to bear : he shall baptize you with the Holy Ghost and with fire."

MARK 1 : 7, 8.

"There cometh one mightier than I after me, the latchet of whose shoes I am not worthy to stoop down and unloose. He shall baptize you with the Holy Ghost."

LUKE 3 : 16.

"One mightier than I cometh, the latchet of whose shoes I am not worthy to unloose. He shall baptize you with the Holy Ghost and with fire."

JOHN 1 : 33.

"Upon whom thou shalt see the Spirit descending, and remaining on him, the same is he which baptizeth with the Holy Ghost."

"Ἀυτος ὑμᾶς βαπτίσει ἐν Πνεύματι Ἁγίῳ καὶ πυρί."—*Matt.* 3 : 11; *Luke* 3 : 16.

"Ἀυτος δὲ βαπτίσει ὑμᾶς ἐν Πνεύματι Ἁγίῳ."—*Mark* 1 : 8.

"Οὗτος ἐστιν ὁ βαπτίζων ἐν Πνεύματι Ἁγίῳ."—*John* 1 : 33.

Importance of this Baptism.

The phraseology of these passages (all agreeing in one) contains elements which being thoroughly mastered will give us partial possession, at least of " the *arx causæ* of this dispute." This being true, we are called upon, in an especial manner, "to seek all aid in its correct interpretation, assuming nothing without proof, and carefully endeavoring to detect the cause of the error, on whichever side it be." This course will require an examination of the verbal elements both separately and in their mutual relations.

We will first examine the baptism and its phraseology as interpreted by friends of the theory.

Baptist Translation and Interpretation.

"He will immerse you in holy spirit and fire"—is the translation by Dr. Conant in the quarto edition of the New Version with critical notes. The translator of John (same edition) says, in a note on 1 : 33, "I would greatly prefer to render these words literally—'immerseth in Holy Spirit'— without the article. I do not consider the πνευμα ἁγιον here spoken of to be *the personal spirit*, contemplated *as such*, but simply *divine essence*, abstracted in the mind of the writer, from all ideas of personal attributes or relations." Dr. Conant, in a note on Matt. 3 : 11, says, "'immerse in *holy spirit*' means, that *divine influence* so often expressed by the Greek words. These translators differ from each other as widely as 'divine essence' differs from 'divine influence.'"

What is "divine essence abstracted from all personal relations and attributes," and how it furnishes a medium for a dipping into it, or what is abstract "holy spirit" and its meetness for a dipping, I confess my entire ignorance. The New Version translators of Mark and Luke are content to "immerse in *the* Holy Spirit." Thus, these four translators give us three essentially different elements for the dipping: 1. Divine influence; 2. Divine essence; 3. The personal Holy Spirit.

Another Baptist writer, Stovel, gives a fourth element in which this dipping is to take place, namely, "*a* holy spirit." To this, however, Dr. Conant will not listen; he says, "It is wholly at variance with the usage and teachings of the New Testament." If these translators are so much embarrassed to find out *the* element *in which* they would make the

Mightier One *to dip*, they might extend some grace to those who can find none at all in which he performs such modal act. None of these translators have anything to say about "the dipping *in fire*," whether it is "influence," or "essence," or actual fire. It is pleasant however to know, that in the final revision all these experimental translations are abandoned, and the third person of the Trinity is allowed to remain in his relations to baptism as heretofore in the old-fashioned English Bible. It is possible that after like experiments with dip, and plunge, and sink, there will be a willingness to accept those words which the Holy Ghost teacheth.

At present, I raise no question as to the translation *dip;* that will come up more fitly hereafter. It is not untimely, however, to call attention to the most remarkable and unheard of character of a "*dipping* in divine essence," a *dipping* in holy spirit, a *dipping* in a holy spirit, or a *dipping* in fire of any kind. There is not much risk in saying, that such rhetoric was never heard of beyond the boundaries of the theory. But it is not merely the peculiar rhetoric which challenges our regard. There is an evident contradiction between the theory and its application, and John and his argumentation. John announces the approach of a Mightier One, and appeals for the evidence of this transcendent mightiness to the wonderful character of his *dipping* (!); so says the theory. Now, it is undoubtedly true that the exclusive ability to dip in one thing, rather than another thing, may show a greater comparative richness of resources, but it fails to make proof of an absolute personal power. A dipping into a divine influence may be of greater worth than a dipping into pure water; but if the dipper can do no more than DIP in divine influence, then his control over divine influence is of the feeblest possible character. Nothing is more certain, than that a dipping into anything is indicative of the object dipped being brought in a most trivial degree under the influence of whatever it may have been dipped into. John, then, is made by the theory, to argue for the unapproachable power and glory of the Coming One, by an appeal to the fact that he will accomplish a certain thing in the feeblest possible manner, to wit, by a dipping! If the friends of the theory are disgusted by such bitter fruits of its logic, and declare themselves wearied beyond farther endurance in the attempt to carry such a burden as " dip and nothing but dip through all Greek literature," and make "immerse " their Hercules on whom they call for help, no objection will be made, provided, 1. That a frank confession be made of error as to the meaning of the word for the past hundred years, and that, on that error, Christians have been required to do an act for the doing of which there is not one syllable in the word of God. 2. That this word shall be accepted, for better or worse, in those points in which it is distinguished from dip: (1.) As without limitation in the form of the act meeting its demand. (2.) As without limitation of time in its accomplished result. (3.) As without limitation in the influence exerted. 3. That there shall be no shifting of meaning or word, but a fair maintenance of the position assumed—" the same meaning in literal and metaphorical use" (Conant). Nothing is more incontrovertible than a boundless difference between *immersion* in essence, in spirit, in a spirit, in the Spirit, in fire, and a *dipping* into these same things. Nothing is more certain, than that the former **may** meet John's reasoning when the latter cannot. And nothing is more certain, than that this difference arises out of the unlimited time during which the immersed object is subjected to the influence of the enveloping element. Those whom " the Coming One" baptizes remain baptized forever and forever! I do not say, that the simple word makes such a result imperative; but I do say, that its essential nature accords with unlimited duration, that it will not of itself terminate that duration, and, as none can undo what God has done, the baptism of the MIGHTIER ONE shall, in fact, never end.

Determining Points of the Interpretation.

The theory claims, that the interpretation of this passage is controlled, 1. By the essential meaning of the preposition ἐν, and 2. By the construction, claimed to exist, in βαπτίζω ἐν

On the first of these points it is said: "The radical meaning of ἐν is *in, resting* within a place. 2. The meaning, *with, by*, is rare. 3. To attribute such meaning to the preposition here is unwarranted and an abuse of an uncommon meaning." On the second point it is affirmed: "This (*in*) is the only sense in which ἐν can be used in connection with βαπτίζω" (Conant).

The radical meaning attributed to ἐν is accepted without reserve. It is also, freely admitted, that the meaning *with, by*, while existing and universally acknowledged in Classical Greek, is, still, comparatively rare. But it is denied that this rare usage obtains in Hellenistic Greek. And if it be not rare there, but on the contrary found on almost every page, then, to attribute such meaning to it, in this class of writings, is not "doing violence to a common use." If there be a marked difference in the frequency with which this preposition is used instrumentally in these two classes of writings, then, it is important that the fact should be established, so as to eliminate from the mind all suspicion of a resort to an extreme meaning in order to meet a controversial exigency.

The position taken as to the force of βαπτίζω ἐν will be met by showing that the relation of these words is misapprehended.

Classical Use of 'Eν.

It is quite unnecessary to cite passages illustrative of the primary meaning of ἐν. But it may be well to call to mind the fact that the withinness belonging to this preposition has no limitation of time, and that, in certain circumstances, influence over the object by the investing material, as well as position, must be a necessary result. This is important to notice as aiding to interpret, in certain cases, the secondary use of this preposition. In the passage—"I am a good helper of the labors ἐν εἰρήνῃ," Xen. Memorab. II, 1, 32, the preposition may be regarded as indicating the labors as done *within the period of time* through which peace lasts, or done *in that condition* of things characterized by peace, and therefore within and *under the influence* of peace.

In Soph. Phil., 102, " Why should you take me away
ἐν δόλῳ," if the preposition here should be supposed to indicate a state or condition within which the party is, still we
cannot rest in the conception of withinness, we must proceed
a step farther, to the influence exerted by such a condition.
The leading away is *in, under, through the influence of* deception.
This development shows us how natural is the transition
from *inness* to instrumentality.   And when influence of a
very absolute and penetrative character is designed to be expressed, there is a fitness in the suggestive use of this preposition.   And, as influence and agency are inseparable, a
usage may find development in which agency or instrumentality is brought into the foreground, if, indeed, it does not
occupy the ground alone.

A single example (see Harrison, On Greek Prepositions,
p. 251) will illustrate the entire class of cases in which ἐν
is used in an instrumental sense.   It is taken from Soph.
Electr., 1128, " I neither washed him (for the burial) with
my loving hands—ἐν φίλῃσι χερσὶν." Here, again, ἐν with its
case does not express, properly speaking, the instrument
with which the bathing of the dead body is performed, but
the manner and conditions of the service.   But while it is
contended that, in such examples, the proper force of ἐν is
almost always discernible, if not in every case, it is not inconsistent with this view to admit that, in cases where the
obvious application and use of the object with which ἐν is
joined suggests the idea of the instrument, as, for instance,
in the example last cited, ἐν and the ablative (locativus) may
have come to be wellnigh equivalent to the expression of
the instrument.   Although ἐν φίλῃσι χερσὶν λουτροῖς ἐκόσμησα
means no more, strictly speaking, than that the washing was
done with the water, or, it may be, with the body "in the
hands," that is, that, in a general way, the washing was conducted in the hands; yet, as it is obvious that the employment of the hands in such case is instrumental, it is possible
that to the Greek mind ἐν χερσίν may have come to convey
directly the notion of the instrument.

As there is an obvious difficulty in connecting the radical

meaning of ἐν with the act of washing (how could the act of washing a dead body be "within the hands?"), would it not be better to make the preposition expository of the condition of ἐγώ? "I," working by the hands, is with great truth "*in* the hands;" and, as the work is under the promptings of love, is "in *loving* hands." It is not the washing, nor the dead body, that is "in the loving hands," but the washer. "Love" is the influence which prompts, and "hands" the instruments employed; and both belong to "I." So, Thucyd. VII, 11, "Ye know ἐν ἄλλαις πολλαῖς ἐπιστολαῖς, in = *with, by,* many other letters."

It is unnecessary to multiply cases of this usage. But it was important to have distinctly before us the fact that a secondary use of ἐν in the Classics is unquestioned, and, also, to glance at the *rationale* of that use.

Hellenistic Use of 'Ἐν.

There are few, if any, who question the more frequent use of ἐν in an instrumental sense by Hellenistic writers in comparison with native Greeks. But it is desirable that the evidence on this point should be presented with sufficient fulness to silence the charge of "a controversial resort to an uncommon meaning to ward off otherwise unanswerable truth."

The poverty of the Hebrew language in respect to particles, prepositions, conjunctions, and adverbs, also, as to the inflections of nouns, pronouns, and verbs, is in marked contrast with the richness of the Greek. Hence arises a necessity for a more varied application of the same word in the former language than in the latter. This fact finds development, especially, in translations from the Hebrew, by Jews, into Greek, as in the case of the Septuagint. But it has, also, marked exemplification in the original compositions of Jews, in Greek, as in the case of books of the Apocrypha and the New Testament.

Dr. Campbell, of Aberdeen (Four Gospels, II, 20), after passing an exceedingly harsh judgment on the translators of our English Bible, because of the translation of ἐν by *with*

instead of *in*, adds, "But I should not lay much stress on the
preposition ἐν, which, answering to the Hebrew בְּ, may denote *with* as well as *in*, did not the whole phraseology concur
in evincing the same thing." The validity of the reasons
for his judgment will be considered hereafter; at present we
have to do simply with the usage of this preposition. Having
found fault with our translators for using *with* instead of *in*,
and lauded Popish translators for "their greater veneration
for the Vulgate" as shown by using *in* instead of *with*, he
condemns that same Vulgate (I, 388) for κακοζηλια, vicious
affectation, "in using the preposition *in* where (Rom. 1 : 4)
the idiom of the Latin and the sense of the expression
required *cum*."

Whatever may be the value of Dr. Campbell's judgment
as to the translation in either of these passages, it is perfectly
clear that he accepts *with* as a translation of ἐν as freely as he
does that of *in*. Father Simon, also, who is quoted (I, 378)
as objecting to the translation by Erasmus of ἐν δυναμει (Rom.
1 : 4), *cum* potentia, and defending that of the Vulgate *in*
virtute, says, "Although the Greek particle ἐν signifies in
the style of the writers of the New Testament, which is conformable to that of the LXX, *in* and *cum*, it had been better
to translate, as it is in the Vulgate, *in virtute* or *in potentia*,
and to write on the margin that *in* also signifies *cum ;* because
there is but one preposition which answers to them both in
the Hebrew or Chaldaic language, with which the Greek of
the New Testament often agrees, especially in this sort of
prepositions." Thus while Protestant and Romanist criticize
the form of translation in particular cases, they unite in the
doctrine that this preposition has a usage which is rooted in
the Jewish intellect and language rather than that of the
Greek.

The use of this preposition comes, also, under the remark
of Winer (p. 36): "A predilection for prepositions where
the Greeks employ cases alone is especially noticeable."
The latter construction implies more abstraction; the former
gives greater explicitness.

It is, also, important to remember that both ἐν and εἰς have an extended usage in the Scriptures growing out of its doctrines. Revealed religion is a spiritual religion. It makes its demands on the innermost being of man. It requires the most intimate soul relations with the Deity, with the redeeming Saviour, and with the regenerating and sanctifying Spirit. To express these relations, and others growing out of them, these prepositions are abundantly used in applications which find no, or but imperfect, parallel in Classic Greek.

Professor Ellicott (Preface to Galatians) justly remarks: "'*Ev* is a difficult preposition in the New Testament. But in the holy Scriptures every peculiar expression, even at the risk of losing an idiomatic turn, *must* be retained. Many words, especially the prepositions, have a positive dogmatical and theological significance, and to qualify them by a popular turn or dilute them by a paraphrase, is dangerous in the extreme." As this usage of these prepositions applies to persons and to things not physical, it follows, that the primary meanings must, of necessity, receive modification. Most commonly there is a suggestion of profound influence which is so naturally associated with inness of position.

That there is a lawless or loose use of these prepositions by the sacred writers is an idea which should receive no tolerance. Many writers and lexicographers seem to imagine that " *Eἰς*, as it happens, may be *into, in, concerning, with, against, before, by, in order to, among, at, towards,* or it may stand without *any* definite meaning—as a mere expletive—and had better be wanted. So also with *ἐν*" (Fairbairn, p. 51).

Septuagint.

A few examples from the Septuagint, illustrative of the use of *ἐν*, will answer our purpose.

" Whom thou hast led forth out of the land of Egypt, *ἐν ἰσχύϊ μεγάλῃ, καὶ ἐν τῷ βραχίονί σου τῷ ὑψηλῷ*" (Exodus 32 : 11). The Vulgate translates—" in fortitudine magna et in manu robusta." But no one would think of interpreting *ἐν* or *in* as having its mere primary meaning. It has, undoubtedly, an instrumental signification, as is attributed to it in our translation from the Hebrew—"*with* great power and *with* a mighty hand." And without a preposition—"Defended *by* thy hand" (Wisd. of Sol. 19 : 8). It is always of interest, and sometimes of vital importance, to trace any particular usage back to the primary meaning, and sometimes, still more important to determine the true logical relation of the preposition. In endeavoring to do this, we must remember the statement of Winer (p. 386)—"The figurative use of ἐν is extremely diversified;" and, also, that of Harrison (p. 246) —"The Latin *in* and the Greek ἐν are not confined to marking the relative position of 'within' with regard to space and time merely, but have this office with reference to any condition or set of circumstances that may invest a person or action." And from withinness, under such circumstances, comes necessarily the suggestion of the full influence belonging to the specified condition. Professor Harrison adds: "If we say in Greek ἐν ὀργῇ εἶναι, 'to be in a state of anger,' the proper force of the preposition is no more difficult to see than in the proposition ἐν τῇ νήσῳ ἐτελεύτησεν, 'he died in the island.'" It is indeed true that the primary idea of the preposition stands out distinctly in both these cases, and yet the force of the preposition, by reason of its relations, differs immensely in the one case and the other. In the latter case, its force is exhausted by pointing out simple locality; in the former position, it is used merely for the sake of developing the influence which invests that position. To declare a man to be "in a state of anger" is not to give him any local position within anger. The phraseology is borrowed from physics, where investiture brings the fullest influence over the invested object. To say, "A man is in the fire," is to make declaration that he is under the influence of fire, which is a necessary consequence of his position. And we employ this same form of expression when we know, and when every one else knows, that withinness is impossible, but where we wish to express the full influence of the term associated with the preposition. While, therefore, we recognize a distant relationship between ἐν ὀργῇ and ἐν νήσῳ, there is one much closer with ἐν πυρί, and without this intermediate link in which influence from position is developed, it would be impossible to show the fitness of associating ἐν with ὀργῇ. While *withinness* in ἐν νήσῳ is everything and influence is nothing; on the other hand *influence* in ἐν ὀργῇ is everything and withinness is nothing. But in ἐν πυρί both withinness and influence meet together and measure each other.

This is illustrated by a case subsequently (p. 254) mentioned by Professor Harrison—"'Εν ὑμῖν ὡς θεῷ κείμεθα, ' we depend on you as on a god,' would literally mean, ' we lie, or are placed in you as in a god,' that is, ' in your power.'" We see, at a glance, that there is no opportunity to apply the primary meaning of the preposition in its present relations; but we can follow back its tracks until we find it in relations where withinness brings helpless dependence, whether it be "in prison," "in chains," or "in a lion's jaws," and, then, we can expound ἐν ὑμῖν κείμεθα as expressing a state of complete dependence, and feel that the phraseology, without any possible inness, is admirably adapted to this end.

In like manner we interpret ἐν ἰσχύϊ, ἐν βραχίονι; we do not look for any withinness in these relations, but we find it elsewhere, in other relations causative of influence; when, therefore, we meet with phraseology which represents the Lord as being "*in* great power" and "*in* an uplifted arm," we know that ἐν has lost its primary meaning, in fact, and expends its strength in suggesting circumstances in which it once appeared in true character and gave opportunity for the development of the full influence of its surroundings. In the present case, shorn of its primary power, it suggests the almightiness of Him who is "*in* the great power and the uplifted arm."

This interpretation only shows the absolute fitness of the translation which makes the preposition instrumental. Jehovah did "in" = *with, by,* great power lead his covenant people.

"Then shall he speak unto them ἐν ὀργῇ αὐτοῦ, καὶ ἐν τῷ θυμῷ αὐτοῦ." (Psalm 2 : 5.) I refer to this passage, especially, to

11

notice the relation of the preposition. It is not the action
of the verb that is done ἐν ὀργῇ, but it is the Lord who is described as being "in wrath," and his speech goes forth from
him in this state, and hence has all its fearful power. Compare Numbers 16 : 46, " Wrath is gone out from the Lord."
Deut. 29 : 28, "And the Lord rooted them out of their land,
ἐν θυμῷ, καὶ ὀργῇ, καὶ παροξυσμῷ μεγάλῳ." Isaiah 54 : 8, " ἐν θυμῳ
μικρῳ, I turned away my face from thee, καὶ ἐν ἐλέει αἰωνίῳ
ἐλεήσω σε." Habakkuk 3 : 2, " ἐν οργῇ ἐλέους μνησθήσῃ." In all of
these passages the preposition refers to the state or condition
of Jehovah, and not to the sphere within which the action of
the verb is executed, as outside of the Deity.

Instrumental means are very clearly exhibited in Deut.
4 : 34, "Hath God assayed to go and take him a nation from
the midst of another nation, ἐν πειρασμῷ, καὶ ἐν σημείοις, καὶ ἐν
τέρασι, καὶ ἐν πολέμῳ, καὶ ἐν χειρὶ κραταιᾷ, καὶ ἐν βραχίονι ὑψηλῷ, καὶ ἐν
ὁράμασι μεγάλοις." The Vulgate translates—per tentationes,
&c. So, Jeremiah 34 : 8; 51 : 12, 13, πεσοῦνται ἐν ῥομφαίᾳ καὶ
ἐν λιμῷ. It is clear that in all such cases (and they are multitudinous) the preposition must be translated instrumentally.
The connection between this meaning, in such cases, and
withinness may or may not be traceable. In III Kings
19 : 11, 12, it is said, "The Lord was not ἐν τῷ πνεύματι, ἐν τῷ
συσσεισμῷ, ἐν τῷ πυρὶ = did not so reveal himself;—but ἐν τῃ
φωνῃ, in, by, the still small voice;" so, the Lord was ἐν
πειρασμῷ, ἐν σημείοις, ἐν τέρασι, &c. (Deut. 4 : 34); that is, he did
reveal himself in, by, temptations, signs, wonders, &c. As a
strong garrison within a fortification makes it an agency
capable of resistance, and as powder and ball in a cannon
makes it an instrument of destruction, so the Lord verbally
represented as "in signs, wonders, tempest, earthquake,
famine, sword," makes them the agencies through which he
works. And under such circumstances the proper translation of ἐν is with, by.

Apocrypha.

"Nebuchadnezzar bound him with a brazen chain—ἐν
χαλκείῳ δεσμῷ." (Esdras 1 : 40.) Here the modification of literal

withinness, and its transition to express instrumentality, is obvious. One who is bound IN a chain occupies a position of very imperfect withinness. His wrists or his ankles may be *in* fetters, and the consequence is that he is within their influence, under their control, bound BY them. By a slight extension of this conception all physical withinness is eliminated. Thus in v. 53, " They slew the young men *with* the sword—ἐν ῥομφαία." The interpretation of ἐν must proceed either on the idea that the slayer is "*in* the sword," thus communicating to it power to kill, or the slain are within the range of the sword, and so come under its power to kill. In either case withinness has disappeared and instrumentality has taken its place. So, also, in v. 55, " They burned the towers of Jerusalem *with* fire, ἐν πυρί." What is put within fire comes under its consuming influence, and therefore, what comes under its consuming influence, although not by being within it, is still expressed by ἐν πυρί. And, so, in v. 57 of the same chapter—"Unto the fulfilment of the word of the Lord *by* the mouth of Jeremiah, ἐν στόματι." And in this same book it is said, " They assisted him *with* gold and *with* silver, ἐν χρυσίῳ καὶ ἐν ἀργυρίῳ." If we pass beyond a direct and absolute instrumentality in our interpretation, we must, I think, place "they" within "the gold and silver" as the source whence was derived the ability to render assistance. They assisted by means of gold and silver. Their power to assist by gold and silver is represented as arising from, being *in*, gold and silver, having it thus within their control. The being within a thing is used to denote that the invested object is under the influence of the investiture, or that he is clothed with the power which belongs to it and can sway it to all its ends. A man who is "rolling in wealth" is invested with all the power which belongs to wealth. "Because they were *in* enmity to them" (ἐν ἔχθρᾳ) (5 : 50). To be *in* enmity is to be under the influence of enmity, to act in its spirit, and by its promptings.

"Which thou gavest *by* the hand of thy servants the prophets" (ἐν χειρί) (8 : 82). However facile it may be to trace this phraseology back to a literal "*in* hand," still, it appears before us in this passage in a simple instrumental character.

"Sennacherib slew many *in* his wrath" (ἐν θυμῷ) (Tobit 1 : 18). Sennacherib was *in* a wrathful condition, therefore under its influence, and so slew many.

"I ate my bread *in* grief" (ἐν λύπῃ) (2 : 5). It is not the "bread" which is *in* grief, nor is it the "eating," but it is "I;" I *in*, under the influence of, grief ate my bread.

"He brought forth the bags *in* the seals" (ἐν σφραγῖσι) (9 : 5). The bags, surely, were not within the seals. But they were in that condition which is effected by sealing. They were in a sealed condition, under the influence of the seals = "in the seals."

"Jerusalem shall be built with sapphires and emeralds, and her walls with precious stones (datives without prepositions), and the towers and the battlements *with* pure gold (ἐν χρυσίῳ). And the streets of Jerusalem shall be paved *with* (ἐν) beryl, and carbuncle, and stone of Ophir (13 : 16, 17).

"And Nebuchadnezzar marched *with* (ἐν) his power against King Arphaxad." (Judith 1 : 13.) The marching was not within his power, but he being "*in* his power" marched. He was *in*—invested with—all the power of a great army. "And he took Arphaxad and pierced him *with* (ἐν) his darts" (v. 15). An explanation of the use of ἐν, in such cases, must place it in relation with Nebuchadnezzar. These "darts" were a part of "the power" in which he went forth, and he was "*in* the darts," and all other agencies, giving them direction on their mission of death. The archer was *in* the arrow *by* which he pierced Philip's eye. "I will go forth *in* (ἐν) my wrath, and I will cover the whole face of the earth *with* (ἐν) the feet of my power." "I will do these things *with* (ἐν) my hand" (v. 12). "To cover the whole face of the earth *with* (ἐν) chariots, and horsemen, and chosen footmen" (v. 19). It was not the act of "going forth" which was within wrath, but Nebuchadnezzar being "*in* wrath" went forth under the influence of it to fulfil its promptings. So, Nebuchadnezzar was "*in* his hand" as that by which he carried out his will. "I, *in* my hand, will do these things."

In the same way it might be said, " I, *in* Holofernes" (my
representative, leader of my armies, executor of my will),
" will do these things." " The whole earth" is not *within*
" the chariots, horsemen, and feet of the infantry," but it is
covered *by* them as effectually as if it were within them, and
therefore sameness of result, although by a different process,
is expressed by *ἐν*. " Their mountains shall be drunken *with*
their blood" (*ἐν αἵματι*) (6 : 4). These mountains are not in
blood really or imaginatively, but if they were, simple inness
of position would not make them drunk. Drunkenness is
not an effect of position, but of influence; the preposition,
therefore, cannot have a local force. The mountains were
to be made drunk *by* blood, not *in* blood. " They shall be
consumed *by* famine" (*ἐν λιμῷ*) (7 : 14). " They gave them
drink *by* measure" (*ἐν μέτρῳ*) (v. 21). The drinking was not
" *in* a measure," nor was the giving " *in* a measure," but
the water was measured; it was given *by* measure, and they
drank *by* measure. " God hath sold us into their hands to
be thrown down before them *by* (*ἐν*) thirst and great destruction" (v. 25). " The Lord will visit Israel *by* (*ἐν*) my hand"
(8 : 33). The visiting is not to be done within Judith's hand,
but, " the Lord *in* her hand" = working through her hand,
giving power to her hand, will visit Israel in bringing deliverance " *by* her hand." " Do thou throw down their strength
by (*ἐν*) thy power" (9 : 8). The preposition here has its relation to " thou" and not to " throw down." The throwing
down is not to be within " power," but the Lord being *in*,
possessed of, controlling, almighty power, is besought to exercise it by throwing down the otherwise resistless strength
of the Assyrian. "Break down their majesty *by* (*ἐν*) the hand
of a woman" (9 : 10). The Lord was to be *in* (make use of
as an instrument) a woman's hand. And that hand, by
reason of its investiture with power from on high, was to do
this great work. " Most gladly, therefore, will I glory in
my infirmities that the power of Christ may rest upon me."
So, " Until the Lord *in* (*by*, *ἐν*) my hand do the things which
he hath purposed" (12 : 4). The Lord is the worker, the
instrument is Judith's hand. " She smote twice upon his

neck *in* (ἐν, *with*) her strength" (13 : 8).   All of Judith was *in* those blows, therefore, she smote *by* them.   So we say, "Throw all your strength (or throw yourself) *into* the blow." "The Lord smote him *in* (*by*, ἐν) the hand of a woman" (13 : 15).   The action of the verb, the smiting, was not within the woman's hand, but the Lord was.   It is of the first importance to apprehend clearly the relations of this preposition.   "And Judith said, 'Praise my God with (ἐν) timbrels, sing unto my Lord *with* (ἐν) cymbals'" (16 : 1). "Assur came *with* (ἐν) ten thousands of his power" (v. 4). "He said that he would destroy my young men *with* (ἐν) the sword" (v. 5).   "The Almighty Lord hath disappointed them *by* (ἐν) the hand of a woman" (v. 6).   "Judith weakened him by (ἐν) the beauty of her countenance" (v. 7). "She anointed her face *with* (ἐν) ointment" (v. 8).   "O, Lord, thou art great and glorious, wonderful *in* (*by*, ἐν) strength" (v. 13).

"And every man of Israel cried unto God *in* (*with*, ἐν) great earnestness, and humbled their souls *in* (*with*, ἐν) great earnestness" (4 : 9).   The relation of ἐν is not with the crying and the humbling as pointing out a space or sphere within which these acts were done.   Such interpretation would eviscerate the statement of all its power.   It would picture shadows going through a dumb show instead of men moved to strong crying and deepest prostration by profound emotion of soul.   The preposition is related to the men of Israel and points out the condition in which they are.   They are in a condition of "great earnestness," and, *by* the influence of this condition, they are constrained to cry out and humble their souls before God.   In such relations *by* can no more be separated from "in" than shadow can be separated from substance, or effect from cause.   If I am *in* fire, I am burned *by* fire.   If I am *in* water, I am drowned *by* water.   If I am *in* pain, I suffer *by* pain.   Thus, this preposition comes to represent agency both where inness can, and where it cannot be traced.

The same Usage.

The results of an examination of all the books of the Apocrypha are before me, but it is unnecessary to give them in detail. The same usage prevails through every book. That ἐν is associated with a great variety of conceptions and is not confined to that of a naked inness, is most obvious on any extended examination. The great variety of physical circumstances in which this particle is used, lays the foundation for the secondary use in which inness disappears or appears only as suggestive of condition affected by influence.

There is a real specific difference in the value of this word in such phrases as the following: *Standing* IN the field, *buried* IN the field; *sailing* IN the sea, *sunk* IN the sea; *walking* IN the flower-garden, *struggling* IN the brier-bush; IN the morass unable to get out with clean boots; IN the morass up to the eyes, unable to get out with life. But it is not merely a modification of a common generic idea which takes place. Its use in certain relations is suggestive of concomitants and influences which overshadow the local thought. Joseph in *a pit* is suggestive of abandonment, incapability of self-deliverance, hunger, and death; Joseph in *a palace* is suggestive of friends, power, abundance, and honor. A son in a father's house with its inmates, is suggestive of the sweetest influences of earth; a son in the banquet hall with the riotous, in the field with swine, is suggestive of guilt, shame, ruin. To be assailed by a pack of wolves in an open plain, is suggestive of their ferocity and of our destruction; but to be thus assailed in a strongly-built and well-equipped structure, is only suggestive of their impotence and of our safety. In such cases the inness is real, but subordinate; the mind does not rest in it, but proceeds by its aid to what lies beyond. Thus the way is prepared for the use of this particle where there is no inness, in fact, but where its presence is suggestive of influences appropriate to and springing out of its adjuncts. When we say, in honor, in shame; in wealth, in poverty; in joy, in sorrow; in strength, in weakness; in sin, in holiness; the particle ceases to express position and is used to give development to the characteristics distinctive of its adjuncts.

Sometimes even this office of suggestion is laid aside or doubtfully revealed, as in, "Many fell *by* (ἐν) the edge of the sword" (Wisd. of Sirach, 28 : 18). " The furnace proves the edge *by* color" (ἐν βαφῇ) (34 : 26). And this direct expression of instrumentality is farther shown by the use or the omission of the preposition in narrating the same transaction. Thus, " Shut the door and seal it *with thy seal*" (τῷ δακτυλίῳ σου) (Bel and Dragon, 1 : 11), is fulfilled in v. 14 in these terms, " They shut the door and sealed it *with the seal of the king* (ἐν τῷ δακτυλίῳ βασιλέως")*. It would be embarrassing to make proof, that the sealing which was effected under the approbation of ἐν, differed one whit from the sealing commanded in which ἐν makes no appearance; or reversely, to show, that if ἐν had appeared in the command, and had made no appearance in the execution of the command, that there would, thereby, be any evidence that the one differed from the other by jot or tittle. And it should be observed, that we do not unify these differing forms by taking inness out of the form in which ἐν appears and introducing it into the form with the nude dative, but the reverse; we preserve the instrumental dative and give to ἐν an instrumental power. The same must be done with the ὕδατι and ἐν ὕδατι of John's baptism.

NEW TESTAMENT.

The New Testament exhibits the same varied usage of ἐν with that which stands out in such bold relief in the Apocrypha and Septuagint.

The evidence adduced will be addressed mainly to two points: 1. To show that the instrumental use is not rare; 2. To show the suggestive use of this particle based on the primary idea, but without its existence in fact, or in conception.

The Instrumental Use of 'Ἐν is not rare.

To avoid all question as to the fitness of the passages

quoted to be regarded as proof passages, I will quote the translations as given in the Baptist Bible. One of the rules of that new version is, that "The exact meaning of the inspired text must be translated by corresponding words with the least possible obscurity or indefiniteness."

In following this guidance we shall be very sure to lose all those cases bearing on baptism in which this particle appears, as well as every other case in which a local meaning can be assigned to it, and, in general, we may be sure that we will get the fewest possible cases in which instrumentality appears. But we may find that when such passages are brought down to their minimum, they are still sufficiently numerous for our purpose.

MATTHEW.

5 : 13. *Wherewith* (ἐν, by what) shall it be salted.

5 : 34. Swear not at all, neither *by* (ἐν) heaven, for it is God's throne.

5 : 35.   "   nor *by* (ἐν) the earth, for it is his footstool.

5 : 36.   "   nor *by* (ἐν) thy head, because thou canst not make one hair white or black.

7 : 2. *With* (ἐν) what measure ye mete it shall be measured to you.

7 : 6. Lest they trample them *with* (ἐν) their feet.

9 : 34. He casts out devils *through* (ἐν) Beelzebub, the Prince of the devils.

12 : 24. Casts out devils *through* (ἐν) Beelzebub, Prince of the devils.

12 : 27. If I *through* (ἐν) Beelzebub cast out devils.

12 : 27. *Through* (ἐν) whom do your children cast them out?

12 : 28. But if I cast out devils *through* (ἐν) the Spirit of God.

14 : 13. He departed thence *by* (ἐν) ship.

17 : 21. This kind goeth not out but *by* (ἐν) prayer and fasting.

20 : 15. To do what I will *with* (ἐν) my own.

21 : 23. *By* (ἐν) what authority doest thou these things?

21 : 24. *By* (ἐν) what authority I do these things.

21 : 27. Neither tell I you *by* (ἐν) what authority I do these things.

22 : 15. How they might ensnare him *with* (ἐν) his talk.

22 : 37. *With* (ἐν) all thy heart, *with* (ἐν) all thy soul, *with* (ἐν) all thy might.

22 : 43. How, then, does David *by* (ἐν) the Spirit call him Lord?

23 : 16. Whosoever shall swear *by* (ἐν) the temple.

23 : 16. Whosoever shall swear *by* (ἐν) the gold of the temple.

23 : 18. Whosoever shall swear *by* (ἐν) the altar—sweareth *by* (ἐν) the gift.

23 : 20. Swear *by* (ἐν) the altar, sweareth *by* (ἐν) it, and *by* (ἐν) all things thereon.

23 : 21. Swear *by* (ἐν) the temple, sweareth *by* (ἐν) it, and *by* (ἐν) him that dwelleth therein.

23 : 22. Swear *by* (ἐν) heaven, sweareth *by* (ἐν) the throne of God and *by* (ἐν) him that sitteth thereon.

25 : 16. Traded *with* (ἐν) them.

26 : 52. They that take the sword shall perish *with* (ἐν) the sword.

Thus, in the first book of the New Testament, we find, according to the testimony of the Baptist Bible, that this preposition is used in a sense not local thirty-seven times, more than once for every chapter, and in one case thirteen times in seven consecutive verses. In a volume (Theodosia, an elaborate argument for dipping baptism), published by the Baptist Publication Society, it is affirmed that there are but forty passages in the New Testament in which ἐν must be translated otherwise than by *in*. If this affirmation be true, then, either these forty passages (less three) are singularly crowded into this gospel by Matthew, or the Baptist translators have failed to give us—" The exact meaning of the inspired text." Let us look into the last book of the New Testament to see whether we can find any, or all, of the three missing passages necessary to complete the "forty."

REVELATION.

In examining the use of ἐν in this last book of the New Testament, we confine ourselves, as in the first book, to the translations of the Baptist Bible.

2 : 16. And will fight against them *with* (ἐν) the sword of my mouth.

2 : 23. And I will kill her children *with* (ἐν) death.

2 : 27. And he shall rule them *with* (ἐν) a rod of iron.

5 : 2. A strong angel proclaiming *with* (ἐν, Cod. Sin.) a loud voice.

5 : 9. And hast redeemed us *by* (ἐν) thy blood.

6 : 8. To kill *with* (ἐν) sword and *with* (ἐν) hunger and *with* (ἐν) death.

9 : 19. And *with* (ἐν) them they do hurt.

10 : 6. And sware *by* (ἐν) him that liveth for ever and ever.

11 : 6. To smite the earth *with* (ἐν, Cod. Sin.) all plagues.

12 : 5. To rule all nations *with* (ἐν) a rod of iron.

13 : 10. He that killeth *with* (ἐν) the sword, must be killed *with* (ἐν) the sword.

14 : 2. The voice of harpers harping *with* (ἐν) their harps.

14 : 7. Saying *with* (ἐν) a loud voice.

14 : 9. The third angel followed them saying *with* (ἐν) a loud voice.

14 : 10. He shall be tormented *with* (ἐν) fire and brimstone.

16 : 8. Power was given unto him to scorch men *with* (ἐν) fire.

17 : 16. And shall burn her *with* (ἐν) fire.

18 : 2. He cried mightily *with* (ἐν) a strong voice.

18 : 16. Decked *with* (ἐν) gold, and *(with)* precious stones, and *(with)* pearls.

19 : 2. Which did corrupt the earth *with* (ἐν) her fornication.

19 : 15. A sharp sword that *with* (ἐν) it he should smite the nations

19 : 15. And he shall rule them *with* (ἐν) a rod of iron.

19 : 20. Wrought miracles, *with* (ἐν) which he deceived them.

19 : 20. A lake of fire burning *with* (ἐν) brimstone.

19 : 21. The remnant were slain *with* (ἐν) the sword.

21 : 24. And the nations will walk *by* (ἐν) its light.

Thus, this last book of the New Testament, like the first, furnishes us, under the rule—"The exact meaning of the inspired text"—with thirty or more cases in which the radical idea of inness is rejected. What, now, becomes of the statement, "There are but forty passages in the New Testament in which ἐν must be translated otherwise than by in?" Is not the Baptist Publication Society strangely at war with the Baptist Bible Translation Society?

In the New Testament there are twenty-seven books. If we average the usage of this preposition in these two books throughout the others, we will have not less than nine hundred cases in which inness makes no appearance. But if this should be thought too large a number, because of the inequality of size in the books, reduce it any proper degree, and the cases must still be computed by hundreds. And in view of such a result what becomes of the assertion that such use of ἐν is so rare that to claim it as possible, or probable, in a doubtful case, is without warrant?

If it should be farther said: "These books are more characterized by a Hebraistic style than some other books of the New Testament, and hence the instrumental use of ἐν is more abounding;" we will not question the position, but accept with pleasure the confession, that New Testament writers less familiar with the Greek employed this preposition more frequently (in accordance with their native tongue) in an instrumental sense.

In confirmation of this we find that the Baptist Bible translates ἐν throughout the gospels of Mark and Luke, instrumentally, with only one-half the frequency with which it translates the same preposition in the gospels of Matthew and John. And, still farther, we have the noticeable fact that while the more Hebraistic Matthew and John use the preposition with water (ἐν ὕδατι) in speaking of baptism, it is rejected (ὕδατι) by the less Hebraistic Mark and Luke.

An examination has been made of all the books of the New Testament with the purpose of presenting them in detail; but it is unnecessary; the result is fairly exhibited in the statements now made. And with these facts before us, it is plainly unwarrantable to affirm, that "The use of ἐν in the New Testament in an instrumental sense is rare," or, that "The proffer of such sense, in any questionable case, is without just warrant."

But these facts carry us still farther. They give unquestionable authority for claiming, that where, in parallel passages, the more Hebraistic writers employ the preposition, and the more Greekly writers use the simple dative, the preposition is used with an instrumental meaning.

More specific Usage.

We will, now, proceed to consider the usage of this preposition in relations bearing more specifically upon the phrase-

ology of the passage under consideration. Is there any reason why ἐν in the phrase ἐν Πνεύματι Ἁγίῳ, and in related
phraseology, should carry with it and be limited to the idea
of inness? In determining the value of the preposition in
this relation, as in its general usage, we shall place under
contribution the learning and fidelity of the translators of
the Baptist Bible.

Septuagint.

We will first take a few exemplifications of this usage from
the Septuagint. Micah 3 : 8 : "I am filled with strength
(ἐν Πνεύματι Κυρίου) by the Spirit of the Lord." *Vulgate:*
Spiritus Domini. English translation of the Hebrew: "I
am full of power by the Spirit of the Lord." Zechariah 4 : 6 :
" Not (ἐν) by great power, nor (ἐν) by strength, but (ἐν Πνεύματι)
by my Spirit, saith the Lord." *Vulgate:* "Non in exercitu,
nec in robore, sed in Spiritu meo." *Douay:* "Not with an
army, nor by might, but by my Spirit." *English:* "Not by
might, nor by power, but by my Spirit." Nehemiah 9 : 30 :
"And testified against them (ἐν Πνεύματι σου, ἐν χειρὶ) by thy
Spirit, by the hand of thy prophets." *Vulgate:* "In Spiritu
tuo, per manum prophetarum tuorum." *Douay:* "By thy
Spirit, by the hand of thy prophets." *English:* "By thy
Spirit in thy prophets." Isaiah 4 : 4 : "When the Lord
(ἐκπλυνεῖ) shall wash out the filth of the sons and daughters
of Zion and shall purge away the blood from their midst
(ἐν πνεύματι) by a Spirit of judgment and a Spirit of burning."
Vulgate: "In Spiritu judicii et Spiritu ardoris." *Douay:*
" By the Spirit of judgment and by the Spirit of burning."
So, the English Bible. So, also, in this and in the preceding
passages, the German, French, Spanish, and Italian translations all express agency by preposition or case to which
inness does not belong.

New Testament.

It will not be necessary to adduce all the passages in the
New Testament where this form appears. Our purpose only
requires that such and so many passages shall be brought

forward as will show that this phrase is used where the thought does not rest in a condition of inness, but is employed where such condition either finds no place, or can only be appealed to as a remote element to aid in expounding a new usage.

Mark 12 : 36 : "For David himself said (ἐν τῷ Πνεύματι τῷ ʿΑγίῳ) by the Holy Ghost." *Vulgate:* "In Spiritu sancto." *Douay:* "*By* the Holy Ghost." *Baptist* (Quarto, Greek text): "David himself said *by* the Holy Spirit," and refers to "chap. 1 : 8, note," where, singularly enough, we read— "ἐν Πνεύματι ʿΑγίω. The preposition should have its ordinary force here as in the phrase ἐν ὕδατι." *By* the Holy Ghost is certainly the "ordinary force" of the preposition in such relation; but Baptist writers are quite unwilling to accept such meaning in ἐν ὕδατι. The note, however, is not referred to by the translator for the purpose of bringing into view an incongruous translation of the preposition, but to vindicate the rejection of "Holy *Ghost*" as the name of the third person in the Trinity on the ground, that, "By present usage 'ghost' is equivalent to '*spectre, apparition*' (*!*)"

The Baptist New Testament (without the Greek text) reads thus: "For David himself said, *in* the Holy Spirit." The difference between these two editions is, that the former (now rejected) gives us a correct translation, while the latter (now adopted) gives us none at all. It gives, in English form, the local Greek preposition without any intimation that out of its local use, under certain circumstances, has grown a secondary meaning expressive of influence, agency, instrumentality, which requires, in English, to be expressed otherwise than by a local preposition. It is impossible that ἐν should, here, express local inness—"*within* the Holy Ghost." It is equally impossible that ἐν should have primary relation to the verb (εἶπεν). The action of the verb was not executed within the Holy Ghost; nor was it the act of speaking which was the immediate object of control. It was *David* who spake, and it was David who was under the control of the Holy Ghost. This idea of control by one person or thing over another person or thing is, in Greek, expressed by a suggestive use of the preposition expressive of inness. Certain objects invested by certain things are brought fully under the influence peculiar to such things. Hence, when it was desired to declare that a person or thing was under some full influence, the usage arose of expressing such thought by saying, it was *in* that thing, although inness, in fact, was impossible, and because it was impossible, it was, at once, understood that no inness was designed, but simply influence suggested by the local word. If, now, with a just understanding of the relation of the preposition, we regard David as "*in*," that is subject fully to the influence of, "the Holy Ghost," we have both an elucidation of the fitness of the usage of this preposition, and an indication of the translation, "David said *by* the Holy Ghost." "David said *in* the Holy Ghost" may be very good Greek. It is not very good English. Bloomfield says (Matt. 22:43, Mark 12:36), "It signifies, *under the influence of* the Holy Spirit." Compare with this passage Mark 13:11: "It is not ye that speak, but the Holy Ghost." And Matt. 10:20: "The Spirit of your Father speaketh (ἐν ὑμῖν) in you." Here the absolute influence of the Divine Spirit is brought to view without the form employed for its expression which was before used. Also, 1 Cor. 12:3: "No man (οὐδεὶς ἐν Πνεύματι Θεοῦ) speaking *by* the Spirit of God calleth Jesus accursed; and no man can say that Jesus is Lord, but *by* the Holy Ghost." The Baptist Bible gives the same translation—"*by* (ἐν) the Spirit of God"—"*by* (ἐν Πνεύματι Ἁγίῳ) the Holy Spirit." Here, it is evident that the relation of the preposition is with οὐδεὶς, "no one in" (subject to the influence of) "the Spirit of God calleth Jesus accursed;" and no one, unless "in" (subject to the influence of) "the Holy Ghost," can say, that "Jesus is the Lord." That it is persons, and not verbs, whose relation to the Holy Spirit is indicated by the preposition is unquestionable. Their condition is affected by this relation. And through this relation to the Holy Ghost is determined their relation to Jesus. And, conversely, as their relations to Jesus are determined by their utterances, so is determined their relation to the Holy Ghost, as in Him = under his con-

trolling influence. The Baptist Bible conforms, in the translation of this passage, to the rule which requires to give—
" The exact meaning with the least possible obscurity or indefiniteness." How it happened that the rule was forgotten
in translating Mark 12 : 36 I do not know.

That this phraseology is designed to give development to
the controlling influence of the Holy Ghost is farther evidenced by parallel passages where the influence is expressed
without this form of its development. Thus, in Acts 1 : 16 :
" This Scripture must needs have been fulfilled, which the
Holy Ghost (διά) by the mouth of David spake." Acts 28 : 25 :
" Well spake the Holy Ghost (διά) by Esaias." In these passages agency is directly expressed as the primary meaning
of (διά) the preposition. In the other cases agency is expressed, yet not as the primary, direct meaning of (ἐν) the
preposition, but one which it has acquired, and with the
modus of acquisition more or less clearly traceable through
inness of position.

Luke 2 : 27 : " He came (ἐν τῷ Πνεύματι) by the Spirit into
the temple." The Baptist translation is the same. Attention is asked to what is so clearly true, namely, that the relation of the preposition is not to the verb, as pointing out a
sphere within which its act is performed, but to Simeon, expressing his condition as under divine influence.

Rom. 15 : 13 : " The God of hope fill you with all joy and
peace in believing, that ye may abound in hope (ἐν) by the
power of the Holy Ghost." The Baptist translation is the
same. I, again, call attention to the relation of the preposition as not being with the verb. The filling does not take
place *in* the power of the Holy Ghost; nor is the filling made
up of the power of the Holy Ghost, but of " joy and peace."
The relation of ἐν is, unquestionably, with " the God of hope "
who in = invested with, capable of wielding " the power of
the Holy Ghost," is, thereby, made competent " to fill with
all joy and peace in believing." In verse 16, we again meet
with, " sanctified (ἐν Πνεύματι Ἁγίῳ) by the Holy Ghost." The
Baptist translation, again, assenting. Rom. 15 : 18, 19 : " For
I will not dare to speak of any of those things which Christ

hath not wrought (διὰ) through me, to make the Gentiles obedient, by word and deed, *by* the power of signs and wonders (ἐν δυνάμει), *by* the power of the Spirit of God (ἐν δυνάμει Πνεύματος Θεοῦ)." The Baptist translation, here, falls back on *in*, "in the power of signs and wonders, *in* the power of the Spirit of God;" why, it is hard to tell. The *Douay* has, "*By* the virtue of signs and wonders, in the power of the Holy Ghost." However these prepositions may be translated, *by* or *in*, their relation is with Christ. He is invested "with the power of these signs and wonders," and "with the power of the Spirit of God," and uses both so that through Paul the Gentiles are made obedient.

1 Cor. 6 : 11 : "But ye are washed, but ye are sanctified, but ye are justified (ἐν) *by* the name of the Lord Jesus, and (ἐν τω Πνεύματι) *by* the Spirit of our God." *Baptist:* "In the name of the Lord Jesus and *by* the Spirit of our God." *Douay:* "In the name of our Lord Jesus and in the Spirit of our God." All Christians are "washed, sanctified, and justified" by being in = under the full influence of, therefore, by the Lord Jesus, as our redeemer from sin, and by being in = under the full influence of, therefore, by the Holy Ghost, as our regenerator from a fallen nature. The prepositions have no local force, but indicate the condition of Christians as affected by the work of the Lord Jesus and the Spirit of our God.

1 Cor. 12 : 9 : "To another, faith (ἐν τῷ Πνεύματι) *by* the same Spirit, to another, gifts of healing (ἐν τῷ Πνεύματι) *by* the same Spirit." *Baptist:* "*By* the same Spirit, *by* the one Spirit." 1 Peter 1 : 12 : "Now reported unto you by them that have preached the gospel unto you *with* the Holy Ghost sent down from heaven." *Vulgate:* "Spiritu sancto misso de cœlo." *Douay:* "The Holy Ghost being sent down from heaven." *Baptist:* "*By* the Holy Spirit sent from heaven." The preposition shows the relation between "the preachers" and the Holy Ghost. It was upon them, upon Peter and his associates, "the Holy Ghost was sent down from heaven," and being thus *in* = under the influence of, the divine Spirit, they were qualified for their work. Jude 1 : 20 : "But ye,

12

beloved . . . (ἐν Πνεύματι ʽΑγίῳ) *by* the Holy Ghost, praying,
keep yourselves in the love of God." The relation of the
preposition is not primarily to (προσευχόμενοι) " praying," but
to (ἀγαπητοὶ) " beloved." They being in = under the influence
of the Holy Ghost, pray under the guidance and control of
that influence.

These passages are abundantly sufficient to prove, Baptist
translators themselves being judges, that ἐν with Πνεύματι ʽΑγίῳ
is not only justifiably, but, if translated at all, must be translated so as to show not locality but condition, the result of
influence exerted by the Holy Ghost.

The Office of the Holy Ghost.

The office of the Divine Spirit in the work of redemption
is one of constant influence and activity among the souls of
men. Since He " moved upon the face of the waters" and
out of the unformed elements brought order, beauty, and
life, until now, He has been the Great Worker in our world.
This truth stands out with towering prominence through all
the plan of redemption. It receives expression through
every form by which active agency can be denoted—by the
use of the Nominative, Genitive, and simple Dative, as well
as by διὰ, ὑπο, and every other appropriate grammatical term
and form. In full accordance with this is the usage and
must be the interpretation of the preposition in question.
The Baptist view, *which assigns to Christ the work of putting
the souls of men in the Holy Ghost as a quiescent receptacle,*
revolutionizes the gospel scheme and, logically, subverts
the cross of Christ. It is not the work of Christ to bring
the souls of men to the Holy Ghost; but it is the work
of the Holy Ghost to bring the souls of men to Christ.
Proof passages for these positions are so abounding that
specification is unnecessary. I only refer to the entire
chapter of 1 Cor. 12, and to the condensed truth in 1 Peter
1 : 2 : " Elect according to the foreknowledge of God the
Father, through sanctification of the Spirit, unto obedience
and sprinkling of the blood of Jesus Christ."

ΒΑΠΤΙΖΩ.

This unquestionable and abounding usage of the phrase under consideration is sought to be nullified by calling in the aid of βαπτίζω. It is said, that the presence of this word in the passage αὐτὸς ὑμᾶς βαπτίσει ἐν Πνεύματι Ἁγίῳ, requires that the preposition should be translated *in*, and Πνεύματι Ἁγίῳ should represent an element in which ὑμᾶς must be dipped. To determine the value of this statement we must consider, 1. The meaning of βαπτίζω. 2. The force of the phrase βαπτίζω ἐν. 3. What is the true relation of ἐν in this passage.

1. What is the meaning of βαπτίζω? This question has been abundantly answered in Classic and Judaic Baptism, but it would be improper in meeting this word for the first time in John's baptism not to notice the elaborate statement of Dr. Conant with which it is accompanied in the "New Version." That statement is embodied in the following fifteen propositions:

" I. This word expressed a particular act, viz., *immersion*, in a fluid or any yielding substance."

Answer. This word does not express any particular act. " Immersion" is not properly used to express a particular act or any act. To immerse does not express any particular act. Immersion is a condition resultant from the act of immersing. The Greek verb does not express a definite or particular form of action, but makes demand for a condition of intusposition unlimited as to the form of act producing it, and also, as to the time of its continuance. Error as to this primary meaning, especially so great error as ties it to " a particular act," must hopelessly vitiate any judgment formed with reference to a secondary usage or a usage beyond the domain of physics.

" II. The word had no other meaning; it expressed this act alone, either literally or in a metaphorical sense, through the whole period of its use in Greek literature."

Answer. " This act" cannot be found anywhere in Greek literature. The error is not verbal, but of substance. It is not trivial, but essential.

"III. Its grammatical construction with other words, and the circumstances connected with its use accord entirely with this meaning and exclude every other."

Answer. Neither grammar nor circumstance testifies to " a particular act."

"IV. In the age of Christ and his Apostles, as in all periods of the language, it was in common use to express the most familiar acts and occurrences of everyday life."

Answer. If it was employed to express diverse acts, then it cannot express " a particular act."

"V. There was nothing sacred in the word itself, or in the act which it expressed. The idea of sacredness belonged solely to the relation in which the act was performed."

Answer. Sacredness is not more absent from the word than is " the act."

"VI. In none of these respects does the word *baptize*, as used by English writers, correspond with the Greek word. For,

" 1. It does not express any one definite act."

Answer. Nor does βαπτίζω; nor does the New Version translation, " immerse."

" 2. It is never used to express any particular act of daily life."

Answer. Nor is the word *Bible* used to denote any book of daily life.

"3. On the contrary it only expresses a religious act; and that not of the private individual, but an ecclesiastical rite, an ordinance of the church."

Answer. When employed to denote a " rite" or " ordinance" it is well employed.

"4. Hence this word has become an ecclesiastical symbol, representing in itself all the ideas comprehended in initiation into the Christian church."

Answer. And just so, pregnantly, it is used in the Scriptures.

"5. And hence, also, it has acquired a mystical sense; with which is associated in many minds, and even in large communities, the idea of an inherent virtue in the rite itself."

Answer. It is greatly to be feared that " the idea of an inherent virtue in the rite" has largely infected "many minds and even large communities" who baptize by walking into the water and dipping the upper part of the body.

" VII. The use of this foreign word, of indefinite meaning and purport in English, tends to perpetuate the fatal error of attaching a mystical sense and efficacy to the rite signified by it."

Answer. These considerations will have special interest when "the Baptist" church shall reject their denominational title because expressed by a "foreign word," fruitful in " mystical sense," and " of indefinite meaning and purport in English."

" VIII. It concerns the purity of Christianity, that its rites should be expressed in terms so clear and explicit, as to guard against such a perversion of their true meaning and intent."

Answer. The purity of Christianity is more interested in the suppression of the novelties of to-day than in the rejection of words venerable with the hallowed associations of eighteen centuries.

" IX. The rendering here given is necessary to show the true significance and purport of the Christian rite, and the obligations to which it binds those who receive it."

Answer. So the translators of the New Version believe. The lovers of the Old Bible believe that their rendering is destructive to "the true significance and purport of the Christian rite," and strongly tends to drown any just apprehension of " the obligations to which it binds those who receive it."

" X. This rendering is also necessary to the correct and full understanding of passages in the New Testament relating to the Christian life."

Answer. No passages of the New Testament can be interpreted on such rendering and give the mind of the Holy Spirit.

" XI. In rendering the Greek word by *immerse*, I follow the example of the leading vernacular versions, made from the Greek, in the languages of Continental Europe, and, also, of the critical versions made for the use of the learned."

Answer. In translating "immerse," and in defining immerse = to express "one definite act," a synonym of dip, the word and the definition are placed in contradiction to each other; and no one who accepts the definition can be accepted as a competent expounder of the word.

"XII. The correctness of this rendering is attested by the requirements and practice of the church in all ages, till within a comparatively short time."

Answer. If the rendering "immerse" is correct, the definition "one definite act" is wrong; if the definition is right, the rendering is wrong. Whatever letters may enter into the orthography of a word, a word is to him who uses it just what he defines it. The man who defines βαπτίζω by "one definite act," thereby takes a position from which the just interpretation of the word is impossible.

"XIII. Its correctness is, also, attested by the expressed opinions of eminent scholars in all communions. For example, Dr. Campbell (Principal of Marischal College, Aberdeen), Translation of Gospels, &c." . . .

Answer. Dr. Campbell was a man of learning and ability, but every man cannot know everything. Dr. Campbell did not know, critically, the meaning of βαπτίζω. He says (*On the Gospels*, II, 203), "The Hebrew טָבַל perfectly corresponds to the Greek βάπτω and βαπτίζω, which are synonymous, and is always rendered by one or other of them in the Septuagint." On this statement I would remark, 1. The Hebrew word does *not* perfectly correspond with βαπτίζω. 2. Βάπτω and βαπτίζω are *not* synonymous. 3. The Hebrew word is *not* always translated by one or the other in the Septuagint. Every statement is an error.

"XIV. This is not a sectarian rendering; for that cannot be called sectarian which is proved, on indisputable philological evidence to be the true rendering of God's word." . . .

Answer. There is no philological evidence to prove that this word expresses "one definite act."

"XV. A duty required of every believer, at his entrance on the Christian life, and plainly expressed in the divine word, should be made equally clear in every version of it.

If it can bɔ proved, on philological evidence, that the writer has not given the true meaning of the word, he will be ready to adopt any other version, that shall be shown to be the correct one."

Answer. Whenever it shall be shown to be "a duty required of every believer, and plainly expressed in the divine word," that he, or she, should walk into the water, to "a proper depth," and have so much of the person as may remain above the water dipped into the water, there will be no objection, from any quarter, to all this being put into the New Version or the Old Version in the plainest possible terms.

These propositions are presented by Dr. Conant at the threshold of his work as expressive of the meaning of this word and as the apologetic ground of the New Version. Elsewhere (p. 104) views are expressed quite foreign from "one definite act." The outstaring fact, as to definition and translation, in every Baptist writer is, SELF-CONTRADICTION.

Translator of Mark.

The translator (anonymous) of Mark presents his views of this word, as follows:

"1. Classic usage. In all instances where an examination has been made by competent scholars who were not biassed by a predilection for a creed, the result has been uniformly in favor of *immerse, dip, dip into;* and secondarily, *drown, sink, overwhelm,* &c. In the process of the scrutiny, it has been settled, that there is no difference, as to signification, between βάπτω and βαπτίζω. The latter is merely a later form of the verb."

Answer. This writer is, no doubt, a very excellent judge of "competent scholars" and of those who are "biassed by a predilection for a creed," but unfortunately his judgment as to the meaning of βαπτίζω is neither clear nor true. Had his views been clear, he would not have mixed up "immerse and dip;" nor perhaps have attempted to distinguish between "dip and dip into;" nor have deduced the modal act of "sinking" from either *immerse* or *dip;* nor perhaps would he have appended, that Baptist novelty, "a secondary meaning" to a word which Conant says, "during the whole existence of the Greek as a spoken language, had a perfectly defined and unvarying import," and which Carson says, meant "dip and nothing but dip through all Greek literature," and never had "a secondary meaning." Certainly if he had had any true conception of the words, he never would have said, "there is no difference as to signification between βάπτω and βαπτίζω."

The other statements made by this writer are embraced in those already mentioned as in Dr. Conant's propositions. It is unnecessary to repeat them. No one can carefully examine the views of Baptist writers on the meaning of this word without being speedily confronted with either absolute error, personal inconsistency, or profound obscurity. I do not see how they can insist upon ἐν, or any other word, having a necessary meaning because of its connection with this word, so loosely and so incongruously treated.

Βαπτίζω ἐν.

In a note, on Matt. 3 : 11 (which is translated, "I indeed immerse you in water"), Dr. Conant says, "This is the only sense in which ἐν can be used in connection with βαπτίζω."

It is true that this is the meaning of ἐν in connection with this word in certain circumstances; but it is not true that this is its meaning in other circumstances and relations essentially diverse.

Where ἐν is employed in connection with βαπτίζω to express the place where a baptism takes place, it is properly translated by "in," as in Mark 1 : 4, βαπτίζων ἐν τῇ ἐρήμῳ, "John did baptize in the wilderness." John 1 : 28, ἐν Βηθαβαρᾷ ὅπου ἦν Ἰωάννης βαπτίζων, "These things were done in Bethabara, where John was baptizing." John 3 : 23, βαπτίζων ἐν Αἰνών, "John, also, was baptizing in Ænon."

No one will claim that the connection between ἐν and βαπτίζω in such passages has the remotest relation to the meaning of the verb, or that the meaning of the preposition is controlled in the slightest degree by the meaning of the verb. If the verb meant any other thing conceivable, to stand, to walk, to sit, to drink, to live, to die, to sprinkle, to pour, the preposition would remain unchanged. It is, then, possible for this preposition to stand in the closest possible juxtaposition with this verb, and yet, be removed to the farthest possible distance from all dependence upon its meaning. So in the Classics, βαπτίζομενον ἐν γαλήνη, the preposition has nothing to do with the meaning of the verb. It denotes a space of time. The vessel was not baptized *in* a calm, but *during*, while the calm lasted.

Where ἐν is employed in connection with βαπτίζω to denote inness of position, it is used with the passive voice indicative of condition already attained, and of rest in that condition. Thus, in *Polybius, Hist.* V, 47, " βαπτιζόμενοι ἐν τοῖς τέλμασιν, baptized in the marshy pools." The preposition, here, marks the place within which these persons were baptized and perished from suffocation. In which places so much of them, or of their armor as may remain, abides in a condition of baptism to the present day. *Plotinus,* " ἐν τῷ σώματι βεβαπτισμένη, baptized in the body." This is a representation of the soul as being within the body, in which condition it rests day after day, and year after year. *Alexander Aphrodisias,* II, 38, " βεβαπτισμένην ἐν τῷ βαθει τοῦ σώματος, baptized in the depth of the body." This, also, represents the spiritual nature as deep within the physical, and, consequently, abiding in an oppressed condition. There is no example, I believe, in the Classics where this verb in an uncompounded active form is used with ἐν when the object is to be put in a condition of baptism. And in all cases where this verb and preposition are used together, the object *abides in the condition*, whatever it may be, which is indicated by the preposition and its noun. Dipping is a suggestion of fatuity.

Now, in the passage to which Dr. Conant's note is appended, neither of these features appears. The verb is in the active voice, the parties to the baptism are not in a condition of baptism, and the nature of the element is such as not to allow of their resting in the condition of baptism, seeing that the object is not to drown. Unless, therefore,

we set at nought Classical usage not only as to the meaning
of the simple word, but, also, as to the phrase, we must conclude, that ἐν with the active form of the verb does not denote
the execution of a baptism. What the executive phraseology
is we shall have occasion to consider hereafter. At present
we confine our attention to the passage immediately before
us. And in doing so we would say, that it is no doctrine
of the Bible that the mission of the Lord Jesus Christ was
to put men within the HOLY GHOST. And, until such doctrine
shall be proved, we must declare, that his Forerunner did
not teach that such was the object of his coming. Besides,
the theory is compelled to abandon the force both of the
verb and the preposition in the phrase βαπτίζω ἐν ὕδατι, giving
them both an evanescent character. How is it in the phrase
βαπτίσει ἐν Πνεύματι 'Αγίῳ? Is this, also, an evanescent thing, a
trivial matter, a dipping? If ἐν Πνεύματι is a baptism which
lasts while immortality endures, and ἐν ὕδατι is a *dipping* (a
thing which is and is not, which perishes in the using), what
unifies such alien conceptions? The theory finds within
itself, as well as in the doctrines of the Bible, and in philology,
insuperable barriers to its dogma.

Βαπτίσει ἐν Πνεύματι 'Αγίῳ.

That "in," in the sense of withinness, is not the only
sense in which ἐν can be used with βαπτίζω, is as certain in
the phrase βαπτίσει ἐν Πνεύματι 'Αγίῳ as in the phrase βαπτίζων ἐν
τῇ ἐρήμῳ, or, in βαπτιζόμενον ἐν γαλήνῃ. And this certainty is
absolute. The simple sequence of words is neither conclusive as to their meaning nor determinative of their
logical relations. There is no warrant, whatever, for the
assumption that ἐν, in this phrase, receives its meaning from
the antecedent βαπτίζω, or that its logical relations are with
that word. In the phrases ἐν ἐρήμῳ, ἐν γαλήνῃ, neither the
meaning nor the logical relation of the preposition is controlled by juxtaposition with the verb. In the first case it
indicates place and is in logical relation with John; and in
the second case it indicates a circumstance whose logical
relation is with "ship." In the case before us the prepo-

s'tion is indicative of agency and its logical relation is with ἀυτὸς, pointing out the condition in which the actor was, and, thus, his fitness for the work attributed to him. As John was *in* the wilderness baptizing, and not baptizing in = within the soil of the wilderness; and as the ship was in = during a calm baptized, and not baptized in = within, a calm, so, the Coming One being himself "in" = under, the influence of, did, therefore, *by the power of* the Holy Ghost baptize, and did not baptize men in, = within, the Holy Ghost. That such must be the interpretation of this passage is susceptible of the most satisfactory proof.

General Evidence.

In evidence for the meaning and relation here attributed to ἐν we may appeal to other passages of Scripture where such meaning and relation are recognized and indubitable. We may take, among very many kindred passages, Rom. 9 : 1, "I speak the truth ἐν Χριστῷ, in Christ, I lie not, my conscience also bearing me witness ἐν Πνεύματι Ἁγίῳ, in the Holy Ghost." Professor Stuart rejects the interpretation of this passage which would make it the formula of an oath. And says, "Abundant analogies are at hand to justify the exegesis which is given to ἐν Χριστῷ here, when we construe it as meaning, *in accordance with Christ, or agreeably to what becomes one who is* IN *Christ, or who belongs to him.*"

He, also, objects to the conjunction of Ψεύδομαι and ἐν Πνεύματι Ἁγίῳ, and establishes the relation of the latter phrase with "conscience." "It was a conscience moved and enlightened by this Spirit, which the Apostle here solemnly declares, testified his affectionate regard for the Jewish nation; ἐν Πνεύματι Ἁγίῳ meaning, *agreeably* TO THE INFLUENCE OF *the Holy Spirit.*"

Professor Hodge, in like manner, disapproves of the oath formula interpretation. He says, ἐν Χριστῷ may be connected with the pronoun *I.* "*I in Christ, i. e.*, as a Christian, or, In consciousness of my union with Christ (1 Cor. 1 : 30, 3 : 1; Rom. 16 : 3, 7). An adverbial interpretation, *after a Christian manner*, would convey much the same meaning. The phrase ἐν Πνεύματι Ἁγίῳ may be connected with *conscience.* ' My conscience *under the influence of* the Holy Ghost;' my sanctified conscience."

Bengel places ἐν Πνεύματι Ἁγίῳ in relation with *conscience.* " The internal testimony of the Holy Spirit enlightens and confirms."

Calvin says, " For to this purpose he hath interposed the name of the Spirit, that he might prove how he did handle the cause of Christ *at the direction and moderation of* the Spirit of Christ."

Olshausen would interpret " ἐν Χριστῷ and ἐν Πνεύματι Ἁγίῳ as having ὤν understood after them." I, *being in* Christ, speak; my conscience, *being in* the Holy Spirit, bears witness. So, Christ being IN the Holy Spirit, baptizes.

Lange says of ἐν Χριστῷ : " He expresses his feeling in the consciousness of the fellowship of Christ while he, so to speak, transfers himself into the feeling of Christ;" ἐν Πνεύματι Ἁγίῳ he connects with *bearing witness.*

Schaaf explains : " ἐν Χριστῷ, *i. e.,* in fellowship with Christ, who is Truth itself, and transfers his members, at all events, into the element of truth and sincerity."

In general accord with these interpretations are Tholuck, Meyer, De Wette, Grotius, Alford, and others. Ellicott (Eph. 4 : 17) says, " By thus sinking his own personality, the solemnity of the Apostle's declaration is greatly enhanced."

The point on which the testimony bears is this : ἐν Πνεύματι Ἁγίῳ may be used to expound the condition in which an actor is, as showing his qualification to perform a certain act, and not to express that into which an act is to pass, or that within which it is to have its development. And in the case before us, it declares the condition in which Christ is and his consequent qualification as a Baptizer = " MAGNUS Baptista."

Winer (p. 390), in expounding the force of ἐν as appearing in this passage (Rom. 9 : 1) and others, says : " It denotes the element in which the speaker lives : *speak the truth in Christ,* as one living in Christ. In so far as the Christian abides (by faith) in living (inward, hence ἐν) fellowship with

Christ, he will do everything in the consciousness of this fellowship, and through the strength which this fellowship confers, *i. e.*, *in* Christ, *in* the Lord" (*in* the Holy Ghost); "*as a Christian, in a Christian spirit*, &c., as the words are frequently rendered, expresses much less than the pregnant phrase *in Christ*" (*in* the Holy Ghost).

The Holy Ghost abode in Christ, and Christ did abide in the Holy Ghost, and "through the strength which this fellowship conferred," he (ἐν Πνεύματι Ἁγίῳ), being in the Holy Ghost, did baptize.

I will add a quotation, made, with warm approval, by the *Baptist Quarterly*:

" The minute study of the Scriptures, in the spirit of devotion, and under the guidance of the Holy Spirit, will lead us to truths and conceptions and emotions, of whose precious value and edifying power we shall not otherwise even dream. The mysteries of the kingdom of God come to us through these words of inspiration. *A doctrine of grace may dwell in the right understanding of a single preposition.* Who can measure the significance and worth of this one expression of the New Testament, IN CHRIST?"

Specific Evidence.

1. The Scriptures teach us that the Lord Jesus Christ was *in* = under the influence of, and acted by the power of, the Holy Ghost. His very name, Messiah, Christ, Anointed, declares this. Isaiah 11:1, 2: "And there shall come forth a rod out of the stem of Jesse, and a branch shall grow out of his roots: and the Spirit of the Lord shall rest upon him." This is a clear declaration that the Son of David shall be under the influence of, and shall act with the power of, the Spirit of the Lord. Isaiah 48:16: "The Lord God and his Spirit hath sent me." John 3:34: "He whom God hath sent speaketh the words of God; for God giveth not the Spirit by measure unto him." The influence of the illimitable possession of the Spirit secures correspondent results. Luke 3:22: "And the Holy Ghost descended in a bodily shape like a dove upon him." The influence of the

Holy Ghost, thus received, is immediately developed. Matt.
4 : 1 : "Then was Jesus led up (ὑπὸ τοῦ Πνεύματος) by the Spirit
into the wilderness." Mark 1 : 12 : "And immediately (τὸ
Πνεῦμα) the Spirit driveth him into the wilderness." Luke
4 : 1 : "And Jesus being full of the Holy Ghost returned
from Jordan, and was led (ἐν τῷ Πνεύματι) 'in,' and therefore
by, the Spirit into the wilderness." Here is both the action
and reaction of the Holy Spirit. The Lord Jesus receives
the Holy Ghost in its fulness of influence upon himself, and
then, under the controlling power of this influence, does
himself act with all the peculiar influence and power of
the Holy Ghost. In Luke ἐν τῷ Πνεύματι takes the place of
the nominative τὸ Πνεῦμα in Mark, and the genitive ὑπο τοῦ
Πνεύματος in Matthew, equally with them, yet not so immə-
diately, expressing the agency of the Holy Spirit. 'Εν τῷ
Πνεύματι represents Christ as "in," and, as a consequence,
under the influence of the Holy Spirit, by whom, therefore,
he is led. His action is invested with the character and
power of the Holy Spirit. "In that wilderness the Good
Spirit, dwelling without measure in Christ, met the Spirit
of Evil face to face. In the power of the Holy Ghost the
Saviour for forty days repulsed the foe." (*Bickersteth, Spirit
of Life*, p. 78.) Is "the foe" repelled until *he* comes "in
the power of the Holy Ghost?" or, does Bickersteth say,
that this is the condition in which is "the Saviour?" It
would be a perfectly Classical use of βαπτίζω, and a perfectly
Scriptural use of ἐν, to say, "Christ, in the wilderness, did
baptize Satan ἐν Πνεύματι 'Αγίῳ." It would, however, be an
infinite blunder to make ἐν Πνεύματι 'Αγίῳ expound the condition into which Satan is to be brought, instead of the
condition in which Christ acts. It is, precisely, this error
which is developed in expounding—"He shall baptize you ἐν
Πνεύματι 'Αγίῳ," mistaking the relation of the defining phrase.
Luke 4 : 14 : "And Jesus returned" (from the wilderness)
(ἐν τῇ δυνάμει τοῦ Πνεύματος) "in the power of the Spirit into
Galilee." This declares the condition of Jesus; he was
"in," = possessed of, and in all that he said and did exercised, "the power of the Spirit;" "And he taught in their

synagogues" (v. 15). How did he teach? Why, of course, he taught "with the power of the Spirit;" therefore, "they were astonished at his teaching, for his word was with power" (v. 32). As the Saviour's teaching was by the Holy Spirit, so, also, were his miracles wrought in like manner—"Jesus of Nazareth, a man approved of God among you by miracles and wonders and signs which God did (διὰ) by him in the midst of you" (Acts 2 : 22). The offering up of himself as an atoning sacrifice was done under the influence of the Spirit—"Who (διὰ Πνεύματος αἰωνίου) through the eternal Spirit offered himself without spot to God" (Heb. 9 : 14). And, in like manner, his final instructions were given— "After that he (διὰ Πνεύματος Ἁγίου) through the Holy Ghost had given commandments unto the Apostles" (Acts 1 : 2). On this phrase, in this passage, the distinguished Baptist commentator, Professor Hackett, says, "*through the Holy Spirit; his influence, guidance.* This passage, in accordance with other passages, represents the Saviour as having been endued abundantly with the influences of the Holy Spirit, and as having acted always in conformity with its dictates (see 10 : 38; Luke 4 : 1; John 3 : 34, &c.). That subjection was one of the laws of his dependent nature." (Comm. in loc.) And on 4 : 26, "*his Christ, his anointed one.* In Hebrew symbology anointing denoted his receiving the spiritual gifts and endowments which he needed for the performance of his duties. He is called *the Anointed,* by way of eminence, because he possessed the gifts of the Spirit without measure, was furnished in a perfect manner for the work which he came into the world to execute." This exposition is confirmatory, in the highest degree, of our interpretation. Christ being ἐν Πνεύματι Ἁγίῳ "was furnished in a perfect manner for the work" (*he shall baptize you*) "which he came into the world to execute."

2. The same phraseology is employed by Scripture, of others, to denote their being under or invested with some influence. Luke 10 : 17 : "Lord, even the devils are subject unto us (ἐν) through thy name." The disciples (not the devils) were "in" (invested with, clothed with, the power

of) the name of Jesus; therefore, BY this name they cast out devils.

The agency of this name is stated, without a preposition, in Mark 9:38 (perhaps, because the disciples did not recognize these persons as deriving their power from being (ἐν) "*in* Christ"): "Master, we saw one casting out devils (τῷ ὀνόματι) by thy name" (Sin. Ms. ἐν). And in Matt. 7:22: "Lord (τῷ σῷ ὀνόματι), by thy name we have cast out devils;" "ὀνόματι χριστοῦ, *i. e.,* non tantum auctoritate Christi, sed etiam potentia et auxilio Christi freti. Sic enim sumitur hæc phrasis etiam Marc. 9:38, coll. Luc. 9:49, ubi aliquis, qui non erat discipulus, ἐπι (Sin. ἐν; Tisch. ἐπί) τῷ ὀνόματι Ἰησοῦ dœmonia ejecisse dicitur. Hic certe non auctoritate, non jussu Christi dœmonia ejecit, sed potentiæ ejus fretus, usus formula, qua discipuli uti solebant: in nomine Iesu volo ut dœmoniacus sanitati restituatur." (*Rosenmul. in loc.*) It is however true, that ἐν τῷ σῷ ὀνόματι may express a profounder meaning, as to condition, than the nude, instrumental dative. Acts 3:6: "In the name (ἐν τῷ ὀνόματι) of Jesus Christ of Nazareth, rise up and walk." The source of power is "the name," as shown in v. **16**, "And his name, through faith in his name, hath made this man strong;" 4:7, "by what means (ἐν τίνι) this person is made whole;" *Baptist*, Quarto, Greek, "In what name;" *Baptist, English, N. T.* returns to the Common Version. v. **10**, "by the name (ἐν τῷ ὀνόματι) of Jesus Christ of Nazareth, by him (ἐν τούτῳ) doth this man stand here before you whole;" *Baptist, Quarto,* "*in* the name;" *Baptist N. T.,* "*by* the name." v. **12**, "*by* which (ἐν ᾧ) we must be saved." Here, again, the two Baptist translations are at contraries; the one adopting "in," the other "by." v. **30**, "that signs and wonders may be done, διά, through the name of thy holy child Jesus." The use of διά shows that ἐν τῷ ὀνόματι is indicative of power.

Matt. 9:34: "He casts out devils (ἐν τῷ ἀρχυντι) through the prince of the devils." This is the Baptist translation, to which this note is appended: "'Ἐν (with *dat.* of *pers.*) denotes the one *in* whom resides the power or authority by which a thing is done; hence *by* or *through.*" But this statement is not clear. It does not show any connecting link between the Prince of demons, in whom the power resides, and the Caster-out of demons, who exercises this power. The statement in the note implies, that the Prince of the demons was the direct and visible actor, just as though δία or ὑπό were used. But this is not the case. The Prince of the demons does not appear in the transaction. But the power exercised is attributed to him, and its transference to the visible actor is accounted for by declaring that he is "in" = under the influence of, invested with the power of, the Prince of the demons, and thus becomes the channel through which this power flows. Matt. 12 : 24 : "This man does not cast out devils except through Beelzebub (ἐν τῷ Βεελζεβὺλ) prince of the devils" (*Baptist Version*). Here, again, the source of power is made to reside "in" Beelzebub, and its transference is exhibited by the verbal form which declares the exercise of the power to be "in Beelzebub." The theory, to be consistent, would connect the verb and the preposition together, and make the casting out of the devils to be a casting of them *in*, within, Beelzebub! v. 27, "And if I (ἐν Βεελζεβουλ) through Beelzebub cast out devils (ἐν τίνι), through whom do your children cast them out?" (*Baptist Version.*) v. 28, "But if I (ἐν πνεύματι θεοῦ) through the Spirit of God cast out devils" (*Baptist Version*). In the parallel passage, Luke 11 : 20, "But if I (ἐν δακτυλῷ θεοῦ) by the finger of God cast out the demons" (*Baptist Version*). Rosenmuller says: " ἐν πνεύματι ἁγίῳ, *per potentiam divinam*, adjuvante Deo. Permutantur notiones spiritus et potentiæ; quod enim uno in loco dictum est fieri spiritu, id in altero potentiæ divinæ tribuitur. Cf. Luc. XI, 20."

It will be observed throughout these passages, that the Baptist translation of ἐν is invariably "through" or "by." It will also be noticed, that this preposition with a person is said to indicate the source of power. And farther we should notice, that the logical relation established by this preposition is with the actor who, through it, becomes clothed with that power which belongs to the adjunct of the preposition. The evidence is absolute as showing that the Jews declared

13

Christ to be ἐν Βεελζεβοὺλ = invested with the power of Beelzebub, while he declared himself to be ἐν Πνεύματι Θεοῦ = invested with the power of God.   The evidence is equally absolute as proving, that the language of John may declare
that Christ is ἐν Πνεύματι Ἁγίῳ = invested with the power of
the Holy Ghost, therefore, able to baptize, to influence controllingly, to change completely the condition of the souls
of men.   The design of John (contrasting Christ's power
and his own) demands this.   And the phraseology imperatively forbids ἐν Πνεύματι Ἁγίῳ being regarded as an element
into which, or within which, the baptism takes place.   Under
this phraseology the "casting out" is indifferently ascribed
to Satan (v. 26) and to Christ (v. 27), and under like phraseology the "baptism" may be indifferently ascribed to the
Holy Ghost or to Christ.

As immediately related to the general subject, and shedding a clear light on this particular aspect of it, we may
refer to the statement made respecting the Forerunner of
Jesus contained in Luke 1 : 17 : "He shall go before him
(ἐν πνεύματι καὶ δυνάμει Ἡλίας) *in* the spirit and power of Elias."
This represents the condition of John, passively.   Two related facts (but not related as cause and effect) are stated.   If
it were designed to declare that "the going" was caused by
"the spirit and power of Elias," then the translation must be,
"he shall go before him *by* the spirit and power of Elias;"
but the design being merely to announce John's personal
fitness for his work, and not his active engagedness in it by
the performance of particular acts, the translation must represent him, simply, as "*in*" = under the influence of, "the
spirit and power of Elias."   In farther illustration we may
take Luke 2 : 27 : "He came (ἐν τῷ πνεύματι) *by* the Spirit into
the temple" (*Common, Baptist,* and *Douay Versions*).   These
translations are correct if "the coming into the temple" be
the outworking of the influence under which Simeon is declared to be; but if the coming into the temple be, as is
quite possible, in the ordinary course of duty, and not from
special influence, then, we must translate, "He came *in* the
Spirit into the temple," and we must refer this statement to

his condition as having reference to what he was about to do after he came into the temple, and as stamping with divine authority his utterance respecting the child Jesus and his mother Mary. But we have not a passive condition, but a state of activity clearly expressed in Matt. 22:43: "How, then, does David *by* the Spirit call him Lord?" This is the Baptist Version, and, in a note, it is added: "*By the Spirit*, is the proper rendering, here, whether we understand ἐν πνεύματι as meaning, under his power and influence (Robinson, New Test. Lex., ἐν, 3, *a. γ.*), or, by his aid or intervention (Ibid. d. a.)." Reference is also made to the fact, that ἐν Πνεύματι appears without the article; but in the parallel passage, Mark 12:36 (ἐν τῷ Πνεύματι τῷ Ἁγίῳ), it appears in the fullest possible form. There is, also, a reference to the note on 9:34, already quoted, limiting ἐν = *by, through*, to persons. This meaning, however, is not limited to persons. Professor Hackett translates Acts 1:3 (ἐν τεκμηρίοις), "*by* proofs;" and Acts 4:7 (ἐν ποίᾳ δυνάμει), "*by* what power;" and Acts 4:12 (ἐν ᾧ) "*by* which," and so in multitudes of cases for precisely the same reason that ἐν Βεελζεβοὺλ is translated "*by* Beelzebub," and ἐν Πνεύματι Ἁγίῳ is translated "*by* the Holy Ghost," to wit, because in these things resides a power which finds development causative of appropriate results. Baptist argumentation necessitates the translation, "he shall baptize *by* the Holy Ghost."

And, now, returning to the Scripture—"Upon whom thou shalt see the Spirit descending, and remaining on him, the same is He which baptizeth ἐν Πνεύματι Ἁγίῳ"—we say, that the evidence is overwhelming that it not only may be, but must be translated so as to show, that the Baptizer is acting under the influence of the Holy Ghost, and by the power of the Holy Ghost effecting a baptism characterized by the efficient power and peculiar nature of that Divine Person, and not so as to represent the subjects of this baptism as put *within* the Holy Ghost. The Jews blasphemed by saying that Christ, himself, was ἐν Βεελζεβοὺλ, not by saying, that he *cast devils within* Beelzebub! John says, Ἀυτὸς βαπτίσει ὑμᾶς ἐν Πνεύματι Ἁγίῳ (Mark 1:8), which is structurally parallel with

Οὗτος εκβαλλει δαιμόνια ἐν τῷ Βεελζεβοὺλ (Matt. 12 : 24). It is certain from the Saviour's form of language in v. 27, *ἐγὼ ἐν Βεελζεβοὺλ*, that this phrase is expository of *Οὗτος*; and from his language in v. 28, *ἐγὼ ἐν Πνεύματι*, it is equally certain that *ἀυτος* in Matt. 3 : 11 is expounded by *ἐν Πνεύματι ʻΑγίῳ*. And this being so, the condition of the Baptizer and the character of the bap·tism are settled.

Summary of Errors.

1. That *βαπτίζω* expresses a definite act or requires a temporary covering, has been disproved in Classic and Judaic Baptism.

2. That *βαπτίζω ἐν* is a formula expressive of the execution of a baptism, is an error entirely without foundation whether in or out of the Classics.

3. That *ἐν*, simply sequent of *βαπτίζω*, must express *withinness*, is an error disproved by Classical usage as well as by that of the New Testament.

4. That there is any necessary logical dependence of *ἐν* on the executive meaning of *βαπτίζω*, by reason of immediate sequence, is a position disproved.

5. That the mission of the Lord Jesus Christ is to put the souls of men " within the Holy Ghost," is a portentous and revolutionary error originated by the theory.

6. That the Holy Ghost is *the passive recipient of the souls of men baptized within it*, is an error subversive of his divinely revealed office work as THE AGENT ever active in applying to the souls of men the fruits of redeeming love.

7. That there is any dipping or immersing of the bodies or souls of men within the Holy Ghost, in this passage, is an entire misconception of its import.

On the other hand we hold as established truths :

1. *ʼΕν*, in the sense *with, by, through*, is of common occurrence in the Septuagint, Apocrypha, and New Testament.

2. *ʼΕν*, in the phrase *ἐν Πνεύματι ʻΑγίῳ*, must ordinarily (and where activity is expressed, invariably) be translated *by ;* such meaning logically proceeding from withinness.

3. *ʼΕν*, in the phrase *ἐν Πνεύματι* (with its variations), con·

nected with an active verb, is logically related to the actor, and denotes with its adjunct, the condition of the actor and the character of the influence or power put forth by him.

4. Βαπτίζω here (as it has been proved it is its office, elsewhere, to do) indicates a complete change in the condition of its objects; the character of that condition being determined, as always, by the nature of the baptizing power.

5. The passage in teaching, that Christ is " in " = under the influence of, the Holy Ghost, and so baptizes *by* the Holy Ghost, harmonizes with all other Scripture teaching.

6. The souls of men being baptized by the Holy Ghost and not in the Holy Ghost, the great office work of the Spirit of God is declared and vindicated.

7. The form of the phraseology (the Hellenistic use of ἐν excepted) is precisely the same with that of related baptisms in the Classics, to wit, the verb with the dative of the influence or agency.

8. The nature and power of the baptism received is, in general, indicated by the condition in which the baptizer is, thus qualifying him to baptize.

Specific baptisms must have specific indications.

As to the precise nature of this baptism I would say, No *specific* character is given to it. Its generic character is declared in the most explicit manner. It is a baptism which is divinely efficient as to its power and generically holy, purifying, in its nature. But within this general character there is room for "multa baptismata" of a specific character, such as εἰς μετανοίαν, εἰς ἀφεσιν ἁμαρτιων, and others, which we shall meet with hereafter. At present I remark, that this avoidance of more specific statement was what the time required. It was necessary for the Forerunner to speak of the Coming One, and to declare him to be mightier than himself, as administering a baptism most real in its nature, while his was but a symbol shadow of that reality; but it was not timely to proclaim, specifically, that baptism which took in the issues of his future life and death. John, therefore, rests in the declaration, that the baptism of his Lord shall be such as is effected " by the Holy Ghost." We shall soon see that he is more specific in announcing the character of the baptism which is distinctive of his own ministry, and so indicates one of the specific baptisms which must be wrought in the soul by the Holy Ghost.

I close this aspect of the subject by the following quotation from Origen, IV, 273, Διὰ τοῦτο λαβὼν τὸ Πνεῦμα μένον ἐπ᾽ αὐτον Ἰησοῦν, ἐν αὐτῷ μείναντι βαπτίζειν τοὺς προσερχομένους αὐτῷ δυνηθῇ, "Therefore, having received the Holy Spirit abiding upon him, he is enabled, by the Holy Spirit abiding in him, to baptize those who come unto him." This passage declares, most explicitly, that Origen regarded Christ as clothed with power to baptize through the influence of the indwelling Spirit; which he had just described as the "pure and true Dove bound unto him and no more able to fly away from him." He did not teach, that Christ dipped the souls of men into, or covered them momentarily within the Holy Ghost, abiding upon him. Compare with this and the other passages, 1 Cor. 12: 12, 13 οὔτω καὶ ὁ Χριστός· καὶ γὰρ ἐν ἑνὶ Πνεύματι ἡμεῖς πάντες εἰς ἓν σῶμα ἐβαπτίσθημεν; where baptism "*in* the Spirit" is excluded by the express statement εἰς ἓν σῶμα; and where ἐν is either directly and simply instrumental, or is so, indirectly, by declaring the relation between Χριστός and Πνεύματι. What John declares Christ would do, Paul declares Christ has done. John came "*in* the spirit and power of Elias," and so symbolly baptized. "The Mightier One" came "*in* the Spirit" and power of Jehovah, and so divinely baptized all his people.

BAPTISM BY FIRE.

MATTHEW 3: 11.

Ἀυτος ὑμᾶς βαπτίσει . . . . . καὶ πυρί.

"He will baptize you . . . . . by fire."

The Theory.

The friends of the theory have very little to say respecting this baptism. After examining some of the most voluminous writers to learn what interpretation they would give to it, I have found it to be either wholly passed by or dismissed with a reference to the "like as of fire" tongues of Pentecost. While this allusion may furnish so much of a point of con tact between the two passages as can be gathered from "fire" and "like as of fire," yet there is not so much as the likeness of a point of contact between dipping the body into fire, and fire-like tongues resting on the head! We have seen the theory maintaining the "one definite act" dogma in the presence of scores of baptisms in the Classics in which no such act was to be found; and we shall find like baptisms in Scripture confronting and repudiating the notion that Bible baptism is and can only be, a dipping into water. There never was a theory more utterly at war with facts than is this dipping into water theory.

Dr. Conant, in his translation of Matthew, has a note on this verse, but says nothing of dipping or immersing "in fire." The translator of Luke, also, has a note on the verse where this fire baptism is announced, but he passes it by in silence. It is pretty certain that no friend of the theory will ever rely upon this passage as a proof text in support of his cause.

The Patristic View.

The early Christian writers have pursued a very different course in relation to this passage from that adopted by our Baptist friends. They have, almost without exception, referred to it and given interpretations of it. Whether their views should commend themselves to our judgment as correct or not, their consideration must be interesting, and can hardly fail to be instructive so far as the use of words is concerned.

Basil.

Basil the Great in commenting on Isaiah 4 : 4, Ἐκπλυνει Κυριος—"The Lord will wash away the filth of the sons and of the daughters of Zion, and purge out the blood of Jerusalem from their midst (ἐν πνευματι κρίσεως, καὶ ἐν πνεύματι καύσεως) by a spirit of judgment and a spirit of burning," adds, "The Scripture clearly foretells the same things by John, saying concerning the Lord—He shall baptize you ἐν Πνεύματι Ἁγίῳ καὶ πυρί." The grammatical structure of these passages is identically the same. Beyond all controversy ἐν πνεύματι κρίσεως καὶ ἐν πνεύματι καύσεως represent the means whereby the washing and purging are to be effected. It is no less certain that the primary and logical relation of these agencies is with "the Lord" who uses them for "washing away" and "purging out." They declare the power of which he is possessed. And if "things which are equal to the same thing are equal to each other," then, the same interpretation must rule in the language of John as in that of Isaiah.

Basil, farther, adds: "But concerning himself he says, 'I indeed baptize you by water into repentance.' Since, then, the Lord has conjoined both, that Ἐκ ὕδατος by means of water into repentance, and that Ἐκ Πνεύματος by means of the Spirit into regeneration, the Scripture also declares both baptisms. Perhaps there are three meanings of baptism, 1. Purification from filth, 2. Regeneration (διὰ) through the Spirit, and 3. The trial by the fire of judgment, so that cleansing for the removal of sin now may be received, but the cleansing by the spirit of judgment and the spirit of burning relates to the test hereafter (διὰ) through fire."

These views of Basil do not point in the remotest degree to a dipping or an immersing "in a spirit of judgment and in a spirit of burning," "in the Holy Spirit and fire," or "in water." It is impossible for language to be used which would more variedly or more absolutely declare all these things to be agencies. We not only have ἐν πνεύματι κρίσεως καὶ ἐν πνεύματι καύσεως used under circumstances which imperatively exclude withinness from the preposition, but we have the same phrase repeated with the preposition thrown aside. We have not only ἐν instrumental in ἐν Πνεύματι Ἁγίῳ, but we have this exchanged for ἐκ Πνεύματος and διὰ Πνεύματος. We have not only ἐν πυρὶ, but also ἐκ τοῦ πυρὸς and διὰ τοῦ πυρὸς. We have not only ἐν ὕδατι, but also ἐξ ὕδατος and ἀπὸ τοῦ ὕδατος. Now, if there be any dipping or immersing in these baptisms, it is not to be found, Basil being judge, in the water, or in the fire, or in the Holy Ghost, or in the spirit of judgment and of burning. It must be looked for somewhere else. In his treatise on Baptism (III, 1541), he defines fire baptism thus, "βαπτισθέντα ἐν τῷ πυρί, τουτ᾽ ἐστιν ἐν τῷ λόγῳ τῆς διδασκαλίας baptized by the fire, that is, by the word of doctrine." As doctrine is instrumentality so must be fire. And in his work on the Holy Spirit (IV, 132), having quoted the passage, "He shall baptize you by the Holy Spirit and fire," he adds: "Calling the trial by the judgment, τὸ τοῦ πυρὸς βάπτισμα, the baptism of fire," according to the saying of the Apostle, τὸ πυρ, "The fire shall try every man's work, what it is," and again, "For the day shall declare it, because it shall be revealed by fire." Thus, again, we have agency expressed by the nominative, and the genitive, as well as by the dative.

Whatever authority belongs to Basil the Great as a Greek scholar, it is directed crushingly against the theory as to its doctrine respecting βαπτίζω, βάπτισμα, and the relation of these words to ἐν πνεύματι ἁγίῳ, ἐν τῷ πυρί, &c.

Jerome.

Jerome (VII, 30) expounds this baptism by saying, "Sive quia ignis est Spiritus sanctus," either because the Holy Spirit is fire, as the Acts of the Apostles teach, "which descending, sat like fire upon each of them;" and the word of the Lord was fulfilled, saying, "I came to send fire upon the earth and how do I desire that it may burn;" or "Because, now, we are baptized (spiritu) by the Spirit, and, hereafter (igne) by fire." V. 686, Translating Origen on Jeremiah, he says, "Perhaps Jesus baptizes by the Holy Spirit and fire, not because he baptizes the same person by both, but while the good are baptized by the Holy Spirit, he who returns to his sins is purged by the torment of burning. Happy is he who receives the cleansing (Spiritus Sancti) of the Holy Spirit and does not need the cleansing of fire. But wretched and worthy of weeping is he who after the cleansing of the Spirit must be baptized (igni) by fire. Jesus has both baptisms: 'For a rod shall come forth from the root of Jesse, and a flower shall rise up from his root' (Is. 11:1);

a rod for transgressors, a flower for the righteous. So the Scriptures say, 'God is both a consuming fire and a light' (Heb. 12 : 20; 1 John 3 : 5); a fire for transgressors, a light for the holy."

Jerome takes his place with Basil against dipping or immersing "in fire," and vindicates agency. The Greek of Origen (III, 281) is, if possible, still more explicit: "Blessed is he who, baptized by the Holy Ghost, does not need (βαπτίσματος τοῦ ἀπὸ πυρός) the baptism which is from fire. But thrice wretched is he who needs (βαπτίσασθαι τῷ πυρί) to be baptized by fire."

Language is better calculated to conceal our thoughts than to reveal them, if a baptism ἀπὸ πυρός or τῷ πυρί is intended to express a dipping into fire, or a temporary covering within fire.

Hilary.

The section (I, 926, 4) which treats of this baptism, by Hilary, bears the heading—"Christus noster *servator* et *judex*." " 'He shall baptize you by the Holy Spirit and fire,' designates the time of our salvation and of judgment by the Lord; because having been baptized by the Holy Spirit, it remains to be completed (igne judicii) by the fire of judgment." It is not within the bounds of possibility that Hilary could by such language intend to indicate a dipping or an immersing in the fire of judgment.

The baptism by the Holy Spirit, evidently, is a condition of the soul in which a certain change is effected, but not adequate to fit it for heaven; and another baptism, *igne judicii*, is required for this end. In all this the performance of "a definite act" never once makes its appearance; but a change of condition confronts us everywhere, and the agencies in effecting this change are the Holy Spirit and a fiery judgment.

Ambrose.

Ambrose (II, 1227) asks: "Quis est qui in hoc igne baptizat? Who is it that baptizes by this fire? Not a Presbyter, not a Bishop, not John, not an Angel, not an Archangel, not Dominions, not Powers, but he, of whom John says: 'He shall baptize you by the Holy Spirit and fire.' . . . And if any one be as holy as Peter, or John, he is baptized by this fire. Then will come the Great Baptist (for so I call him, as Gabriel called him, saying, 'He shall be great,' Luke 1 : 15), he will see many standing before the entrance of Paradise, he will wave the sword turning every way, he will say to them on the right, not having heinous sins: 'Enter, ye of good courage, who fear not the sword.' For I foretold you: 'Behold I come as a fire' (Isaiah 56 : 15); and by Ezekiel I said: 'I will blow upon you with the fire of my anger, that ye may be melted from lead and iron' (22 : 21). He comes, therefore, as a consuming fire, he burns up in us the lead of iniquity, the iron of sin, and makes us pure gold. . . . Each one of us is burned by that flaming sword, not burned up. . . . That is one kind of fire by which involuntary and undesigned sins are burned up, and that is another kind of fire appointed to the devil and his angels."

The view of Ambrose as to this fire baptism is, that the condition of the soul is by it thoroughly changed and fitted for Paradise. That this fire must do its work by the soul being dipped into it or covered over by it, is disproved, so far as Ambrose is concerned, by its being effected by *a flaming sword*, which can neither dip nor immerse.

Origen.

Origen (III, 704), in like manner, expounds this baptism by a reference to the flaming sword. He appeals, also, in illustration, to the knife and cautery used in surgery for the extirpation of a cancer, and then quotes: "I came not to send peace on the earth, but a sword;" and, "I came to send fire upon the earth." These passages he expounds thus: "The Saviour uses both sword and fire" (*et baptizat quæ non potuerunt Spiritus Sancti purificatione purgari*) "and baptizes those sins which could not be purged by the purification of the Holy Spirit."

This exposition settles several points: **1.** This Greek scholar did not believe, that a baptism required (in fact or in fiction) a dipping or an immersing. 2. He did believe, that baptize meant *to purify.* 3. He also believed, that in this fire baptism the fire was used as an agency by which the baptism (purification) was effected, and not as a receiving element within which the object was to be dipped or covered up.

Tertullian.

Tertullian (III, 1202) says: "On the day of Pentecost, when the Holy Ghost descended upon the disciples that they might be baptized by him, tongues like fire were seen resting on each one, that it might be evident that they (Spiritu Sancto et in igne baptizatos) were baptized by the Holy Ghost and by fire."

The absence of the preposition with "Spiritu Sancto," and its presence with "igne," together with the well-known facts of the case, show that Tertullian had no thought of a baptism carrying the Apostles within the one or the other.

Heretical Fire Baptism.

Irenæus (1292) quotes from Clement of Alexandria: "Some, as Heracleon says, πυρὶ τὰ ὦτα τῶν σφραγιζομένων κατεσημήναντο" (which is translated by a commentator on Tertullian, "*igne aures siggillatorum* (baptizatorum) *adurebant*"), "marked with fire the ears of the sealed (baptized)."

Epiphanius (I, 372) says: "Those who are under Carpocras attach a seal (ἐν καυτῆρι) by a red-hot iron to the right lobe of the ear."

Augustin (de Hær., 59) says: "The Seleucian heretics (*igne Baptismum contulisse*) confer baptism by fire."

If this baptism was to be by fire, then, these heretics did not err in employing *bonâ fide* fire, instead of referring it to the *quasi* fire of Pentecost as do our Baptist friends. And it seems to be quite as clear, that the theorists must accept, in logical consistency, the cauterization of the ear by a hot iron as an equally honest fire baptism with the resting of a tongue of *quasi* fire over the head. And more, the reasoning by which they seek to justify a *dipping* into water as a substitute for *baptism* in water, namely, "because a baptism would drown," is reasoning equally apologetic for these ancient heretics. If water baptism will drown, fire baptism will burn up. If to escape drowning baptism may be converted into a dipping, then, to escape burning up, baptism may be converted into a cauterization of the ear. It is no less a heresy to convert Bible baptism into water dipping, than it is to convert baptism "by the Holy Ghost and fire" into a "burning of the right lobe of the ear." The two heresies are of precisely the same nature. They both arise from a misapprehension (equally honest no doubt in both cases) of the nature of Bible baptism. And when they find that the true idea of a baptism cannot be applied to their misapprehension without destroying life, instead of abandoning their error (as thus proved to be error), they carry out their notion with as little mischief as possible, by abandoning the Bible baptism, and, in the one case, dipping the upper part of the body into water, and, in the other case, touching the end of the ear with a burning coal.

Of the two heresies that of the fire Baptists is the less; for there is no evidence that they regarded the fire as appointed to be the element within which the baptism was to take place, but only as a symbol means by which the true baptism was to be set forth; while the water Baptists declare, that water is that within which the baptism is commanded to take place, and that such withinness is the baptism. The fire Baptists are justified, under their view, in employing a coal of fire, but the water Baptists have no justification, under their view, for dipping into water. They say, that God does clearly and imperatively demand a baptism in water; but a *dipping* into water is no *baptism* in water. If they are right as to God's command, they are wrong as to their obedience. The two things are irreconcilable. The one or the other must be given up. These old fire Baptists had a baptism; but it was heathenish, not Christian. Our modern water Baptists have no baptism; whether of heathenism, or of Judaism, or of Christianity. They refuse water in the character in which the Bible offers it—*a symbol agency,*

and they dare not use it in the character which they themselves assign to it—*a mersing element*—and, therefore, change
the meaning of the word ($\beta\alpha\pi\tau\dot\iota\zeta\omega$), and with it change the
ordinance of God, substituting for it an ordinance of their
own devising; an ordinance never before heard of either
in history or in Scripture.   It is utterly vain to appeal to
Patristic water covering to justify such a baptism.   Dipping
into water is no more patristic baptism than is the dipping
of white linen in spring water, the same thing as covering
the same white linen in a purple dye.   Every Patrist that
ever lived would reject, at a word, the notion, that a dipping
into water was, or was of the essence of, Christian baptism.
Use it in whatever form they may, they do universally and
always use it *as the means*, very generally in the faith, that
it is filled with the influence of the Holy Ghost, and *so*, has
power, as a means, to baptize the soul; which soul baptism,
thoroughly changing its condition by the remission of sins,
was, in their view, Christian baptism.   Therefore they could
and did baptize, as absolutely and as literally, the dying by
sprinkling as the living by covering.   And for the same
reason, the "lobe of the ear" touched by a burning coal was
as truly a fire baptism as would have been a world wrapped
in flames.

Agency.

The essential idea in every baptism is complete change of
condition.   In every baptism there is some agency operative to effect the demanded condition and (where the agency
alone is stated) to give character to that condition.   In all
the quotations made there is a universal representation of
the Holy Spirit and fire, as agencies effecting and giving
character to the baptisms.

I will add a few more references of a similar character.

Gregory Naz. (II, 357): "There they will be baptized, $\tau\tilde\omega$
$\pi\upsilon\rho\dot\iota,\ \tau\tilde\omega\ \tau\varepsilon\lambda\varepsilon\upsilon\tau\alpha\dot\iota\omega\ \beta\alpha\pi\tau\dot\iota\sigma\mu\alpha\tau\iota$, by fire, the final baptism."   To
translate this "In fire, in the final baptism," would be
beyond all justification.

Cyril of Jerusalem (440): "The Saviour baptized the Apos-

tles, Πνεύματι Ἁγίῳ καὶ πυρί, by the Holy Ghost and by fire."
This is of the same clear character with the preceding.

Didymus (673): "He shall baptize you by the Holy Ghost
and fire. For man being an earthen vessel he needs first the
purification, ἀπὸ ὕδατος, by water, and, then, the hardening
and perfecting, νοητοῦ πυρός, of spiritual fire (for God is a
consuming fire)." The genitive, here, indicates the source
whence the baptizing power proceeds. It must be ever
borne in mind, that in the view of these writers water had
a power to baptize entirely distinct from its receptive
quality as a fluid.

Macarius Ægyptus (*Hom.*, 32): "The baptism πυρὸς καὶ
πνεύματος of fire and of Spirit purifies and cleanses the polluted mind."

(*Hom.*, 47): "But with us is the baptism ἁγίου πνεύματος καὶ
πυρός." If the dative form of this phrase, with the preposition, was local, it could not be changed for this genitive
form; but if it express agency, then it is unexceptionable.

Gregory Thaumaturgus (X, 1187): "Christ says to John,
'Baptize me who am about to baptize those who believe,
δἰ ὕδατος, καὶ πνεύματος, καὶ πυρός, *through* water, and the Spirit,
and fire, ὕδατι, *by water,* which is able to wash away the filth
of sin, Πνεύματι, *by the Spirit,* who can make the earthly
spiritual, πυρί, *by fire,* whose nature it is to burn up the
thorns of sin.'"

Here we have the genitive with διὰ interchanged with the
causal dative expressing in the strongest possible manner,
that water, fire, and the Holy Spirit, stand related to baptism as agencies.

Classical Use of the Dative for Agency.

As the varied grammatical forms, πυρὶ, πυρός, ἀπὸ πυρός, διὰ
πυρός, indifferently used by the early Christian Greek writers
to express baptism ἐν πυρὶ, show that they understood "fire"
to occupy the position of agency effecting such baptism, so,
the use of the dative without a preposition, and of the genitive with its preposition, by Classic Greek writers, vindicates
the correctness of their view.

In order that this may be made clearly apparent, I will present all the passages in which these cases appear in Classic and other writers outside of the Scriptures (together with their translations as given by Dr. Conant), where the Greek verb is uncompounded.

Libanius. A general desertion *whereby* the city would have been baptized.

Chrysostom. Baptized the soul of the poor man as *with* successive waves.

Basil. Being baptized *with* wine.

Chrysostom. Not baptized *by* the troubles of the present life.

" Baptized *by* none of the present evils.

Heliodorus. Baptized *by* the calamity.

Achilles Tat. To be baptized *with* such a multitude of evils.

" And he, baptized *by* anger.

Evenus. Baptized in Sleep, neighbor of Death.

Heliodorus. When midnight had baptized the city in sleep.

Chrysostom. Being a king and baptized *with* ten thousand cares.

Libanius. The congregation baptized in ignorance.

Isidorus. Most men, therefore, baptized in ignorance.

Clement. More senseless than stones is a man baptized in ignorance.

Chrysostom. How were we baptized in wickedness.

" Baptized *with* ten thousand sins.

Justin Mart. Baptized *with* most grievous sins.

Diodorus. They do not baptize the common people *with* taxes.

Plutarch. Baptized *with* debts amounting to fifty millions.

" The soul is baptized *by* such (labors) as are excessive.

Philo. As though the reason were baptized *by* the things overlying it.

Plotinus. Baptized either *with* diseases or *with* arts of magians.

Chrysostom. Neither to be baptized *with* poverty, nor puffed up *with* wealth.

Athenæus. Flooded *with* vehement words and baptized *with* undiluted wine.

Conon. And having baptized Alexander *with* much wine.

Proclus. The Io Bacchus baptized *with* much wantonness.

None of these baptisms are regarded by Dr. Conant (not even those in which the physical element, *Wine*, appears) as physical baptisms. In this respect they are like the baptisms under consideration = baptisms ἐν Πνεύματι, ἐν πυρὶ. I have given, I believe, all of this class mentioned by Dr. Conant in which the dative without a preposition appears. The passages in all are twenty-six. Of this number six are translated by *in;* once, "*in* wickedness;" twice, "*in* sleep;" thrice, "*in* ignorance." Twenty times the translation is *with, by.* It is most remarkable, if these writers wished to give these baptisms a *within* character, that they should have so employed the dative as to constrain so earnest an advocate for that idea to give a translation from which *withinness* is wholly eliminated. This is, confessedly, the case in twenty instances out of twenty-six. But why the other six or, rather, the other three (" wickedness," " sleep," " ignorance ") are not included, it would be hard to tell. If baptism may be "*by* care," why not *by* " sleep ?" If baptism may be "*by* calamity," why not *by* "ignorance ?" If baptism may be "*by* sin," why not *by* " wickedness ? "

The cases in which the genitive, with ὑπὸ, appears are fewer in number.

Libanius. I am one of those baptized *by* that great wave (of calamity).

Chariton. Although baptized *by* desire.

Libanius. Would be baptized *by* a slight addition.

Plutarch. We, baptized *by* worldly affairs.

Chrysostom. Should be baptized *by* the annoyances of passion.

Themistius. Whenever she observed me baptized *by* grief.

Josephus. Baptized *by* drunkenness into stupor and sleep.

Clement. Baptized *by* drunkenness into sleep.

Chrysostom. Before thou art deeply baptized *by* this intoxication.

    "   Job was neither baptized *by* poverty nor elated *by* riches.

Professor Harrison (Greek Prepositions and Cases, p. 52) says: " The genitive case has one uniform office, namely, that of defining a preceding term or statement by introducing an object or class of objects to which specifically it is to be referred for a more exact qualification of its sense. . . .

The more exact definition made by the genitive case serves to designate what particular kind or variety is intended of a thing capable of having many kinds or varieties."

And p. 468: "The proper signification of ὑπὸ is *under;* but corresponds, also, to the English *by, by means of,* introducing the person by whom an action is performed; the person 'under' whom, that is, under whose active power, anything is represented as occurring, being naturally regarded as the agent 'by' whom it is done. *E. g.,* Herod. 9, 98, ὑπὸ κήρυκος προηγόρευε, 'he proclaimed by a herald,' or 'by the agency of a herald.' The herald 'under' whom, that is under whom considered in his proper character and office, the proclamation was made, may be regarded as the agent of the proclamation. As in Xen. Cyrop., VI, 1, 35, ἐδάκρυε ὑπὸ λύπης, 'he shed tears from (under) grief,' the nature of the feeling expressed by λύπη is such, and such its obvious natural relation to δάκρυα, that, when it is said that a person 'shed tears under grief,' it is plain that grief is the moving cause of the tears; so, when it is said that 'a proclamation was made under a herald,' it is readily inferred, that the proclamation represented as made 'under' him was made 'by' him, or by his agency."

Under the principles thus laid down by this high authority, these genitives define the baptisms with which they are respectively associated, while the preposition indicates that the baptisms are effected "under" = "by means of," "by reason of" the influence or agency of its adjunct. In other words, in βαπτιζόμενον ὑπὸ τῆς ὀδύνης the nature of the baptism is defined by ὀδύνης, it is "a grief baptism;" and the cause of the baptism we find, under the guidance of the preposition, in that which gives character to the baptism = *grief.* The same is true of anger, sleep, &c.

Now, these baptisms expressed by the genitive and preposition differ in form only, not in reality, from those baptisms which are expressed by the dative without a preposition. Harrison (p. 70) says: "The dative (ablative) has other significations different from that which belongs to the dative proper, and incapable of being reconciled with it. In the second class of examples in which the ablative is employed in Greek, it may be called the instrumentalis, as marking the instrument, means, or agent by which an action is performed" (p. 78).

The long list of datives which has been given, in connection with baptisms, clearly belong to this instrumentalis class, and do, by their own proper force, declare that the baptisms are effected by the means and agencies which they represent. The truth of this is shown by Dr. Conant's translations, which, almost without exception, express agency. And it is shown by the identity of the agencies which are expressed under the two grammatical forms.

How is it possible to distinguish, beyond form, in the statements: "Baptized the soul of the poor man (by unkind acts) as by successive waves" (dative), and, "I am one baptized by that great wave (of calamity")) (gen. with prep.)? "Baptized by wantonness" (dative), and, "Baptized by desire" (gen. with prep.)? "Baptized by undiluted wine" (dative), and, "Baptized by drunkenness" (gen. with prep.)? "Baptized by much wine" (dative), and, "Baptized by intoxication" (gen. with prep.)? "Baptized by poverty" (dative), and, "Baptized by poverty" (gen. with prep.)?

If any one thinks that he can point out any essential distinction, under these varying grammatical forms, either as to the nature or cause of the baptisms, the way is open for the attempt.

But we may go farther and confidently affirm, that there are phrases in which ἐν with the dative appears, by which cause is evolved as truly and as legitimately as in phrases which exhibit the simple dative or the genitive with its preposition. And this is sustained by Classical as well as by Scriptural authority.

Harrison (p. 250) says: "'Ἐν with the ablative (locativus) case expresses that on which a thing depends, or in the power of which it lies, where in English we use such phrases as 'in the hands of,' 'in the power of.' E. g., Œdip. Tyr., 314, ἐν σοὶ ἐσμεν, 'on you we depend,' 'we are in your hands;' properly, 'we, as regards our salvation, are in you,' that is,

in the condition afforded by your personal qualities, your
ability and willingness to save. It is not intended to be
said literally that we are 'in' or 'within' you, but the person is employed for the properties belonging to him, and
that may be the ground of confidence for those seeking
safety" (p. 246). "Œdip. Col., 247, ἐν ὑμῖν ὡς θεῷ κείμεθα, 'we
depend on you, as on a god,' literally (254), 'we lie or are
placed in . . . namely, in you,' that is, 'in your power.'"

Both these passages are quite parallel with those passages
of the gospel in which the Pharisees declare that Christ is
ἐν βεελζεβοὺλ, "in his hands," "acts under his control;" and
in which Christ claims to be ἐν Πνεύματι Θεοῦ, "in the Spirit
of God," "to act under his control." And all these passages
are parallel with the passage under consideration, 'Αυτος ἐν
Πνεύματι 'Αγίῳ καὶ πυρί. As being in the condition represented
by this phraseology the Lord Jesus Christ acts in the execution of his baptism; acts in the double character of Saviour
and Judge. (See, as parallel, 2 Thess. 2: 7–9.) It is I think
evident, that under these diverse forms there is evolved the
common idea of power to effect baptism, whether the form
be βεβαπτισμένον οἰνῷ, βεβαπτισμένον εν οἰνῷ, or βεβαπτισένον ὑπὸ οἰνοῦ.
But suppose that the theory insists on "one meaning through
all Greek literature, alike in physical and in metaphorical
uses" (Conant, p. 60), and declares, that the first form represents a man "in a wine river flowing with a strong current
by which he is swept away from sobriety into the gulf of intoxication;" while the second form represents a man in a
wine pool laboring under a heavy burden by which he slowly
sinks until he rests *in* the depths of drunkenness; and the
third form represents him in a wine ocean deeply stirred by
a convivial tempest until some huge wine billow falls upon
him bearing him down *under* its power into the lowest caverns
of drunken stupor; what, after all this peculiar exegetical
wisdom, is the conclusion of the matter? Why, nothing
more or less than that, under all these forms there is a representation of the power of wine to make drunk. And so,
under all the forms, βεβαπτισμένον πυρί, πνεύματι; βεβαπτισμένον ἐν
πυρί, ἐν Πνεύματι; βεβαπτισμένον πυρος, ἀπὸ, ὑπὸ, διὰ πυρος; βεβαπτισμένον

Πνεύματος, ἀπὸ, ὑπὸ, διὰ Πνεύματος; there is nothing, more or less, than a representation of the power of fire and the Spirit to baptize = to thoroughly change the condition of their objects according to their respective characteristics. It is remarkable, that while Dr. Conant translates these cases thirty times out of thirty-six, *with, by,* yet he writes over them as a heading, "To plunge, to immerse, to whelm (as *in* ingulfing floods) *in* calamities, *in* ruin, *in* troubles, *in* cares, *in* poverty, *in* debts, *in* stupor, *in* sleep, *in* ignorance, *in* pollution, &c."

That is to say, What in the translation is made active agency to effect the baptism, is, in the heading, converted into a receiving element—an "ingulfing flood." The hard demand of theory wrote the heading. The inexorable requirement of fact made the translation. Dr. Conant the Scholar is in severe antagonism with Dr. Conant the Baptist.

The Nature of this Baptizing Power.

It being in proof, 1. That ἐν is used in the Classics, and abundantly in the New Testament, in the sense *with, by;* 2. That, in connection with persons and things in which reside power or influence, it is used to give development to such power or influence (such usage being profoundly characteristic of the New Testament, and especially revealed in the phrase ἐν Πνεύματι with its variations); 3. That the Lord Jesus Christ is, thus, represented as being "without measure" ἐν Πνεύματι Ἁγίῳ and acting under the influence consequent upon such condition in effecting the salvation of his people; 4. That he is also represented as a Judge (ἐν πυρί φλογὸς) "in flaming fire" destroying his enemies; 5. That the phrase *βαπτίζω* ἐν has no Classical usage for denoting the execution of a baptism; it is of necessary consequence in proof, That the power to baptize, under consideration, is of such a nature as may proceed from "the Holy Ghost and fire." The general character of this baptism, beyond all rational controversy, is that of purification. And this is all that could be fairly expected to be announced by the Forerunner as the baptism of the Coming One. It was not timely for him to enter into more specific characteristics. Our Lord himself was compelled, at the beginning of his ministry, to veil the profoundest characteristics of his mission; how much more, then, must he do so who is only preparing the way of the Lord.

There is, however, somewhat of specialty thrown into this Messiah baptism by the association of πυρί with Πνεύματι which claims attention.

Among various interpretations suggested are the following: 1. Literal fire. 2. The firelike tongues of Pentecost. 3. The sufferings of Christians, intense and purifying as by fire. 4. The sufferings of lost souls in eternal fire.

The first of these interpretations may be dismissed with the suggestion, that literal fire cannot purify the soul, and, as a symbol, it can have no place, for the baptism is by the Lord Jesus Christ, who does not baptize by symbol, but in reality. The second interpretation has but the semblance of a claim to a hearing. The "firelike" tongues were not fire, and therefore are out of the question, unless in the interpretation of Scripture we are at liberty to take away reality and substitute semblance. Besides, these "tongues" had nothing to do with effecting the baptism; they were but symbols, as "tongues," of the most outstanding feature of the baptism (the power of speaking in diverse languages), while their "firelike" character symbolized the glowing nature of the utterances; but the "fire" of Christ's baptism is executory of the baptism. It can only find its representative in fire most real and most intense.

The notion of Dr. Carson and friends, that "they were literally covered with the appearance(!) of wind and fire," belongs to that class of eccentricities sometimes perpetrated by the human intellect, but never witnessed by sober onlookers without commingled feelings of sadness and humiliation. The third interpretation which identifies this "fire" with the sufferings of Christians cannot be accepted, because sufferings have no essential power to purify, and if they had, could never be associated with the Holy Ghost as a joint purifying power; while without an inherent power they could not be disjoined from the Holy Ghost who alone gives efficiency to anything to purify the soul. The fourth interpretation is substantially correct, but is too limited by a restriction to " eternal fire."

A satisfactory interpretation can only be reached by a just determination of the persons represented by ὑμας. If this word is to be resolved into individual souls to each of whom is to be applied the purifying baptism " by the Holy Ghost and fire," it is difficult to separate it from theological error. Suffering disjoined from the Holy Spirit cannot purify. To say, " It is not meant to disjoin them," is met by the inquiry, Why, then, disjoin in statement what must be conjoined in interpretation? But if this pronoun represent a collective body, whom John addresses as representing the collective Jewish people, then, all difficulty is removed. This pronoun, then, becomes a threshing-floor where is massed together the wheat and the chaff, and which, as a mass, is to be purified by the fan and the fire.

John declares, that the Jewish people, as a collective body, was to be purified by the Holy Ghost and fire—by redemption and by judgment, which beginning on earth would reach into the ages of eternity. This twofold representation of the Lord Jesus Christ as a Saviour and a Judge is the representation met with everywhere in the Scripture. He is the Lamb of God and the Lion of the tribe of Judah. As the Forerunner proclaimed to the Jewish masses Christ, their baptizer by the Holy Ghost and fire, so, they who follow after Him who has come, now preach to the masses of the Gentiles that same Christ as their baptizing Redeemer and Judge. " He that believeth shall be saved by Him who baptizes ἐν Πνεύματι ‘Αγίῳ; he that believeth not shall be damned by Him who baptizes ἐν πυρὶ." This baptism, then, in the simplest language, denotes the purification of the Jewish people (and so, also, of all others) by the twofold operation of mercy and judgment.

What a dipping has to do with this baptism, they who have a more fruitful imagination than myself may be able to determine. We, rejecting the theory " of a definite act," behold in this twain-one baptism, as on every page of the New Testament, the majestic moving of the Holy Ghost, as a Divine Agent, among the souls of men, baptizing the chosen ones by the sprinkling of the precious blood of atonement, while in the background there are the lurid gleamings of those fires by which the righteous Judge of all will finally baptize the impenitent. The purging of our world from sin is effected only by the conjoint baptism " of the Holy Ghost and of fire."

THE PERSONAL BAPTISM OF JOHN.

MATTHEW 3 : 14.

" I have need to be baptized of thee, and comest thou to me? "

" Ἐγω χρείαν ἔχω ὑπὸ σοῦ βαπτισθῆναι, καὶ σὺ ἔρχη πρὸς μέ; "

Illustrative of John's Knowledge of the Word.

It is important to show that John was thoroughly acquainted with this Greek word and did familiarly use it in other than its primary and physical applications.

Does John, here, use βαπτίζω in its primary sense and with a physical application? A negative answer must be given to this question.

I am not aware that any friend of the theory has ever suggested the idea that John expressed his sense of a "need" for being *dipped into the Jordan* by the Saviour. Many of this class sadly err as to the mode, and nature, and power of water baptism; but John does not belong to them. Roger Williams and others who have, at different times and in different parts of the world, entertained the idea that a covering of the body with water was essential to baptism, have secured this end for themselves either by walking into the water " to a convenient depth " and dipping the remainder of the body. themselves, or by getting some one else to do it for them.

There is no account of John's thus baptizing himself, nor

can he be understood as, now, asking the Saviour to do it for him. He cannot be so understood, because John knew that for one person to baptize another in water must, by the simple force of its terms, destroy life; and because he knew that water baptism was but a symbol baptism, and that it was not the office of the Lord Jesus Christ to deal with symbols, but to work out and to give the realities. This he had taught when he said, " He shall baptize by the Holy Ghost and fire." This was a real not a symbol baptism. It was this baptism of which John feels his " need." He had been baptized in infancy, " filled with the Holy Ghost" from his birth-hour; but baptism by the Holy Ghost is manifold in its nature, and John amid the responsibilities of his public ministry may feel the need of a special baptism; or his language may be understood as declarative of his profound sense of dependence for all fitness for his work, whether received in the past or to be received in the future, on his divine Lord.

John did not feel any " need" for water baptism for himself as God's minister. And had Roger Williams and others, who inaugurated a momentary covering of the body with water, been called of God to this work, they would have understood that they who are called of God to such service do not need to receive the rite at the hand of themselves or of others, any more than John or Peter.

But this baptism desired by John for his own spirit, by the Holy Spirit, gives a sore test as to the merits of the doctrine—Every baptism, not physical, is still to be understood as a " plunging in ingulfing floods." In what " ingulfing floods" are we to picture John, as plunged, in receiving baptism by the Holy Ghost? The human intellect will not only bear, but will, most strangely, load itself with the most unbearable burdens.

John could not have desired water baptism under any idea of spiritual power being attached to it. If he had believed that the mere administration of the rite washed away sin from the soul, he would have welcomed and not driven away the Pharisee and the Sadducee in all their unrepented sins.

Dr. Conant gives as a reason for expunging " baptize"

from the English Bible, that it fosters "the idea in many minds of an inherent virtue in the rite."

I am afraid that the getting rid of this word from our Bibles will not suffice for getting rid of such error from many minds. There are "many minds" which have substituted, very effectually, a dipping for a baptism, who, notwithstanding, nay, who thereby have become entangled in the notion of "an inherent virtue in the rite."

This statement will be made sufficiently plain by the following extracts from a tract placed in the hands of a member of my congregation, and just now handed to me while visiting in her sick-room.

"Baptism."

"1. The word Baptism is Greek and signifies a dipping.

"2. There is but one Baptism, for Paul so says, Eph. 4 : 5.

"3. That one Baptism is in *water;* so says Peter, Acts 10 : 47.

"4. This one Baptism in water, is a *burial.* Rom. 6 : 4; Colos. 2 : 12.

"5. A man is not in Christ before he is baptized, for we are plainly taught that we must be baptized INTO HIM. Galat. 3 : 27.

"6. Baptism is for the *remission of sins* that are past. Acts 2 : 38.

"7. Baptism like all God's commands is essential to salvation. 1 Pet. 3 : 21."

The italics and capitals are all as they stand in the tract. These extracts speak for themselves. It is very far from my purpose to controvert them. They are all false in the sense intended, and yet all susceptible of a specious vindication from Scripture by verbal and isolated quotations. It is evident, that the "remission of sins by water dipping" is just as easy of proof, by these theologians, as is the "dipping" and the "burial." And the proof for the latter is worth just as much as is the proof for the former; no more. Dr. Conant will see that the substitution of "dipping" for baptism will not free "many minds from the idea that there is inherent virtue in the rite."

I only add, that the forefront announcement, "The word Baptism is Greek and signifies a *dipping,*" is a statement which has been flung in the face of the Christian world, as absolute truth, for more than a hundred years, but which its friends are now as loth to whisper in the chamber as they once were zealous to proclaim it on the housetops. Yet, strange to say, while most anxious to get rid of it, they are just as anxious to keep it. They, therefore, resort to a new mode of spelling. And old " dipping" is made to do valiant service under the new spelling i m m e r s i o n!

If John the Baptist had been such a Baptist as these Baptists, then, most assuredly, he would have besought at the hands of the Lord a dipping into water in order to secure, " in the only way," union " into Christ," " the remission of sins," and " the salvation" of his soul. But such is not the " need" which he expressed. He longs to be baptized by one who is clothed with all the influence and power of the Holy Ghost, to be brought under the full influence and assimilating power of this Divine Agent. But in such baptism a dipping or a covering, in fact, is impossible. If it should be said, " No claim is made for either of these things in fact, but only in imagination," then we ask, Of what use to John was a mere dipping or covering? If, again, it should be replied, " It is not a mere dipping or covering that is contemplated, but the effects consequent upon a dipping into or covering by the Holy Ghost," then, again, we reply with Dr. Carson, " There is a radical difference between the act of dipping or covering and the effects consequent upon such acts." If it is the effect, and not the act, which is contemplated by the word, then the word has undergone an essential change of meaning, in which case the demand upon the imagination to conceive of the act as done is lawless, and, if it were possible, is worthless, and must be rejected as rubbish, in order that we may reach what is beyond, and is the truth in view, namely, effect. There is no such roundabout and essentially valueless statement made by John. He declares his " need" of being baptized, brought under the purifying power of the Holy Ghost, by one whose character as " Mightier than I" is displayed by the gift of such divine influence. John knew the meaning of βαπτίζω.

In full harmony with this view we have the following comment on the passage by Hippolytus (X, 856), "Βάπτισον με τῷ πυρὶ τῆς θεότητος—Baptize me by the fire of the divine nature; why dost thou desire the water? Φώτισόν τῷ Πνεύματι. Illumine me by the Holy Spirit; why dost thou wait on the creature?" Can this use of the simple dative be rationally translated, "Dip me in, cover me for a moment in the fire of the divine nature?" Must we also translate, "Illumine me in the Holy Ghost?" In the petition for "illumination" there is no request for "a definite act" to be performed, but for a condition to be effected; and in like manner, in the petition "Baptize me" there is no request for the performance of "a definite act," but for a condition of purification to be effected. "The fire of the divine nature" is not a receiving element within which an act is to be performed, or in which a covering is to take place, but it is an agency by which a change of condition is to be accomplished. And, in like manner, "the Holy Ghost" is not a person, or place, or sphere within which "illumination" is to take place, but Light by which John was to be enlightened. In every aspect in which we can look at the subject the theory breaks down.

PATRISTIC VIEW OF THE ACCOMPLISHMENT OF THIS BAPTISM.

"'Εβαπτίσθη 'Ιωάννης τὴν χεῖρα ἐπιθεὶς ἐπὶ τὴν θείαν τοῦ δεσπότου κορυφήν, καὶ τῷ ἰδίῳ αἵματι."

"John was baptized by putting his hand upon the divine head of his Master, and by his own blood."—*John of Damascus*, I, 261, Paris (see Beecher, 194).

A passage like this takes hold of the pillars of the theory, as with the strong arms of Manoah's son, and shakes it down into hopeless ruin.

John was baptized by touching the head of his Lord.
Where was the dipping or covering? "Where? why,
plainly enough in the descending and ascending of John's
hand there was a dipping, and, if he kept his hand on 'long
enough,' virtue could flow along it until John should be
covered by it. Can anything be plainer?" No, nothing;
the excellent virtue of the theory could not be made plainer.
And yet it is somewhat remarkable, that such plain passages
are never adduced by the theory to illustrate and enforce its
claims. In this respect it does not follow in the footsteps
of the old Greeks. They did not hesitate, very freely and
very frequently, to speak of baptism as effected by *the touch
of the hand*. In witness of this take the following:

Acti Sancti Thomæ.—"*Καὶ ἐπιθεὶς ἐπ' αὐτῇ τὴν χεῖρα αὐτοῦ ἐσφράγισεν
αὐτὴν εἰς ὄνομα πατρὸς καὶ υἱου καὶ ἁγίου πνεύματος.*" "And putting
his hand upon her he sealed her into the name of the Father,
and of the Son, and of the Holy Ghost. And many others were
sealed with her. But the Apostle ordered his deacon to spread
a table"—for the administration of the Lord's Supper, as common after baptism.

As to the use of "seal" and "sealing," for "baptism"
and "baptizing," all will admit the correctness of the statement made in a note by the Editor: "Antiquissima enim
est atque frequentissima illa baptismi et rituum baptismalium
appellatio apud ecclesiæ catholicæ doctores, Such appellation
is a most ancient and most frequent designation of baptism
and the rites of baptism among the teachers of the Catholic
church." A fuller form is sometimes used—"sealed by
baptism." This would naturally take an abbreviated form
as above.

This passage presents precisely the same form of expression, as to the manner in which baptism was effected, as in
the case of John "touching the divine head of his Lord with
his hand."

Firmilian.—"Paulus eos qui ab Joanne baptizati fuerant, pri-
usquam missus Spiritus sanctus a Domino, baptizavit denuo
spiritali Baptismo et sic eis manum imposuit ut acciperent

Spiritum sanctum; Paul baptized those who had been baptized by John (before the Holy Spirit had been sent by the Lord) again, by Spiritual Baptism, and put his hand upon them that they might receive the Holy Ghost."

Is this "baptism by the hand" another kind of immersion to be expounded after the model of that "immersion in a house full of sound like wind?"

Anonymi Liber.—This anonymous writer, whose work on "Re-baptism" is contained in the third volume of Tertullian, after stating that all the disciples were baptized, having been baptized by water, were baptized again after the resurrection, by the Holy Spirit, says, that others also may be baptized again, "with Spiritual baptism, that is by the imposition of hands and conferring the Holy Ghost—Baptismate spiritali, id est manus impositione episcopi et Spiritus sancti subministratione" (1195).

It is unnecessary to multiply quotations. It is beyond dispute, that the placing of the hand upon the head was competent to effect spiritual baptism. There is a parallel and complementary passage, however, which is not without interest, and I give it.

Hippolytus.—Ἐκλινεν τὴν κεφαλὴν ἀυτοῦ βαπτισθῆναι ὑπὸ Ἰωάννου (X, 856). "He bowed his head to be baptized by John."

It is clear from these passages that in the days of their writers baptism was administered by the hand of the baptizer being placed upon the head of the baptized person. If it should be said, that it was put upon the head to press it down into the water, then, 1. We encounter the assertion of Dr. Carson, that "to press down" is not to baptize. 2. To baptize by pressing down the head is not the baptism practiced under the theory. 3. This baptism by placing the hand upon the head was practiced in unnumbered cases when there was no water present, more or less, into which to press down the head.

No solution of these hand baptisms can be given without an overthrow of the theory.

John wished to be baptized in that only way in which his
Lord baptized—by the Holy Ghost. It was, indeed, true
that he had been baptized in infancy (Luke 1 : 15); but that
baptism which had conferred upon him "the Spirit and
power of Elias" might now be magnified by the bestowal
of a double measure of the spirit of the ascended prophet.
And while John's word was apparently not met, yet it was
really granted (if we may trust to John of Damascus), without a dipping, by his obediently laying his hand upon the
head of his divine Master. A strange baptism for the theory.

THE BAPTISM OF JOHN BY HIS BLOOD.

'Εβαπτίσθη 'Ιωάννης . . . . . καὶ τῷ ἰδίῳ ἅιματι.

"John was baptized, also, by his own blood."

The utter impossibility of dipping John into his own blood
or of covering him in it, reminds us of that analogous case
of impossibility in the dipping of the lake in the blood of a
frog. Dr. Carson declared such a conception "monstrous,"
and a piece of extravagance beyond the bounds of all rational rhetoric. He unhesitatingly declared, that the passage ἐβάπτετο δ' ἅιματι λίμνη was, of itself, sufficient to establish
a secondary meaning for βάπτω, and to prove, that the lake
was not "dipped in blood," as Gale affirmed to be the literal
statement, but was "DYED by blood." If there is any value
in the reasoning on this case (and all Baptists now accept
it), then, by parity of reasoning, it is monstrous and intolerable rhetoric to dip or cover John in his own blood; and
ἐβαπτίσθη 'Ιωάννης τῷ ἰδίῳ ἅιματι, is "of itself sufficient to establish a secondary meaning for" βαπτίζω, "and to prove, that
John was not dipped or covered in his own blood, but was"
PURIFIED "by his own blood."

The phraseology in which this blood baptism is expressed
by Patristic writers is instructive and confirmatory of this
conclusion.

Patristic Blood Baptism.

Gregory Nazianzen.—Ἤδει γὰρ τῷ μαρτυρίῳ βαπτισθησόμενος. "I have need to be baptized by thee: Add this, and for thee. For he knew that he would be baptized by martyrdom" (352).

How can a dipping or a covering be secured within "martyrdom?" "And what says Jesus? 'Suffer it to be so now.' For he knew that after a little while" (αὐτὸς βαπτίσων Βαπτιστήν) "he would baptize the Baptist." This does not say, that "he would dip the Dipper," or "cover the Coverer," or "put in and take out Him who was the Putter in and Taker out," but (as the language of Gregory Nazianzen can only mean, as has been incontestably proved in Judaic Baptism), "He would purify the Purifier." And this is in perfect harmony with the Patristic doctrine as to the eminently purifying character of martyrdom.

Cyril of Jerusalem.—Ὅι μὲν ἐν καιροῖς εἰρήνης ἐν ὕδατι βαπτισθῶσιν, ὅι δὲ ἐν καιροῖς διωγμῶν ἐν οἰκείοις αἵμασι βαπτισθῶσι. "He that does not receive baptism, has not salvation, except martyrs, only, who receive the kingdom without water. For the Saviour redeeming the world by the cross, and wounded in his side, shed forth water and blood; that some in times of peace, might be baptized with water, and others, in times of persecution, might be baptized with their own blood. For the Saviour calls martyrdom baptism, saying, 'Can ye drink of the cup that I drink of, and be baptized with the baptism that I am baptized with?'" (440.)

Does the Saviour call "martyrdom" a dipping, a covering over, an immersion? The theory is driven, at every turn, into the greatest possible extravagance. Again, the theory insists upon it that Cyril by ἐν καιροῖς εἰρήνης ἐν ὕδατι βαπτισθῶσιν, affirms, clearly and literally, that in times of peace Christians must be "momentarily *covered over in* water;" well, does Cyril also, by ἐν καιροῖς διωγμῶν ἐν οἰκείος αἵμασι βαπτισθῶσι, affirm, clearly and literally, that in times of persecution Christians "must be momentarily *covered over in* their own blood?"

"No, he does not say that they must be, literally, covered over in their own blood." He does not say so? Why? Does he not use identically the same grammatical forms? Does he not use identically the same words? Is not blood, and water, equally a physical element? Have they not both, equally, "covering over" power? Are they not both traced to the same fountain head—the Saviour's wounded side? "This is all true, and exegetical law would seem to require that both baptisms should receive a like interpretation, but our theory will not allow of this; so, we interpret the first literally, and make the other a kind of figure by which blood is changed into suffering, and out of this suffering we construct a 'covering' which we throw over the weakness of our theory." Well, as this "weakness" seems to be sufficiently obvious to engage attention and to elicit confession, it would be ungenerous to press it farther. We make our interpretation in harmony with exegetical law, historical fact, and the theological sentiment of the writer, and say, that neither water nor blood are spoken of as receptive elements, but as purifying agencies, and that in peace Christians "must be *purified* BY WATER, and in persecution they must be *purified* BY BLOOD." And if there be any "weakness" in this interpretation we will not "cover it over," but welcome the sharp arrow to test the joints of the harness. The interpretation of the use of βαπτίζω by Cyril and his associates must not be confounded with the use of that word by New Testament writers. With sameness of grammatical usage there is, also, difference in verbal meaning.

Basil Magnus.—᾽Εν τῷ ἰδίῳ αἵματι βαπτισθέντες· καὶ οὐκ ἀθετῶν τὸ ἐν τῷ ὕδατι βάπτισμα. "There are some who in striving for piety have undergone death for Christ, in reality not in semblance, needing for salvation nothing of the water symbols, being baptized by their own blood. I say these things without disesteeming baptism by water" (IV, 132).

It is only necessary, in addition to what has been already said, to call attention to what is most evident, that blood and water are spoken of as agencies.

Didymus Alexandrinus.—Τῷ ἰδίῳ ἀπολουσάμενοι ἅιματι, οὕτως ὑπὸ τοῦ ἁγίου Πνεύματος τοῦ Θεοῦ ἐζωοποιήθησαν. "But without being born again by baptism, through the Spirit of God, and sealed by sanctification, and made his temple, no one can partake of the heavenly blessings, although his life should be found, in other respects, blameless. However they who have attained martyrdom before baptism, being cleansed by their own blood, are thus made to live by the Spirit of God" (IV, 132).

In this passage ἀπολουω is substituted for βαπτίζω. The mere interchange of words cannot prove sameness of meaning. But it is in proof, that βαπτίζω was used by these early Christian writers in the sense *to purify*. Its interchange, therefore, in the same phrase, with a word which signifies, confessedly, to purify, is proof that such is its meaning in such phrase.

The agency of blood and of water is again brought to view as that through which the Spirit of God regenerates the soul, cleanses it from sin, and fits it for heaven. We are not, now, to adjudicate on their theology, but their usage of Greek words.

Origen.—"Exeamus loti sanguine nostro. Baptisma enim sanguinis solum est quod nos puriores reddat, quam aquæ baptismus redidit." "That we may die washed by our own blood. For it is the baptism of blood, only, which makes us purer than the baptism of water made us" (II, 980).

With some change of phraseology the purifying agency of blood and water is, if possible, brought out with increased clearness. He adds, "This is not a sentiment of my own, but is declared by the Scriptures, the Lord saying to his disciples, 'I have a baptism to be baptized with which ye know not. And how am I straitened until it be accomplished.' You see, therefore, that he called the shedding of his blood baptism." The "shedding of blood" could not be called a *dipping*, nor a *covering* over. It was called *purification*, and rightly, as that in which and by which purification was to be found. Thus, Nehemiah (Jud. Bapt., 345) called "the thick water" found in the pit, with which the altar was purified, καθαρισμός "purification." This affords additional and conclusive evidence for the secondary meaning of this Greek word as used by Patristic writers.

Cyprian.—"Ut quis coram hominibus Christum confiteatur, et sanguine suo baptizetur? . . . Quod si hæretico nec Baptisma publicæ confessionis et sanguinis proficere ad salutem potest" . . . (1123).

"Baptizentur gloriosissimo et maximo sanguinis Baptismo." ...

"Sanguine autem suo baptizatos et passione" (1124).

"Can the power of Baptism (vis Baptismi) be greater or better than Confession, than Martyrdom, when one confesses Christ before men and is baptized by his own blood?"

"But if the Baptism of public confession and of blood cannot profit a heretic for salvation, because salvation is not out of the church, how much more shall it profit him nothing, if infected by the contagion of impure water (tinctus adulteræ aquæ contagione) in the covert and den of robbers."

"They who are baptized by that most glorious and chiefest baptism of blood. The Lord declares in the Gospel, that those baptized by his blood and passion are sanctified and attain the grace of the divine promise, when he speaks to the thief, believing and trusting in the very passion, and promises that he shall be with him in Paradise."

In this extract we have the "baptism of confession" as well as of blood. How will the theory extract a dipping or a covering over out of this baptism?

We have, also, the VIS *Baptismi*, "the POWER of Baptism," which is an express declaration that the water occupies the position of agency in Baptism, whatever may be the manner of its use. We are, also, told that it is "the power" in Confession, in Martyrdom, which makes them Baptisms. In other words, it is the *influence* which belongs to the Water, to the Confession, to the Martyrdom, which affects and changes the condition of the soul—baptizing it. Such a mode of speech finds nothing in the theory which is responsive to it. The view which we have presented as the meaning of the word could hardly be more distinctly stated.

And we have, also, *tingo* ("tinctus") used in its secondary meaning *to stain, to infect*, in which sense it is used not un-frequently in connection with baptism in a good or bad sense. The act (*dip*) is lost, and *effect* (*influence*) only remains.

Jerome.—"Tu me in aqua baptizas, ut ego te baptizem pro me in sanguine tuo." " 'Suffer it to be so now,' says the Lord Jesus, I have also another baptism with which I must be baptized. Thou dost baptize me with water, that I may baptize thee, for myself, with thy blood" (VII, 50).

The crucifixion on Calvary, and the beheading of John in prison are here declared to be blood baptisms. To convert such statements into "ingulfing floods" is a confession that the facts, as they stand, are unmanageable.

This identification, by early Christian writers, of the baptism desired by John with his death as a baptism by blood, shows, most unmistakably, that a fluid element may be present in baptism and have the "vis baptismi," the power of baptizing, without dipping or covering over.

The correctness of this position is illustrated by many baptisms. *Wine is a fluid* which, by its nature, allows of a dipping into it; but the drunkard is baptized by wine with-out being dipped into it. *Tears are a fluid* which, by their nature, allow of a dipping into them; but the penitent bap-tized by tears is not dipped into them. *Ashes-water is a fluid* which, by its nature, allows of a dipping into it; but the de-filed Israelite was baptized by it without being dipped into it. *Blood is a fluid* which, by its nature, allows of a dipping into it; but John the Baptist "baptized by his own blood" was not dipped into it.

COROLLARY.—*The presence of a* FLUID *element in baptism is no evidence that it is there as a* RECEIVING ELEMENT INTO WHICH *some object is to be dipped.*

JOHN'S COMMISSION.

THE COMMISSION OF JOHN TO BAPTIZE.

'Αλλ' ὁ πέμψας με βαπτίζειν ἐν ὕδατι.

" But he that sent me to baptize with water."—*John* 1 : 33.

This language is a reference, in brief, by John, to his divine commission to employ a ritual ordinance in the furtherance of his ministry.

The object of this rite and of the entire ministry of John, was, as he himself declares (vv. 29–31): " That the Lamb of God, which taketh away the sin of the world, should be made manifest to Israel, *therefore* am I come baptizing with water." We have, then, divine authority for the object and nature of the rite. The object of the rite was to direct the attention of the people, not only by words, but by the additional help of a visible symbol, to the Lamb of God as in himself most pure, as vindicating the divine purity by his work, and as demanding and securing purification in all who should share in the fruits of that work. The rite was designed by the use of symbol water to set forth PURIFICATION FROM SIN as the great and vital thought connected with and effected by the coming LAMB OF GOD.

The nature of the rite, as to its own inherent power to purify or otherwise, we are also clearly taught. Any power in itself to purify is disclaimed. That power is expressly and exclusively assigned to the Lamb of God. The purification by the Lamb of God is declared to be a spiritual purification—" Which taketh away the sin of the world." " To make manifest " this purification, not to effect it, nor to

effect any other, but *to make manifest* that purification which
was to be effected by the Lamb of God, "I come baptizing
with water." The nature of this ordinance, therefore, was
neither that of the Jew effectively purifying ceremonially,
nor of the Patrist effectively purifying spiritually, but such
as pertains to simple water which by its nature cleanses from
physical defilement, and so by its nature becomes, in its sim-
plicity, a fit symbol for absolute purification.

The rite, then, is not in itself a purifying rite, but "makes
manifest" a purification which is to proceed from another
source. Physical purification is a reality. Spiritual purification is a reality. Ceremonial purification is a reality.
Symbol purification is not a reality. It is but the falling of
a shadow from the purification symbolized. But it is not,
therefore, without value. It was but a shadow which rested
on the tents of Israel; but that shadow came from a cloud
in which Jehovah dwelt. There was a blessing in "the
shadow." The symbol rite of John was but a shadow; but
it was a shadow forecasted by the coming "Lamb of God
that taketh away the sin of the world," and so "made him
manifest." There was a blessing in the symbol shadow.

There are some who are by no means satisfied with this
divine teaching as to the nature and design of John's baptism; but who confidently affirm, that the essence of the rite
centres in the manner in which the water is used. According to this doctrine the Lamb of God will not "be made
manifest" except the water be used in one definite mode.
And the nature of water as purifying is of so little value,
and is so mere an accident, that the rite has no existence,
without a certain mode of use.

If this be true, then, surely it is one of the most marvellous things ever attributed to our most holy religion.

But what is that mode of act which works with such
magical power as to swallow up all other good?

For more than a hundred years it has been said, The act
is most definite in its form, and is absolutely expressed by
to dip. Recently, this has been found to be a mistake, and
it is corrected thus: "It is of no consequence what is the

form of the act, so that the whole body is put in and taken out of the water." More recently still, there has been this amendment: " Put the body under the water in any way; but there being no provision in the command for taking it out, we must, for this, trust to the God of nature and muscular effort."

Whether this remarkable interpretation of a divine command (attained only through some centuries of embarrassment and obscurity) be correct or not, we will continue to inquire by examining the language in which John refers to his divine commission.

Water.

1. 'Υδατι. The first question to be determined is this: Does the presence of water in John's baptism, thereby, show that the baptism must be physical, and the water must be used as and for a receptive element, and not as a symbol?

This question is answered most absolutely, by facts, in the negative. Such facts have already been referred to.

Wine is a fluid; and we have seen it to be present in many baptisms without being treated as a receptive element. It was there as an agency producing a baptism in which receptivity had no existence. Wine can be used in baptism as a receptacle, but the baptism is deadly whether the experiment be tried on the live chicken of the Roman poet, or on the princely Duke of Clarence. Baptism *in* wine drowns; baptism *by* wine makes drunk.

Blood is a fluid; and we have met with it in many baptisms, but not as a receptive element. It was there, if the Greek language is capable of expressing anything by case or preposition, as the agency effecting a baptism in which there was no receptacle, much less was the blood such a receptacle.

Tears are a fluid; and we encounter them abundantly in baptisms; but never are men or women dipped into them, covered over temporarily in them by some indefinite act, or covered over in them and left to their own resources to get out. They are not a receptacle.

Water is a fluid; and as such was present in the baptism of Carmel's altar, but the altar was neither dipped into it, nor covered over by it in any way. It was not a receptacle.

It is, then, a point settled beyond disturbance, that the simple presence of water, or of any other fluid, in baptism gives no evidence whatever to prove, or to allow the affirmation, that the baptism must be *in* such fluid. It may be grievous to the theory to acknowledge this; but acknowledged or unacknowledged, it is, still, the truth. There is a "power" in wine, blood, tears, water (ceremonial of the Jew, symbol of John), to baptize apart from receptivity.

'Ἐν. Does the presence of ἐν in the record of a baptism, having as its adjunct a fluid element, make a physical baptism necessary, and require that the baptized object shall be placed within such fluid element?

This question, also, must be answered in the negative. We have met with many baptisms ἐν αἵματι, in none of which was the baptism physical, nor was the baptized object placed within the blood. The martyr who laid down his life for the love of Christ found in his shed blood a "vis baptismi" by which his soul was (as supposed) baptized and fitted for heaven. It follows, therefore, that ἐν ὕδατι cannot, by reason simply of its fluid character and preposition, make the baptism with which it may be connected a physical rather than a symbol baptism, nor make the water to fill the part of a receptive element. This conclusion is farther established by the use, in these same baptisms, of αἵματι and ὕδατι, αἵματος and ὕδατος, ἀπὸ αἵματος and ἀπὸ ὕδατος, δι' αἵματος and δι' ὕδατος, in which cases receptivity is out of the question, and "power" is expressed.

Βαπτίζω. Does the presence of βαπτίζω necessitate a physical baptism and require withinness to be present as its characteristic feature? No. In "baptizat quæ non potuerunt purificatione sancti Spiritus purgari," the transferred Greek word appears without a physical baptism and without any real or conceivable withinness. But if the verb be followed by a preposition, βαπτίζω ἐν, how then? Well, πλοῖον βαπτιζόμενον ἐν γαλήνῃ (C. B., 278) meets the condition; and yet the preposition and its adjunct, immediately sequent to the verb, have no more to do with the form of the baptism, or with being a receptacle within which the baptism takes place, than if they were in the moon.

But if such phraseology and a fluid element are conjoined, must not the baptism be physical and with a covering? It must not be either. We have a score of times just such phraseology = βαπτιζόμενον ἐν αἵματι; and there is neither physical baptism nor covering. And there may be a βαπτιζόμενον ἐν ὕδατι in which there will be just as little appearance of either. Water is just as capable of being used for religious purposes in other character than that of a receptive element, as is blood. Ἐν ὕδατι, with βαπτίζω, may denote merely a circumstance belonging to the baptism, a symbol with "power" to show the purifying nature of a baptism εἰς μετάνοιαν, as ἐν τῷ πλῷ βαπτίσαι (C. B., p. 266) denotes a circumstance as to the period during which the baptism (drowning) took place, which baptism was ἐν τῷ πλῷ, during the voyage as to the time, and εἰς θάλασσαν into the sea as the enveloping element.

In the phrase βαπτίζειν ἐν ὕδατι it is not only possible, in Classic Greek, that the preposition and noun may indicate the position of the baptizer and not of the baptized object, but it is possible that they should indicate the means by which, and not the element in which, the baptism took place. In Hellenistic Greek this possibility becomes a probability; and when this phrase occurs in the administration of a religious ordinance in the narration of which one writer (Matthew) of Hebrew training uses ἐν ὕδατι, and another (Luke) of Greek culture, uses the simple ὕδατι, a lower probability rises into a violent probability; and when, in addition to this, other writers, native-born Greeks of the highest culture, describe the same transaction, indifferently, by ἐν ὕδατι, ὕδατι, ὕδατος, ἀπὸ ὕδατος, ἐξ ὕδατος, δι' ὕδατος, probability passes into moral certainty. If this moral certainty requires any addition to make it absolute, it could only be by express statement declaring that *the* BAPTISM was *into another wholly different element*, and not into water; and this absolute proof we shall find is not lacking.

Proof of the *agency* of water in baptism is found in another form. Augustin (IX, 176) says, " Sacramentum, quod ministrorum opere corporaliter adhibetur, sed *per hoc* Deus hominis consecrationem spiritualiter operatur." The physical element is here declared through preposition and case ("per hoc") in the strongest possible manner to be the agency by which a spiritual change of condition is effected. Also (276): "Baptizandum esse professus est iterum, non jam aqua, nec spiritu, sed sanguinis baptismo, cruce passionis." Here, water, Spirit, blood, and cross are declared to be agencies by which, and not elements in which, baptism takes place. If martyrs may be baptized by blood and not in blood, as a symbol of consecration unto death; and if Christ may be baptized by his cross and not in his cross, as the symbol of woe, and shame, and death; then, his people may be baptized by water and not in water, as the symbol of that purification received through his blood.

Again (276): " Similes Christo martyres facitis, quos post aquam vere baptismatis sanguis baptista perfundit." This passage teaches, 1. That blood is the agency in baptism. 2. That "baptista" has a secondary meaning. It is as impossible for "sanguis baptista" to denote *dipping* blood, *covering over* blood, as it is impossible that "Baptista Magnus" (Jud. Bapt., 223) can mean "Great Dipper," when baptism is by "waving a flaming sword." 3. It expressly declares, that the baptism was not *in* the blood, or in anything else, whether of fact, or of imagination, because it declares the manner in which the blood was applied (*perfunditur*), by sprinkling or affusion. Baptism was effected by water, almost daily, applied in the same way—" non desunt qui prope quotidie baptizentur aegri" (Hilary, 1 Tim. 3 : 12, 13; Beecher, 175). The sick were baptized in the same way (*perfusione*), by the sprinkling or affusion of water, and not by dipping in, or covering over in water. The Emperor Constantius (ἀποθνήσκων ἐδοξε βαπτίζεσθαι) "when dying wished to be baptized." Dying men are baptized by water, not in water. In this direction, also, we have absolute proof that water was used as an agency in baptism.

Again : It is in proof, that the Classics did not use the formula βαπτίζειν ἐν to express the execution of a baptism, the causing of an object to pass out of one condition into another; neither is such phraseology suitable to express any such conception. It is an incongruous combination of movement and of rest. The preposition with the active form of the verb could, fitly, be employed by Hellenistic writers to express the agency in baptism. The Classics with the passive form used this preposition to denote the condition in which the baptized object was at rest—βεβαπτισμένην ἐν τῷ βάθει τοῦ σώματος —ἐν τῷ σώματι βεβαπτισμένη (Class. Bapt., 254). If it be insisted upon, that in John's commission βαπτίζειν ἐν ὕδατι refers to the execution of a physical baptism, the element of the baptism being water, and the verb used in its primary, literal sense, then, it is as certain as that Greek is Greek, that John was commissioned to drown every person whom he baptized. Not only does not the Greek word ever take out of the condition in which it once places its object, and not only is this Greek word employed expressly to denote the drowning of men, but, according to the interpretation of the theory, the very language of John's commission represents as the result of his baptism, his disciples as *resting within the water* in a drowned condition.

If this conclusion, from these premises, can be avoided it must be done in some other way than by making the verb take out what it puts in, for this we cannot allow, as " βαπτίζω never does take its subject out of the water" (Baptist Quart., April, 1869, 142), nor can this be done by an appeal to the " God of nature" and the baptized man's " normal muscular action" (*ibid.*), for we baptize under the God of grace, and he has made no provision for escape *from that baptism which he enjoins*, whether by the "normal muscular action" of the baptized, or in any other way.

Whether, then, we look at this Commission of John through a Classic, a Hellenistic, or a Patristic medium,

there is an imperative arrest of that interpretation which
would command John to baptize men and women *in* water.

JOHN'S COMMISSION ILLUSTRATED BY HISTORICAL ALLUSION.

Τὸ βάπτισμα 'Ιωάννου—The baptism of John, whence was it?—
Matthew 21 : 25; *Mark* 11 : 30; *Luke* 20 : 4.

Βαπτισθέντες τὸ βάπτισμα 'Ιωάννου—Being baptized with the baptism of John, the publicans justified God.—*Luke* 7 : 29.

'Απὸ τοῦ βαπτίσματος 'Ιωαννου—From the baptism of John.—
Acts 1 : 22.

Τὸ βάπτισμα 'Ιωαννου—Knowing only the baptism of John.—
Acts 18 : 25.

'Ιωαννης μὲν ἐβάπτισε βάπτισμα μετανοίας—John verily baptized
with the baptism of repentance.—*Acts* 19 : 4.

Baptisms are Distinctive.

These passages do not require any detailed discussion.
They are adduced for the purpose of showing that throughout the Scripture when "the baptism of JOHN" is spoken
of it is in a manner to indicate its possession of a distinctive
character separating it from all other baptisms.

We say, that this is the force and design of the phrase
βάπτισμα 'Ιωαννου. The character of the baptism is pointed out
by the adjunct and defining genitive. "John" the origi-
nator and preacher of the baptism stands for the peculiar
character which he gave to that baptism.

The theory says: All baptisms are alike; and John's baptism did not differ, by jot or tittle, from any other baptism,
heathen or Christian; the phrase "baptism of John" merely
points out John as a dipper in, or coverer over in, water,
just as "baptism of Moses" would represent Moses in the
same aspect, and baptism of Bacchus would make Bacchus
a dipper in, or coverer over in, water, or wine, or some
equivalent "ingulfing flood;" baptism, by whomsoever or

by whatsoever effected, is one and the same thing, "a dipping" (Carson), "a momentary covering" (Fuller), "a definite act" (Conant), "a specific act" (Alex. Campbell), "a plunge" (Arnold-Stourdza).

Suppose that it should be granted, that in all baptisms an elementary thought, more or less attenuated, might be traceable, would that prove or begin to justify the conclusion, that all baptisms are alike? What would be thought of the man who should say—"A related elementary thought may be traced through every usage of the word *condition*, therefore, all conditions are one and the same?"

Is it true, that because an abstract idea can be attached to a word, therefore nothing but such abstract idea can enter into it when used in concrete relations? Was the "condition" of Israel under Pharaoh, one and the same with the "condition" of Israel under David? Is a "condition of bondage" the same as a "condition of freedom?" "a condition of woe" the same as "a condition of joy?" "a condition of death" the same as "a condition of life?" Such questions answer themselves. Baptism has just the same unity, and just the same diversity, as has "condition." Baptism is condition limited to that phase characterized by controlling assimilative influence, the specific nature of which is determined by adjunct terms.

In support of this position I would appeal to the statements of Ambrose, "Baptisma non est unum;" "Multa sunt genera baptismatum;" and to the endlessly varied specific baptisms scattered through Classic writings. Among these Classic baptisms are found: 1. Baptism of wine, a drunken condition. 2. Baptism of war, a desolated condition. 3. Baptism of care, an anxious condition. 4. Baptism of trouble, a harassed condition. 5. Baptism of passion, an excited condition. 6. Baptism of grief, a sorrowful condition. 7. Baptism of ignorance, an unenlightened condition. 8. Baptism of wickedness, a depraved condition. 9. Baptism of taxes, an oppressed condition. 10. Baptism of debts, a bankrupt condition. 11. Baptism of mental labor, an imbecile condition. 12. Baptism of questions, a

bewildered condition. 13. Baptism of disease, a sickly condition. 14. Baptism of Magian arts, a superstitious condition. 15. Baptism of poverty, an impoverished condition.
16. Baptism of a drug, a somnolent condition. 17. Baptism
of pleasure, a joyous condition. 18. Baptism of fright, an
alarmed condition. 19. Baptism of surprise, a startled condition. 20. Baptism of heifer ashes, a ceremonially pure
condition.

There is no truth in the statement—" Baptism is one, is
mode and nothing but mode; what is baptism in one case is
baptism in another case; there can be no difference in a
mode, a definite act."

Here are a score of baptisms of which no two are alike;
and in no one of which has mode, or definite act, any place
whatever. Baptism is no more one than is condition one.
Is it replied to this: " These baptisms are not physical baptisms and therefore not in point." We rejoin: 1. The assumption, that John's baptism was a dipping or covering in
water, we cannot allow. It is the point at issue. It must
be proved. 2. All physical baptisms are diversified by reason of a diverse nature in the baptized object, and a diverse
character in the enveloping medium; whence originates an
endless diversity in the condition of baptized objects.

This resultant diversity of condition among physically
baptized objects (due, 1. To the nature of the object; 2. To
the character of the influential cause; 3. To the form in
which such influence was brought to bear) gave origin to
those baptisms in which the condition of objects was changed
by controlling influences not operating in the same method
as in the case of physical baptisms. These baptisms are
characterized by the peculiarity of the influences operating
to produce them, and hence are as diversified as are the influences. The distinctive baptism which is so clearly involved in the phrase, " baptism of John," was (as we are told
in Acts 19 : 3, 4) that of repentance. In reply to the inquiry,
" Into what were ye baptized?" The reply was given,
" Into John's baptism;" on which the Apostle interprets
this language by declaring, " John verily baptized the bap-

tism of repentance." It is, then, by inspired authority that we say, "the baptism of John," and "the baptism of repentance" are equivalent expressions. It becomes, therefore, a point of the first moment to determine the true value of the phrase, "baptism of repentance."

Βάπτισμα μετανοίας.

The translation which the New Version gives of this phrase is "immersion of repentance." A note is appended to vindicate "immersion" (*in water*, of course) as the translation of βάπτισμα. This is done by an appeal to eminent names. The best appeal for the meaning of words is to the usage of the words. The usage of this word is so restricted, that there is less reason than usual for turning aside from the highest authority. The following, I believe, are facts: 1. This word is never met with in the Classics. 2. Its use originates in the Scriptures, in which it is never used with a physical defining adjunct. 3. It is never employed in Patristic writings to denote a simple physical mersion. 4. The usage of the word shows that it is not derived from the primary but secondary use of βαπτίζω, of which secondary use its own usage is a proof, and the highest proof. If βάπτισμα had originated with βαπτίζω *to merse*, it would have indicated (according to its form) the condition demanded by that word, namely, an indefinitely prolonged physical envelopment; but it has no such usage, and, therefore, can have no such origin. If it sprung out of the secondary use of this word, *to influence controllingly*, then, it would denote a condition resultant from such influence; and such, with essentially related usage, marks the entire history of the word. In such origin and usage βάπτισμα shows a perfect parallelism with the related word βάμμα. This word is not derived from that stem of βάπτω which signifies *to dip*, but from that which signifies *to dye;* and hence, it signifies not *a dip*, but *a dye*, and *a color* made by a dye.

In the passage, "'Ινα μή σε βάψω βάμμα Σαρδιανικόν, Lest I dye you a purple dye," I presume few would feel it desirable to make a new version by rendering it, "Lest I dye you a purple *dip*." Would the phrase βάμμα πορφύρης, *a dye of purple*, be improved by the translation, " a *dip* of purple?" But such translation is not more erroneous and unintelligible, than is the translation of βάπτισμα μετανοίας by "*immersion* of repentance." Βάμμα is qualified and defined by πορφύρης; and βάπτισμα, in like manner, is qualified and defined by μετανόιας.

But again: This translation is not only a philological error, but is, also, a moral impossibility in its relations. If βάπτισμα be derived from βαπτίζω *to merse*, then, it cannot rationally mean a dipping, a *temporary* covering, for there is no such thing in the verb. It might as well be said, that βάμμα means a temporary dye. There is nothing temporary in the verb or in its derivative. This is not merely true as a philological deduction, but it is true as a matter of fact shown in all the usage of the word. There is no such thing to be met with anywhere in the New Testament, where this word originates, as a dipping βάπτισμα. And to put men as demanded by the word in a condition of water baptism, would be to them certain destruction. From this there is no escape if we are governed by the force of terms; and if we are not, then, it is not a " New Version" that is needed, but a New Bible altogether.

Still farther: The translation "immersion of repentance" must be rejected as no translation. It is neither English nor Greek, nor any other language in the long list of Babel's offspring. To make it something by dashing in pieces the divine mould in which inspiration has cast this phrase, and casting it over again after a model fashioned according to the theory, we can never allow. If the dependence of βάπτισμα on μετανοίας is to be ruthlessly severed, and an unlawful union is to be established between it and *water*, so as to make an immersion *in water* (a βάπτισμα ὕδατος, of which the Word of God knows absolutely nothing), then, let such immersion be reserved for the theory itself; and when it shall have perished by such immersion, spare others from undergoing any such like experiment.

Let us take these words of the Holy Ghost just as they

stand, adding nothing to them nor taking anything from them, and, as becomes faithful expositors of the Word of God, humbly ask, What do they teach? and not, How can we alter them so as to make them teach some notion of our own?

Do these words, βάπτισμα μετανοίας, express a complete thought in themselves, and one which is in harmony with the general tenor of the Scriptures, and demanded by the particular passage in which they stand? We answer affirmatively. And in evidence now say: The proof already furnished by this Inquiry is clear and full, that βάπτισμα does and must express condition marked by controlling influence. Such a term is susceptible of being placed in relation with, and thus receiving specific coloring from, an almost indefinitely wide range of influences. In the present case it is allied with μετανοίας, the genitive form (according to the law already stated) defining the specific character of the baptism, namely, a baptism (= *a thoroughly changed condition*) *under the influence of repentance.* Now, whether this be a complete thought, whether it be in harmony with the tenor of Scripture, whether it is that which the particular passages, in which the phrase occurs, demand, and whether this be fairly deduced from the teachings of a true philology and the just interpretation of grammatical forms, I cheerfully submit to the judgment of those who are competent to decide.

It may be observed, that while the particular grammatical form in this case defining the nature of the baptism, is that of the simple genitive, the baptism may, also, be defined, as to its character, by other forms. In the early Christian writers we meet with βάπτισμα ἐν αἵματι, αἵματι, αἵματος, ἐξ αἵματος δι' αἵματος, and, with the same forms, in connection with a great variety of influences; all of which are equally capable of indicating the particular character of the baptism. Thus, Origen speaks of a baptism "through the mystery of Christ's suffering," genitive with διά; Athanasius of a "baptism through tears," genitive with διά; Eusebius of a "baptism through fire," genitive with διά; John of Damascus of a

16

"baptism through blood and martyrdom," genitive with διά; also, of a "baptism through repentance," genitive with διά; Cyril of a "baptism through faith," genitive with διά; and Justin Martyr confirms the clear usage of John of Damascus, which makes repentance the efficient agency in constituting the baptism, by the parallel phrase τὸ λοῦτρον τῆς μετανοίας, "the washing of repentance," which baptizes, cleanses, the soul from unholy affections.

Such phrases, by eminent Greek scholars, determine the meaning of βάπτισμα to be such, that it may be effected by suffering, by blood, by tears, by fire, by martyrdom, by faith, by repentance. This is beyond controversy. It has already been shown, that βάπτισμα is, also, used with the simple genitive, defining the baptism in these same relations; as also with the simple dative in its instrumental force. Such usage and such forms prove, incontestably, that βάπτισμα μετανοίας indicates neither more nor less than its own express declaration—a repentance baptism, just as βάμμα πορφύρης indicates—a purple dye. As confirmatory of this conclusion may be adduced the fact, that writers of all classes abandon the idea, that the phrases "baptism of John," "baptism of repentance," can be interpreted on a mere water basis. Thus, Dr. Halley (p. 162) says, "John had to teach a new doctrine. So closely were the baptism and the new doctrine connected, that the one term seems to be employed for the other. 'The baptism of John' (the new doctrine) 'was it from heaven or of men?' 'After the baptism' (the new doctrine) 'which John preached.' To be baptized was to be initiated as a disciple or learner of the new doctrine—the speedy coming of Christ." Professor Wilson (p. 343) says, "The Scriptures, more than once, identify the doctrine and the baptism of John."

The Christian Standard (Baptist) says, "This phrase, 'baptism of John,' is to be taken for the doctrine of this great herald of Jesus." Professor Ripley, an eminent Baptist commentator, says (Acts 18 : 25), "The baptism of John is here put for all the ministry of John the Baptist; and all the doctrine he taught." And (Acts 19 : 3), "We received the doctrine which John the Baptist taught." . . . So, Professor Hackett (Acts 18 : 25), "Knowing only the baptism of John, which differed from that of the Apostles mainly in these respects; first, that theirs recognized a Messiah who had come, and, secondly, that it was attested by the extraordinary gifts of the Spirit. Since John, however, taught that the Saviour was about to appear, and that repentance, faith in him, and holiness were necessary to salvation, Apollos, though acquainted only with his teaching, could be said, with entire truth, to be 'instructed in the way of the Lord.'"

Thus, these distinguished Baptist scholars unite in declaring, that "the baptism of John" as used in the Scriptures, sometimes at least, does not mean a dipping into water. By this we are to understand, that in some instances the separation of this phrase from water is so plain, that the fact *must* be acknowledged. Now, we ask in turn, for a single instance in which βάπτισμα stands so related to water that there *must* be a baptism in the water, and a separation cannot be made between the baptism and a covering over in the water. We say, that there is no such case in John's ministry. The statement by Professor Ripley, that "the baptism of John" is put for all the ministry of John is too broad. "The baptism of John" was the baptism which John introduced; and that baptism was *a doctrine*, to wit, thorough repentance in preparation for the Messiah, which doctrine was illustrated and enforced by a rite in which water was used as a symbol. This doctrine Apollos knew, and it being the central truth of John's preaching, could well represent "all the doctrine he taught." The distinction made by Professor Hackett between "John's baptism" and the Apostles' baptism, is a distinction as to certain accidents pertaining to those baptisms, and not as to the baptisms themselves. John's baptism had an existence independent of its relation to the coming of Christ; that coming was a mighty argument to enforce the baptism, but it did not enter into its existence. John's baptism was preached by the Apostles as well as by himself. The coming of the Messiah did not annul that baptism; it only changed the form of the motive. When he had come and accomplished the work of atonement the preacher could no longer cry, "Repent, for the kingdom of heaven is at hand;" but must say, "Repent, and be baptized every one of you in the name of Jesus Christ." "The extraordinary gifts of the Spirit" did not enter into the essence of the Apostles' baptism. Their baptism had an existence apart from "extraordinary gifts." In fact these gifts constituted another, and quite different, baptism, which might or might not be present with the special baptism of their commission. If a theorist, Professor Hackett would say, "Between John's baptism and the Apostles' baptism, considered simply as baptisms, there was not, nor could there be, any difference whatever; both were, alike, coverings over in water." But being a most learned and truly admirable commentator he offers no such interpretation.

Nor is this the representation which is given by the Scriptures. They represent everywhere *the baptism* (not some accident pertaining to it, but), the very baptism of John as having a distinctive character. If the view of baptism entertained by Baptists will not allow of any distinction between the baptism of pots and cups and couches, insisted on by the Pharisees, and the baptism preached by John to prepare the souls of men for the coming of the Son of God, and the baptism into a crucified Redeemer preached by the Apostles, then, their view as to what constitutes a baptism must be an error, because the Scriptures teach, that all these were baptisms, and, *as baptisms*, differed from each other. John's baptism was not Jewish baptism, which went before it, nor Christian baptism which came after it; it had, *as a baptism*, a distinguishing character of its own. Jewish baptism was a baptism of ceremonial purification, as has been proved; and John's baptism was a baptism of repentance, as has been, in part, and will be hereafter, more fully, proved. None can deny the essential difference between thorough ceremonial purity and thorough godly sorrow for sin; our view, then, meets the demand of Scripture for diversity *in the baptism*, in the condition of the body in the one case and of the soul in the other; the Baptist view cannot possibly do it, for with them it is an axiom, that "a baptism is a baptism." This is conceded when, unable to find under the theory any possible distinction in the baptisms, resort is had to distinction in the *accidental appendages* of the baptism. If I want to know the difference in nature between the baptism of Ishmael and the baptism of Satyrus, I do not want a dissertation on the time, or place, or persons, or circumstances of any kind gathering around those baptisms; but I want to know, what difference there is between those things which make them baptisms, and without which there would be no baptism. To this the only answer that can be given is, that the one baptism is a condition of thorough intoxication induced by wine; and the other baptism is a condition of thorough stupefaction induced by an opiate. If the theory can present nothing but difference of accident, when the demand is for difference of essence, it is necessarily a failure. It cannot take the first step toward the expounding of the baptisms of the Bible.

Subjective Genitive.

Winer (p. 186) says (and other grammarians agree with him), that the simple grammatical form of a defining genitive does not decide whether the relation of the defining word be that of a subjective or objective genitive. "The decision between the subjective and the objective genitive rests in many passages not with the grammarian but with the exegete, and the latter in making it must give careful attention to parallel passages also."

"In Phil. 4 : 7 εἰρήνη θεοῦ can only mean *the peace* (of soul) *that God gives*, according to the custom of the Apostles to wish their readers εἰρήνην ἀπὸ θεοῦ. That δικαιοσύνη πίστεως (a *single* notion : *faith-righteousness*), Romans 4 : 13, signifies *righteousness* which *faith* brings with it, is manifest from the more frequent expression 'the righteousness which is ἐκ πίστεως' (Rom. 9 : 30; 10 : 6). In Heb. 3 : 13 ἀπάτη τῆς ἁμαρτίας is the subjective genitive." So, we say, βάπτισμα μετανοίας is the subjective genitive. If "faith" and "sin" can produce such changed conditions of the soul as are denoted by "righteousness" on the one hand, and by "deceit" on the other hand, then there can be no embarrassment in attributing to "repentance" the office of changing the condition of the soul in that thorough manner indicated by βάπτισμα. Winer, however (p. 188), places this phrase under the head of "more remote internal relations," and translates "*baptism engaging to repentance.*"

If this baptism to which we are to be engaged were a baptism effected by divine truth, or by the divine Spirit, it would come to the same thing as in our interpretation; but this, very clearly, is not the idea; it is a ritual baptism. And against this there are objections, philological, exeget-ical, and theological. 1. It is yet to be proved, that βάπτισμα has any usage which identifies its origin with the primary, physical, use of βαπτίζω. If such proof can be adduced, it remains to be proved, that such usage can apply to living men and women who are not to be deprived of life. 2. The exegete who will observe the counsel of Winer and "give careful attention to parallel passages before he decides," will find his way barred against an exegesis which would put men and women within a water covering. Some of these passages will soon claim our attention, and are, therefore, now passed by; but there is one, Heb. 6 : 2, βαπτισμῶν διδαχῆς *baptisms of doctrine*, which lies without our present range of inquiry, at which we may glance.

Winer says, that this is a difficult passage, and in this judgment commentators, generally, are agreed. Will not the passage receive elucidation by accepting the defining word, διδαχῆς, as the subjective genitive, and the phrase βαπτισμῶν διδαχῆς as explicative of the preceding "repentance from dead works," and "faith toward God" = baptisms of doctrine? Does not the structure of the passage call for such interpretation? Is not the plural form, βαπτισμῶν, thus accounted for? Was not the doctrine of repentance the baptizing power in John's ministry, and the doctrines of repentance and faith the conjoint baptizing power in the Apostles' ministry = "Testifying both to the Jews and also to the Greeks repentance toward God and faith toward our

Lord Jesus Christ?" Does not such interpretation place
the passage in the most absolute harmony with all other
Scripture? If such interpretation be accepted, then, we
deliver the βάπτισμα μετανοίας from the cold and deadly embrace of the waters (see Winer, pp. 192, 551). 3. Theologically a ritual baptism "engaging to repentance" is objectionable; because the language implies that those baptized
are (at their baptism) impenitent. But John forbids men living impenitently in their sins to come to his baptism. They
must first "bring forth fruit meet for repentance."

This was well understood by the Jews, as is conclusively
shown by the language of Josephus, "βαπτισμῷ συνίεναι—τῆς
ψυχῆς προεκκεκαθαρμένης to come for baptism, *the soul having been
first* purified by righteousness." It would be difficult to
present a more correct statement of John's Repentance-bap-
tism of the soul (as a prerequisite to the reception of the rite
in which this soul baptism was symbolized in its purifying
nature by the application of pure water to the body) than is
done by this statement of Josephus.

If it be understood, that ritual baptism is to effect a soul
baptism and make it penitent, then, I answer: This is not
within the power of any rite to do; but belongs to "Him
who is exalted to the right hand of God to give repentance"
to the souls of men. If this baptism be resolved into a
naked profession of repentance, the answer of Scripture is:
God demands the heart and will be satisfied with nothing
else: "A broken and a contrite heart, O God, thou wilt not
despise;" and precisely this, no more, no less, is βάπτισμα
μετανοίας, and it was essential that such baptism should be
preached. John did so preach.

4. This interpretation is farther established by that of the
kindred phrase, καρποὺς τῆς μετανοίας (Matt. 3 : 8; Luke 3 : 8).
Here the adjunct cannot possibly be anything else than a
defining subjective genitive. The "fruits" are not such as
spring out of τῶν δένδρων, but τῆς μετανοίας; they are not figs
and olives, but justice and mercy. And as the nature of a
fig-tree determines the character of its fruit; and the nature
of the olive-tree, in like manner, determines the character

of its fruit; so, the nature of repentance determines the character of its fruit, and of the character of its baptism, issuing, by the grace of God, εἰς ἀφεσιν ἀμαρτιῶν.

Pasov, in his lexicon, says, that it is the subjective genitive which appears in this phrase.

JOHN'S COMMISSION ILLUSTRATED BY THE BAPTISM WHICH HE PREACHED.

Τὸ βάπτισμα ὃ ἐκήρυξεν Ἰωάννης—The baptism which John preached.—*Acts* 10 : 37.

Προκηρύξαντος Ἰωάννου βάπτισμα μετανοίας—John having first preached the baptism of repentance.—*Acts* 13 : 24.

Ἰωάννης ὁ βαπτιστής, κηρύσσων καὶ λέγων, Μετανοεῖτε—John the Baptist came preaching and saying, Repent!—*Matthew* 3 : 1, 2.

Moral Impossibility.

It is a moral impossibility that the ministry of the Forerunner heralding the coming of the Lord Jesus Christ should consist in the proclamation of a mere ritual ordinance. It has, already, been shown, that the βάπτισμα of which Peter speaks in Acts 10 : 37 could not, philologically, be a dipping in or covering over in water. We now add, that John's mission, as the Forerunner of Christ, could not have been to preach the dipping in or covering over of the Jews in water, because 1. Such preaching is inconsistent with the spirit of Christianity. John's ministry was not a fully developed Christian ministry, but it was Christian in contradistinction from Jewish; it was twilight Christianity, the beginning of the kingdom of heaven. Under Judaism rite and ceremonial had a prime importance. It was by and through them that truth was reached. Under Christianity truth is brought into the foreground and directly taught; while the observance of rite, as such, is not taught at all by Christianity. Ritual observance never appears but as the shadow of truth, and by itself is as worthless as a shadow. It may be received in all its shadowy perfectness and leave the receiver "in the gall of bitterness and bonds of iniquity;" and on the other hand, there may be an utter destitution of it and the soul pass " to-day into Paradise." It is morally impossible that such a system could be introduced by concentrating the attention of the Jewish people upon a ritual ordinance, and insisting on its outward observance as a preparation to receive Christ.

If to this it should be replied: "John did not preach merely the observance of a rite, but truth, also, as connected with the rite," I answer: John's ministry is characterized as "the preaching of a baptism;" it is so characterized not once merely, but many times; not by one person only, but by Mark, and Luke, and Peter, and Paul; not before Christianity, but after Christianity; not as something alien from Christianity, but as in full harmony with it; and such baptism so proclaimed by John, and so appealed to by Peter and Paul, must have constituted the substance of his preaching; and if so, then, it is morally certain that "the baptism" was not a dipping in, or covering over in, water. This conclusion is, farther, established by the fuller form $\beta \acute{a} \pi \tau \iota \sigma \mu a$ $\mu \varepsilon \tau a \nu o i a \varsigma$ which appears in Acts 13 : 24. Peter in Acts 10 : 37 only speaks of $\tau \grave{o} \ \beta \acute{a} \pi \tau \iota \sigma \mu a$, the well-known baptism which John preached; but Paul defines the nature of the baptism by joining with it a limiting term, which gives to it the greatest possible precision; it was the $\beta \acute{a} \pi \tau \iota \sigma \mu a \cdot \ \mu \varepsilon \tau a \nu o i a \varsigma =$ *Repentance* baptism, and not *water* baptism. If it should be said: "This phrase is elliptical, and the ellipsis is to be supplied by the introduction of *water* to form the baptism and making repentance an accident, a shadowed end," I answer: The expression has the most absolute completeness as indicating the nature of the baptism, and the introduction of water, or of anything else, to change the nature of the baptism, is nothing more nor less than a sheer change of the word of God. If it be rejoined: " We are at liberty to supply an ellipsis from other parallel and more fully stated passages, and in such 'water' is found," I answer: The former part of this statement I accept; the latter part I deny. I deny, that "water" can be found in any statement made to declare the character of John's *preaching*. The point before us is, "the baptism which John PREACHED." Passages which refer to baptism in other relations are not parallel passages. A baptism preached and a baptism administered may have no more identity than a substance and the shadow which it casts. A reference to baptisms administered to take out of them "water," for the purpose of incorporating it with a baptism preached, is as wise as the taking of Omega out of the alphabet to expound Alpha on the ground that they are both Greek letters; or the taking of flesh out of the body and insisting upon incorporating it with the soul on the plea that soul and body make up one person. What God hath made twain no man may make one. To put water into the baptism which John preached is to write a history of John's ministry under some other authority than that of the Holy Ghost.

The Baptist Church declares it to be her glory above all her fellows, that she sternly adheres to the very word of God. If this be, in very deed, her position among her brethren, then she is, truly, invested with a pre-eminent glory; but let her see to it, that she puts no water into the baptism preached by John, lest she take the testimony of the Holy Ghost to the baptism of John and drown it in the pool of her theory, and for this great wrong she be discrowned by John's Lord as no longer the pre-eminently faithful witness to the letter of his truth.

Does any one, in alarm, ask, "Do you mean to deny that water was used by John in administering baptism?" I mean to deny just what the word of God denies, and to affirm just what the word of God affirms. I mean to be very jealous for that excellent glory claimed by our Baptist brethren, and, therefore, to follow very humbly and very adoringly (as otherwise knowing nothing) the very words which the Holy Ghost teacheth. And in doing so I mean to distinguish, just so much and no more, as the Holy Spirit distinguishes between the baptism which John preached in which

there was no water, and the ritual baptism which John administered in which there was water. John's mission did
not consist in the administration of a ritual ordinance. It
did include the administration of a rite in which water, as a
symbol, appeared illustrative of and lending force to that
repentance baptism in the preaching of which (water not
entering into it) his mission did so pre-eminently consist
that it is ever used by the Holy Spirit to characterize it.
But of this hereafter; I conclude what is, now, to be said
on the baptism preached, so far as brought to view by the
Scriptures quoted, by one other reference. 3. John was not
sent to administer a ritual water baptism, but was sent to
preach repentance baptism, just as Paul "was not sent to
baptize, but to preach the gospel" (1 Cor. 1 : 17). The
phrase βάπτισμα μετανοίας means nothing more or less than a
pervading and controlling penitential condition of the soul.
This was what John was commissioned to preach, and this
was what he did preach, Mark, Luke, Peter, and Paul being
witnesses. He both denies, that he was sent to administer
water baptism as his ministry, and affirms, that his mission
was to preach repentance baptism, when he refuses water
baptism to the Pharisee and Sadducee, and calls them to repentance baptism, to be evidenced by its appropriate fruits.
And this interpretation of the phrase used by Mark and
Luke, and of the great mission of John, is confirmed in the
most absolute manner by Matthew when he says (3 : 1, 2),
"In those days came John the Baptist, preaching in the wilderness of Judea, and saying, Repent ye." Matthew never
uses the phrase βάπτισμα μετανοίας; but when Mark says, "John
preached in the wilderness the *baptism of* REPENTANCE;" and
when Luke says, "John preached in all the country about
Jordan the *baptism of* REPENTANCE;" Matthew says, "John
preached in the wilderness of Judea, REPENT ye!" We
are thus led by another route, guided by inspiration, to
the identical conclusion to which we had previously been
conducted by philology and grammatical law, namely, that
βάπτισμα μετανοίας and μετανοεῖτε are but different forms for
expressing the same conception—a thorough change in the

condition of the soul effected by repentance. How much "water" is there in Μετανοεῖτε? Just so much is there in βάπτισμα μετανόιας and no more.

JOHN'S PREACHING FARTHER DEVELOPED.

Κηρύσσων βάπτισμα μετανοίας ἐις ἀφεσιν ἁμαρτιῶν—Preaching the baptism of repentance into the remission of sins.—*Mark* 1 : 4; *Luke* 3 : 3.

The Text.

The change in the received reading of Mark made by Tischendorf, Alford, and others, ἐγένετο Ἰωάννης ὁ βαπτίζων ἐν τῇ ἐρήμῳ καὶ κηρύσσων, brings Mark into closer conformity with the statement of Luke, who does not speak of John's "baptizing" but only of his "preaching the baptism of repentance into the remission of sins." Mark generally (1 : 4; 6 : 14, 25) according to the Codex Sinaiticus, uses ὁ βαπτίζων to express the title of John as "the Baptist."

Whether Mark and Luke unite in stating merely the fact of John's preaching, or Mark be accepted as stating both the fact of John's ritually baptizing, and the fact of John's "preaching the baptism of repentance into the remission of sins," we have a broad distinction made, tacitly in the one case and expressly in the other, between preaching and baptizing. That John did ritually baptize is unquestionable. That his oral addresses consisted in the proclamation of a ritual baptism, and a call upon the people to receive such baptism, is (in view of the nature of his mission) a simple absurdity. But all inspired writers unite in testifying, that the grand feature of John's ministry was the *preaching a* BAPTISM; that baptism, then, could not have been a water baptism, but must have been, as we are expressly told, a RE-PENTANCE *baptism.* Of course, the ritual ordinance in connection with this preached baptism (which was its visible, symbol exposition) had to be announced; but it did not have to be made the grand theme of preaching. There is a ritual baptism pertaining to Christianity, but, whatever the theory may think upon the matter, neither Paul, nor any other minister of Christ, was ever sent to preach a ritual baptism. The Christian commission is to preach Christ and his baptism (who never baptized with water), announcing the existence and requiring the observance of a corresponding ritual baptism; and the man of whose ministry it can be justly said, "his preaching is the preaching of a ritual ordinance," cannot be one of those whom Christ has sent to preach the gospel. And inasmuch as the ministry of the Forerunner is evermore described as the preaching of "the baptism of John," "the baptism of repentance," "the baptism of repentance into the remission of sins," it follows (just as certainly as that there was no absurdly incongruous relationship between the preaching of John and the preparation of the way of the Lord) that ritual baptism was not the theme of the preaching of him who was "filled with the Holy Ghost from his mother's womb," and who entered upon his work "in the Spirit and power of Elias" "to prepare the way of the Lord and to give the knowledge of salvation unto his people."

Translation.

The "New Version" translates these passages—"preaching the immersion of repentance unto remission of sins." Alexander Campbell translates a parallel passage—"immersion *in water into*" (Christian Baptism, p. **116**).

Εἰς unto. The translation of εἰς, in connection with "immersion," by "unto" is something remarkable for Baptists. There is not a single case, outside of the Scriptures, in which, in such relation, they translate εἰς by "unto." The proper translation, as shown by the character of the Greek verb, is *into.* And on this, up to this point, the theory has insisted in the most imperative manner. This principle has not been disregarded, and this universal practice has not been discarded, without some strong reason. What that strong reason is, is sufficiently obvious. A translation in harmony with the translation of this preposition in every case of Classic use would cut up the theory by the roots. Try it: "He preached the immersion of repentance *into* THE REMISSION OF SINS." This makes an end to the theory so far as John's preaching is concerned. The "immersion" is made not "into *water*," but "into *the remission of sins*," and, of necessity, the baptism cannot be physical. What reason, it may be asked, is assigned for so marked a departure from an asserted law of translation? The reply must be given, There is none. If a friend of "the New Version" should interpose and say, "The old version translates 'for the remission of sins.'" The statement of fact is admitted and we add: No friend of the old version ever claimed for it perfection in its translation. "*For* the remission of sins" states a truth under a proper interpretation of "baptism of repentance," but "immersion (in water) unto the remission of sins," states, on its face, an untruth ruinous to the gospel and to the soul which confides in it.

Lovers of the blessed old English Bible, and highly accomplished scholars, have not failed to see, and to declare, an imperfection in the translation of this particular passage. The translators of the New Version have appealed to Professor Campbell of Scotland as authority for changing "*with* water" into *in* water; why was not Professor Wilson of Ireland, no less a scholar, accepted as authority for changing "*for* the remission of sins" into the better form, "*into* the remission of sins?" As Dr. Campbell, wrong, is quoted, let us hear Professor Wilson, right:

"This rendering of εἰς after βαπτίζω or any of its derivatives by 'for,' as in 'I baptize εἰς μετανοίαν,' and 'Baptism of repentance εἰς ἀφεσιν ἁμαρτιῶν,' we consider wholly unauthorized. The correct translation is *into*" (On Baptism, p. 341).

And, so, wherever εἰς occurs, literal or figurative, in a hundred quotations outside of the Scriptures, given by Dr. Conant, he uniformly translates it by *into*. Why was another translation reserved for the Scriptures?

No defence can be set up by appealing to the old Bible,

because the new Bible was to be made by "scholars competent" to amend the imperfections which were declared to be
in it, and also to be of so serious a character as to be intolerable; and, because they have made their emendation (?) here
and should have left it perfect. "Baptism of repentance"
has been converted into "*immersion* of repentance," and "*for*
the remission of sins" has been changed into "*unto* the remission of sins." A defence of this translation by an appeal
to certain possible meanings of the preposition is untenable
for reasons assigned in Jud. Baptism, pp. 95–100.

Far be it from me, in accounting for this remarkable departure from a uniform translation of the Classics, to retort
the language flung at those noble men who gave us the old
English Bible, and say:

"They virtually combine to obscure a part, at least, of divine
revelation, that the real meaning of the words should be pur-
posely kept out of sight."

It is, indeed, a fact, that "divine revelation is obscured;"
and it is a fact, that "the real meaning of the words is kept
out of sight;" but I do not say, I do not believe, that this
was of design. The translators of the New Version believed
that they were giving a correct translation; but they were
mistaken. They entered upon their work with full faith in
the never to be questioned axiom—baptism is a dipping into
water; and when they came to this passage, they reasoned
thus:

"Βάπτισμα must be translated *immersion*, but if we translate εἰς
(as we have always insisted it should be translated) *into*, we
take away *water* from our 'immersion' by giving to it a purely
ideal element which would ruin our doctrine, and as our doctrine cannot be wrong, εἰς cannot mean 'into;' therefore, we
are justified in translating it *unto*. And it will be better to confront the self-contradiction in our translations than to abandon
a baptism *into* WATER for a baptism *into* REMISSION OF SINS."

This explanation impugns neither the learning nor the
integrity of these translators. It only brings them within
the range of those infirmities which belong to our common

humanity when preconceived errors cloud the perception of truth, and are, unhappily, taken as infallible rules whereby all questions that arise must be adjudicated.

The translation proposed by the President of Bethany College, as applied to this case, is an impossible translation, "Preaching the immersion *in water* of repentance *into* the remission of sins." This translation is impossible, 1. Because, there is no fully stated passage in which "in water" occurs in connection with βάπτισμα out of which it could be taken to supply an imagined ellipsis. 2. Because, philologically, a βάπτισμα "in water" can do nothing but drown. 3. Because, grammatically, βάπτισμα cannot stand related to two incongruous elements, "*in* water" and "*into* the remission of sins." 4. Because, if a second ellipsis is sought to give "into" another relation, we are not interpreting the Word of God, but making it a waxy mass to be moulded after the forms of our ignorance or of our prejudice.

"NEW VERSION."

Remarkable Collocation of Words.

An examination of the entire phraseology, as given in the New Version—"preaching the immersion of repentance unto remission of sins"—shows, certainly, a very remarkable combination of words. No one, untaught in the mysteries of the theory, could ever venture to undertake their resolution into any intelligible conception. What is to guide in the interpretation? Are we to understand the language as complete or as elliptical? Is the "immersion" literal or figurative? Does "repentance" define the immersion and immerse some object, or is repentance itself to be immersed? What is the force of "unto?" Does it denote the depth of the "immersion," reaching down *unto* something, or, in general, an end to be attained? Does "immersion" attain unto "remission of sins" actually and absolutely, or, only, possibly and conditionally? These are some of the inquiries suggested by the terms, but to which they return no rational answers.

But here we are told, that we do wrong to look upon the language as complete and self-interpretative. It is highly elliptical. "Immersion" is to be made complete by the addition of *in water*. John preached "the immersion (*in water*)." Of what? "Why, of men and women." Well, "immersion in water" expresses, and expresses only, the condition of an object resting in repose within water. Is it meant, that John preached that men and women must occupy such a condition? "No, for then they must be drowned; therefore the meaning of βάπτισμα is changed to one (not, to be sure, found in Greek writings, but, which being quite necessary to make out our case must be right) from which the inherent idea of the word is entirely eliminated." Certainly that is most heroic practice. And what of repentance? "This, also, is eviscerated of its life, and we convert the repentance of inspiration into a *profession* of 're-pentance.'" And what of "remission of sins?" "Why we say, The immersion of men and women in water making a profession of repentance never reaches 'unto remission of sins' (that is Campbellism), therefore, we make a double ellipsis and say: 'The immersion' (of men and women in water, making a profession) 'of repentance' will not, but true soul repentance will, avail 'unto the remission of sins.'" Well, this is keeping up a good courage to the end. Some would shrink from so flat a contradiction of John as to deny what he affirms, namely, that the baptism which he *preached* did issue in the remission of sins. But inasmuch as the theory necessitates this contradiction of John, I suppose the theory must be sustained rather than the Preacher in the Wilderness. And, yet, notwithstanding all this lofty imperialism of interpretation which transforms βάπτισμα into an immersion in which there is no immersion but only an evanescent dipping; which divorces βάπτισμα from μετανοίας, and establishes an unlawful union with water; which takes away μετανοίας and gives us in its stead an empty "profession;" which denies, what John affirms, namely, that his preached baptism issued in the remission of sins; I say, notwithstanding this imperialistic downtreading of every word

17

of this Scripture, and the mangled rending of its members
from their living relations, I am disposed to gather up the
torn fragments that they may be restored to their divinely
appointed relations, and to accept of them, just as the Holy
Spirit has given them, without any attempt at re-writing in
order to make them square with a theory.

I say then, that βάπτισμα μετανοίας εἰς ἄφεσιν ἁμαρτιῶν is a complete statement needing no addition, and that it is the fullest
and most vividly distinct statement of the distinguishing
characteristics of John's preaching to be found anywhere in
the Scriptures. The theory can neither destroy it nor escape
destruction by it. The meaning of βάπτισμα has been sufficiently established both philologically and by usage. There
is not a particle of evidence that it does ever, in the Scriptures, enter into physical relations. And, so far as my examination goes, it is never used in physics out of the Scriptures. There is no one who will deny, that in βάπτισμα
μετανοίας the latter word may define, and be causative of, the
former word. That this must be the explanation of the
relation of these terms, in the present case, is proved by
parallel phrases of whose import there is no doubt; such
as βάπτισμα πυρὸς καὶ πνεύματος, this can be nothing else than
" baptism of (by) fire and Spirit;" βάπτισμα αἵματος, βάπτισμα
δακρύων, " baptism of (by) blood," " baptism of (by) tears;"
βάπτισμα μαρτυροῦ, otherwise stated, in immediate connection,
τὸ μαρτυρον βάπτισμα, " baptism of (by) martyrdom," otherwise
stated, " the martyr baptism;" baptismum publicæ confessionis, "the baptism of (by) public confession." And in the
parallel phrases, Lavacrum pœnitentiæ, " the washing of
(by) repentance;" Lavacrum sanctæ regenerationis, "the
washing of (by) holy regeneration;" Lavacrum fidei, "the
washing of (by) faith." In all of these cases the genitive
adjunct defines and establishes the baptism or washing;
and in no instance is the baptism or washing within a
physical element. The reference is only and always to a
condition of the soul. That εἰς ἄφεσιν ἁμαρτιων may mean
"into the remission of sins" is unquestioned; that it must
mean this, in the relation in which it here stands, is estab-

lished by parallel passages and by Baptist translations of those passages.

What, now is the sentiment of the whole? "John preached the baptism of (by) repentance into the remission of sins," in other words, John preached *a thorough change in the condition of the soul to be effected by repentance and to be accompanied with the complete forgiveness of sins.* "Repentance is the gift of God," and "baptism by repentance" is baptism by the Spirit of God, and by none other. Is this scriptural preaching? Was it a kind of preaching suitable to prepare the way of the Lord? Was it preaching becoming him who while he cried in the wilderness "Repent," also, with uplifted finger, pointed out the Coming One, already in their midst, exclaiming—"Behold the LAMB OF GOD *that* TAKETH AWAY THE SIN of the world?"

John preached a baptism which he did not execute; a baptism which he attributes to repentance, and thus, to the Holy Ghost, the fruit of which is, pardoned sin through the Lamb of God. Is this preaching so unsound or so unintelligible that it must be converted into water dipping before it can be received?

Parallel Passages.

The disproof of the translation and interpretation of the theory, and the proof of the translation and interpretation offered instead, scarcely need to be strengthened; yet it may be well to adduce some parallel passages outside of the Scriptures.

Βεβαπτισμένον εἰς ἀναισθησίαν καὶ ὕπνον ὑπὸ τῆς μέθης—Baptized by drunkenness into insensibility and sleep.—*Josephus, J. A., X, 9.*

This passage has been considered, at length, in Judaic Baptism (pp. 92–100). I refer to it now as being identical, in general structure, with the passage under consideration, and as receiving the same translation and interpretation by all parties. It affords, thus, common standing ground from which to look at this debated passage. No one questions but that Josephus, here, represents a baptism as effected ὑπὸ τῆς μέθης; that the element within which, by verbal form, the baptism takes place is ἀναισθησίαν καὶ ὕπνον as indicated by εἰς; and that the full development of the influence of this verbal element is expressed by βεβαπτισμένον. Dr. Conant accordingly translates, " plunged *by drunkenness* INTO STUPOR *and* SLEEP." For the translation of βεβαπτισμένον by the definite act " plunged" there is no authority in the word; but as plunge does not, like dip, take its object out of the element into which it puts it, the result is the same, whether an object gets into a condition of " insensibility and sleep" by *plunging*, or in any other way. It will remain within and, therefore, be under the fullest influence of the investing element. Dr. Conant recognizes " drunkenness" as the power effecting the baptism, and " insensibility and sleep" as the verbal element investing and influencing the object, by their peculiar characteristics, in the completest manner. The plunging part of the exposition the theory is responsible for, and not βαπτίζω nor the method of putting to sleep; at least this is not the mode of the cradle hymn—" Hush, my babe, lie still and slumber." If, however, the theory does inexorably demand, that cradle and babe, drunkard and cups, shall be *plunged*, even so let it be.

If Josephus had written βάπτισμα μέθης εἰς ἀναισθησίαν καὶ ὕπνον neither the sentiment nor the form of the conception would have been affected in the slightest degree. The genitive, with or without a preposition, is constantly met with in these baptisms. The points which demand attention, and which are uncontroverted, are, 1. The baptizing power, μέθης. 2. The element within which (verbally) the baptism takes place, ἀναισθησίαν καὶ ὕπνον. 3. That no provision is made for taking out of this baptism, as there never is in any βάπτισμα. 4. Deliverance from this baptism must come from the self-exhaustion of the drunken-making power, or from some foreign counteracting influence. A baptism by drunkenness is a definite baptism so far as excluding other and diverse baptisms, such as baptism of grief, baptism of passion, &c., is concerned; but it is not definite so far as the range of its own power is concerned. Drunkenness may produce a diversity of conditions. Therefore, Josephus makes his statement specific, as to the varied baptisms of which drunkenness is capable, by saying, I mean, specifically, that result of drunkenness which is expressed by εἰς ἀνασθησίαν καὶ ὕπνον. In like manner John announces in the most specific manner possible, one out of many baptisms of which repentance is capable, namely, baptism εἰς αφεσιν αμαρτιῶν.

Ὑπὸ μέθης βαπτιζόμενος εἰς ὕπνον—Baptized by drunkenness into sleep.—*Clemens Alex.*, II, 421.

This passage from Clement Dr. Conant, again, translates, "Plunged by drunkenness into sleep," and thus, again, accepts "drunkenness" as the baptizing power; "sleep" as the verbal element; and a baptism, as expressing a condition in which there is no self-limitation as to continuance.

Ἐκ σωφροσύνης εἰς πορνείαν βαπτίζουσι ταῖς ἡδοναῖς καὶ τοῖς πάθεσι χαρίζεσθαι δογματίζοντες—Teaching the practice of pleasure and passion they baptize out of chastity into fornication.—*Clemens Alex.*, II, 1212.

This passage Dr. Conant translates, "They *immerse* from sobriety into fornication, teaching to indulge the pleasures and passions."

We will not stop to inquire why "plunge" in the previous translations has been displaced by "immerse" in this, but call attention to the more important point that εἰς is still recognized in the office of indicator of the verbal element of baptism, "*into* fornication." The baptizing power in this baptism does not appear in the genitive, nor by any one word, but is represented by ταῖς ἡδοναῖς καὶ τοῖς πάθεσι χαρίζεσθαι. The agency may be expressed by the dative (and often is in these baptisms) as well as by the genitive. Those persons who accepted such false teaching as inculcated the indulgence of pleasure and passion, were baptized (ἡδοναῖς καὶ πάθεσι) "by pleasures and passions into fornication" εἰς πορνείαν. In every baptism we have a thorough change of condition. It may be out of a condition of chastity into a condition of unchastity, or out of a condition of impenitence into a condition of penitence. These are all the passages exhibiting this character of baptism which are referred to and translated by Dr. Conant. As my present purpose is to frame an argument from Baptist translations, I will add no other quotations.

The passages now cited are in perfect accord as to structure with that under consideration, βάπτισμα μετανοίας εἰς ἀφεσιν ἁμαρτιων, which cannot possibly be translated by Baptists, in consistency with their own translations, in any other way than, "the baptism by repentance into the remission of sins." To introduce "water" or "a profession of" repentance, is, in so far, to make a new Bible. To make "remission of sins" depend on a water rite and a profession, is to subvert the Gospel. To convert βάπτισμα into an evanescent introduction into and withdrawal out of water, is an utter disregard both of philology and of usage.

On the other hand; to translate these words, just as they stand, by the severest grammatical and exegetical laws, develops a sentiment which is in the most absolute harmony with the general teachings of Scripture, and, in especial, with all that is demanded by the mission of the Messenger who was "to prepare a people for the Lord." The letter and the spirit, philology and theology, make common demand for the interpretation assigned. All the genitives, μέθης, πυρὸς, αἵματος, δάχρυων, μαρτυροῦ, publicæ confessionis, sanctæ regenerationis, pænitentiæ, fidei, as well as μετανοίας, are subjective, and not objective, in their character.

If the evidence is not adequate to sustain the position claimed, the deficiency must be pointed out by others; I am unable to perceive it. If the evidence adduced be adequate to vindicate the ends for which it is adduced, then, the theory has no standing place. The case must be dismissed.

Alexander Campbell.

Alexander Campbell, of Bethany, Virginia, has occupied so prominent and influential a position in sections of our country, and his peculiar views as to the "design of baptism" are so largely based on the passage under consideration, which views are practically inseparable from very serious error, if, indeed, they be not essentially and purely erroneous, that a consideration of this passage would hardly be considered complete without a statement and consideration of those views.

My knowledge of this, certainly in some respects, very remarkable man is derived entirely from his writings. I have never been brought into contact with those holding his views. The impression which I have received from his writings is, that he was a man of much more than ordinary intellect, and of real honesty of purpose; but that his history is deeply colored by an imperial will and a profound confidence in himself, which, however noble in themselves, yet, do always jeopard the reception of truth " as a little child." The quotations made are taken from " Campbell on Baptism, Bethany, Va., 1853; Book IV, chap. 1, 2." This " Fourth Book" bears the title *Design of Baptism,* and these two chapters are all that is written on that subject.

" DESIGN OF BAPTISM."

" The *design* of baptism, and not the *action,* or the *subject,* is the transcendent question in this discussion. What, then, is the design of New Testament baptism? We say of *New Testament* baptism, because we have in that book ' THE BAPTISM OF JOHN,' and the baptism ordained by Jesus Christ. The Harbinger proclaimed ' the baptism of repentance *for the remission of sins.'* This form of expression is exceedingly familiar and intelligible; and were it not for an imaginary incongruity between the means and the end, or the thing done and the alleged purpose or result, no one could, for a moment, doubt that the design of baptism was ' for the remission of sins.' This is *the only purpose* for which baptism was ordained. John's baptism was as certainly '*for the remission of sins,'* as it was ' *the baptism of repentance.'* Baptism is not ' for the remission of sins ' *in the same sense* as is the death of the Messiah, but it is in some sense. If Jesus died *because* men's sins were remitted, then, John's baptism was for those who were already cleansed from their pollutions. Translate the preposition *into* or *unto,* and it still shows a connection between baptism and remission of sin. To baptize *into* remission intimates that the subject of that act is about to pass into a new state.

The only divinely instituted baptism is for the remission of sins. **To** be baptized *for* Christ or *into* Christ, *for* his death or *into* his death, is to be baptized for the sake of the rights, privileges, and honors accruing from himself or his death. Of all these remission of sins is the leading blessing. We are not commanded to be baptized for faith, for repentance, &c., but we are commanded to be baptized ' for the remission of sins,' not for the remission of 'original sin,' not for the remission of sins yet to be committed, but for the remission of sins that are past. Through faith and repentance, we are commanded to be baptized for one specific purpose.

" 2. Our second leading inquiry must be, *In what sense is baptism for the remission of sins?* Causes are various, *original, efficient, meritorious, instrumental, concurrent, final.* For most minds, it is enough to read the precept, ' Repent and be baptized, every one of you, for the remission of sins,' without presuming to comprehend or develop the necessity for it. It is not a meritorious or an efficient cause, but an instrumental cause, in which repentance and faith are developed and made fruitful and effectual in the changing of our state and spiritual relations. It is also a *seal* and pledge that, through faith in the blood of the slain Lamb of God, and through repentance, by the virtues of the great Mediator, we are thus publicly declared forgiven. Baptism is ' for the remission of sins;' to give us through repentance and faith a solemn pledge and assurance of pardon: any other baptism is a human invention. ' He that believeth and is baptized shall be saved' associates faith and baptism as antecedents, whose consequent is salvation. The Apostles in their epistles allude to baptism as a symbol of moral purification—a washing away of sin in a figure, declarative of a true and real remission of sin—*a formal and definite release of the conscience from the feeling of guilt and all its condemnatory power.* Baptism was for the *true, real,* and *formal remission of sins,* through faith in the Messiah, and a genuine repentance towards God.

" Baptism was designed for the remission of sins, for a pledge and an assurance of pardon through the Messiah, our Lord and Saviour Jesus Christ. Baptism is a sign and seal; it is *a seal* of the righteousness of faith, or the remission of all our past sins, through faith in his blood, then, and in that act publicly expressed and confirmed. This, most unquestionably, is its place, its meaning, and importance in the Christian institution.

' Baptism doth save us.' Not that there is anything in the mere element of water, or in the act, or in the administrator, or in the formula, but all its virtue and efficacy is in the faith and intelligence of him that receives it.

" To him that believeth and repenteth of his sins, and to none else, then, we may safely say, ' Be baptized for the remission of your sins,' and it will surely be granted by the Lord, and enjoyed by the subject with an assurance and an evidence which the word and ordinances of the Lord alone can bestow."

I have, thus, endeavored to give a faithful abstract, generally in his own words, of the two chapters which Alexander Campbell has written on " the Design of Baptism." After an attentive perusal of the whole, the impression left upon my mind is that of bewilderment. And I think that that is only a shadow from the state of mind of the writer. If Alexander Campbell had not been bewildered on this subject he never could have started out with the italicized premise, " baptism is *for the remission of sins*," and then concluded with the declaration—" To him that *believeth* and *repenteth* of his sins, and *to none else*, we may safely say, ' Be baptized for the remission of your sins.' " Was ever premise and conclusion farther removed, logically, from each other? The body of these chapters, also, contain statements which in their relations to each other are so indefinite, so ambiguous, so incongruous, and so irreconcilable, that the conviction is forced upon the mind that the writer is painfully struggling to establish harmony between admitted vital truth and the pernicious error of a sadly misinterpreted text of Scripture. I am heartily glad, however, that by a courageous sacrifice of logic he does save alive in his conclusion so much of God's precious truth as was given over to death in his premise. There was too much of essential truth lodged in the mind of this strong man to allow so bald and so portentous an error as, that " dipping into water was designed of God for the remission of sins," to fruit out in its logical results. But the danger is, that Alexander Campbell would be less of a " Campbellite" than any of his followers. It is impossible to sow among the masses such seed as *water dipping for*

sin remission, without a crop springing up which will call for
tears to drown it out. I have already said, that I have had
no opportunity to observe the practical operation of this
doctrine; but if it does not turn the soul away from a crucified Redeemer as the source of remission of sin, and induce
the substitution of a water-pool, I shall be agreeably surprised.

The President of Bethany has embarrassed himself, and
imperilled others, by a misunderstanding of that great announcement of John—the βάπτισμα μετανοίας ἐις ἀφεσιν ἁμαρτιῶν.
It is he, not John, that has put water into that βάπτισμα. It
is he, and not John, that has put "design" into that εἰς.
When these errors shall have been corrected and the true
announcement of the Holy Ghost, through the Forerunner,
is allowed to be made, of a baptism, not into water but, into
the remission of sins, effected not by a human administrator
but, by the Holy Spirit working through repentance, then,
human error will be eliminated and the pure truth of God
will be revealed. Then, it will be no longer necessary to
plead against " an imaginary incongruity between the means
and the end," but the divine harmony in the analogy of
revealed truth will be so obvious that none will think of
"imagining" incongruity. When John says, I baptize (εἰς
μετανοίαν) *for* (?) REPENTANCE; if, "in some sense," then, in
what sense is baptism "for" *repentance?* And if not "*for*
repentance," how does εἰς ἀφεσιν become "*for* the remission
of sins?"

It is with great pleasure that I present the following just
views of Professor J. H. Godwin (Notes on Mark, London,
1869):

"John was both a prophet and priest. As prophet he preached,
and as priest he used a rite of purification similar to those used
by the priests. All public purifications with water, and all in
which one person acted on another, were by sprinkling or
affusion. These and only these were appointed by the law, and
were called baptisms (Heb. 9 : 10). The same term which is
used for the *rite* is also used for the *reality* of which it is an
emblem. As there was a circumcision of the body, so there was
a circumcision of the mind. The baptism which was the *subject*

of John's preaching, and which was *for* the remission of sins, was that of the mind. Justin Martyr speaks of the cleansing of repentance and of the knowledge of God, and declares this to be the only baptism which can purify the person. The baptism of repentance is a purification which consists in this or comes from this."

The reference to Justin Martyr may be found in Judaic Baptism, p. 277. As it is a very admirable exposition of the phrase under consideration I will here quote a portion of it:

"Through the washing of repentance and of the knowledge of God . . . we have believed and make known that this very baptism which he foreannounced is the only one able to cleanse the repenting. . . . For of what use is that baptism which cleanses the flesh and the body only? Baptize the soul from anger, and from covetousness, and from envy, and from hate, and behold the body is pure."

This earnest testimony of the Martyr witness is the very truth of God. And whether it be the special theory of Alexander Campbell, or the general theory, which he shares with others, converting those precious words—βάπτισμα μετανοίας εἰς ἄφεσιν ἁμαρτιῶν into a water dipping (!)—the one and the other alike antagonize, if they do not subvert, the teachings of the Word of God.

JOHN'S COMMISSION ILLUSTRATED BY THE RITUAL BAPTISM WHICH HE ADMINISTERED.

'Εγὼ μὲν βαπτίζω ὑμᾶς, ἐν ὕδατι, εἰς μετανοίαν—I, indeed baptize you with water, into repentance.—*Matt.* 3 : 11.

'Εγὼ μὲν ἐβάπτισασα ὑμᾶς (ἐν) ὕδατι—I, indeed, have baptized you with water.—*Mark* 1 : 8.

'Εγὼ μὲν ὕδατι βαπτίζω ὑμᾶς—I, indeed, baptize you with water. —*Luke* 3 : 16.

These passages of Scripture show the presence of water in the ritual baptism administered by John. It is put there

by divine authority. Its presence is essential to the rite.
To take away the water is to destroy the rite. This water
is used by John. He is the administrator of the ritual baptism. In the baptism which John preached there was no
water. Of that baptism John was not the executive. He
was only its Proclaimer. The agency effecting it was repentance. And as repentance is the work of the Holy
Spirit, the Holy Spirit was the Author of the baptism.
Into that baptism water cannot be introduced without destroying it. We have, then, a twofold baptism, or one baptism under a twofold aspect. In the one water has no place,
and in the other water is of divine appointment. The
question which presses on us for solution is this: "What is
the position occupied and the purpose served by water in
this ritual baptism?"

Before entering upon a detailed consideration of the elements entering into a solution of this question, as furnished
by these passages, it will be well to note the circumstances
under which, and the ends for which they were spoken.
The three passages were evidently spoken at the same time
and for the same ends. Mark is less definite as to time and
circumstance than the other Evangelists. He (1 : 7, 8) only
represents the person and baptism of John, as contrasted
with the person and baptism of Christ, without assigning
any special reason for this being done. It was not necessary
to assign any special cause as giving origin to such contrast.
The contrast was, in itself, most momentous and necessary
to be taught to all persons and through all ages.

Matthew, however, informs us both as to the reason and
the purpose of the statement. "A generation of vipers,"
impenitent in their sins, had come to his baptism, and John,
in the glowing spirit and jealous power of Elias, confronts
them and declares, that his baptism is not for such as they
are; that his baptism has no power to give repentance; it
is not the very βάπτισμα μετανοίας, but only a symbol of it
(ἐν ὕδατι); before they can receive this latter they must first
have received the former, "bringing forth fruits meet for repentance." Thus, John separates all spiritual power from

t.is baptism, declaring that it has no other power than that which belongs to water. Luke presents a yet fuller view of the case than does Matthew. In addition to the clear teaching of the essential difference between the βάπτισμα μετανοίας and the βάπτισμα ἐν ὕδατι εἰς μετανοίαν, and the necessity for the former to be received before the latter can be administered, he, also (3 : 15), teaches us, that "the people mused in their hearts of John, whether he were the Christ or not;" and therefore it became necessary to place himself, as administering a powerless symbol baptism, in the boldest contrast with Him who wielded a divine baptizing power controlling all the soul. It is under these circumstances, and for these ends, that John says, "'I, indeed, baptize into repentance with water'—a powerless symbol; the Coming One, mightier than I, shall baptize not with an empty symbol but 'by the Holy Ghost,' giving repentance and remission of sins to his people as a Saviour, and executing judgment 'by fire' upon the impenitent, in the character of a righteous Judge."

With this exhibition of the circumstances which originate the statement, we are prepared to enter upon a more particular examination of the phraseology in which it is made. The statement as bearing upon our inquiry is one of the very highest importance. There is not a word in it which has not a special value both in itself and in its relations. It claims, and it will richly repay, a full and fair examination.

New Version Translation.

A just translation is essential to a true interpretation; and such a translation is, itself, an interpretation. It is well, then, to know and to examine carefully the translation which the theory offers through its New Version. It reads thus: "I, indeed, immerse you in water unto repentance."

The objection which stands out on the face of this translation is, that it is destructive to life. Immersion in water deprives of life any human being. To this it is answered: We do not mean to keep under the water. And we rejoin: Is there any limitation of time in "immerse?" No. Is there any other word limiting the time of the immersion?

No. Is immerse used in English (without any expressed limitation) to denote the drowning of men? Yes: It is so used in the following quotations: "*Submersion* (which is the French for drowning) leads off as the most fatal of accidents."

> " And *immersed*
> Deep in the flood, found, when he sought it not,
> The death he had deserved, and died alone."

> "At length, when all had long supposed him dead
> By cold *submersion*, razor, rope, or lead."

There can be no doubt that the word is used in English, without limitation and by its own proper force, to denote death by drowning.

How is it in the Latin language from which "immerse" is derived? The usage is the same; *immergo*, without limitation, is used to express the drowning of men in the following passages:

> Tyberinus, qui in trajectu Albulæ amnis submersus.
> "Tyberinus *submersed* (drowned) in passing the river Albula."

> —— pelagoque immergere nautas.
> —— " and *immerse* (drown) the sailors in the sea."

And how is it with the Greek βαπτίζω of which "immerse" is given as the translation? Greek usage is precisely the same as the Latin, and the English; βαπτίζω, without limitation, drowns, as in the following citations:

> Βαπτίζων αὐτὸν ἀπέκτεινεν.
> " *Baptizing* him he killed him."

> Σε κύμασι πόντου βαπτίζων, ὀλέσω.
> "*Baptizing* in the sea, I will destroy thee."

Then, this translation, according to the admitted usage of the English, Latin, and Greek languages, does, of its own proper force, express a drowning; and it cannot therefore be a true translation, for John could not say, "I drown you." No, of course not; and, therefore, we change the meaning of the word which the Holy Spirit uses and which refuses to give any limitation to its immersion, and substitute another which will answer our purposes, by limiting the immersion to the shortest possible time, as our theory requires.

And so, at the demands of a theory, which confessedly is murderous under the word of God as it stands, God's word is remorselessly changed as to its express purport, under the plea, that it must be done to escape violating the command, "Thou shalt not kill!"

The theory which involves its friends in such a dilemma seems to be not a little objectionable.

I have another objection to this translation on the ground of impracticability. It is said, that it was made the commanded duty of John to immerse these people; so the New Version reads (John 1:26), "He that sent me to immerse in water." Does that language divide the duty of immersing between John and anybody else? No. Does it intimate, that the duty made incumbent upon him was one which he was unable to perform, and to do which he must call in the aid of somebody else? No. Then did John, of himself, do what it is said he was here commanded in his official character to do? The theorists must answer, "Why no, of course he did not and could not; and therefore our theory compels us to add to the commission of John, that he *and the people jointly*, were to baptize; they immersing a part of their body by walking into the water, and he dipping so much of the upper part of the body as they may have left unimmersed." And in what part of the Word of God do you find all this? "Well, in that part of the commission which was omitted by 'holy men of old who spake as they were moved by the Holy Ghost,' but which has been added since as a supplement demanded by the theory."

I entirely agree, that the theory makes the duty, which it says was imposed upon John, an impossibility; but before I accept the joint offices of others to help John do the work which was committed to him alone, I would like to be better satisfied that the Word of God does indeed impose a duty upon one, and yet mean that it should not be performed by him, but by somebody else. "But if he was commanded to immerse men and women how otherwise could it be done

except in some such *quasi* manner as this?" I cannot pretend to say how it could be done. I can only say, that if
John was commanded to immerse the people in water, *John*
did not do it. This may be a trifle in the view of the theory,
but that theory is not well calculated to make friends which
announces a very express command from God, and then
lightly proffers to us something else on the ground that the
command cannot be obeyed. Before leaving this point of
interference with John's official duty let me say, that to one
on the seashore who proposed to go into the ocean and baptize herself, a Baptist friend objected, "But you have no
right to baptize yourself." Now I would ask: If I, being
without Scriptural authority to baptize, do nullify the ordinance by covering all my body in water, what precise portion of my body will the Scriptures tolerate me in unofficially
covering, and the ordinance be unharmed?

We offer a third objection to the translation, questioning
the fidelity of the report as to this divine command.

We object to the translation—"I immerse you *in* water,"
1. Because the form of the Greek does not express, what
the nature of the case would demand, the transition of an
object from one position into another. 2. Because the preposition may denote only the position of the baptizer; in
which case there is no provision left for putting ὑμᾶς in the
water. 3. Because if the preposition be made to give
position to ὑμᾶς, then, although the language as the language
of inspiration may be treated lightly, and ὑμᾶς may be taken
out of the position in which we were told John was commanded to put them, still, there is too much of stiffness in
heathen Greek forms to allow of any such manipulation.
If the forms of Greek are so much disregarded as to give
these people position *in* water, there is no help for them but
to stay there. The passive form of the verb βεβαπτισμένῃ ἐν
τῷ σώματι—βεβαπτισμένην ἐν τῷ βάθει τοῦ σώματος—βεβαπτισμένοι ἐν τῇ
κακίᾳ—gives position to the soul "*in* the body"—"*in* the depth
of the body"—"*in* depravity"—but it leaves it where it finds
it. If ἐμβάπτισον ἄλμῃ (with the preposition in composition and
with the active verb) be regarded as an equivalent form,

"the pickles" will still remain immovable "in the brine."
And, in like manner, if it be insisted upon, that βαπτίζω ἐν
ὕδατι ὑμᾶς should place its luckless objects "*in* the water,"
there is no outcome for them. If to this it be replied:
Although inspiration has omitted to make provision for
bringing men and women out of the water, and although
Greek forms do refuse to lend any aid for their recovery,
notwithstanding, they must come out or—the theory must
be wrong. We accept the alternative. And in proving that
alternative to be the truth, will proceed to show, that men
and women were never put *in* the water by any command
of God.

This we do by offering a fourth objection to the translation, having respect to εἰς μετανοίαν "*unto* repentance."

This objection is based, in addition to the merits of the
case, upon a patent inconsistency with a long series of
uniform translations made, in similar cases, by Baptist
writers.

Whenever an object is to be physically baptized by being
moved out of one position into another position, the appropriate Greek form to express such change of position is the
preposition εἰς with the investing element. The following
passages, with their translations by Dr. Conant, will establish
this point:

Βαπτισθέντι εἰς αὐτὸ—Immersed *into* it (Lake Tatta).
Βάπτισον εἰς θάλασσην—Plunge thyself *into* the sea.
Βαπτίζων εἰς τὴν λίμνην—Plunging *into* the Lake Copais.
Βαπτίσας εἰς τὸ αἷμα—Dipping his hand *into* the blood.
'Εβάπτισε εἰς τὴν σφαγὴν—Plunged the sword *into* his own neck.
Βαπτίζειν εἰς γάλα—Immerse it *into* breast milk.
Βαπτίζετο εἰς ῥοόν—Immersed himself *into* the ocean stream.
Βαπτίσαι εἰς τὸ στῆθος—Plunge the sword *into* the enemies' breast.
Βαπτιζόντων εἰς τὴν λίμνην—Plunging others *into* the lake.
Βαπτίζουσι εἰς τὸ ὕδωρ—Plunge a pole *into* the water.
'Εβάπτισ εἰς τὸν οἶνον—Immersed him *into* the wine.
Βεβαπτισμένον εἰς αὐτήν—Immersed *into* it.
'Εβαπτίσθην εἰς καταδύσεις—Plunged *into* bottomless depths.

These are all the passages, so far as I know, in which the

18

baptized object is spoken of as moved in order to its baptism, and, in all cases, the preposition εἰς is used, and the translation by Dr. Conant is invariably *into*. Indeed, he says, that the distinct office of this preposition, in such cases, is to express the transition and entrance of the object within the medium to which it points—"The preposition *into* before the name of the element into which an object is plunged or immersed expressing fully the act of *passing* from one element into another" (p. 62). Now the theory says, that in the baptism under consideration the objects to be baptized (men and women) pass from one element (they say, "out of the investing atmosphere") into another, the investing water; then, according to Greek usage, we should have this preposition with the element (εἰς ὕδωρ); but there is no such phraseology to be found in the entire history of John's baptism; and since ἐν ὕδατι cannot express the passing of men and women *into* the water, and cannot express the resting of men and women *in* the water (1, because it is not a fact that they do so rest; 2, because if they did so rest they must perish) we conclude, that ἐν ὕδατι is illegitimately united with βαπτίζω to express the element *within* which the baptism takes place; the true relation of the verb being with μετανοίαν, which presents, in εἰς, a certificate of wedlock which cannot be set aside.

Objection.

If it should be objected, that εἰς μετάνοιαν is not a physical element and therefore cannot represent the element of John's ritual baptism; it may be replied: 1. To say that John's ritual baptism must be *within* a physical element is an assumption of the whole question. 2. Baptisms are abundantly met with in which physical elements (water, wine, blood, tears,) appear without the baptism taking place *within* those elements. They are present, solely, in the character of agencies. If it be objected: Water cannot effect a baptism εἰς μετάνοιαν. I answer: That is precisely the doctrine which John makes to ring in the ears of impenitent Pharisees and Sadducees. It cannot give repentance nor remit sins. But water has a power which makes it meet to appear in a ritual baptism εἰς μετανοίαν. It has a symbol power. It can symbolize the purifying nature of "repentance," and the purified condition consequent upon "the remission of sins," and the purifying power of the atoning blood of "the Lamb of God that taketh away the sins of the world." Water, then, may appear in John's ritual baptism as fulfilling an office which such ritual baptism demands, and which is properly expressed by ἐν ὕδατι εἰς μετανοίαν. The exigency of the case requires the presence of water as a symbol agency, and the language of inspiration responds to the demand most absolutely. 3. Εἰς μετανοίαν, as a verbal element, may as truly indicate a baptism and point out its essential thought, as can a physical element; and in doing so it requires the same translation.

This is acknowledged by Dr. Conant, both in principle and in practice, in all cases outside of the Scriptures. The following are examples of such passages:

> Βεβαπτισμένον εἰς ἀναισθησίαν—"Plunged *into stupor.*"
> Βαπτιζόμενος εἰς ὕπνον—"Plunged *into sleep.*"
> Βαπτίζουσι εἰς πορνείαν—"Immerse *into fornication.*"

None of these are baptisms within a physical element. They have, however, the same verbal form and require the same translation. But while not *within* physical elements, two of them are effected *by* wine, a physical element, as the agency; not, however, simply as a fluid, but as a fluid possessed of a quality which, when drunk, is capable of inducing, 1, a condition of drunkenness; 2, a condition of stupor. To express this complete influence (not to express *immersion*, which has no existence) an admirably adapted verbal form, borrowed from physical baptisms, is employed —εἰς ἀναισθησίαν—εἰς ὕπνον. Wine is the efficient cause of these baptisms. It has the power, not through immersion but through drinking, to cause the conditions of complete stupor and profound sleep. Water has no power, either simply as a fluid or by its use in any particular form, to effect soul repentance. It cannot, therefore, be used for any such purpose. But when water, in certain religious rites, is applied to objects, it has a power which wine has not, namely, to make such objects *ceremonially* pure, or, to *symbolize* spiritual purity. For this reason (because of its symbolly purifying power) John was commissioned to use water in the ritual administration of his baptism εἰς μετανοίαν. And to express this the language of inspiration has the most perfect adaptation, ἐν ὕδατι εἰς μετανοίαν. We insist, therefore, upon our objection to the translation *unto* repentance, and declare it to be indefensible whether viewed philologically, grammatically, theologically, or in the light of the translation of all kindred passages, outside of the Scriptures, by Baptists themselves.

Dr. Carson.

Dr. Carson being of supreme authority among the friends of the theory, and having no superior in the ability which he has brought to its support, it would be unsatisfactory not to present, in full, his views on this most important passage. I will therefore make an exhibit of all his points.

His translation (p. 121) of Matt. 3 : 11, " I baptize you *in* water," leaves out εἰς μετανοίαν, nor does he once in all his discussion of the passage allude to these vital words. To leave out Hamlet from Hamlet is the merest trifle compared with the omission of these words in a critical consideration of this passage. Dr. Carson might as well take out from the Bible all that it says of the Lamb slain, from Abel's altar in Genesis to " the Lamb slain, as it were, in the midst of the throne," in Revelation, and hold forth to the world the mangled fragment which remained as the Word of God, as to take εἰς μετανοίαν out of this passage, and present Ἐγω βαπτίζω ἐν ὕδατι as the baptism of John. Having, thus, summarily dismissed the defendant and his witnesses from the court-room, he goes on to hear the plaintiff and his testimony, arriving at a result as self-satisfying as might be anticipated under so full and impartial a hearing.

The whole discussion proceeds, 1. On the assumption of the primary and literal meaning attributed to βαπτίζω; which may well be done in the enforced absence of εἰς μετανοίαν;

and, 2. On the assumption of a union between βαπτίζω and ὕδατι through the vinculum ἐν; against which invasion of his rights the silenced εἰς can offer no plea.

The interpretation is made to hinge on ἐν, and we will see what can be said in favor of this *ex parte* case.

Dr. Carson admits (p. 291), that "βαπτίζω ἐν is not so definite as βαπτίζω εἰς. It designates merely the place or substance in which the action is performed. It is the verb *immerse* and the circumstances which must prove the mode."

Thus Dr. Carson rejects from the passage βαπτίζω εἰς, confessedly the stronger form, and adopts βαπτίζω ἐν, confessedly the weaker form, and which could not lift up its head in the presence of its sturdier opponent.

He adds (p. 121): "It may be surprising after all that has been said on the subject, I should still lay any stress on ἐν *in*. I may be asked, Do you deny that it may be translated *with?* I do not deny this; yet I am, still, disposed to lay stress on it. A word may be used variously, yet be in each of its applications capable of being definitely ascertained. To ascertain its meaning here I shall submit the following observations:

" 1. *In* is the primary and most usual signification of ἐν."

This is cheerfully admitted with the necessary appendage, that *in this same Gospel* it is used *thirty-six* times in the sense *with, by*, as is acknowledged by the Baptist translators of the New Version.

" 2. In Matt. 3 : 11 all the words in connection admit the primary and usual meaning of ἐν. The most extravagant of our opponents admit, that βαπτίζω signifies *to dip*. . . . I contend, then, that though ἐν may sometimes be translated *with*, yet, it cannot be so used here."

On this position I observe : 1. Among " all the words in connection" with ἐν, the Greek verb is not to be numbered. It is in juxtaposition with it, but not in such syntactical relation as to bear any part in determining the meaning of the preposition ἐν. Its relations, in this regard, are with the elided εἰς μετανοίαν, and can give no determining character to the translation of ἐν ὕδατι. 2. Going beyond " the most extravagant of our opponents," I make no admission that βαπτίζω means *to dip*.

"3. I have produced innumerable examples in which ἐν is construed with this verb incontestably in the sense of dipping. What can forbid the phrase to have its usual meaning?"

These "innumerable examples," on examination, are reduced to the quite computable number—*none, no not one*. And as to the "usual meaning of the phrase βαπτίζω ἐν ὕδατι," if Dr. Carson, or any friend of the theory, can find one example in Classic, Jewish, Inspired, or Patristic literature, in which it means to put momentarily within and withdraw from a fluid, he will find what has eluded all my investigations.

"4. Even Mr. Ewing's translation——"

This we pass as having no concern with it

"5. Any translation that can be given to ἐν is inconsistent with the supposition that βαπτίζω signifies *to pour*."

It is in proof by evidence that never has been and never can be gainsaid (see Judaic Baptism), that baptism may be effected by pouring. No designed momentary introduction of an object into a fluid and its withdrawal (= a dipping) was ever called a baptism by any Classic Greek writer. But while a baptism may be effected by pouring (without the remotest reference to a covering), still, neither this modal act, nor any other modal act, is the *meaning* of the Greek verb.

"6. I maintain that ἐν in the sense *with* is not a Hebraism from *beth* which signifies *with* as well as *in*. 'Εν signifies *with* in Classical Greek as well as in the Septuagint and the New Testament; and just in the same circumstances."

New Testament writers do not give to ἐν a new meaning, but they use it very frequently in a sense in which it is more rarely used by Classical writers; they, also, use it with the dative case where Greek writers would only use the case. "The more frequent use of prepositions to mark relations indicated in Classic Greek by cases is characteristic of the style of the New Testament" (Fairbairn, Herm. Man., p.

38). "A predilection for prepositions where the Greeks employ cases alone is especially noticeable" (Winer, p. 36).

"7. Equally groundless and equally absurd is the assertion that the fact that the preposition is sometimes omitted, recommends the sense of with. Such an omission can cast no light upon the subject."

This "groundless and absurd assertion" we venture to make our own. If Classic writers usually employ the case alone to express instrumentality, and, usually, limit the preposition to mark locality, and if New Testament writers very frequently use the preposition with the case in expressing instrumentality, then, when New Testament writers in narrating the same thing use the dative, the one with, and the other without the preposition, the conclusion is overwhelming that the nude case must determine the wavering usage of the preposition. This conclusion is strongly enforced when the preposition is used by one with so strong Hebraistic tendencies as Matthew, and rejected by one of such Greekly tendencies as Luke. In such case the Hellenistic use of the preposition by the former in ἐν ὕδατι is made little short of certainty by the Classical use of ὕδατι by the latter. "When the dative case is employed without a preposition no other version than that which recognizes the instrumental dative ought to be admitted without a necessity" (Halley, p. 415). "In all cases of the New Testament where the element of the Baptism is expressed by the dative, only the element by which, not the mode in which Baptism is performed, is designated by the sacred writers" (Prof. Stuart). "But the dative, by a further extension of its import, is made to denote whatever accompanies the action, and this becomes a real ablative of the *mode* and *manner*, or of the instrument as Acts 1 : 5 ἐβάπτισεν ὕδατι. We often find ἐν used for the instrumental dative" (Winer, § 31, 7). Thus Winer adopts the "groundless and absurd" idea, that the simple dative countenances the sense of instrumentality, and that where the instrumental dative is employed by one writer and the dative with ἐν is employed to express the same thing by another writer, that we should regard the latter use as a case of " ἐν used for the instrumental dat. ⌣;" in other words, that the ἐν ὕδατι of Matthew and the ὕδατι of Luke are equivalent expressions indicative of instrumentality. While Winer does not apply the principle to this particular case, the presence of εἰς μετανοίαν and all the exigencies of the case require, that ἐν ὕδατι should be regarded as a circumstance or symbol instrument attendant on the baptism.

But while Dr. Carson elides from the text εἰς μετανοίαν, without note or comment by way of defence or apology, he elsewhere (p. 298) lays violent hands on βαπτίζω εἰς, and declares it to be an unquestionable " immerse *into*." The passage in which he finds this phrase (Mark 1:9) will be hereafter considered on its merits; at present, I refer to it only as the occasion for the expression of Dr. Carson's views as to the legitimate force of this phrase.

He asks : " If in common syntax such a phrase has such a meaning, why should it not have this meaning in the syntax of Scripture ?"

A very pertinent question, certainly; and just such as I would like to ask of Dr. Carson and friends in regard to Matt. 3:11, and Mark 1:4.

He adds : " But this syntax is not confined to *one* instance; it is found in many instances. Εἰς is connected with βαπτίζω in the commission (Matt. 28:19). Now, though water is not the regimen, yet it is the meaning of the preposition in reference to the performance of the rite which must regulate its meaning in all cases."

" Must regulate its meaning in all cases though water is not the regimen." Very good. And " this syntax is not confined to one instance; it is found in many instances." Very true. Now, let us turn our eye, for a moment, toward the " many instances of this syntax" together with their translations :

Βαπτίζω ἐν ὕδατι εἰς μετανοίαν—Immerse *unto* repentance. *Matt.* 3:11.

Βάπτισμα μετανοίας εἰς ἄφεσιν ἁμαρτιῶν—Immersion *unto* remission of sins. *Mark* 1:4.

Βαπτίζοντες εἰς τὸ ὄνομα τοῦ Πατρὸς . . . .—Immersing *in* the name of the Father . . . . *Matt.* 28 : 19.

Βαπτισθήτω . . . . *εἰς ἄφεσιν ἁμαρτιῶν*—Immersed *unto* remission of sins. *Acts* 2 : 38.

Βεβαπτισμένοι εἰς τὸ ὄνομα τοῦ κυρίου Ἰησοῦ—Immersed *in* the name of the Lord Jesus. *Acts* 8 : 16.

Ἐβαπτίσθητε, οὖν εἰς τί;—Immersed, then, *unto* what? *Acts* 19 : 3.

(Ἐβαπτίσθημεν) εἰς τὸ Ἰωάννου βάπτισμα—Immersed *unto* John's immersion. *Acts* 19 : 3.

Ἐβαπτίσθημεν εἰς Χριστὸν Ἰησοῦν—Immersed *into* Jesus Christ. *Rom.* 6 : 3.

Ἐβαπτίσθημεν εἰς τὸν θάνατον αὐτοῦ—Immersed *into* his death. *Rom.* 6 : 3.

Βαπτίσματος εἰς τὸν θάνατον—Immersion *into* his death. *Rom.* 6 : 4.

Ἐβαπτίσθητε εἰς τὸ ὄνομα Παύλου;—Immersed *in* the name of Paul? 1 *Cor.* 1 : 13.

Ἐβάπτισα εἰς τὸ ἐμὸν ὄνομα—Immersed *in* my own name. 1 *Cor.* 1 : 16.

Ἐβαπτίσαντο εἰς τὸν Μωυσῆν—Immersed *unto* Moses. 1 *Cor.* 10 : 2.

Ἐβαπτίσθημεν εἰς ἓν σῶμα—Immersed *into* one body. 1 *Cor.* 12 : 13.

Ἐβαπτίσθητε εἰς Χριστὸν—Immersed *unto* Christ. *Gal.* 3 : 27.

We have, here, I believe, all the cases of the New Testament in which the syntax *βαπτίζω εἰς* occurs with a difference in the adjunct, or with a difference in the circumstances under which the same adjunct is employed.

The cases are fifteen in number. The New Version translates these fifteen passages in four instances by "into," and in the remaining eleven by "unto" and "in." And such translation is given while loudly affirming, that such syntax demands *into* for its translation, and that even the feebler form, *βαπτίζω ἐν*, "will not admit of any other translation;" such translation is given while in every like case in the Classics the translation *into* is invariably made; and such translation is given, too, in the face of Carson's protesting inquiry—"If to produce such a meaning, such a syntax is necessary in common language, why should it be thought probable that where such syntax occurs in Scripture, it has not the same meaning? If the syntax is necessary to the meaning, why is the meaning denied it where the syntax is found?"

And what apology is offered for such marvellous departure from principle, from practice, and from protest? Just none at all; we are left to guess. And what shall we guess? Well, 1. This strawy reason: "The adjunct of the syntax is not a physical element." But has not Dr. Carson forestalled any such objection by his declaration—"though water is not the regimen, the meaning of the preposition is the same?" Besides, if Dr. Carson had never stated this truth, do not such baptisms superabound in the Classics? Why, then, should they not abound in the Scriptures? True, in the Classics the verbal form of the element in such baptisms is not stated; this, however, only shows how profoundly familiar were such baptisms, how long they had been in use, and with what familiarity they were employed. It could not be so, in the nature of the case, with these baptisms of the Holy Scriptures. These baptisms were all novelties as to their peculiar nature. They are now announced in the ears of men for the first time. It is an absolute necessity that the statement of their character should be, to the last degree, specific. And this is done to the exhaustion of the power of language when they are announced as βάπτισμα μετανοίας, βάπτισμα εἰς μετανοίαν, βάπτισμα εἰς ἄφεσιν ἁμαρτιῶν, βάπτισμα εἰς Χριστόν, &c., &c.

If our "guess" be right as to this reason, it is not of much worth.

We guess, again: 2. "A physical element appears in the rite symbolizing Repentance baptism, and therefore the baptism must be *within* that element." To which we reply: If men and women are to be thus baptized, then, of necessity, they must *pass into* this water element; but to express the passing into such element βαπτίζω εἰς is essential, while such phraseology with water as the adjunct is not to be found in the New Testament. The phraseology which is found (erroneously interpreted however by the theory as to syntactical relations) βαπτίζω ἐν is incapable of expressing "passing into," and does express *resting in*. Besides, what are the facts with regard to this phraseology? Just this: it is found some three or four times in the whole New Testament, all of which are repetitions of one utterance, or at the most by one person on two occasions, and such utterance, confessedly incapable of expressing the act declared to take place, and confessedly competent to and necessarily issuing in the destruction of life without foreign intervention; this phraseology, once uttered, is taken to the rejection, and to the subversion of phraseology which declares expressly and explicitly from the lips of the Forerunner, from the lips of the Mightier One come in his redeeming power, and from the lips of his commissioned Apostles, a baptism *into* REPENTANCE, *into* THE REMISSION OF SINS, *into* JESUS CHRIST, *into* THE NAME OF THE FATHER, SON, AND HOLY GHOST. What a reason!

We make one more guess: 3. " Our theory must perish if we carry into the Scriptures the principles and the practice which we observe in our Classic translations."

There can be no doubt about that conclusion; but as it must perish, anyway, it might as well perish in the observance of consistency. It does not save the bird of the desert to hide her head in the bush when the hunter is upon her. She must die. The bomb-ketch on which ten thousand Paixhan guns are playing must be "blown out of the water." The theory can never live under such dread artillery as is let loose upon it from the open mouths of words which the Holy Ghost teacheth.

Baptism into Repentance no Model for Dipping into Water.

Some might imagine that the phraseology " baptism *into* repentance" would furnish a basis on the ground of resemblance for using the water in the rite by dipping "into" it. But this is not so. There is nothing in " baptism into repentance" bearing a resemblance to *dipping into* water any more than there is a resemblance to a square or a circle. Dr. Carson objects to an argument in favor of pouring water in ritual baptism being grounded on a resemblance to the " pouring out of the Holy Spirit." He says (p. 105), " Baptism, whatever be the mode, cannot represent either the manner of conveying the Spirit, or his operations in the soul. These things cannot be represented by natural things. There is no likeness to the Spirit or the mode of his opera- tions. It is blasphemy to attempt a representation. Bap- tism, then, cannot be pouring or dipping, for the sake of representing the *manner* of the conveyance of the Holy Spirit; for there is no such likeness. Pouring of the Spirit is itself a figure, not a reality to be represented by a figure."

All this is true, so far as any imagined resemblance of form is concerned between the pouring out of water and the pouring out of the Spirit; but an argument based on the harmony of words and of conception in thought would be perfectly legitimate. But in the case of " baptism into re- pentance" and "dipping into water," there is not merely the absence of resemblance in form, but there is no resem- blance in words, or in conception of thought. There is no such language as " baptizing into *water*" known to the Scriptures; and between the conception of a " *baptism* into repentance" and a " *dipping* into water" there is a great gulf fixed. The one expresses the most complete, penetra- ting, pervading, and assimilating influence of which lan- guage is capable; while the other expresses a momentary act and a superficial result. There is, therefore, no ground in any aspect for deducing a water dipping from a repent- ance baptizing.

It is possible that some might imagine, that the phrase- ology " baptism into repentance" was derived from the use of the water in the rite; this, however, is as impossible as that the foundation of a house should rest on its roof. The baptism which John preached was antecedent to, and the foundation of the rite which he administered. The rite grew out of the preaching, not the preaching out of the rite.

It must, also, be clearly understood, that there are not two (really or verbally) diverse baptisms in the preaching and in the rite. The baptism is but one. The diversity is to be sought in the agencies. In the baptism preached the agency is appropriate in nature and adequate in power, namely, the Spirit of God, and he effects a true baptism εἰς μετανοίαν. In the baptism ritually administered the agency, water, has neither appropriateness of nature nor adequacy of power to effect such true baptism; but it has both appropriateness of nature and adequacy of power to symbolize such true baptism. The baptism then, in both cases, is verbally the same; but in the one case the baptism is realized, and in the other case only symbolized. It is manifestly absurd to suppose, that John should preach one baptism and ritually administer a wholly diverse baptism. Whatever baptism was in his preaching that same baptism was in his ritual administration. And this the Scriptures declare *totidem verbis*, when they announce that John *preached* τὸ βάπτισμα μετανοίας (Mark 1 : 4; Luke 3 : 3; Acts 13 : 24), and, in the same express and identical words, announce that he *baptized* τὸ βάπτισμα μετανοίας (Matt. 3 : 11; Acts 19 : 4). The proof is absolute, that there neither was nor could be any baptism into water; and to convert these Bible baptisms *into* WATER DIPPINGS is to reject the revelation of God and to make one for ourselves.

We have, now, passed in review all that Dr. Carson has to say on this passage which, so largely, pivots the whole question, and we find nothing to justify his mutilation of it by excising εἰς μετανοίαν, and thus converting the passage into its contradictory—"I baptize you *in water.*" We have found as little to approve in the New Version of Matthew, "I *immerse* you *in* water *unto* repentance," or that of Mark (the translator of which informs us that, "it has been settled that there is no difference in signification between βάπτω and βαπτίζω"), "I *dip* you in water." To make repentance the end of the ritual use of water ("*unto* repentance"), is to sow seed which must logically fruit out in all the errors of Campbell-baptism or something worse, for Campbell denies that water dipping is "*for* repentance," while inconsistently affirming that it is "*for* the remission of sins."

I am not aware of any other objections likely to be made against the translation which has been given—"I baptize you with water into repentance;" a translation sustained by grammatical law, conformed to Classical usage, harmonious with parallel passages, accordant with the spiritual nature of all other New Testament baptisms, and demanded by the very nature of John's ministry.   We will therefore adhere, for reasons both positive and negative, to our position, that John did baptize *into* repentance *with* water used as a symbol—"repentance" being the complement of βαπτίζω, and "water" being a circumstantial adjunct setting forth, symbolly, the nature of repentance baptism in its purifying character.

'Εγὼ μὲν ὕδατι βαπτίζω ὑμᾶς—I indeed, with water, baptize you. *Luke* 3 : 16.

This passage claims consideration in so far as it presents differences as compared with the parallel passage just considered.

1. One of the differences consists in the elliptical character of this passage of Luke compared with that of Matthew. The ellipsis consists in the omission of εἰς μετανοίαν.   A hasty judgment might lead to the conclusion that it would be the less important words which would be omitted, but the contrary of this is the truth.

Professor Crosby, in his Greek Grammar, observes : "It is a remarkable but general truth that ellipsis omits that word which is most essential to the grammatical structure of the sentence.   The reason is such word will be more readily missed and more easily supplied."

Dr. Carson is in accord with Professor Crosby in this doctrine of ellipsis.   He says, " This figure always grounds on the fact that the elliptical matter will always be suggested by the frequency of the use of the phrase, so that it cannot be either wanted or mistaken.   If it does not necessarily and obviously present itself, it is essentially vicious in rhetoric and utterly unworthy of revelation " (p. 328).

Now, the ellipsis in this passage answers very squarely to this doctrine.   What is more essential to the structure of the sentence than the absent words εἰς μετανοίαν, or βαπτισμα μετανοίας, which are absolutely essential to give completeness to βαπτίζω?   And what could be more readily supplied by reason of the frequency of the use of the phrase either formally stated or more briefly referred to? Let us look at the frequency of this usage, not throughout all the gospels, but by Luke alone:

Luke 3: 3. Preaching the baptism *of repentance* into the re-
        mission of sins.
 " 7 : 29. Being baptized with the baptism *of John*.
 " 20 : 4. The baptism *of John* was it from heaven or of men?

The latter briefer statements are completed by the former fuller one. The same writer, in the book of Acts, furnishes us with the following passages:

Acts 1 : 22. Beginning from the baptism *of John*.
 " 10 : 13. Preaching peace by Jesus Christ . . . . . after the
          baptism *which John* preached.
 " 13 : 24. When John had first preached before his coming
          the baptism *of repentance*.
 " 18 : 25. Apollos . . . . . knowing only the baptism *of John*.
 " 19 : 3. Into what, then, were ye baptized? And they said,
          Into *John's* baptism.
 " 19 : 4. Then, said Paul, John, verily, baptized the baptism
          of repentance.

We see, by these frequent allusions by Luke to the baptism of John, "what," to use the language of Dr. Carson, "can neither be wanted nor mistaken." The ellipsis to be supplied must be from Matthew, εἰς μετανοίαν, or, as furnished by Luke himself, βάπτισμα μετανοίας εἰς ἄφεσιν ἁμαρτιων, which differ in letter only, not in spirit. These are the essential words which we cannot do without. And, thus, by the doctrine of ellipsis, we are brought again to the conclusion, that the vital part of John's baptism is to be sought not in ἐν ὕδατι, but in εἰς μετανοίαν.

2. A second point of difference is found in the use of the simple dative.

Luke is persistent in this usage. It appears in his Acts of the Apostles (1 : 5; 11 : 16) as well as in his Gospel. He never uses ἐν ὕδατι. This is readily accounted for by his more Greekly style. Mark also (1 : 8) uses the simple da-

tive according to the Cod. Sin. and other authority, which
is received by Tischendorf and Alford as the true reading.
Origen also (IV, 253), while quoting Matthew and John as
using ἐν ὕδατι, quotes, at the same time, Mark and Luke as
using ὕδατι. The latter form is more frequent than the former according to these authorities.

The New Version translates this nude form, in every instance, "*in* water." Such translation is contrary to the general consent of scholars. Winer (p. 216) gives Acts 1 : 5,
11 : 16, as cases in which the dative "has passed over altogether into the ablative." He adds, "In all these relations
prepositions are not rarely and sometimes more usually employed with or without a modification of the meaning. Thus
we find ἐν ὕδατι instead of ὕδατι. The identity of the two expressions in *sense* is manifest; yet we must not consider one
as put for the other" (p. 412).

The reason assigned by the New Version for the translation in Luke 3 : 16, namely, "The preposition ἐν is obviously
understood before ὕδατι," is neither sustained by the general
merits of the case nor by the doctrine of ellipsis. The conclusion reached by the New Version in Acts 1 : 5, "The in-
sertion or omission, therefore, of the preposition does not
alter the construction or the sense," has an inadequate foundation in the reason assigned, namely, that Matthew and
John use the preposition and Mark and Luke do not.

The phrases may differ immediately, both in construction
and in sense, yet agree ultimately in a common thought. It
is not the same form of thought which is expressed by "Seal
ἐν τῷ δακτυλίῳ," and "Seal τῷ δακτυλίῳ;" "Kill ἐν ῥομφαίᾳ," and
"Kill ῥομφαίᾳ;" "Nourish ἐν γάλακτι," and "Nourish γάλακτι;"
"Baptize ἐν ὕδατι εἰς μετανοίαν," and "Baptize ὕδατι εἰς μετανοίαν."
There is a power and authority which belongs to "the ring"
(king's) with which "the sealer" is represented as invested
by ἐν, and *in* this power and authority performing the act
of sealing. In the nude dative this conception is wanting; while the sealing is quite as effectively done "*by* the
ring." So, "the sword" has a power to slay, with which
"the killer" is represented as invested and as controlling.

"Milk" has a quality for nourishing, and "the Nourisher" gives direction to the development of that quality. "Water" has a symbol power to baptize into repentance, and the Baptizer is represented as invested with and exercising just that symbol power. This conception has no statement in the simple dative.

It is noticeable, that the preposition is never omitted by any of the sacred writers in speaking of the baptism by Christ ἐν Πνεύματι Ἁγίῳ. This finds a perfect explanation in the relation between Christ and the Holy Ghost. He is ever "in the Holy Ghost," invested with and acting through his divine influence, and it would not be so suitable to say, that he baptizes Πνεύματι Ἁγίῳ, separating him from that divine inness taught by the Scriptures. The contrast between ἐν ὕδατι and ἐν Πνεύματι Ἁγίῳ is absolute. John was invested with the mere shadow power belonging to symbol water; Christ was invested with all the real power belonging to the Spirit of God. John came "in the Spirit and power of Elias," and baptized with the power of symbol water; Christ came, "God manifest in the flesh," and baptized in (invested with) the power of the Holy Ghost. Under any aspect in which the case can be considered, the nude form ὕδατι sustains the conclusion that ἐν ὕδατι is, mediately or immediately, expressive of instrumentality.

3. A third point of difference is the order of the words. In so far as any difference of interpretation is suggested by the order of the words—βαπτίζω ἐν ὕδατι εἰς μετανοίαν, and ὕδατι βαπτίζω εἰς μετανοίαν, the latter order brings βαπτίζω and εἰς μετανοίαν into more obvious relationship. Thus the language of Luke, by the ellipsis of the most essential feature of the phrase, by the nude dative, and by the change in the order of the words, does at every point sustain the interpretation which has been given of the passage in Matthew.

The order of the words (using the preposition) ἐν τῷ ὕδατι βαπτίζων (εἰς μετανοίαν) is the same in John 1 : 31 as in Luke 3 : 16.

The New Version translator of Acts says, in a note on 1 : 5, "As ὕδατι stands to the immersion by John, so precisely

does ἐν Πνεύματι stand to the immersion of Christ." This is
true; and the converse is, also, true: As ἐν Πνεύματι stands to
the baptism of Christ, so, precisely, does ὕδατι stand to the
baptism of John. Now, there are few things, if there be
anything, having more absolute proof of their truth, than
that of the executive agency of the Holy Spirit in the baptism of the soul into repentance, εἰς μετανοίαν, or into the remission of sins, εἰς ἀφεσιν ἁμαρτιων. It must, then, be true,
that water occupies the position of symbol agency in reference to the ritual administration of these same baptisms.

This view is confirmed by the painful absurdity which has
ever characterized the attempts of those friends of the theory
who have sought to transform this agency into an investing element, as well as by the necessity which has been felt
by other of its friends to abandon this irrational endeavor
and to expound it as a penetrating, pervading, and controlling power. Thus Professor Ripley (Acts 1:5) says, "To be
baptized with the Holy Spirit, means *to receive the influences
of the Holy Spirit in great abundance*—to be most plente-
ously *endued with divine influence*—the promised *effusion* of the
Holy Spirit took place. v. 8. The supernatural ability with
which the Apostles *were to be endowed by* the Holy Spirit—It
was *by the Holy Spirit's agency* that the Apostles were to be
fully prepared for their office. (2:4.) The Spirit was imparted so copiously, that the disciples are said to have been
filled with it. New and unusual mental power was possessed
by them. Their religious views became clearer, and their
religious fervor was greatly increased." Professor Ripley
eschews the ludicrous absurdity of " a house filled with the
sound of wind in which the Apostles are immersed." He
also interprets " the *immersion* of Christ," of which the New
Version translator speaks, as having no " immersion" in it,
whether of fact or of imagination; but resolves it into effect
produced, to wit, changed condition of the soul. In this
view this distinguished Baptist commentator is undoubtedly
correct; and it follows, as a necessary consequence, that
there was no " immersion," of fact or of imagination, in
" the *immersion* of John;" but that the pure water symbol-

ized the purifying nature of this "changed condition of the soul." The preposition in ε'ς μετανοίαν—εἰς ἀφεσιν—is introduced as suggestive of such cases of physical baptism as exhibit the baptized object penetrated, pervaded, and assimilated by the qualities of the investing element; and having performed this duty its functions are exhausted.

JOHN'S COMMISSION ILLUSTRATED BY HIS FORMULA OF BAPTISM.

Εἰς μετανοίαν.

It is not certain that John used any formula of words which he repeated in the case of every individual baptism. There is no such express statement, nor is there any absolute necessity for it. The ministry of John was not like the subsequent ministry of Christianity, one which embraced a broad field of varied truth and duty; but was severely limited to a single particular—the coming of Christ and preparation for it by true soul repentance. A ritual ordinance based on such a ministry could have but one character, and therefore could not need the repetition of a word formula for its exposition.

If, however, a formula was used, its terms must, of necessity, have been such as to be a reannouncement of the object and end of his ministry. Some have thought with Olshausen that the formula of John announced a baptism εἰς τὸν ἐρχόμενον —"I baptize thee into the Coming One." If this were so, then it is as certain that John said nothing of a baptism into water, by such formula, as that true words express true things.

It is simply impossible that in 'Εγω ὕδατι βαπτίζω ὑμας εἰς τὸν ἐρχομενον, that βαπτίζω can occupy a double and identical relation to ὕδατι and εἰς τὸν ἐρχόμενον. Its complementary relation must be with the one or the other exclusively. If the baptism be, as declared, "into the Coming One," then, the verb has absolutely nothing to do with expounding the manner in which ὕδατι is employed in the rite. Its power is exhausted by the declaration, that the baptized are to be brought under the controlling influence of "the Coming One."

Beza, and others, have thought that John baptized, ritually, εἰς τὸ ὄνομα τοῦ κυρίου 'Ιησοῦ. Now it is obvious, that the difference between the baptism of Olshausen and of Beza lies precisely in the difference between εἰς τόν ἐρχόμενον and εἰς τὸ ὄνομα τοῦ κυρίου 'Ιησοῦ; ὕδατι has nothing in the world to do with it, cannot by any possibility enter into it; so far as the baptisms depend on it they do not differ, but are identical. If these baptisms, therefore, differ in any wise, they differ by reason of the words indicated and in them must we look for the baptism, just as we look to εἰς γάλα, εἰς αἷμα, for the difference between a "baptism *into* MILK" and a "baptism *into* BLOOD."

But there is no Scriptural authority for saying, that John "baptized, with water, into the Coming One," or "baptized, with water, into the name of the Lord Jesus;" the declaration is express, "I baptize, with water, into REPENTANCE" (εἰς μετανοίαν). The formula of baptism must declare the nature of the baptism, and this is here done in the most explicit manner. Water is introduced merely as a symbol agency with whose manner of use the verb has no concern.

Baptist writers, when they forget themselves and speak according to the record, use the language of Scripture and say, as does Stovel, "John baptized them into repentance, without which none can be accepted of God in the Redeemer." Now, as Mr. Stovel did not teach, that "immersing in water" made the soul "accepted of God in the Redeemer," he could not refer to ritual baptism, and must use this language, "baptized them *into repentance*," just as John preached it, and just as the phraseology expresses it = the soul brought under the controlling influence of repentance; such are, none other are, "accepted of God in the Redeemer." Such a baptism became the Forerunner of the Mightier One; such a baptism was a fit preparation for the coming Lord; to preach and to administer a dipping in water was neither becoming to the character of John, nor a preparation for the presence of Christ. If Stovel had said: "John *immersed them in* WATER, without which none can be accepted of God," what an infinitely different sentiment would he have uttered compared with the words which he has employed—"John *baptized them into* REPENTANCE, without which none can be accepted of God." I repeat, then, that the nature of the baptism must be found in εἰς τὸν ἐρχόμενον—εἰς τὸ ὄνομα—εἰς μετανοίαν—and while John said, ritually, "I baptize *into* REPENTANCE, with water," as a symbol; he never said, I baptize *into* WATER (εἰς ὕδωρ).

John may have used the formula, "I baptize thee into repentance," saying nothing about the water, in words, but leaving the use of the water to speak for itself, as showing that a symbol baptism, only, was contemplated; or, he may have said, "I, *with water*, baptize thee into repentance;" thus, calling attention to the water, as a symbol, that they might the more surely avoid the error of supposing, that there was any spiritual efficacy in the rite. But while the words of Scripture remain as they are, it is beyond the power of any sound interpretation to deduce from them a dipping *into water*. So far, therefore, as the evidence for a formula of baptism goes, it is in support, clearly and exclusively, of a baptism "into repentance" and not into water.

*Parallel usage—*καταπίνω, βυθίζω, ποντίζω.

The principles which enter into the preceding interpretations receive confirmation by their acceptance in parallel cases.

Καταπίνω exhibits in many respects a usage parallel with that of βαπτίζω (καταβαπτίζω).

1. This word expresses etymologically, the act of drinking, swallowing down a liquid.

2. It drops the limiting *liquid* element, and is applied to swallowing *solids:* Matt. 23 : 24, "and swallow a *camel;*" Josephus, de Bello, V, 10, 1, "they swallowed *pieces of gold* that they might not be found by the robbers;" VI, 7, 3, "swallowed down *food* fouled with blood."

3. It drops the distinctive character of the *act* as well as

of fluid substance: Is. 28 : 7, "The priest and the prophet are swallowed up (κατεπόθησαν) of (διὰ) wine;" Josephus, V, 13 : 6, "Jerusalem would have been swallowed up by a yawning gulf." Swallow *up* expresses *result*, beyond what is done by swallow *down*, which expresses *act*.

4. All form of descending action is lost, and resultant covered condition substituted: Hebrews 11:29, "The Egyptians were swallowed up κατεπόθησαν = drowned." The Egyptians were already within and on the bottom of the sea. They were not "swallowed *down*." The waters returning swal·lowed them up = destroyed them by drowning.

5. Covered condition, as well as form of action, is lost and destruction remains: 1 Peter 5 : 8, "The devil as a roar· ing lion seeketh whom he may *devour*" (καταπίη). The lion may or may not swallow what he destroys. "A roaring lion" destroys more than he swallows. It is to his destroying and not swallowing character to which reference is here made. Destruction precedes swallowing in the case of a roaring lion. It follows swallowing in the case of the returning waters of the sea. The devil *destroys* many; he "swallows" none. Wine swallowed *down* by priest or prophet, swallows *up* priest and prophet; wine baptized *in the stomach* by drinking, baptizes the drinker in *drunkenness*.

Secondary use of καταπίνω.

As destruction of the thing swallowed is the natural and ordinary result of swallowing, such expression therefore is very naturally used of things in which there can be no swallowing, but whose destruction we wish to signify.

1. This is expressed fully and clearly by verbal figure: 1 Cor. 15 : 54, κατεπόθη ὁ θάνατος εἰς νῖκος, "Death is swallowed up *into victory*." Here, death is not merely represented as "swallowed up," this would have been sufficient to express, generally, its destruction; but not the specific character of the destruction. But this is done in the completest manner by the statement—"swallowed up *into* VICTORY." This expresses not merely the death of death, but the triumphant circumstances attendant upon that death.

Now, will any one say, on the ground of the verbal figure εἰς νῖκος, that νῖκος must represent a man's stomach, and "death" must represent a drink of cold water going down into it? or a lion's paunch and a torn sheep passing down into it? This is the rhetoric of the theory. Is not the phrase exhausted, when it guides us to its physical origin and we take therefrom the thought of destruction which there confronts us?

2. VERBAL figure, grounded in the *swallowing*, finds no place by statement or imagination; but a power capable of effecting, by other means than swallowing, a condition of like characteristics, is brought into view.

As in 2 Cor. 5:4, "that mortality might be swallowed up *by life*." That which is swallowed up is not necessarily swallowed up within that which is causative of such condition. It was sin which caused Jerusalem to be in danger of being swallowed up, not within itself, but within "a yawning chasm." One may be swallowed up by intemperance into the profoundest debasement, or by luxury into utter effeminacy. To be swallowed up *by* a thing, in secondary usage, is a phrase of very different value from being swallowed *down by* or *in* a thing. To be swallowed *up by* ambition, *by* avarice, *by* selfishness, is indicative of the supreme control of such influences; they have the mastery. This ends the idea. There is no imaginary stomach to be constructed. In 2 Cor. 5:4, the controlling agency is in the genitive with ὑπό; but in 2 Cor. 2:7, it is in the dative without a preposition, "swallowed up *by overmuch sorrow*." This expresses directly the supremacy of sorrow. There is no formal figure. Figure is only present in that sense in which a word is diverted from its primary, physical application, and so much of the original thought as is adapted to the case is accepted, and the remainder rejected. It might be converted into verbal figure and give greater specialty to the statement by saying—"swallowed up by overmuch sorrow *into* DESPONDENCY, *into* LETHARGY, *into* DESPAIR." Either of these conditions might result from "overmuch sorrow," and by their differences they show the neces-

sity for specific statement when it cannot be otherwise certainly learned.

3. The result consequent upon the swallowing up of an
object, literally, is not a destructive influence over such object always; but on the contrary a powerful influence may
proceed from such object by reason of its new position.

This is true with regard to food swallowed. It, thereby,
exerts an influence over the whole physical system which is
preservative of life. The same in principle, although the
opposite as to the character of the influence exerted, is the
influence of wine or poisons swallowed. On this literal
foundation we have that usage which appears in Ar. Ach.,
484, "to drink or swallow down Euripides;" where the purpose is to express the influence to be derived from Euripides,
and not that which should be exerted over Euripides. Of
precisely the same character is the transaction in Julian,
Egypt, p. 223, "I mersed Cupid into the wine and swallowed
him." Cupid having first been swallowed up in the wine
was, then, swallowed down by the drinker for the purpose
of securing the influence which the God of Love would
thereby exert over the drinker, and which is expressed by
his "titillating wings." So in all cases of wine-drinking;
the wine is swallowed down not for any influence to be exerted upon the swallowed-down wine, but for the swallow-
ing-up influence of the wine which, hereby, finds development, not envelopment.

Influence may be exerted controllingly by the enveloping
substance over the enveloped object, or, reversely, the enveloped object may exert a controlling influence over the
enveloping substance. The Scriptures afford exemplifications of both cases. Dr. Conant says, " Βαπτίζω expresses
the being swallowed up" (not the being swallowed *down*)
" wholly in a new state or life." This would be a remarkable meaning for a *dipping*. But it is the most absolute vindication of our interpretation which places the object under
the complete influence of " the new state or life." John
preached a " new state," a " new life," and symbolly baptized into it, and not into water.

Βυθίζω, ποντίζω.

All words having a literal meaning of such a character as βυθίζω, ποντίζω, βαπτίζω, &c., must carry with them the idea of influence, and come in the exigencies of language to express influence directly. Robinson (N. T. Lex.) says, καταποντίζω, Matt. 18 : 6, "is used to indicate the highest degree of misery and suffering." In II Mac. 12 : 4, βυθίζω is used to express, directly, *drowning*, the influence of throwing men and women "into the deep." And in 1 Tim. 6 : 9, ἅιτενες βυθίζουσι τυὸς ἀνθρώπους εἰς ὄλεθραν καὶ ἀπώλειαν, we have (through verbal figure) the nature of the engulfing influence of "many foolish and hurtful lusts." And just as Paul says, the influence of such lusts issues εἰς ὄλεθρον καὶ ἀπώλειαν, so Josephus says, the influence of wine-drinking issues εἰς ἀναισθησίαν καὶ ὕπνον, and John says, the influence of the Holy Ghost issues εἰς μετανοίαν παὶ ἄφεσιν ἁμαρτιῶν.

Such words express a *general controlling influence which receives specific character from the adjunct.* A general usage, belonging to this entire class of verbs as now indicated, gives to the interpretation assigned to βαπτίζω the highest certainty. We ask nothing for this word which does not belong to every other word of its class as shown by usage both in and out of the Scriptures.

PLACES OF JOHN'S BAPTISM.

PLACE WITHOUT MENTION OF WATER.

Ἰωάννης βαπτίζων ἐν τῇ ἐρήμῳ.
John was baptizing in the wilderness.—*Mark* 1 : 4.

Ἐν Βηθανίᾳ . . . . . ὅπου ἦν Ἰωάννης βαπτίζων.
In Bethany beyond Jordan where John was baptizing.—*John* 1 : 28.

Εἰς τὸν τόπον, ὅπου ἦν Ἰωάννης τὸ πρῶτον βαπτίζων.
Into the place, where John was first baptizing.—*John* 10 : 40.

ARGUMENT FROM PLACES OF BAPTISM.

"*In the Wilderness.*"

ALL who urge the essential duty of "walking into the water and dipping the upper part of the body" give bold relief to the places where John baptized. These places were the wilderness, two villages, and a river. The Scriptures declare the. place, the symbol, and the nature of the baptism; the friends of the theory see nothing but a *river* and a *dipping* into it.

They who call upon the world to perform "a definite act" under penalty of "violated fealty to God," assume no ordinary responsibility; and they who yield to such demands become partners in such responsibilities. We will obey the commands of the Lord adoringly; we will reject the commands of men absolutely.

New Version Translation.

Some of the best critical editions of the New Testament make the text of Mark 1 : 4 to read, ὁ βαπτίζων the Baptist, and not βαπτίζων *baptizing;* we shall, however, now consider the passage as it stands.

The New Version translates thus: "John was immersing in the desert" (Quarto); "came immersing in the wilderness and preaching the immersion of repentance unto the remission of sins" (later edition).

We object to the translation "*im*-mersing," because the original is βαπτίζων and not ἐμ-βαπτίζων. If to this it should be answered, "We have no word *merse,* uncompounded with a preposition in the English language, and must do the best we can;" then, What is this but a confession that the English language does not, in this direction, furnish a suitable translating word? It is idle to say, that there is no difference of power between βαπτίζω and ἐμ-βαπτίζω, mergo and *im*-mergo. And it is worse than idle to say, that the Greek usage of βαπτίζω and ἐμ-βαπτίζω is the same. But, although we have not in English *to merse* uncompounded, we have *to merge* both simple and compound, and Dr. Conant says this uncompounded Greek word means "im-*merse,* im-*merge.*" Why not, then, take the uncompounded *merge?* Why not say, "John came *merging* in the wilderness?" Is it replied, "This is not English; this is nonsense?" I respond, This may be so; and yet it does more nearly express the truth than, "John came im-*mersing* in the wilderness." *To im-merse,* primary, means to put an object within some *physical medium* for an indefinite period of time; while *to merge* has no such English usage, but is applied ordinarily (if not without exception by good writers) to things which are not physical, and denotes the passing of an object into new relations, with which it thenceforth becomes incorporated and assimilated. "Feeble-mindedness *merging* into idiocy," expresses an intellectual condition passing into and becoming assimilated unto the condition of idiocy. It is boundlessly absurd, in view of English usage, to speak of "feeble-mindedness merging (!) *into water*," not merely because the intellect cannot pass into a fluid, but because the intellect cannot become incorporated with and assimilated unto water. We enter a peremptory denial, in the name of the whole New Testament, against βαπτίζω any more than "merge" carrying its object *into water*. And we demand by all the authority of the express Word of God, that this word shall be allowed to carry its object *into the condition of* REPENTANCE (to be made subject to its controlling influence in the remission of sins through the Lamb of God), which condition shall be ritually set forth by pure symbol water.

But again: Why take a compound word to express an uncompounded word when there are simple forms, *plunge*, *dip*, which we are told do express in the most perfect manner the meaning of the Greek word? Why not get rid of the preposition (which is not in the Word of God) by translating, according to Professor Arnold, "John came *plunging* in the wilderness and preaching the *plunging* of repentance *unto* the remission of sins?" Thus conforming to the solemn declaration of Professor Arnold, of the Baptist Theological Seminary, Chicago (Bapt. Quar., Jan., 1870, p. 81), "In fact, the verb βαπτίζω, *immergo*, has but one meaning. It signifies literally and perpetually *to plunge*." Or, why not translate, "*dipping* in the wilderness and preaching the *dipping* of repentance *unto* the remission of sins?" And so conform to the affirmation of Dr. Carson, versus Arnold, "*Βαπτίζω* means dip and nothing but dip through all Greek literature." "Preaching the *immersion* of repentance *unto* the remission of sins" is neither English, nor Greek, nor Christianity.

The translation "immersing" is objectionable on another ground. It does not accord with the affirmation made as to the meaning of the Greek word by Baptists.

The translator of Matthew says, the word means "a definite act." But there is no one definite act in "immerse." Why, then, translate by a word which does not express the meaning of the translated word? The translator of Mark and Luke says, "It has been settled, that there is no difference as to signification between βάπτω and βαπτίζω." Then,

why translate by "immerse?" Everybody (and these translators not less than others) admits, that βάπτω means *to dip;*
but no one who understands the English or the Latin language will say, that *to dip* and *to immerse* are equivalent
words. Why then, I repeat, originate this incongruity between definition and translation? I have no doubt whatever
of the good general Greek scholarship of this translator, but
when engaging in a New Version which was to be, emphatically, a new and true version of βαπτίζω, he should have
sought such a special mastery of the use of this particular
word as would have saved him from so patent an error as
that in the declaration, "It has been settled, that there is no
difference, as to signification, between βάπτω and βαπτίζω.
The latter is merely a later *form* of the word." This statement is, truly, surprising.

The translator of Acts says, "*Dip, bap,* and *plunge,* indicate
the sounds made by variously applying any solid substance
to water. The air echoes *plunge* when a person is suddenly
immersed in water—it echoes *dip* and *bap* when persons or
other solid substances are suddenly submerged. Being
words of *action,* and not of *mode, they can have but one literal
and proper meaning.*" It is cause for wonder, that this scholar
after looking upon Dr. Carson's crucifixion of Professor Ewing on the cross of ridicule, driving in through every available point the tenpenny nails of sarcasm and of contempt,
did not shrink from adopting the Professor's idea, that *bap*
and *pop* were expository of βαπτίζω; but we have neither
cross nor "scalping knife" for the erring friends of the
theory. It is painful enough for them to see a cherished
theory perish through its own falsity. We would, however,
like to ask: How it happens, that while *bap,* and *dip,* and
plunge, are the "echoes" of the Greek word, yet these
echoes are all rejected, and "im-merse," which makes no
such "echo," is taken in their stead? Carson flays alive
the luckless friend of *pop;* the Baptist Quarterly repudiates
dip as too contemptible a word to give name to a Christian
ordinance; and Booth will have nothing to do with *plunge,*
because "it makes our views ridiculous." And yet these

words are pronounced by these translators to be the very words which, above all others, represent βαπτίζω, while, in translation, they are all set aside for another word essentially different in radical thought from *pop*, *dip*, or *plunge*, as they and it are, all alike, heaven-wide diverse from βαπτίζω in nature and in language development.

The New Version translator of Ephes. 5 : 26 (note), translates βαπτιζόμενος "*he that dippeth.*" We object to this statement in notes, that a word means one thing, and "can have but one literal and proper meaning," and, then, giving in the text a word to which usage has assigned a very different meaning. It is as easy to unify midnight and noon, as it is to unify the usage of dip and immerse. And yet we are enjoined, in God's dread name, to believe that βαπτίζω means, indifferently, "dip or immerse." So long as we fear God and retain the use of reason we shall decline the absurdity.

The translation "immersing" is objectionable, if used in the sense of *dipping* (a designed momentary putting into and taking out of the water), because such is not the Classic use of the translated word. The element of momentariness belongs and gives character to βάπτω *to dip;* but this element has utterly disappeared from βάπτω *to dye.* The same is true with regard to βαπτίζω; and while the absence of momentariness is not all which distinguishes it from βάπτω, it is its most essential element, and that without which it would be wholly incompetent for its developed usage. If on the other hand, "immersing" is not used for "a *designed* momentary putting into and taking out of," then, it is objectionable that it should be conjoined with *water*, because to put a human being under water without withdrawal is to destroy life. In either case the translation is an error.

The Scriptures have neither changed the essential meaning of the word, nor have they allied it with water as its exponential adjunct. There is not an instance of the use of βάπτω (primary) in the New Testament to which the idea of momentariness does not belong; and there is not an instance of the use of βαπτίζω in the New Testament to which the idea of momentariness does belong. If this be true the theory falls into a shapeless ruin. I know that assertion is not proof. Were it otherwise proof of the theory would long since have out-topped the stars. I accept all the burden which this assertion brings; I will give the proof.

Baptism of the Passage.

The baptism which is announced by Mark is not a baptism in water, but is, *totidem verbis*, declared to be a "*baptism through* REPENTANCE *into* THE REMISSION OF SINS."

The possibility of such a baptism will be questioned by no one acquainted with the usage of βαπτίζω. And the possibility of the language of Mark expressing such a baptism will be questioned by no one acquainted with the Greek language. We claim that what is possible is true in fact. It will be seen, at once, that such a baptism has this superiority over the baptism of the theory—*there is no need to take any one out of this baptism in a twinkling in order to save life.* The soul may remain under the full controlling influence of remitted sins forever. The redeemed once introduced into this condition will, in fact, so abide forever. Thus far, then, we have the advantage of giving an exhaustive development to the full power of this forcible word, while the theory mocks at its high character and substitutes for it a sham.

The difference between baptism εἰς μετανοίαν, and "baptism of repentance εἰς ἀφεσιν ἁμαρτιων," is only the difference between a bud and its blossom, an antecedent and its consequent. Repentance and remission of sins are inseparable. There cannot be, under God's system of grace, a baptism into the one without a baptism into the other. And although John was, emphatically, the reprover of sin, and the preacher of repentance, he was, also, commissioned to proclaim "the beginning of the gospel" in making announcement of the remission of sins. "His name is John. And thou, child, shalt be called the prophet of the Highest: for thou shalt go before the face of the Lord to prepare his ways; to give knowledge of salvation unto his people by the remission of their sins" (Luke 1 : 76, 77). It was not his commission to preach a baptism into water, but a baptism into the remis-

sion of sins, through a baptism into repentance. And this
he did preach, as Luke 3 : 3 expressly states—"He came
into all the country about Jordan preaching *the baptism of*
REPENTANCE *into* THE REMISSION OF SINS." The baptism mentioned by Josephus εἰς ἀναισθησίαν was preceded and caused
by a baptism εἰς μέθην, and the two are conjoined as a baptism
ὑπὸ μέθης εἰς ἀναισθησίαν; so, the baptism "into remitted sins,"
and the precedent baptism "into repentance," are thrown
together as βάπτισμα μετανοίας εἰς ἄφεσιν ἁμαρτιῶν. The baptism
which John preached, and the baptism which John administered, were one and the same baptism. So Mark 1 : 4
says; so Luke 3 : 3 says; so Paul, Acts 19 : 4, says; and so
John himself, Matt. 3 : 11, says. John disclaims all power
to confer repentance, or to remit sins. He proclaims his
nothingness in these respects. He declares his inability to
baptize in any other way than symbolly, by water. He
points all who wait upon his ministry to the Coming One in
whom, and in whom only, they must "Behold! the Lamb
of God THAT TAKETH AWAY THE SINS OF THE WORLD."

How John ritually used this symbol water we are not,
here, told. It will hardly be insisted upon in the present
case, as it has been done heretofore, that ἐν following βαπτίζω
expounds the meaning of βαπτίζω. Dr. Conant in translating
βαπτίζω ἐν ὕδατι says, "in" is the only sense in which this
preposition can be used in connection with βαπτίζω. The
implication in this statement is, that whenever ἐν is used
with this verb the element for a dipping must be indicated,
and consequently ὕδατι must be used for a dipping. These
things are not only assumptions, but they are erroneous assumptions. In the present passage ἐν stands in closest juxtaposition with βαπτίζων, but it does not point out the element
in which the baptism takes place; it merely declares where
John was, and where John baptized. He was ἐν τῇ ἐρήμῳ;
and whether he there ate, or drank, or slept, sprinkled,
poured, or dipped, is a matter of infinite indifference to
ἐν τῇ ἐρήμῳ. It is as little warranted to assume, that ἐν with
βαπτίζω must be translated "in." The New Version translates 1 Cor. 12 : 13, ἐν ἑνὶ Πνεύματι .... ἐβαπτίσθημεν "*by* one

Spirit we were all immersed into one body." The friends of the theory being judges, then, we may supply the ellipsis in this passage from Matt. 3 : 11, by ἐν ὕδατι, and translate— "John came baptizing, *with* water, in the wilderness and preaching the baptism of repentance *into* the remission of sins." Attention has, already, been called to the impropriety of making a ritual baptism the great theme of John's preaching, as, also, of connecting remission of sins with the administration of a rite, as is done by the translation "immersion of repentance *unto* remission of sins," and nothing more need, now, be added.

There is nothing in the character of this place of John's baptism, nor in anything said in connection with it, which looks like a dipping into water; but there is express statement of a baptism *by* REPENTANCE *into* THE REMISSION OF SINS, which, unless there were two baptisms, must be the baptism of the passage and of the place. We may add : If absolute uniformity of translation be any authoritative rule for the judgment, then we must judge it to be an absolute certainty, that if this language of Mark were found in any Classic author, every Baptist would translate the passage as I have translated it, and interpret it on the principles by which I have interpreted it. They would translate εἰς by *into*, and make it point out the ideal element of baptism, under whose influence the baptized must come. But inasmuch as there is a theory about the mode of Bible baptism, the translation and interpretation of that holy volume must proceed on a new basis, and be made conformable to human notions.

In Bethany.

John 1 : 28. Ταῦτα ἐν Βηθανίᾳ ἐγένετο πέραν τοῦ Ἰορδάνου, ὅπου ἦν Ἰωάννης βαπτίζων—These things were done in Bethany, beyond the Jordan, where John was baptizing.

John 10 : 40. Εἰς τὸν τόπον, ὅπου ἦν Ἰωάννης τὸ πρῶτον βαπτίζων—And went away again, beyond Jordan, into the place where John at first baptized.

The place where John was baptizing is, here, very definitely expressed. The baptizing was "in Bethany" (or Bethabara), a small village "beyond the Jordan."

The friends of the theory are not satisfied with the language of Scripture as it stands. They would change it in several particulars. For example:

'Εν. While Dr. Carson admits that ἐν should be translated *in* and not *at,* yet he insists that the baptism was not "*in* Bethany." He claims, that the preposition may take in an indefinite space around the village.

It is undoubtedly true, as Matthies and others state, that ἐν is used with the names of places, sometimes, when proximity only is implied.

Jordan. But for what purpose is it that the natural boundaries of the preposition are sought to be enlarged? Dr. Carson answers, "To take in the Jordan which was a short distance off." But why take in the Jordan? "To get enough water for 'the definite act,' the dipping." But where does the dipping come from? "It is in the theory, and we cannot do without it." Well, then let it be understood, that the Jordan is to be brought within the limits of Bethany not by the demands of Scripture statement, but in order to accommodate the assumptions and necessities of the theory.

But the Scriptures do not merely state, that this baptizing took place "in Bethany;" they have something to say about Jordan; and what they say is, that the baptizing was "in Bethany *beyond* the Jordan." Now, if the sacred writer wished to say, that the rite was administered *in* the Jordan, why has he said, "in Bethany, *beyond* the Jordan?" If we make such addition to the text, we have this awkward construction—"baptizing in Bethany beyond the Jordan, in the Jordan." To the suggestion that it is elsewhere said, that baptizing took place "in the Jordan," I answer: And so it is said elsewhere, that baptizing took place "in the wilderness." And if it should be rejoined, "Jordan implies a dipping," the answer is—*Assumption.*

Origen (IV, 280) says, "τοῦ παρὰ τῷ Ἰορδάνῃ βαπτίσματος, ἐν Βηθαβαρᾷ ὑπὸ τοῦ Ἰωάννου γινομένου, ἐξεταζομένου. I think that all

these things are presented, not untimely, in inquiring concerning the baptism alongside the Jordan, effected by John
in Bethabara."

Origen here exchanges πέραν for παρὰ, which is not done
unwittingly but of design, for he had just quoted the text as
it stands. · This shows, that Origen's idea of the relation of
this baptism to the Jordan was not that of the theory, *in* the
Jordan, but "*alongside* the Jordan." Besides, it is of the
first importance to note, that this inquiry into the baptism
effected by John is no more made to turn upon the manner
in which John used the water, than would an inquiry into
the quenching of his thirst be made to turn upon his lapping
up water out of the Jordan or taking it up with his hollowed
hand. The power of water to quench thirst does not depend
upon the manner of drinking. It made no difference to
Gideon's men, as to the slaking of their thirst, whether they
" lapped putting their hand to their mouth, or bowed down
upon their knees to drink water;" and to the Patrists it
made no difference how the water was used by John; the
power to baptize which belonged (in their view) to the water
had no dependence upon the manner of its use. Hence in
Patristic writings you do not meet with the question of the
mode of baptism as a question on its own merits, but merely,
and that rarely, as to the power of a given mode to effect
a certain character of baptism; and the decision was, that
the character of the baptism is not affected by the manner
of using the water, any more than the quenching of thirst
is affected by the quaffing of water from a goblet or suck-
ing it through a straw. The Patristic writers know nothing whatever of a Christian baptism whose essence centred
in a covering of the body in water. Their baptism was effected by water as an agency through a special power communicated to it; the development of which power did not
depend upon a dipping into it, any more than the power of
water to make hot iron cold depends upon the iron being
dipped into it.

The sacred writers do not raise the question of the manner
of using the water, for the same general but not for the same

specific reason which influenced the early Christian writers, namely, because there was, in their view, no room for any such question. The latter regarded the water as receiving *a power to take away sin and to regenerate the soul*, which did not depend on manner of use, and this new condition of the soul was in their view Christian baptism; the former regarded water as having *the power of a symbol* to show forth the condition of the soul penitent, pardoned, and made regenerate by the Spirit of God, which power being wholly independent of manner of use, and pertaining to its nature, the mode of using the water is left, as of will and not as of commandment, to be gathered from terms used to express the *shedding forth*, and *pouring out* of the Spirit, and the *sprinkling* of the blood of Jesus.

The idea of a baptism produced, brought into existence by some power, is shown by the word (γινομένου) used by Origen, a term which he would never have used had he regarded the baptism as consisting of a physical dipping into water.

To all these considerations as bearing upon *place*, may be added the historical fact stated in John 10:40, "Jesus went away again *into the place where* John, at first, baptized." Now, it is absolutely certain that Jesus did not go *into the river*: 1. From the dictates of common sense; 2. From the express declaration that the place into which he went was "beyond the river," and, yet, we are most explicitly told, that "he went *into the place where* John baptized." Here again the theory, not satisfied with the language of Scripture as it stands, must enter a plea for a liberal interpretation of this new preposition (εἰς) or abandon ἐν Ἰορδάνῃ as full of water into which John baptized.

1. If we take the simple language of Scripture in narrating the fact of this baptizing, then John baptized "in Bethany," and not in the Jordan. 2. If we take the historical account of Jesus coming "into the place" where John baptized, then John baptized "in Bethany," and not in the Jordan. 3. If we supply the ellipsis as placed in our hands by other Scripture (ἐν ὕδατι εἰς μετανοίαν), then John baptized in Bethany

"with water, *into* REPENTANCE," and not into the Jordan. We are satisfied with the words of inspiration as they stand. Can the theory say so?

PLACE OF BAPTISM AND MANY SPRINGS.

JOHN 3 : 22, 23.

Μετὰ ταῦτα ἦλθεν ὁ ᾿Ιησοῦς . . . . εἰς τὴν ᾿Ιουδαίαν γῆν . . . . καὶ ἐβάπτιζεν.

"After these things came Jesus . . . . into the land of Judea . . . . and baptized."

῍Ην δὲ καὶ ᾿Ιωάννης βαπτίζων ἐν Αἰνὼν ἐγγὺς τοῦ Σαλεὶμ, ὅτι ὕδατα πολλὰ ἦν ἐκεῖ, καὶ παρεγίνοντο καὶ ἐβαπτίζοντο.

"And John, also, was baptizing in Ænon near to Salim, for there were many springs there, and they came and were baptized."

MANY SPRINGS.

Translation and Punctuation.

A just translation is essential to a true interpretation of any passage. To make a proper translation it is necessary that there should be a proper adjustment of the relations of words and sentences by punctuation and otherwise.

The arrangement of the text and its punctuation as given by Tyndale is much to be preferred to that of our common English Bible.

The common version disjoins vv. 22 and 23 by marking them as distinct paragraphs. The close of v. 22 is marked by a period. The last line of v. 23 is separated from the preceding part by a colon: all this is wrong. Tyndale, Campbell, Townshend, and others, throw these two verses into one paragraph as containing closely related facts. Tyndale, also, includes in the paragraph, very properly, v. 23. But he makes vv. 22, 23 to constitute a single sentence with, I think, no less propriety. The whole passage, as rendered by him, reads thus:

"After that came Jesus and his disciples into the Jews' land, and there abode with them and baptized, and John also baptized in Enon beside Salim, because there was much water there, and they came, and were baptized. For John was not yet cast into prison."

This arrangement and punctuation is a very great improvement. It brings Jesus and John with their baptizings into the closest local relation, and by the comma preceding and succeeding "because there was much water there," gives to those words a proper parenthetic character which (with the better translation "for there were many springs there") throws an explanatory light over the entire preceding statement.

Olshausen (Comm. in loc.) recognizes the proximity of Jesus and John. He says, "Jesus left the city and baptized, remaining, however, in the country of the Jews. John, also, was baptizing in the neighborhood, and the proximity of the two messengers of God occasioned the following dispute." This last statement lacks evidence for its support. Tischendorf sustains (both in the Cod. Sin. and in his Critical Edition of the New Testament) the punctuation which makes, ὅτι ὕδατα πολλὰ ἦν ἐχεῖ, parenthetical. And Bengel (1 : 24) says, " John is wont to use parentheses, as to causes, as to place, by means of which the subject may the more clearly be understood."

New Version.

The New Version adopts the arrangement of Tyndale so far as the throwing of vv. 22, 23, and 24 into one paragraph is concerned; but in punctuation it follows the Common Version. It translates, as usual, "immersing in Ænon," and in the quarto edition, " many waters," in the sense "*a great abundance of water*," but in the later and revised edition, " much water." This latter translation stands alone when compared with that made of all other passages (Rev. 1 : 15; 14 : 2; 17 : 1) in the New Testament where the expression πολλὰ ὕδατα is found. In these passages the New Version always translates " many waters."

Of the translation, " immersing in Ænon," nothing need be said so far as "immersing" is concerned, except to call attention to the fact, that here, again, the adjunct word says nothing of a dipping. The place of baptism is designated by precisely the same phraseology as in every other case, heretofore, considered. As John baptized "in the *wilderness*," and "in *Bethany*," so, also, he baptized "in *Ænon*." The juxtaposition of βαπτίζω ἐν is guarded against misinterpretation, in the most careful manner, by the sacred writers. The theory insists that ἐν with βαπτίζω must be translated *in;* but this position to be worth anything to those who make it must assume a dipping in the adjunct; but how is there to be a dipping *in* the waste lands of a wilderness, or *in* the houses and streets of villages? In all such cases the language of Scripture is effectually guarded against misinterpretation. The guard against error is no less real (though it seems to have proved less effectual), where water is the near neighbor of this word (βαπτίζω ἐν ὕδατι), by the introduction of εἰς μετανοίαν; for grammatical law and the facts of usage do as absolutely preclude the appropriation of βαπτίζω by ἐν ὕδατι in the presence of εἰς μετανοίαν, as the laws of gravitation preclude the inferior though nearer moon from making the earth its satellite against the higher claims of the more distant sun. The verb is related to both phrases, but the relation is greatly diverse; the relation being toward εἰς μετανοίαν as its verbal element, and toward ἐν ὕδατι as its symbol agency. Thus, there is no case of the use of βαπτίζω ἐν which is left in doubt.

Πόλλα ὕδατα.

But some zealous friend of the theory may say, "As to this matter of water, we have it all here, and plenty of it (πόλλα ὕδατα), *much water*, and this must be a case of dipping or of physical covering, because there is a physical element involved." I answer: Is not *wine* a physical element? Is not *blood* a physical element? Are not *tears* a physical element? And are not all these used scores of times in baptisms where there is no dipping or physical covering? "This cannot be denied; but wine, and blood, and tears, are used because having some quality, or representative char-

acter apart from simple fluidity, and the dipping was not to
be in the wine, or the blood, or the tears, but into something
else." Then it is admitted, that a fluid may be present in a
baptism without the baptism being in the fluid, provided it
has some special quality, or representative character. What,
then, hinders water from being present in a religious baptism without any dipping into the water? Has it not had a
distinctive character as a symbol of religious purity for a
period so long that the memory of man runneth not to the
contrary? May it not be present, therefore, in a baptism as
a symbol representative of purification, just as wine is present as an effective agency? "It would seem that it might
be so." Then let me ask, Is there any syntactic relation between βαπτίζω and πόλλα ὕδατα which requires the water to be
used for dipping? "There is no such syntax; but why was
'much water' needed for *sprinkling?*" I have not said that
it was needed for sprinkling. "Or for *pouring?*" I have
not said that it was needed for pouring. "What, then, will
you do with this 'much water?'" Pardon me for questioning whether the sacred writer speaks of *much* water, and for
doubting whether *much* water would be competent to meet the
end which he has in view in speaking of πόλλα ὕδατα. If the
intention was to state, that there was enough water in which
to dip men and women, the statement would have a strange
sound for an inspired writer, and the language chosen to express the fact would be no less strange. For reasons which
will be given, and which I hope will be satisfactory, I think
that the sacred writer does neither of these strange things;
but speaks not of a *quantity* of water, but of a *number* of
springs. To quantity in itself considered, or as a thing of
fact, I make no objection. My objection is, that the exigency
of the case does not call for a quantity of water, but does
call for a number of waters, springs, fountains, streams; and
whether they had much water or little water in them, was a
point on which the sacred writer had no occasion to say
anything and, as a matter of fact, does not say anything.
This I will endeavor to establish by adequate proof drawn
from the record.

Ænon.

That the phrase πόλλα ὔδατα is introduced for the purpose of declaring the existence of a *number* of springs in close proximity to each other, and not to make announcement of the *quantity* of water, is very conclusively shown by the plural form of the name (Ænon) given to the locality. There is some diversity of opinion in explaining the form of this name, but there is general consent in regarding it as a plural form (Ezek. 47:17) and as meaning *fountains, springs.* Evidence could scarcely be more complete to establish the fact of a plurality of water-courses.

En, or Ain, the singular of Ænon, is very frequently employed as the name of a town or locality near to a fountain or spring. As springs were numerous some distinctive term was usually added in order to avoid confusion. Thus we have:

En-Mishpat	Fountain of Judgment	*Genesis* 14 :	7.
En-Shemesh. . . .	Fountain of the Sun	*Joshua* 15 :	7.
En-Rogel	Fountain of the Fuller . . .	" 15 :	7.
En-Om	Two Fountains	" 15 :	34.
En-Gannim	Fountain of the Gardens . .	" 15 :	34.
En-Geddi	Fountain of the Kid	" 15 :	62.
En-Dor	Fountain of the Dwelling . .	" 17 :	11.
En-Haddah	Fountain of Swiftness	" 19 :	21.
En-Eglaim	Fountain of Two Pools . . .	*Ezekiel* 47 :	10.

As it is much less common to meet with a number of springs in close proximity than with a single spring, the plural form is much more rare than the singular form in connection with the names of places. It is found, however, in Ezekiel 47:17, 48:1, in composition with Hazar, a village—Hazar Ænon the Village of Fountains. Ænon, uncompounded, would be much more distinctive than En, as there would be fewer places which could be so designated; yet more than one place, it would seem, bore this title, and therefore John (exemplifying that trait attributed to him by Bengel), parenthetically adds to the statement "John, also, was baptizing in Ænon" (I mean that Ænon which is "near to Salim), for there were many springs there." In the like spirit we find the parenthetic explanation (1 : 28), I mean that Bethany which is "beyond Jordan," in order to avoid confusion because of another Bethany near Jerusalem.

The principal members of the sentence are the first and the last—"John, also, was baptizing in Ænon . . . and they came and were baptized." The whole might be paraphrased thus: "John, also, as well as Jesus, was baptizing in Ænon (I mean that Ænon near to Salim, so called, because of its many springs, which furnished separate baptizing places for John and his Lord), and they came and were baptized." Thus the words, which are thrown in between the principal clauses, become explanatory of two important particulars, 1. Of the name Ænon; 2. How John could "also" baptize at Ænon at the same time with Jesus.

Hebrew Phrase.

The usage of the Hebrew phrase, of which πόλλα ὕδατα is but a Greek form, shows that it does not refer merely to a large body of water, much less to any particular form in which it is to be used.

The Hebrew (noun and adjective in the plural) is found in Ezekiel (19 : 10) in speaking of a vine planted by the waters and made fruitful by reason of "many waters."

The translation by the Septuagint, ὕδατος πολλοῦ, is in the singular number, showing that the plural form does not, necessarily, express quantity, or, that it may be equally well expressed by the singular. This vine was not dipped into the "many waters," but was planted by them, although the Septuagint has ἐν ὕδατι πεφυτευμέν, while the Hebrew preposition corresponds with ἐπί; another evidence that this phrase is not to be pressed on as of the exclusive sense in water. A vine planted in water would not flourish, but die. The quantity of water furnished by the "many waters" of Ezekiel was so much as was necessary for the nurture of a vine. The manner in which the water was used was by taking it up by means of the rootlets. John (for anything said to the contrary) may have used the many waters of Ænon in the same way, namely, by taking up and baptizing with it.

In Judith (17 : 17), τὰ ὕδατα καὶ τὰς πηγὰς τῶν ὑδάτων denotes a variety of sources, not quantity. The plural form is not necessary to express quantity. In 2 Chron. 32 : 4, ὕδωρ πολὺ is used for this purpose, and in the Wisdom of Solomon, 10 : 18, ὕδατος πολλοῦ is adequate to express all the waters of the Red Sea. Naaman, 2 Kings 5 : 12, uses the plural to express number and not quantity—"Are not Abana and Pharpar rivers of Damascus better than, πάντα τὰ ὕδατα, all the waters (rivers) of Israel?" Luther translates, "Are not *the waters* Abana and Pharpar better than all *waters* in Israel?" making "waters" in both cases equivalent to rivers.

Number and not quantity is, also, very distinctly stated by the plural form in Exodus 15 : 27, "And they came to Elim where were twelve springs of waters and threescore and ten palm trees; and they encamped there, παρὰ τὰ ὕδατα, by the waters." The encampment is by "*many* springs," not by a *quantity* of water.

This passage does not leave us in doubt as to whether quantity or number is intended. The "τὰ ὕδατα" are counted, and they number just " twelve."

Ambrose (II, 1432) understood the πολλὰ ὕδατα of Ænon to be many springs, and not a large aggregation of waters; he says, " Etsi baptizabat Joannes in Ennon, baptizabat juxta Salim, ubi erat aquarum abundantia, *duodecim fontes*, et septuaginta Palmarum arbores—an abundance of waters, *twelve springs*." So, Ambrose counts them.

In a note on Tertullian (II, 1157), a spot is described which would seem to answer very well for Ænon—" Antrum Corycium describens, ait: Multi hinc illic e vivis fontibus fluitant rivi—Many streams, out of living springs, flow this way and that."

These references establish conclusively that the many waters of Ænon have no necessary connection with " much water" collected into one body, or to " many great streams, the sound of which resembles mighty thunderings, or may resemble the sound of a cataract, or the roaring of the sea, but cannot resemble a tinkling rill" (Dr. Ryland).

The only interpretation which can receive justification is one which recognizes the presence of "many springs" adequate for the purposes of baptism, however administered, *and accommodating two distinct parties engaged in baptizing at the same time,* without interfering with each other.

It may be added, that quantity (πολύς, πλῆθος) may be used in cases of baptism, and the quantity be no greater than what can be drunk. Both these terms are used in wine baptisms, and a quart, or a pint, was sufficient for the accomplishment of the baptism. Men could not be dipped into a quart pot of wine; but they were baptized by it with all ease. The many springs of Ænon may have furnished enough water for a dipping, but if not they may still have furnished quite enough for a baptizing. The very mention of number precludes the idea that the mention of the springs is for the sake of a dipping. If they were as many as the springs, or the palm trees, at Elim, there would be no increased facility, thereby, for a dipping. If any one of the "twelve," or the "seventy," was sufficient for a dipping, the other eleven, or sixty-nine, could be dispensed with. If no one was sufficient, what benefit would accrue from a multiple of nothing by nothing? Carson says, that they might be all made tributary to a common stock and so enough be secured? I answer, 1. This method of getting up enough water for a dipping is only another illustration of the truth that the Scriptures, as they stand, do not answer for the theory. 2. The question is not, Whether or no there was enough water for the dipping of men and women, but whether a dipping into water is declared, by the Word of God, to have taken place in fact.

Ambrose, undoubtedly, believed that twelve springs furnished any reasonable quantity of water, and yet he did not feel that, however great the quantity, there was, therefore, any need for dipping men into them in order to secure their virtues. This is the use which he makes of these twelve springs: "Hos fontes habet Ecclesia, hoc est, in veteri Testamento duodecim patriarchas, et in novo duodecim apostolos. His fontibus ante perfunditur quicunque Christi mysteriæ sacrosancta consequitur—The church has these fountains, that is, in the Old Testament the twelve Patriarchs, and in the New Testament the twelve Apostles. Whosoever attains to the sacred mysteries of Christ must be first *besprinkled* by these fountains." In the same spirit Lactantius (I, 491) says: "Sic etiam gentes baptismo, id est, purifici roris perfusione, salvaret—So, also, he would save the Gentiles by baptism, that is, *by the sprinkling of the purifying dew.*" Thus we have this spring-water used according to Ambrose by the verb (perfundo) for sprinkling, and baptism declared by Lactantius to be administered by sprinkling pure water, not only by the use of the noun (perfusio) correspondent with the verb (perfundo), but as if to exclude all possibility of doubt as the mode of use, he likens it to the sprinkling of the dew-drops. Did any one ever hear of "dew" in the shape of a dipping? except, indeed, when the theory performs the feat of dipping Nebuchadnezzar into it!

These quotations are not offered as proof that John did, in fact, baptize in Ænon by sprinkling water from its springs. I am under no obligation to adduce such proof. My business is to show that there is no such usage of βαπτίζω in this passage as demands a dipping of men and women into these "many springs." The mention of *many* springs might be better adduced to show that John dipped frequentatively, rather than that he dipped at all. If these "many springs" were converted into "much water" as vast as the ocean, there would not be a hair's breadth advance toward a dipping. Not only does not this Greek word signify *to dip*, but it is not in any such grammatical relation to this water as to make water complementary of the meaning of the verb be that meaning what it may. To make claim for any such relation is the most absolute assumption. To claim that any such relation exists anywhere in the New Testament between this verb and water, is the purest assumption without evidence. To claim that βαπτίζω, of itself, does anywhere, in the Scriptures or out of the Scriptures, demand any such relation to water or any other fluid, is intolerable assumption. Quantity of water can show, that there was enough for a dipping or a drowning, if there was any disposition to use it for such purpose; but it can never prove any such use, in fact. Alexander of Pheræ had a sufficient quantity of wine in his vaults to have sufficed for the dipping of himself or of any number besides; and we are told that he was, in fact, baptized (πολλῷ ὄινω) "by much wine;" and, yet, he was not dipped in wine to the extent of the tip of his finger.

Now, apply to this transaction the reasoning of the theory: "Wine is a fluid suitable for dipping into; we are expressly told that Alexander was baptized, and therefore dipped, for baptize means nothing but dip; there was no lack of wine for the dipping, as we are distinctly told there was 'much wine,' and that much wine was used in the baptism; therefore, it is 'not want of evidence but want of honesty' which denies that Alexander was dipped in wine." So logicizes the theory.

The case, as presented, is, certainly, not open to the objection of impossibility. It is, unquestionable, that dipping into "much wine" is just as practicable as dipping into "much water." Nor is such dipping open to the objection that it has never taken place. The Duke of Clarence was more than dipped in "much wine;" he was truly baptized. Nor can it be objected that such a baptism as that of the Duke of Clarence would be inappropriate since he was drowned by his baptism; for just such a murderous baptism meets the case precisely; Alexander was baptized for the very purpose of taking his life. Why now, may not, must not, all friends of the theory exclaim, "Alexander was dipped into much wine, and whoever denies this, 'forces the conviction upon us, that, on this subject, it is not light that is most wanted . . . but religious honesty'" (Mem. of Carson, Bapt. Pub. Soc., xxxvii).

On Baptist principles we are shut up to the putting of Alexander in this much wine where he must be drowned. according to the legitimate force of the terms, as was Clarence, or be saved by some foreign intervention, as Cupid was saved by his godship when undergoing a like wine baptism, as related by Julian (C. B., p. 245). And in being shut up to such conclusion we are shut up to the most absolute error. The facts of the case were, that Alexander was baptized by drinking (not by being dipped into) this "much wine," and when thus thoroughly baptized, was murdered.

Now, what element of proof for a dipping into water can be found in this Ænon baptism, which does not appear for a dipping into wine in this Pheræ baptism? Is water, by its fluid nature, suitable for dipping into? So is wine. Was there "much water" in Ænon? So was there "much wine" in Pheræ. Is baptize competent to dip, to cover over? It was equally present in both cases. Have men been put into water, of literal fact? So have they been put into wine. What then, I ask, was the discriminating difference in the two cases which gives certain proof that the Ænon disciple must be baptized by *dipping*, while the Pheræ tyrant was effectually baptized by *drinking?*

Is it said in reply, "Wine drunk can, by figure, baptize *into drunkenness?*" I answer, Water sprinkled can, by symbol, baptize *into repentance.* The question then returns, Why must John in his baptism be ironly bound to use "much water" by dipping, while Thebe, in her baptism, has not a green withe to restrain her liberty in using "much wine," by drinking?

While waiting for an answer to this question I will venture the affirmation, that there is not one word in this account of the baptism at Ænon which would prevent John using the water in precisely the same manner that Alexander used the wine, namely, by *drinking;* and if he had so used it βαπτίζω would have kept an everlasting silence as having no concern in the matter.

The theory must find evidence for baptizing by dipping into water somewhere else than in the account of this baptism in Ænon.

Proximity of John and Jesus.

There is strong evidence in this passage and the context to show, that John and Jesus were both baptizing in Ænon.

In v. 22 we are told that Jesus left Jerusalem and went into the country region of Judea. The particular locality reached, however, is not stated. But in v. 23 we are told, that "John *also* was baptizing in Ænon near to Salim." Here, a particular locality is stated, but not so as to determine, definitely, its relations to "the land of Judea," unless such relation is indicated by "also" interpreted as expressive of John's being in the same place and being engaged in the same duty.

This interpretation is strengthened by the 26 v., which represents John's disciples as coming to him and saying of Jesus, "Behold, the same baptizeth and all men come to him." This statement very clearly implies, 1. That these disciples of John had been eye-witnesses of the baptism of Jesus of which they spake. 2. That they had just seen it, and that it was still going on. 3. That John himself might have ocular demonstration of the truth of the statement, if he would,—"Behold! all come to him."

After this fact, namely, "that Jesus made and baptized more disciples than John," became more generally known, we are told (4 : 1), that "Jesus left Judea and departed again into Galilee." Now, the relative number of disciples made and baptized by John and Jesus would be most readily learned by their close proximity, in which case any striking disparity of numbers would force itself upon the attention. And since, on the development of this·fact and as a consequence of it, Jesus leaves Judea, the inference is, that John was in Judea and was left there by Jesus to avoid such invidious comparisons as had been already made by John's disciples, and to preclude any course of procedure which the Pharisees might be disposed to take thereupon.

A difficulty which would at once suggest itself, arising out of the unavoidable confusion of two distinct parties baptizing at the same place, is met in the fullest manner by the remarkable parenthetic statement, "for there were many springs there." Our Baptist friends say, πόλλα ὕδατα indicates a large body of water; but there is no such large body of water in the whole land of Judea, not the Jordan itself, which could claim the application of these words in that large sense in which they are, sometimes, applied to the Euphrates or to the sea; while understood in relation to number the exigency of the case is perfectly met. Ambrose seems to think that there is something kindred between the "twelve springs" of Elim and these "many springs" of Ænon; whether this be so or not it is clear, that as all Israel encamped παρὰ ὕδατα, by the springs of Elim, without interfering with each other, having a spring for every tribe, so, the disciples of Jesus and of John may have encamped at Ænon, παρὰ ὕδατα, without interfering with each other, both parties being accommodated by one of the "many springs."

There was, however, one difficulty in the way of an entirely satisfactory conclusion on this subject, owing to the uncertainty of the geographical position of Ænon.

The more common view of the locality did not place it within Judea at all; but where it was, there was confessedly no certain knowledge. Unable to arrive at any certain result from the resources within my immediate reach, I addressed a communication on the subject to Rev. Lyman Coleman, D.D., of La Fayette College, so well known as an accomplished Biblical Geographer, Classical scholar, and Christian gentleman. The following communication, which I take pleasure in submitting, was received in reply:

" Few localities have more perplexed geographers than Ænon. Dr. Robinson went on his second tour chiefly to settle this point. I have many times reconsidered this question, and have an unvarying conviction that Dr. Barclay has brought to light this long-lost locality. About four or five miles northeast of Jerusalem, beyond the Mount of Olives, two or three below Anata, the ancient Anathoth, birthplace of Jeremiah, he found in the desert a succession of fountains for a mile or two gushing out from under high cliffs, πολλά ὕδατα, many pools deep enough for wading. swimming, and all the immersions of the Baptists.

21

Both (John and Jesus, with their disciples), here, would be nigh to each other, and have ample space. Indeed all the conditions of the narrative are fully met here. I was at Anata and should surely have gone down to these waters, but I knew not of them. I have since conversed with Dr. Barclay abundantly on this subject.

"The name is either a Greek plural, as I believe, or a secondary form, as in Ezekiel 47 : 17.

"See Barclay's City of the Great King, pp. 558–570."

DR. BARCLAY.

The following extract, somewhat condensed, is the passage in Dr. Barclay's work referred to by Dr. Coleman:

"Aiyûn or Ainyûn—Wadah Farah—Fountains of the Valley of Delight. Of all the fountains in the neighborhood of Jerusalem, the most copious and interesting by far are those which burst forth within a short distance of each other in Wady Farah, about six miles northeast of the city. It is a very interesting spot entirely unknown to Christendom. We passed some half dozen expansions of the stream, the water varying in depth from a few inches to a fathom or more. These pools are supplied by some half dozen springs bursting from rocky crevices at various intervals. Verily, I thought, we have stumbled on Ænon! 'Many fountains,' I believe, is what Professor Robinson, the great lexicographer, prefers rendering the πολλά ὕδατα of Ænon; and here are not only 'many fountains,' but literally 'much water,' thus accommodating each translation.

"Although this conjecture (that Ain Farah was Ænon) must be set down to the random conjecture of the moment, yet a more intimate acquaintance with the geography of the neighborhood has brought me to the assured conviction that the place is none other than the 'Ænon near to Salim, where John was baptizing because there was much water there.' Eusebius and Jerome supposed Ænon to be near a town in Galilee, called Alim, Shalim, Salim, Shulimias, Salimias. But, surely, never was tradition so poorly sustained; indeed it is self-refuted. Instead of being 'near to Salim and Jordan,' it is, at least, sixteen miles from Salim, and ten miles from the Jordan.

"On inquiry, when within a mile and a half of the fountains, 'What is the name of this Wady?' I had the satisfaction to hear the Arab pronounce the identical word (Salim), and was conducted to the site of an ancient city. Others pronounced it Sillim, Selim, Sulim, Saleim, Sallem, Selam, &c. This valley, Wady Selim, commences on the eastern slope of Mount Olivet, rather more than a mile above the city, and runs east three miles. The position of Ænon would be well known by the Apostles' reference to this ' city set on a hill.' "

Dr. Barclay, farther, says, that his view of this locality is confirmed by an interesting passage from Lightfoot, which he quotes, and adds :

" The obscurity has been dissipated by the discovery of the Wady Salim, which affords the clue to the identification of this interesting locality. Its Hebrew name is A i n o o n and not Enon; and this is, almost exactly, the Chaldee Hebrew for fountains.

" The waters, after tumbling eastward ten miles, empty into the Jordan under the name Kelt, an Arabic corruption of Cherith. Dr. Robinson (Bib. Researches, II, 288) says, both the name and locality may answer to that of the brook Cherith, where the prophet Elijah hid himself. A more admirable place of seclusion could nowhere be found. It dries up in summer, as was now the case."

The identification of this locality seems to be complete. Its position, " in the land of Judea," "its many springs," their " bursting from rocky crevices at various intervals" along a distance of some miles, expounds the name Ænon, and squares perfectly with every conclusion reached by a previous direct examination of the passage, and especially accounts for the introduction of πολλά ὕδατα as explanatory of "John also," as well as Jesus, " was baptizing in Ænon."

While it is true, that there was much water at Ænon, that is not the truth which is stated by the inspired writer, nor one which would have answered his purpose to state; it would not account for the simultaneous baptizing of two independent companies at the same place; the presence of " many springs," separated from each other by short distances, will do this; and the existence of such a marked peculiarity in that locality is what the Scripture states. As to the amount of water in these springs the statement says nothing; and the fact to explain which it is introduced did not require that anything should be said.

As there is nothing said of the quantity of water (we are ready to admit the greatest amount which any one could desire), so, there is nothing said of the manner in which the water was used. There is nothing in the construction which makes βαπτίζω and ὕδατα expository of each other; and as there is no necessary dependence of these words upon each other, it is a pure addition to the Word of God to assume any such relation. We may go farther and say: It is not merely an addition, but a substitution for and an abrogation of the direct testimony of the Holy Spirit, which never places these words in a complementary relation to each other; but establishes other relations wholly diverse in nature. This is done by the declaration through John, "Βαπτίζω ἐν ὕδατι εἰς μετανόιαν (Matt. 3 : 11), ὕδατι βαπτίζω (εἰς μετανοίαν) (Luke 3 : 16), I, with water, baptize into repentance;" where βαπτίζω finds its complement in μετανόιαν; and water (disjoined from the verb in such relation) expounds, as a symbol instrument, the purifying character of repentance baptism.

If, then, we place ourselves under the guidance of the Holy Ghost, we must say in the words which he teacheth, "John was baptizing in Ænon (with water as a symbol) *into* REPENTANCE." And John and Jesus were baptizing at the same time, in the same locality, without interfering with each other, " because there were *many* springs there."

Why Baptizing at Ænon?

It only remains to inquire, Why John was baptizing at Ænon rather than at the Jordan?

The Scriptures do not give any direct answer to this question; but we can find one which is highly probable, if not certain, by a reference to facts which are stated.

The first fact which claims attention is the time of the year. It was the spring, in or immediately after March. The Passover, celebrated in the first of the ecclesiastical year, was just passed. Jesus had gone up to Jerusalem (John 2 : 13, 23) in order to its observance. After its termination he left Jerusalem (3 : 22) "and came into the country re- gion of Judæa." Now, it was in this month of March that the Jordan overflowed its banks, and John, as well as the lion from his fastnesses, would be driven into the country region of Judæa by "the swellings of Jordan." "The Jor- dan may be said to have two banks, of which the inner marks the ordinary height of the stream, and the outer its elevation during the rainy season, or the melting of the snows on the summits of Lebanon. This happens in the first month of the Jewish year, which corresponds with March (1 Chron. 12 : 15). Maundrell, after descending the outer bank, went about a furlong upon the level strand, before he came to the immediate bank of the river. This inner bank is thickly covered with bushes and trees. . . . . In this entangled thicket, so conveniently planted near the cooling stream, and remote from the habitations of men, several kinds of wild beasts were accustomed to repose, till the swelling of the river drove them from their retreat." (*Ency. Rel. Knowl.*) This condition of things affords a highly probable reason for John's leaving the Jordan at this time.

A second fact is connected with Jewish views of purifica- tion and the fitness of things.

The Jews regarded running or living water as especially adapted for religious purifications. All running water, how- ever, was not equally pure. The Jordan itself was not re- garded as technically pure. The Talmudists say, that "the waters of the Jordan are not fit to sprinkle the unclean be- cause they are mixed waters," meaning, mixed with the waters of other rivers and brooks which empty themselves into it.

But at the time of its overflow the waters of the Jordan lose their purity not merely by mixture with other waters, but by sweeping along with its swollen flood all the unclean things which were the result of a year's accumulation within its widely extended outer banks. No thorough Jew would use such water for legal purifications; nor can we imagine that John (much as we may suppose him to be free from a purely Jewish feeling) would be likely to use these turbid waters, without necessity, in a religious rite for symbol purification.

We have, then, in the overflow of the Jordan (and consequent flooding of all that space between the outer and the inner bank within which John and the people were, probably, wont to congregate), together with the consequent real as well as technical impurity of its waters, an adequate reason for the abandonment of the Jordan, and the presence of John at one of the pure springs of Ænon.

Thus the argument for a dipping from the "much water" of Ænon passes like a swollen torrent, loud while it lasts, but also like it passes away, never to return.

JORDAN.

PLACE OF BAPTISM, A RIVER.

Καὶ ἐβαπτίζοντο ἐν τῷ Ἰορδάνῃ ὑπ᾽ αὐτοῦ.
And were baptized by him in the Jordan.—*Matt.* 3 : 6.

Καὶ ἐβαπτίζοντο ἐν τῷ Ἰορδάνῃ ποταμῷ ὑπ᾽ αὐτοῦ.
And were baptized by him in the river Jordan.—*Mark* 1 : 5.

The Jordan.

While no Baptist was ever known to base an argument for dipping on the Scripture statement, that John was baptizing *ἐν τῇ ἐρήμῳ* in the wilderness, *ἐν Βηθανίᾳ* in Bethany, *ἐν Αἰνὼν* in Ænon (admitting that such phraseology is expressive of nothing more than locality, and makes no approach toward a statement of a dipping within or a covering over by the wilderness, Bethany, or Ænon), yet the same identical form of statement, *ἐν τῷ Ἰορδάνῃ*, is made the basis of a universal argument for dipping into, covering over with *water*, although intelligent friends of the theory admit, that *ἐν τῷ Ἰορδάνῃ* does as truly and as absolutely express locality as does ἐν τῇ ἐρήμῳ. It is our business, now, to inquire into the authority by which "in the Jordan," a locality, is metamorphosed into *in the water*, which is no locality.

We very cheerfully admit, that of all the local statements, "in the wilderness," "in Bethany," "in Ænon," "in Jordan," the last affords, by far, the greatest facility for constructing a popular argument in which locality may be ignored, and *water* may be surreptitiously substituted.

General Argument of the Theory.

The general argument of the theory is of this sort: "To go to a river for baptism, when water could be had in smaller quantities elsewhere, necessitates the conclusion or, at least, induces a violent presumption, that a large quantity of water was necessary for baptism, and that the mode of its use was by dipping men and women into it."

The points which are involved in this statement are as follows: 1. The parties did go to a river. 2. They did go to a river for the purpose of baptism. 3. They did leave a place where there was a small quantity of water because of the small quantity of the water, and did go to a place where there was a large quantity of water because of the large quantity of the water. 4. The quantity of water can be accounted for in no other way than by its use for dipping men and women into it.

Let us look at these points in their order and try to gauge their worth.

1. "The parties did go to a river."

It is customary for our Baptist friends (or was so in old-fashioned times) to leave their homes and their churches (baptizer, candidates for baptism, and attendant throng) to go forth to some river, more or less distant, for the sake of baptizing.

Now, such a sight as this is nowhere to be met with in the Bible. Never is John represented as heading a company and leading them from some remote point to a river. Never is John, or any one else in Scripture, represented as leaving his usual place of preaching to go to a river to complete the functions of his ministry. Such things belong exclusively to a Baptist ministry. They have no place in a Bible ministry.

But it may be asked: "Do you mean to deny that John was at the river Jordan?" Certainly not. John was at the Jordan; John preached at the Jordan; John lived at the Jordan; and where John was, where John preached, where John lived, there John baptized. What I deny is this, namely, that John was accustomed or did ever preach at some remote point, and afterward lead away his converts to a river for the accomplishment of some end which could not be accomplished on the spot where he preached.

Dr. Carson says: John's baptizing at a river can never be satisfactorily accounted for except on the acknowledgment that baptism was by dipping men and women into water. In contradiction of this position we aver: That John's presence at the Jordan, and his consequent baptism there, is fully accounted for without any reference to the mode of baptism. In support of this statement we adduce the fact, that the Jordan and the vicinity of the Jordan was John's home, and the appointed field within which he should exercise his ministry. Luke (3:2) says: "The word of God came unto John the son of Zacharias in the wilderness. And he came into all the country about Jordan preaching the baptism of repentance into the remission of sins. As it is written in the book of the words of Esaias the prophet, saying, The voice of one crying in the wilderness, Prepare ye the way of the Lord . . . and all flesh shall see the salvation of God."

We are here taught, that John was already in the wilderness (and may have been there for years, Luke 1:80) when "the word of the Lord came upon him," calling him to, and qualifying him for, his ministry. When and where he was called, then and there he entered upon the work of his ministry as foretold by Isaiah. In his preaching, as here announced, there was not a particle of water; it was not a ritual baptism which he preached, but a repentance baptism. It is by such baptism only, that "the way of the Lord" is prepared, " remission of sins" graciously secured, and "the salvation of God" made ours. The ministry of the Forerunner of the Lord Jesus Christ was not a ministry whose great business was to make proclamation, that men and women must be dipped into water!

It is, then, a matter settled as absolutely as Scripture can settle it, that John was in the wilderness through which the Jordan flowed, not for the purpose of dipping into its waters, but because it was his home.

There is, then, a great gulf separating John's position in relation to the river from the Baptist position. Baptists leave their preaching places and seek out a river in whose waters they may baptize " by walking in to a convenient depth," and dipping the upper part of the body. There is not one word of any such doing in all the history of John's ministry. Where he preached, there he baptized. But it may be urged: "Although John did not go to the Jordan from some distant point of preaching, carrying his converts with him in long procession, he may have gone into the wilderness in anticipation of his call and of the need of the river." To this suggestion it may be replied: (1.) If John did, thus, go into the wilderness some years, more or less, beforehand, in order that he might be close by a river, it was certainly a very remarkable piece of forethought; and none the less remarkable in that he has never since had any imitator, inspired or uninspired, in any such prudential arrangement. (2.) If John went into the wilderness beforehand, in anticipation of the coming exigency when the river would be needed for dipping, *why did his great prototype, Elias, go into the same wilderness and make his home by the banks of the same river?* Did he, also, want water for dipping?

The Scriptures teach us, that Elias for a long period together made his home by the brook Cherith, which empties into the Jordan (precisely the spot occupied by John); but the only use which he made of its waters, so far as we are informed, was for " drinking." It is possible, then, that he who " came in the spirit and power of Elias" frequented the same wilderness, and the same river-banks, without being governed by the singular forethought of securing waters for a dipping. And this possibility excluding dipping "accounts, rationally, for the baptism of John at a river." (3.) The notion that John went into the wilderness (like a good general to secure a favorable base for future operations in ritual service) is, in view of his preparation work for the kingdom, as absurd as the building of a pyramid with its apex on the earth and its base in the air. Such conceit proves conclusively that the theory out of which it springs falls far below the level of John's preparation ministry, and that in relation to a developed Christianity it is purely anti-christian. I say this with no unkindness toward those who hold this theory, but in all kindness, that they may apprehend how absolute and how profound is the error which they hold.

(4.) The idea that John went beforehand to live and preach in the wilderness, anticipating the necessity which otherwise would arise of his coming with his converts to the river for a dipping, is another of the constantly recurring evidences that the Bible, as it stands, does not suit the theory.

It is most manifest, that so far as the "going to the river" part of this argument is concerned, it is all in the air.

2. "They went to the river *for the purpose of baptism.*"

So far as "they" is intended to include John the statement has, already, been disproved. The simple fact of John's baptizing at a river (that river being his home previous to his entering upon such ministry) takes away from the river all specialty so far as argument from place is concerned. Olshausen (I, 259) says: "The wilderness is spoken of as the place where he preached, which is not to be understood, of course, as literally void of men, but rather as pasture-ground. But in the fact that John preached in the wilderness and not in towns, we discover the peculiar character of this witness to the truth. It belongs to John's character to flee from men and to preach to those that seek him; while the Redeemer himself seeks men. The wilderness of Judæa bordered on the Jordan and the Dead Sea." Olshausen thinks that the ministry and the place of John's ministry has some other characteristic than that of dipping and its conveniences. John's wilderness home, his camel's hair apparel, his locust food, his repentance preaching, all told of the severity of the law and preparation for the welcome reception of "grace and truth by Jesus Christ." To put aside all these things and to give us a dipping in their stead is a blank repudiation of the Scriptures. We cannot accept a stone for bread.

Did others "go to *the river* for baptism" because there were no water facilities for a baptism at the places from which they came? There is no shadow of such an intimation in the Scriptures. Some, we are told, went out "to see John;" and some went to inquire of him, "Who art thou?" and some went to hear him preach; and some "came forth to be baptized of him;" but it is nowhere said, they came out to the Jordan to be baptized because it was a river and there was not means for baptizing in the places which they left. It was not the river which attracted them, but John; and John was at the river, and baptized at the river, not because it was a river, but because it was his home, and because it furnished the nearest and most natural supply of water. "Jesus came from Galilee to Jordan unto John, to be baptized of him" (Matt. 3:13). He did not come to Jordan because there was no river, or no water in Galilee, but because there was no John there. The theory patronizes Jordan at the expense of John. The Bible magnifies the Baptizer and puts the place of baptism, "in the Jordan," in a common list with other places of baptism, "in the wilderness," "in Bethany," "in Ænon," declaring that in all these places, alike, John did baptize ἐν ὕδατι εἰς μετανοίαν.

3. "They left a place where there was a small quantity of water, because of the small quantity of water, and went to a place where there was a large quantity of water because of the large quantity of water."

To sustain this position there is no evidence, jot or tittle, in Scripture. If we should grant, what cannot be proved, that John and his converts left one place for baptism in another place, and if we should farther grant, that there was

more water in such latter place than in the former, still, it
would not follow by any necessary consequence, that the
reason for leaving the one place and going to the other, was
to be found in the relative quantities of water; the reason
might be in the *character* of the water, standing or running,
impure or pure.

It is notorious, that both Gentile and Jew attached a
specially purifying value to *running* water. Thus, the Roman high priest addresses the Sabine, " Quidnam tu, hospes,
paras ? Inceste sacrificium Dianæ facere ? Quin tu ante
vivo perfunderis flumine. Infima valle præfluit Tiberis (Livy,
I, 45)—What are you about to do, O Stranger ? Would you
sacrifice impurely to Diana ? Sprinkle yourself first with
the *living* stream. The Tiber flows before you in the bottom
of the valley."

Philo, the Jew (de Sacrificantibus), says: " It is the custom
of nearly all others to *sprinkle* themselves for purification
with pure water; many with that of the sea, some with that
of *rivers*, and some with that which in vessels they have
drawn up from wells."

The Old Testament requires the use of running or living
water for religious purification. "And he shall dip them in
the *running* water and sprinkle the house seven times : And
he shall cleanse the house with the blood of the bird, and
with the *running* water" (Levit. 14 : 51, 52).

These extracts disprove the reasoning which says, " They
went to the river for a religious purification, and *therefore*
went for a dipping because there was *much* water there."
The conclusion is not in the premise. The Gentile and the
Jew alike went to the flowing stream, not because of the
quantity of the water to be found there, but because of its
character. They sought for *running, living*, therefore pure
water, and having found this, so much as would suffice for
a *sprinkling*, was a quantity sufficient for them.

Thus, " a rational explanation " is given for the presence
of John and the people at the banks of the Jordan without
any reference to the " quantity" of water flowing within its
banks.

The reply made by Dr. Carson to this reasoning, "We are not to suppose that John would be influenced by such peculiarities," is unsatisfactory: (1) because there is no reason why John, a Jew, exercising his ministry within Judaism, should not conform to Jewish usage in employing running water for religious rites; and (2) because, the use of running water was more convenient for John and would meet the views of the people, even supposing that John in the use of the running water did not design to discriminate as to the fitness of one kind of water rather than another kind for religious uses.

If now it should be admitted, that the presence of a river does not *necessitate* either the use of a quantity of water or of a dipping into it, while it is still urged, that this is the most *probable* conclusion, we again dissent and appeal to facts.

Homer says: That Telemachus went to the sea for a religious purification by means of its waters. Now, the theory argues, "The quantity of water in the sea was quite enough for a dipping, and as the son of Ulysses took the trouble to go to the sea rather than have a little sea-water brought to him, it is 'probable' that he went to the sea because of the quantity of its waters, and used them by dipping his person into them." The only trouble in the way of this reasoning is, that we happen to have a statement of the manner of using these sea-waters, and we find that this Greek, after going to the sea, was satisfied to use its waters for *washing his hands.*

Hesiod: "Before prayer the *hands* should be washed in pure, *flowing* water." Virgil: "Sprinkling the body with *river* water." Ovid: "The hands should be washed with *living* water." The Roman priest directs the Sabine to go to the *river* Tiber to *sprinkle* himself with its water. Philo: "It was customary for the Jews to *sprinkle* themselves with *river* water." The Old Testament enjoins, sprinkling with river water.

In view of these facts it may be asked, If it is "probable" that when river water is used for religious purification, it is used for dipping the body into it, then, how does it happen, that this probability is persistently violated from the days of Hesiod until the present hour? I say "until the present hour," for the custom of going to running water for religious purification by using the water in other forms than that of dipping, is an unquestionable historical fact extending by an unbroken series through more than three thousand years.

Customs in the East have a fixedness like to that of the everlasting hills. The custom of resorting to rivers for religious purification, because of the greater purifying power of running water, is a custom of Eastern origin, and is continued to the present day. The evidence for this is found in the following statements of missionaries laboring in India.

The Rev. R. S. Fullerton: "While the Pittar Pukhs lasts, he goes every morning to the Ganges, wades into it, and while a Pundit reads the Sankalap, takes up handfuls of water, and pours them out again into the stream, repeating the names of his father, grandfather, and great-grandfather."

The Rev. Mr. Löwenthal: "A lotâ is a brass urn, holding between a pint and a quart, which no Hindoo can well be without. The Hindoo bathes every day, that is he pours the water from his lotâ over his body, usually at some stream. The secret meetings of the Sepoys took place, generally, when they went to bathe, all with their lotâs in their hands."

The Rev. Dr. Jamieson: "The usual mode of bathing by the Hindoos is by *pouring* water over their persons from a vessel called a *lota*, even when they stand on the brink of a river. In washing hands both Hindoos and Mohammedans always *pour* water on them. They say, that to dip them into the water defiles the water, and the more you wash the more unclean they are."

What becomes, in view of such facts, of the argument, "They went to the river, therefore, they were dipped into its waters?"

Baptists go to the river for a dipping; and on this practice of theirs as a foundation (a foundation as unstable as water) they build the conclusion, that John, living on the banks of the river, could use its waters in no other way than by dipping.

This is the same illogicism with that which carries back our ordinary mode of bathing through some millenaries of years and insists that the bath of the olden time must be modelled after ours. If we had been simply told that the Sepoy went to the Ganges to bathe, the theory would have insisted upon it, that no " rational explanation" could be given for his going to the river except that which dips him into its waters. And yet, whether it be rational or irrational, he did go to the river, he did bathe there, and he did not dip into the river; but he did pour " a pint or a quart" of water over his body. If the Rev. C. S. Stewart had only told us, that the " bath of a Japanese noble lasts for an hour," the theory would have insisted, most uncompromisingly, that there could be nothing else than a dipping in such a bath. Unfortunately, however, for this theorizing the witness has gone into particulars and his testimony is as follows : " The chief butler sits down before his lord with a large teapot of warm water. After a decorous interval he fills his capacious mouth with the liquid, and then purls it in a spirting stream over the tawny skin of his master. The operation lasts about an hour." This Eastern nobleman only escapes a dipping bath at the hands of the theory in some river, or its equiva- lent, by the recorded presence of a *teapot!*

This use of the " lotá," and the " teapot," reminds me of a very neat argument deduced from the language of the Forerunner in John 3 : 34, " God giveth not the Spirit (ἐκ μέτρου) *out of a measure* unto him." The argument is this: Ancient pictures represent John as baptizing by pouring water " out of a measure" (a vessel resembling a shell), and as suggested by this and in contrast with it, he declares, that the Lord Jesus Christ is baptized with the Holy Spirit, not " out of a measure," but immeasurably. The argument, if accepted, would prove that John used the water in bap- tizing by pouring it out of a vessel of limited capacity. Evidence deduced from incidental allusions is often most striking and satisfactory in its character. I do not know of

anything which can prove, that John did not make allusion
to the fact of his using "a measure," or vessel of small capacity, in administering baptism; still, no more than a possible, though possibly a high, value should be attached to
the reasoning. If the theory could present as satisfactory
evidence for a dipping, as is hereby given for a pouring, it
would present a more satisfactory front.

In view of this examination, now made, we are fully
justified in concluding, that there is neither necessity, nor
violent presumption, nor probability, that John dipped men
and women into water merely because a river was one of
the places where he made his home, where he preached,
and where he baptized.

In addition to the facts already stated in support of this
conclusion we may add the following: "Those admitted
into the lesser or introductory mysteries of Eleusis were
previously purified on the banks of the Ilyssus, by water
poured upon them by the Udranos" (Prof. Wilson, p. 242).
They went to the river and still there was no immersion.
"And the daughter of Pharaoh came down to wash herself
at the river" (Exod. 3 : 5). In addition to the violent im-
probability against Pharaoh's daughter going into the Nile
to wash, we have the fact, that the preposition of the Hebrew and Greek arrests her going at the bank of the river,
while there is nothing in the verb which requires her to be
covered with the water. We have, also, seen that the mode
of female washing in Egypt was not by going into a river,
or into water at all, but by the application of water to the
person (see Jud. Bapt., p. 121).

If there is any deficiency in this "rational explanation"
of religious purification at a river without dipping into it,
I know not what it is. We rely on facts; the theory on
assertion.

4. "The quantity of water necessitates the idea of a dipping." Answer: 1. The word "dip" is not to be found in
the New Testament in connection with baptism. 2. The
word baptize is not to be found in the New Testament in
complementary relation with water. 3. Facts trample such

statement under foot. "The hoary sea," the Ilyssus, the Tiber, the Nile, the Ganges, the bath in the midst of the Atlantic Ocean *out of a teapot*, say such reasoning is baseless.

Going down to the River.

The friends of the theory press hard upon the phraseology "going down to the river" as evidence for a dipping. There is, confessedly, no dipping in the language, but neither is there in anything else; so every possible, and indeed impossible thing, must be laid under contribution.

Dr. Carson, on Matt. 3 : 6–13, p. 126, urges this point with much earnestness. He says: "I perfectly agree with Mr. Ewing that ἀπό would have its meaning fully verified if they had only gone down to the edge of the water. How, then, can I deduce dipping from the phrases *going down* and *coming up from?* My argument is this: If baptism had not been by immersion, there can be no adequate cause alleged for going to the river. Can sober judgment, can candor suppose, that if a handful of water would suffice for baptism, they would have gone to the river? Many evasions have been alleged to get rid of this argument, but it never will be fairly answered. I have strong suspicions that these evasions are hardly satisfactory even to those who make them. Mr. Ewing attempts to account for this phraseology by the fact that fountains and rivers are in hollow places. This indeed accounts for the phraseology, but does it account for this fact! Whether the river was on a hill or in a valley, why did they go to it, when a handful of water would have sufficed?"

This is Dr. Carson's unanswerable argument. We can only promise that our answer to it shall have the merit of being without "evasion" and "satisfactory to ourselves." Our appeal is to facts. Telemachus did go to the sea not for a dipping, but for a hand-washing for which "a handful of water would have sufficed." The Eleusinian disciples did go to the river Ilyssus for an onpouring of water for which "a handful would have sufficed." The Sabine did go down

22

to the river Tiber for a sprinkling when "a handful of water would have sufficed." Pharaoh's daughter did go down to the river Nile to wash when, according to Egyptian custom, "a handful of water would have sufficed." The Hindoo during the Pittar Pukhs did go down to the river Ganges for an object for which "handfuls of water did suffice." The Sepoy did go to the river for "a pint or a quart" of water when "a handful," in his tent or on a hilltop, "would have sufficed." Greek and Latin writers say, that men did, daily, go down to the river for hand-washing and water sprinkling, when "a handful of water would have sufficed." Philo and Josephus, Old Testament and Apocrypha, substantiate the fact, that Jews went down to running streams not to dip into them, but for purposes for which "a handful of water would suffice."

What, now, in view of facts like these, becomes of Dr. Carson's inquiry, "Can sober judgment, can candor suppose, that if a handful of water would have sufficed for baptism that they would have gone to the river?" The answer may not be very satisfactory to the friends of the theory, but, certainly, there is no "evasion" when Romans, Greeks, Egyptians, Hindoos, and Jews are all shown in long procession "going down to the river," not for a dipping, but for a sprinkling, a pouring, and a washing, for which "a handful of water would have sufficed."

Dr. Carson has said repeatedly, that possibility is all that is necessary in order to give validity to an objection. Now, we have not only shown it to be possible for persons to go down to a river to make use of its water in other ways than by dipping, but have shown that to do so was a common practice in various nations and in various ages extending through thrice ten hundred years. And this three thousand year old practice we throw across the path of the argument of Dr. Carson, as an objection, to bar forever access to the conclusion—"dipping is the necessary end of 'going down to a river.'"

Justin Martyr.

Justin Martyr is quoted in support of a dipping from "going to the water." In speaking on the subject of baptism he says, "ἔπειτα ἄγονται ὑφ᾿ ἡμῶν ἔνθα ὕδωρ ἐστὶ—Then they are led away by us where there is water."

Our Baptist friends say, "They are led to the water to be dipped into it." But, unhappily, Justin, like all others, omitted the statement of any such fact. The leading away is very plainly stated, and the presence of water is no less explicitly stated, but the place where should be found the "dipping" is an absolute blank.

There is a passage from Irenæus quite parallel with this from Justin: "But some of them say, τὸ μὲν ἄγειν ἐπὶ τὸ ὕδωρ περισσὸν εἶναι, to lead away to the water is superfluous, and mixing oil and water together, they sprinkle it upon the head of the perfected (baptized.)" (664.)

Irenæus is speaking of certain heretics. They were heretical in their baptism in that they did not baptize into the Trinity; but they are not charged with heresy for the manner in which they used the water in ritual baptism.

Irenæus had just spoken of other heretics in this language: Οἱ δὲ ἄγουσιν ἐφ᾿ ὕδωρ, καὶ βαπτιζόντες ὕτως ἐπιλέγουσιν Εἰς ὄνομα . . . . "Others lead away to water, and baptizing, speak thus—Into the name of the unknown Father of all, into Truth mother of all, into Him descending upon Jesus, into Unity, and Redemption, and Communion of the powers."

These heretics "conducted their disciples to water and baptized them saying"—What? We dip you into water? That, certainly, is what they must have said, if dipping into water is baptism; but they said no such thing, but instead of a dipping-into-water-baptism, they declare that they baptize *into the name of the unknown Father*, &c. This was a most heretical baptism, and Irenæus had the good sense to attach the heresy not to the manner of using the water, whatever that may have been, but precisely to that to which it did belong, namely, to the substitution of another (false and wicked) verbal element for that appointed by the Scriptures

into which the soul was to be baptized, made subject to its
control, and assimilated to its likeness.

But to "the leading to water" some objected on the
ground that it was "superfluous." On what specific ground
they based this objection we are not told; but Dr. Carson
and friends say, "It is superfluous to go to the water unless
you dip into it." If we suppose that these heretics reasoned
in the same way, then, it would follow, that after leading to
water there was a failure to dip into it, and hence arose the
complaint, that "going to the water was superfluous."
Whether the friends of the theory will give up their claim,
that "sober judgment and candor" must confess a dipping
as the issue of going to the water, or will allow that things
were managed otherwise in the days of Irenæus, I do not
know.

In farther illustration of this "leading to water" and consequent dipping into it, we may refer to 3 Kings 1 : 33,
καταγάγετε αὐτὸν εἰς τὴν Γιὼν, v. 38, κατέβη Σαδὼκ ὁ ἱερεὺς .... καὶ
ἀπήγαγον αὐτὸν εἰς τὴν Γιὼν, v. 45, καὶ ἔχρισαν αὐτὸν ἐν τῇ Γιὼν, καὶ
ἀνέβησαν —"lead him down to the Gihon .... Zadok the high
priest went down—and they led him away to the Gihon—
and anointed him at (ἐν) the Gihon, and they came up."

We have here a case of "leading to the water." Will the
theory insist upon it that "sober judgment and candor"
must declare that Solomon was *dipped into* the Gihon. Will
it insist upon his being led *into* the Gihon by those strongest
possible words εἰς τὴν Γιὼν? Will it insist upon the kingly
anointing taking place *within the waters* of the Gihon by
reason of those unreserved words, ἐν τῇ Γιὼν?

If Solomon was "led away to where there was water," if
he was led into the water (so far as εἰς τὴν Γιὼν, by any necessity, puts him into water), if he was anointed within the
water (so far as ἐν τῇ Γιὼν has any absolute force to put him
within water), if he went down to the water and came up
from the water, when but "a handful would suffice," what
becomes of "the unanswerable argument" for a dipping
from "going down to and coming up from?"

If it should continue to be said, that this reply, like all

others which have gone before, presents " many evasions to
get rid of the argument without making a fair answer," I
can only plead, that I have answered according to the
measure of my understanding, and that whatever remains
unanswered must be set down as too profound for my apprehension.

Responsibility.

As the theory insists upon a dipping of men and women
into water, it does, thereby, make itself responsible for all
the consequences which unavoidably attach to such dipping.

They refuse to be responsible for a drowning (while confessing that βαπτίζω does drown), on the plea that God never
meant that Christians should be drowned; and refusing to
give up the theory that men and women are to be put into
water, they change the word which the Holy Spirit has used
and for baptizing substitute dipping, which term will allow
living persons to be brought into an unscriptural relation
with water without depriving them of life.

They like just as little, to be made responsible for a promiscuous multitude disrobing and enrobing on the banks
of a river, or for its alternative, to be dipped into the water
without any change of garments before or after the dipping.

Dr. Carson (p. 337) vents his indignation under the pressure of this responsibility after this manner: " Must we go
back eighteen centuries to find a change of raiment? We
have nothing to do with inquiries of this kind. I prove
that they were immersed. I care not from what sources
they had suitable conveniences."

There is an abundance of *nonchalance* in this language,
but the responsibility is too firmly fixed to be either denied
or evaded. Dr. Carson sets out joyously to traverse the
track of eighteen centuries to discover a dipping into water;
is the journey any harder, or any longer, to find out whether
the dipped were disrobed or enrobed? The National Baptist quotes a Jewish Rabbi as saying, "Jews were baptized
in a nude state, and by a submersion of the whole body in
water. And John the Baptist surely performed it in the

same way that the Jews did." Is this the accepted solution?
I know of no Baptist authority which attempts, directly, to
resolve the difficulty. Dr. Fuller, very thoughtfully, sees
that this difficulty is met in the case of Judith. He says:
"Had it been in the day, and in a place where she could be
seen, there would have been no indelicacy, for she was, of
course, dressed in proper apparel." This "of course dressed
in proper apparel" sounds very much like exposition from
a Baptist vestry-room.

I presume no one questions whether the multitudes baptized by John were baptized in the daytime or not; or
whether they were baptized in a place where they could be
seen or not; were they, also, "of course dressed in proper
apparel?" If they were dressed "in proper apparel" (Jewish Rabbi to the contrary notwithstanding) when they went
into the water, what is to be done with this, now, *im*proper
apparel when they come out of the water? Is it to be kept
on? If not, how is it to be removed and other apparel put
on there on the banks of the river? The difficulty is real
and practical. The theory is vexed by it.

The Bible narrative does not meet the wants of the theory.
It leaves them in a dilemma. It may be the best thing that
Dr. Carson can say under difficulties, "We have nothing to
do with such inquiries;" but such utterance shows that the
last bullet has been fired from his pouch, and he is driven to
the necessity of tearing a button from his coat. He knew
both the importance of this point and the impossibility of
giving it a satisfactory solution, not by reason of the eighteen
centuries which have elapsed, nor yet because of the silence
of the Scriptures, but *because of what the Scriptures have said.*
It is not time, nor silence, which gives the trouble when
promiscuous multitudes, distance from home, and wilderness, are spoken of. It is *the statement of these positive facts*
which constitute a condition of things in which while a
change of raiment is necessary to a dipping into water, how
such a change of raiment is to be effected, in such circumstances, becomes a thing all inexplicable. Dr. Carson, therefore, with controversial skill, makes light of an unmanage-

able difficulty and declares, " I care not from what sources they had suitable conveniences. I prove that they were immersed." Well, if it is indeed proved that these multitudes were dipped into water, I will throw in the raiment and be dumb with silence on that point. But "proof" will be required. We cannot accept assumption, nor assertion, nor evasion. Dipping into the river evokes the raiment question. The Bible says nothing about either dipping or raiment. Rabbi Kalisch says, John dipped; and he disposes of the raiment question by saying, he dipped the people " naked." The theory supplements the Bible by saying, John dipped; but pleads ignorance about the raiment, and adds, " I don't care ! "

I close this view of the subject by the general remark, that " the Jordan" comes into view as belonging to the same class with " the wilderness," " the locusts and wild honey," " the camel's hair raiment and leathern girdle," all of which pertain to John in his peculiar individuality and Elias character, and have nothing more than incidental relation to his baptism. This is conclusively shown by the fact, that while baptism survived John, neither " wilderness," "locusts," " wild honey," "camel's hair," " leathern girdle," or "Jordan" survived him. All passed away together. There was thenceforth no more known of any one in the Scriptures going out into the wilderness, or going to the Jordan, or going to any river, to seek for baptism.

EXEGETICAL EXAMINATION.

We proceed to a more detailed consideration of the phraseology in which this case of baptizing is stated. No passages are made more frequently the subjects of popular appeal in order to confound opponents and to magnify the theory.

TRANSLATION.

Ἐβαπτίζοντο ἐν τῷ Ἰορδάνῃ . . . . . ἐν τῷ Ἰορδάνῃ ποταμῷ.

" Were baptized in the Jordan . . . . . in the river Jordan."

'Ἐν.

Dr. Conant and Dr. Carson complain of the diverse trans·
lations of the preposition ἐν in the phrase ἐν ὕδατι *with* water,
and in the phrase ἐν Ἰορδάνῃ *in* Jordan. They claim to know,
that the reason why the translation of the former phrase was
not used in the latter phrase was, because the wrong would
have been "too glaring." They also aver, that the unfaith-
fulness of the translators of our English Bible is rebuked by
the more faithful adherence to the original by Popish translators. This condemnation is pressed by the quotation of a
passage from Dr. Campbell, which these gentlemen very
cordially indorse. Dr. Conant, in his Version of Matthew
for the Baptist Bible Union, gives the following quotation
in a note on Matt. 3:11—"Campbell (Dr. George Campbell,
President of Mareschal College, Aberdeen) says, with just
severity, I am sorry to observe that the Popish translators
from the Vulgate have shown greater veneration for the
style of that version than the generality of Protestant translators have shown for that of the original. For in this the
Latin is not more explicit than the Greek. Yet so inconsistent are the interpreters last mentioned, that none of them
have scrupled to render ἐν τῷ Ἰορδάνῃ, in the sixth verse, 'in
Jordan;' though nothing can be plainer, than that if there
be any incongruity in the expression 'in water,' this 'in
Jordan' must be equally incongruous. But they have seen
that the preposition *in* could not be avoided there without
adopting a circumlocution, and saying, 'with the water of
Jordan,' which would have made their deviation from the
text too glaring."

The translators of the English Bible were not infallible.
This will hardly be claimed for themselves by the New
Version translators, whatever may be claimed for the Vulgate and its Popish translators. It is seldom, however, that
such charges against the integrity of the translators of the
English Bible are brought from any quarter, much less from
such quarters as those where we naturally look for that noble
sympathy which is inherent in the highest learning and the
truest piety.

Dr. Conant did not give the sentence following the quotation which he made. It runs thus: "The true partisan of whatever denomination always inclines to correct the diction of the Spirit by that of the party." Now, I do not say, that there was a "just severity" in this remark, which was "seen" by Dr. Conant, and under the consciousness that the application was "too glaring" to the work of the Baptist Bible Union, "in correcting the diction of the Spirit by that of the party" in promoting whose object Dr. Conant was himself engaged, and, *therefore* he omitted the passage.

Such charge might involve great wrong. But does Dr. Conant do less wrong to the memory of the translators of the English Bible when he indorses such charges against them. Who was it told Dr. Campbell or Dr. Conant, that it was a less veneration for the words of the Holy Ghost than Papists felt for the words of men, which made the difference between the one translation and the other? Who certified either Doctor, that there is any inconsistency in the renderings "with water" and "in Jordan?" Who assured either of these writers, that our translators gave the rendering "with water" in a blundering attempt to escape from "in water?" By what authority is it said, that the translation "in Jordan" was not made on its merits, but because the translators were shut up to it by an otherwise unavoidable circumlocution which would have made their treachery to God's truth "too glaring?" It does not belong to me to answer for the motives influencing those men whom God raised up to do, in his name, one of the grandest works of all the ages of time. They and their impugners may, in this regard, be safely left to the revelation of secrets in the last great day, when He who knows the heart shall be upon the judgment seat. But—I was about to say, as to their competency as translators in comparison with fault-finders, I was reminded of a contemporaneous anecdote, but the narration would not be in place, for I perceive that the charge is not made against their competency, but, sheerly, against their integrity. Then, of this, let God be the judge.

Inasmuch, however, as it has been my lot to adopt substantially the same translations of these phrases, which are here with "just severity" condemned, it becomes necessary to defend them against the charge of being wrested from the truth to the injury of baptism by dipping into water.

1. As to the charge of irreverence for God's words compared with "the veneration of Popish translators for man's words."

Does this mean that when the Holy Spirit uses one word in two different passages, it is a want of veneration toward God to use two words in translating such passages into English?

In attempting to find an answer to this inquiry I have opened the New Version, and the first passage to which I have turned is 1 Thess. 4 : 16, in which the Holy Spirit has used one word (ἐν) four times, and the New Version has translated three times, "*with* (ἐν) a shout," "*with* (ἐν) voice of archangel," "*with* (ἐν) trumpet of God," and once "*in* (ἐν) Christ." Was it a lack of veneration for the word of God which prompted the diverse translations "with," "in," when there was no diversity of letter in the original?

For farther light I turn to the version of this same passage by the Popish translators, and find, "*with* commandment," "*with* the voice of the archangel," "*with* the trumpet of God," and "*in* Christ." To learn whether they maintain their veneration for the words of men above the veneration of our translators for the word of God, I open the Vulgate and there read, "*in* jussu," "*in* voce archangeli," "*in* tubæ Dei," "IN Christo." Alas! their higher veneration has been as a morning cloud. They have irreverently translated one word (*in*) by two words "with" and "in."

And why may not Ellicott bring the charge alike against the New Versionists, and the Popish translators, of lack of veneration toward both God and man, seeing that he says, ἐν may mean "*in* a shout, *in* the voice of the archangel, *in* the trump of God," meaning, that *during* these occurrences the descent of Christ shall take place?

Is it prudent to throw stones up into the air when our own pate is uncovered?

2. There is a charge of inconsistency. And what is the evidence? It is this: They would have perverted the word of God by translating *with* Jordan, but they found they could not do it without exposure; because they would have been under the necessity of introducing an intolerable circumlocution ("with the water of"), and therefore, they were shut up to honesty in this translation at the expense of consistency when compared with the previously made dishonest one, "*with* water."

And, now, as to the worth of this reasoning. Is there any truth in the statement, that it was necessary to introduce a circumlocution into the translation "*with* Jordan?" Does the Roman priest feel it necessary to introduce any circumlocution when he says, "vivo perfunderis flumine, sprinkled *with the river?*"

Clemens Romanus (988) speaks, without any circumlocution, of washing "with the whole sea and *with all rivers.*"

Didymus Alexandrinus (697) feels no need of circumlocution when he says, "immortal baptism is *by the Jordan.*"

Why is it, then, that the translators of the English Bible have turned back affrighted at circumlocutionary terrors which have had no existence, or no power to alarm any one else?

But on what is this charge grounded? Is it in the naked fact of a diverse translation of the same word when met with in different passages? Then the New Version is guilty of like wrong in wellnigh twoscore passages in the one gospel of Matthew, and times without number throughout the New Testament.

Is it because the word has identically the same relations and of necessity the same meaning? Who makes this affirmation? By whomsoever made it is made erroneously. The relations of the two passages are not ἐν ὕδατι and ἐν ὕδατι, or ἐν Ἰορδάνῃ and ἐν Ἰορδάνῃ; but ἐν ὕδατι in the one case, and ἐν Ἰορδάνῃ in the other. Is this an identical sameness of relation?

But it may be pleaded, Although not the same in letter, yet they are the same in substance, and have of necessity the same meaning. What is the proof? There is none. But as a substitute for proof we have the assertion that "nothing can be plainer" than that ἐν ὕδατι, and ἐν 'Ιορδάνῃ, are the same thing and demand the same translation; which assertion puffs away the integrity of all Protestant translators, "none of whom have scrupled to render" these identities as diversities! And on what does this *assertion* rest? Why, on the *assumption*, that the terms "water" and "Jordan" are absolute and necessary equivalents. Never was assumption more gross or more groundless. John speaks of "water" in the most abstract terms possible (ἐν ὕδατι) stripped of all quality and locality, beyond what pertains to simple and universal *water*. Now, is "Jordan" an abstract term of like character, simple in its nature, universal in its existence, and without local habitation? Is it not a concrete term? has it not a complex nature? and is it not most definitely local in position? These questions answer themselves. Then we have the assertion, that an abstract, universal, and unlocalized term is identical with a concrete, limited, and local term. This, certainly, is assertion enough for one occasion. Is the farther plea entered, "We do not mean to say, that water and Jordan are alike in all respects, but only in one respect; *water* is in both terms." That is to say: You *assert out of* "Jordan" all those things in which it differs from "water" and *assume into it* that one thing in which it agrees, and which can be made to suit a purpose. We can submit neither to such assertion, nor to such assumption.

We are ready to admit, that "Jordan" ordinarily, not necessarily nor by any means always, includes *water*. Sometimes, under this term the banks of the river only are referred to; sometimes, only the dried channel; and sometimes, only a locality without specific reference to banks, or channel, or stream. Now, in "water" there is neither bank, nor channel, nor stream, nor locality. *It is possible*, beyond all possible denial, that when John uses the phrases ἐν ὕδατι, and ἐν 'Ιορδάνῃ, that he used them not because of that particular in which they agreed, but because of that in which they differed. That is to say, he speaks of "water" as the symbol element employed in ritual baptism, while "Jordan" is spoken of as the place where the ritual baptism took place, without any reference to anything else than the simple determination of the locality.

This possibility, even if it should be carried no farther than a possibility, is adequate to crush all assertions and assumptions by which the integrity of our translators is stolen away.

But we do not stop at a bare possibility; we go much farther.

1. It is usual for the Scriptures to state the place of baptism. They mention "the Wilderness," "Bethany," and "Ænon," as places of baptism. Now "Jordan" is a locality, as truly as is the Wilderness, or Bethany, or Ænon; and the same precise form which is used to denote Wilderness, Bethany, Ænon, as localities where baptism took place, is also used in speaking of "Jordan;" therefore we say, it is denoted as a locality.

2. "Jordan" is constantly spoken of as a locality in connection with baptism. *Matt.* 3 : 13, "Then cometh Jesus from Galilee to (ἐπὶ) Jordan." *John* 1 : 28, "These things were done in Bethabara beyond Jordan *where* John was baptizing." *John* 3 : 26, "He that was with thee beyond Jordan." *John* 10 : 40, "And went away again beyond Jordan *into the place where* John at first baptized." We say that ἐν ᾽Ιορδάνῃ denotes locality just as all other localities, ἐν ἐρημῷ, ἐν Βηθανιᾳ, ἐν ᾽Αινῶν, are designated.

3. Dr. Carson admits that ἐν ᾽Ιορδάνῃ denotes locality and nothing but locality. He says (p. 351) "When we wish *merely to designate the place* we always use *in*. They were baptized in the Thames." (p. 291.) "'Εν never has the signification *into*. When construed with βάπτω or βαπτίζω, it is not so definite as εἰς. It designates *merely the place* or substance in which the action of the verb is performed. When I say that such a man was immersed in the river Thames, all that I assert is that the action of the verb was performed in the river. It is the verb immersed and the circumstances

that must prove the mode. This will appear clear to any one who takes an example in which the verb is changed. Such a man was *killed* in the river."

Thus we have Dr. Carson's clear testimony, that ἐν Ἰορδάνῃ can denote nothing but locality. This is all we have to do with at present. Dr. Gill, Matt. 3 : 6, says, " *The place where* they were baptized of him was the Jordan." Now, ἐν ὕδατι never did and never can express *the place where* a thing was done. And to say, that a preposition with an abstract element, and the same preposition with a locality, must receive the same translation, is a statement which has no self-evidencing support.

What help, in support of this error, is to be derived from "the verb and from circumstances" has been already noticed, in part, and will receive farther attention in its place.

I now only add, in vindication of this translation, that it bears the marks of the most thorough consistency.

1. "The Jordan" is always regarded by our translators as a locality, and is translated, precisely, as are all other localities—*in* the Wilderness, *in* Bethany, *in* Ænon, *in* Jordan. Can this be denied? Is not this consistency?

2. "Water" is always regarded by our translators as an abstract element, the symbol instrument, with which ritual baptism is effected; and it is always translated accordingly, "*with* water." Can this be denied? Is not this consistency?

3. The Holy Ghost is always regarded as the divine Agent by whom real baptism, the changed condition of the soul, is effected; and the associated preposition is always translated in conformity with this idea, "*with* the Holy Ghost." Can this be denied? Is not this consistency?

What, then, becomes of the charges of "want of veneration for the Word of God," the lack of Christian integrity, and the destitution of personal consistency?

These charges, also, are made utterly to evaporate under an admission of Campbell not quoted by Conant. It is as follows: "But I should not lay much stress upon the preposition (ἐν) which answering to the Hebrew בְּ, may denote *with* as well as *in*." Then after all, there is not necessarily any more of dishonesty than of ignorance in the translation "*with* water." But Dr. Campbell thinks that "the whole phraseology in regard to this ceremony" favors a dipping. In my poor judgment, however, it is the very contradictory of this which is the truth. It is only in a partial phraseology that dipping finds the shadow of support. This will, presently, be shown to be true by a general exhibit; the specification by Campbell may, here, be disposed of. He says, "Accordingly the baptized are said ἀναβαινειν *to arise, emerge, ascend* (v. 16) ἀπὸ τοῦ ὕδατος, and (Acts 8 : 39) ἐκ τοῦ ὕδατος *from* or *out* of the water." It is marvellous how sane men will dig pits and then, with open vision, plunge headforemost into them. This argument of Campbell deserves to be placed highest in the long list of extraordinary arguments for dipping. How any one, much less such a one as Dr. Campbell, could get from the Scriptures the idea that ἀνα βάινω indicated an *emersion from beneath the surface of the water*, passes my wit to comprehend. Any reader of the Greek text maintaining such a notion is beyond argument from me. Professor Stuart (Mode of Baptism, p. 36) thus disposes of the "conceit": "But who will venture to introduce such a conceit as this? Yet if any one should wish to do so, the verb ἀναβάινω will hardly permit such an interpretation. This verb means *to ascend, mount, go up*, viz., a ship, a hill, an eminence, a chariot, &c.; and as applied to trees and vegetables, *to spring up, shoot up, grow up*. But as to *emerging from the water*, I can find no such meaning attached to it." But, alas! Moses Stuart it may be must, with the translators of our English Bible, yield the palm for veneration of the Word of God to Popish translators!

Having, now, endeavored to defend the varying translation "*with*," "*in*," of the preposition ἐν, on the ground of its association with the widely varying terms ὕδατι, and Ἰορδάνη (the one an abstract element and the other a definite locality), I now proceed to show, that the conjunction of this preposition with the name of a river does not require, as is assumed, that that name should **be** used as the equivalent of *Water*.

'Εν 'Ιορδάνη.

Dr. Carson, while admitting that "Jordan" is a locality, presses the point that this locality is a *river*, and assumingly concludes, that the name of the river is the representative of water solely; so that "in the Jordan" means nothing more nor less than *in the water*.

We freely admit that water is one of the elements which enter into our idea of a river; but water, alone, cannot make a river; there must be banks and channel, and these are as essential to the existence of a river as is water. The name of a river may be used as the representative of any one of its essential constituents, whether water, bank, or channel, when it is desirable to refer to either to the exclusion of the others. When, therefore, we meet with the name of a river, the assumption that it represents water, solely, is an assumption against the ordinary and universal usage of language.

As to the force of ἐν, with the name of a river, I hope our Baptist friends will bear in mind the declaration of their (for all popular effect) *facile princeps* leader, "When we wish merely to designate the place we always use (ἐν) *in.*" Such is the usage of the Scriptures in denoting the places of baptism, ἐν ἐρημῷ, ἐν Βηθανια, ἐν Αινων, ἐν 'Ιορδάνη. In connection with the names of rivers and other bodies of water it may be only proximate position and not absolute inness which is denoted. But, whether it be interpreted with a severe literality or more freely, we shall adduce evidence to prove that it may be construed with the name of a river without meaning *in water*.

Professor Harrison (Greek Prepositions, p. 243), in discussing the import of the preposition ἐν, assigns to it the meaning *at, on, near.* After having quoted Il., XVIII, 521, ἐν ποταμῷ *at* the river; Herod., I, 76, πολιν ἐν Εὐξείνω πόντῳ a city *on* the Euxine Sea; Xen. Anab., IV, 8, 22, πόλιν 'Ελληνίδα ἐν τῷ Εὐξείνω Πόντῳ a Grecian city *on* the Pontus Euxinus; he says, "In such examples ἐν has really the meaning of 'in,' but in the accommodated sense in which it marks with its case the circumstances or conditions in which an action occurs or an object stands. The phrase ἐν Ἐυξείνω πόντῳ, and such like, are not to be understood literally as meaning *in*, *within*, the Euxine Sea, but as descriptive generally of the circumstances of an action or object as regards its place, *and so as to embrace also the adjoining region* as well as the place itself."

We have, then, the authority of Professor Harrison, as the interpreter of Homer, and Herodotus, and Xenophon, for saying, that a man may be ἐν ποταμῷ without being in the *water* of a river; and a city may be ἐν πόντῳ without being in the *water* of the sea.

Cyrus (Xen., VII, 5) gives command to descend " εἰς τὸ ξηρὸν τοῦ πόταμου into the dry part of the river." In this passage " river," certainly, is not the equivalent of *water*, unless some part of water is " dry." But the channel being an essential part of a river, when a portion of the channel is dry it is perfectly legitimate to say, that a part of the *river* is dry. A parallel passage is found in 3 Kings 17 : 7, " καὶ ἐξηράνθη ὁ χειμάῤῥους, and the brook was dried up." The *water* was not made dry, but the channel was, by drought and evaporation. " Brook," here, is not the equivalent of *water*.

Dr. Carson, himself, presents in the strongest possible manner evidence for the truth for which we contend. In speaking of the ambuscade represented (Il., XVIII, 520) on the shield of Achilles, he says (p. 339), " The ambuscade is represented as placed, ' ἐν ποταμῷ, in the river.' It was within the banks of the river that the ambuscade lodged. This is a much better place for an ambuscade than the bank of a river." These soldiers lodged, so Dr. Carson insists, ἐν ποταμῷ *in* the river, and not *on* the river, nor *at* the river. Did they lodge in the *water?* If they did not, then neither " river," nor " in the river," means *water, in the water.* It seems that there is no difficulty in finding in this phrase of Homer a fine, dry camping ground; while the same phrase in the New Testament is full of *water* to the brim and fit for nothing but a dipping. It would be difficult, in our day, for soldiers to camp " in a river" and keep their powder dry, if " river" must be the equivalent of *water.*

23

Dr. Carson, also, notices the passage which speaks of Ulysses escaped from shipwreck, with the following comment: "He has only the choice whether to watch all the rueful night, ἐν πόταμῳ in the river, or to ascend the acclivity. But why in the river? Is he not out of the river? Why does he suppose a necessity for going into it again? The reason is obvious. If he does not choose to ascend the acclivity, and go into the wood for shelter, and make a leafy couch, he must lodge in the river, under the cover of its banks. It is not *at* the river, but *in* the river that he supposes himself to watch. On the bank he could have no shelter; in the river he could have the shelter of the bank. He might be *in the* RIVER, yet *not in the* WATER; *all within the banks* is the river."

And so ends, most squarely, all controversy on this point so far as Dr. Carson is concerned. Whatever other Baptists may say, their great leader declares in the most explicit terms, that "river" and *water* are not convertible; a man may be *in the river* all night long and not come in contact with a particle of *water*. And John may have baptized "in the river Jordan" all his life long and never, so far as "in the river" is concerned, have dipped anybody in its *water*.

As do the classic Homer, Herodotus, and Xenophon write, so do the inspired penmen of the Holy Scriptures.

Sacred Writers.

3 Kings 17 : 3 (Septuagint), "Elijah is commanded to hide himself, ἐν τῷ χειμάρρῳ Χορράθ, in the brook Cherith that is before Jordan."

It is undoubtedly competent for a man to hide himself most effectually in the water of a brook; water will be the winding-sheet of a drowned man; but was the Prophet directed to thus hide himself? We have just seen a company of Greeks hiding themselves in a river without being troubled by water; why may not this Hebrew prophet do the same? We are not left to conjecture. We are told (v. 5), that Elijah "did according to the word of the Lord and sat down (camped, dwelt) ἐν χειμάρρῳ Χορράθ *in the brook* Cherith."

If Elijah was " in the brook," he was somewhere else than in the *water;* and yet there was water as well as a prophet " in the brook," for while the ravens brought him food, " he drank water out of the brook."

The brief comment by Dr. Carson on this historical fact is this: " Could not the prophet take up his residence *within the banks* of the brook?"

We answer this question very cheerfully and say, We think that he could; and are happy to know that Dr. Carson, also, thinks that he could live " in the brook" and not be incommoded by *water.* Barclay thinks that a more admirable hiding-place could nowhere be found, and that " ravens," only, could bring food to some of the recesses in its lofty and precipitous boundary walls.

But if Dr. Carson feels no embarrassment in finding a home for the first Elias by the Jordan, " in the brook Cherith," for so much of those years of drought as served to " dry up" the brook, why need he be troubled if the second Elias should make his residence " in the river Jordan" during the brief period of his ministry?

And if Elias lived " in the brook," and " drank water out of the brook," what was to hinder him who came " in the spirit and power of Elias" from living " in the Jordan," and taking water out of the Jordan both to drink and to baptize?

If when the first Elias was hiding from his enemies it had been said, that he lived and baptized ἐν τῷ χειμάρῥῳ Χοῤῥὰθ, why might not (not to say must not) the statement refer to locality merely and not to *water?* And if this is true of the first Elias, why not also true of the second, when he lived and baptized ἐν τῷ 'Ιορδάνῃ πόταμῳ?

It is declared of John, that he " dwelt upon the Jordan," as it is said of Elijah, that he " dwelt in the brook Cherith." This is the language of Justin Martyr (588), " John dwelt (καθίζω, the same word used by the Septuagint to denote Elijah's dwelling in the brook Cherith), ἐπὶ τὸν 'Ιορδάνην πόταμὸν, upon the river Jordan." And it is this same preposition and phrase, ἐπὶ τὸν 'Ιορδάνην, which the Scriptures (Matt. 3 : 13) use to express the coming of the Lord Jesus " from Galilee

to John *upon the Jordan* to be baptized of him." Again,
proving, in the most absolute manner, that "Jordan" is
used to express locality and not *water*. There is just as
much water in ἐπὶ τὸν 'Ιορδάνην as there is in ἐν τῷ 'Ιορδάνῃ, and
just as little, that is, there is, by the necessity of the terms,
just none at all in either.

1 Kings 15 : 5. "Saul having gathered together his hosts, a
quarter or a half million of men, against Amalek, formed an
ambuscade ἐν τῷ χειμάρρῳ, in the brook."

It would seem from this statement that the Greeks were
not peculiar in using water-courses as places for ambuscades.
The comment of Dr. Carson is, again, very brief. He asks,
"What is to hinder the place of ambush from being in the
brook?" Nothing, according to the views which we hold.
Everything according to the views of those who make "in
the brook" equivalent to *in the water*.

If Dr. Carson wields a wand which, with a brief question,
waves off all difficulty in disposing of some hundreds of
thousands of men "within the banks of a brook" without
troubling them with water, why should he stumble at the
difficulty of putting "all Jerusalem, and Judæa, and the
region round about Jordan," within the banks of the Jordan
without putting them into the water? and, more especially,
since "he finds no evidence in the Scripture that there was
ever, at one time, a multitude with John?" Is it said, that
the word *baptize* makes the difference? Then, we answer:
The point of inquiry now is, what is the precise value of
the phrase, ἐν 'Ιορδάνῃ, ἐν 'Ιορδάνῃ πόταμᾳ, and we cannot allow
our friends to elude our hold upon them or upon the issues
of the case, by slipping away from things in a half-settled
condition. It is too much the custom of the friends of the
theory, when pressed with unanswerable evidence on a particular point, to slip away to something else without confession of wrong, and, thus, to pass from baptize to river, and
from river to much water, and from much water to went
down to and came up from, and from these to burial and
resurrection, and so circling round again to baptize. There

must be an end of this. Let us take one thing at a time, and make thorough work of it, and dispose of it in finality. Now we discuss " in the river." Is *water* so in this phrase as to be inseparable from it, and to allow the assumption, without proofs, of its equivalence with " *in the water?* " or, Is this phrase of such a nature as to allow Saul to put a quarter of a million of men in a river, " within the banks of a brook," without putting so much as the soles of their feet in *water?* And if this be true, as Dr. Carson says that it unquestionably is, then, Why may not John receive *in the river*, " within the banks of the Jordan," so many as come for baptism, without one of them being in the *water*, while "in the river?" That is the question. What is the answer?

Psalms 83 : 10. " Do to them as to Midian and to Sisera, as to Jabin (ἐν τῷ χειμάῤῥῳ Κεισῶν), in the brook Kison."

" Sisera (Judges 4 : 13) had collected nine hundred chariots of iron and all the people that were with him from Harosheth of the Gentiles (εἰς τὸν χειμάῤῥουν Κισῶν) into the brook Kison."

Few, I presume, will say, that the battle which followed was fought *in the water* although it was fought "in the brook." Professor J. A. Alexander translates, "In the valley of the Kishon." Rosenmuller, "In valle, s. ad torrentem Kischon, in the valley, or at the brook Kishon." Gesenius says, that "the Hebrew ב (as here, and in the other passages) with a river, is represented by the Greek ἐν πόταμῳ, and by the Latin *ad* fluvium." But if we were to translate ἐν τῷ 'Ιορδάνῃ πόταμῳ *at* the river Jordan, what would become of the choicest popular utterance of the theory? Surely, in that case, we would be doubly in danger of having, " less veneration than Popish translators," " designedly obscuring the Word of God," " not light that is needed but honesty," together with other beauties of the vocabulary, thrown heavily at us. And this must be patiently endured while it is seriously held, that the theory is the Word of God and the Word of God is the theory, "if the Holy Spirit reports truly" (C., p. 367); and, " to deny it, is to give the lie to the inspired narrator" (p. 450); and the enjoyment of infallibility requires that every argument should be held fast though an angel were to reject it (p. 420).

1 Kings 15 : 13. "Asa destroyed her idol and burnt it (ἐν τῷ χειμάῤῥῳ τῶν Κέδρων) in the brook Kedron."

Is it usual to "burn" things in the *water?* If not, then "in the brook" and *in the water* are not altogether equivalents.

Jeremiah 13 : 4–7. "Arise, go to the Euphrates (ἐπὶ τὸν Εὐφράτην) and hide it (girdle) there in a hole of the rock. So I went and hid it (ἐν τῷ Εὐφράτῃ) in the Euphrates, as the Lord commanded me. And it came to pass after many days, that the Lord said unto me, Arise, go to the Euphrates (ἐπὶ τὸν Εὐφράτην) and take the girdle from thence, which I commanded thee to hide there. Then I went to the Euphrates (ἐπὶ τὸν Εὐφράτην πόταμον) and digged, and took the girdle from the place where I had hid it."

When Jeremiah hid his girdle "in the Euphrates," as the Lord commanded him, he did not hide it in the *water*, but "in a hole of the rock." When Elijah was commanded "to hide" (the same word as here, κρύπτω) "himself in the brook Cherith," he, no doubt, hid himself "in a hole of the rock," and not in the *water*. The name of a river, then, is not the equivalent of *water*. When Jeremiah went "upon the river Euphrates," he did not go upon the *water*, for where he went there he "digged," and we are not in the habit of digging in the *water*. "The *river* Euphrates," then, and "water" are not equivalents.

We may notice in passing, that when Elijah was commanded "to hide" himself in the brook Cherith, he did not hide himself in the same mode as Jeremiah hid his girdle in the Euphrates. The prophet did not dig a hole and bury himself, as Jeremiah digged a hole and buried his girdle. Yet they both "hid" (the one himself and the other his girdle) and both obeyed the divine command to the letter. Now, to hide and to baptize belong to the same class of words, namely, that class which makes demand for condition. *To hide* demands for its object a condition of concealment; the time and the manner of concealment being unlimited

To baptize demands, primarily, for its object a condition of intusposition without limitation of duration or mode of accomplishment; and secondarily, condition without intusposition, the result of some controlling influence, equally without limit of duration. Elijah was not sent into the brook Cherith *to play at bo-peep* with Ahab; nor was John sent upon the Jordan *to dip* men and women into water. "Bo-peep" has precisely the same family likeness to "hide" as "dip" has to "baptize." Interchange has the same possibility and impossibility in the one case as in the other.

It must be admitted that "in the Euphrates" is not exactly *in the water.*

The Jordan with Various Prepositions yet without Water.

The same phraseology which is employed in connection with the Cherith, the Kedron, the Kishon, and the Euphrates, is also used in connection with the Jordan, and in like manner without using the name of the river as the equivalent of water.

'Εν.

Joshua 3 : 8. "When ye are come upon (ἐπὶ) the brink of the water of Jordan, ye shall stand still (ἐν τῷ 'Ιορδάνῃ) in the Jordan."

A nicely defined line is here drawn separating, by a hair's breadth, "in the Jordan" from "in the water." They were to come (εἰσέλθητε) to the water, even to the very brink, but to stop short (ἐπὶ μέρους τοῦ ὕδατος) "*upon* the brink of the water;" and in this position they were said to stand (ἐν τῷ 'Ιορδάνῃ) in the Jordan.

Could language discriminate more markedly, and at the same time more sharply?

The same thing is shown in v. 13: "As soon as the feet of the priests rest ἐν τῷ ὕδατι τοῦ 'Ιορδάνου, the water of the Jordan shall flow away." This translation of the Septuagint, "*feet* of the priests," is not so nicely accurate as that of our English Bible, "*soles* of the feet." The water flowed away as soon as the soles of the feet of the priests bearing the ark of Jehovah, Lord of the whole earth, came in contact with the brim of the water. When they stood "in the Jordan," they did not stand "in the water." So in v. 15, "When the priests came ἐπὶ τὸν Ἰορδάνην, upon the Jordan, and their feet (ἐβάφησαν) were dipped into the brim of the water of the Jordan, (v. 16) the waters flowed away, (v. 17) and the priests stood (ἐπὶ ξηρᾶς ἐν μέσῳ τοῦ Ἰορδάνου) upon dry ground in the midst of the Jordan."

Throughout this very precise description there is a contrast made between in the water and in the Jordan; and we are guarded against the notion that the priests stood in the water, while it is expressly declared that they stood "in the midst of the Jordan."

It may be well to observe the use of βάπτω (טָבַל) in v. 15 as exhibiting, very strikingly, the discriminating difference between this word and βαπτίζω. The dipping of the soles of the feet into the brim of the water involves an act, feeble in force, an entrance into the element the least possible in extent, a continuance within it the briefest period possible in duration, and issuing, necessarily, in the least possible measure of influence. This is an extreme case; but extreme cases show the possible power of words, and oftentimes reveal most clearly their essential nature. A similar case is that of dipping the feet of a flea into wax in order to measure the distance of its leap (Aristophams, Nubes I, 2); and of Lazarus dipping the *tip* of his finger in water (Luke 16: 24).

There are no such cases of the usage of βαπτίζω, nor could there be while the word remains what it is and has ever been. Current usage shows these words to be antipodal of each other as to restricted form of action, restricted time of continuance within the element, and consequent restricted influence over the object; the one is severely limited in all these respects, while the other has no restriction. Hence the former when applied, secondarily, to effect, or condition, can only be used where the result or influence is of the most limited and feeble character; while the latter has a capacity competent to measure results which are ultimate, and influences which are most profound.

Δια.

Verse 11. "Behold the ark of the covenant of the Lord of the whole earth (δια-βαινει τον 'Ιορδάνην) passes through the Jordan."

The ark passed "through the Jordan," but it did not pass through the *water*. In v. 17 we find this preposition used both independently and in composition to express the same fact. "And all the children of Israel (διεβαινον δια ξηρας) passed through, through the dry (channel), until all the people finished passing through the Jordan." Passing "through the Jordan" has no more power to wet the people than has "in the Jordan." The point at issue, namely, the right to assume, in any controverted case, that Jordan and water are equivalents, is, here, settled most flatly in the negative by the identification of Jordan and *dry* channel. The same thing is repeated in this same verse by the statement that "the priests stood (ἐπὶ ξηρᾶς ἐν μέσῳ τοῦ 'Ιορδάνου) upon the dry channel, in the midst of the Jordan." This passage is entirely parallel with that from Xenophon (εἰς ξηραν τοῦ πόταμου), "into the *dry* part of the river."

Such use of language shows how worthless is any argument which is based on the phrases "through the Jordan," "in the Jordan," as the necessary equivalents of "in the *water*," "through the *water*."

'Εx.

Joshua 4 : 3. "Take up, ἐκ μέσου τοῦ 'Ιορδάνου, out of the midst of Jordan, twelve stones."

There are some prepositions on which Baptist writers rely with especial confidence to prove a dipping in water. Highest on this list is ἐκ. On this preposition Dr. Carson depends with such unbounded faith as to make it the determining pivot of the whole controversy. It would not be proper here to enter into any extended discussion of the essential power and use of this preposition, but inasmuch as it now crosses our path, it becomes necessary to recognize its presence and to observe its functions in this particular case.

Dr. Carson says, that never under any circumstances in all Greek literature, does it mean anything else than *out of*. Well; then, according to the assumption, "out of (ἐκ) the midst of Jordan" must mean out of the midst of *water*. For is not Jordan the name of a river? And is not river *water?* And what can "out of the midst of Jordan" be but out of the midst of its watery depths? Such reasoning is very admirable and very unanswerable until we come to the facts, and then it is neither admirable, nor does it require any answer. For, notwithstanding the presence of the Jordan, and our standing in the very midst of it, and notwithstanding the presence and help of that sturdy little univocal ἐκ, we cannot manage to get one of these twelve stones out of the *water*. They are dry, and on dry ground, in the midst of a river.

It is clear, then, that a stone, or a person, may pass out of the midst of Jordan, without passing out of a state of immersion into a state of emersion. But, however irresistible this inference may be, we are not left to any inference. It is a matter of the most express and reiterated statement that the coming out of the Jordan did not involve any coming out of *water*.

Joshua is directed (v. 16) to command the priests (ἐκ βῆναι ἐκ τοῦ 'Ιορδάνου) "to come out, out of the Jordan." This command is given (v. 17) ('Εκ βῆτε ἐκ τοῦ 'Ιορδάνου), "Come out of the Jordan." Obedience to this command is announced (v. 18) ('Εξέβησαν ἐκ τοῦ 'Ιορδάνου καὶ ἔθηκαν τοὺς πόδας ἐπὶ τῆς γῆς), "they went out of, out of the Jordan and placed their feet upon land." The Septuagint speaks of their feet being placed on the land in contradistinction from the river, although there was no water in the river. The Hebrew says, they placed "the soles of their feet on dry ground," using the same word with that which had been employed to express the dried up channel of the river.

It is impossible to use the preposition in greater strength than in the double form in which it is here presented, and yet the priests and the people "come out, out of the midst of Jordan" without the sprinkling of water upon them, and with the soles of their feet, at every step, resting on dry ground.

Ἀνέβη ἐκ.

Verse 19. "And the people, ἀνέβη ἐκ τοῦ Ἰορδάνου, went up out of the Jordan."

Dr. Carson is greatly dissatisfied with an interpretation which refuses to identify "Jordan" and *water*. This is his language: "As if the Holy Spirit had anticipated Mr. Ewing's perversion of the word *Jordan*, by converting it, without any authority, into Jordan-dale, the word river is added to it by Mark. . . . It would be a strange explanation that would explain the *river Jordan* not to be the *river Jordan*, but something else. This would be a neological explanation" (p. 126).

The argument of Carson is, that the addition of *river* to Jordan makes the presence of water so certain that to refuse its recognition is nothing else than an infidel perversion. But we have seen that this assumption is contradicted by incontrovertible facts. And no man has more utterly repudiated the idea, that "river" does by any necessity include water, than has been done by Dr. Carson himself. Has not Dr. Carson said, that "the river" in which the Grecian ambuscade was placed was "not a river" (water) at all? Has he not said, that "the river" in which Ulysses lodged was "not a river" (water) at all? Has he not said, that "the brook" in which Elijah dwelt was "not a brook" (water) at all? Has he not said, that "the brook" in which Saul placed his ambuscade was "not a brook" (water) at all? Is this "neological perversion?" or, has Dr. Carson a reserved right "to explain a river not to be a river" while for others to do so is a "perversion" of the word of God?

But Dr. Carson does not seem to be entirely satisfied with this charge of neology, as he adds: "There is in the passage under consideration other evidence that baptism was performed by immersion. It is said, that 'Jesus when he was baptized went *up* straightway from the water.' I admit the proper translation of ἀπὸ is *from* and not *out of:* and that the argument founded on the former is not the same with that which is founded on ἐx, *out of.* 'Aπὀ would have its meaning fully verified, if they had only gone down to the edge of the water."

Dr. Carson evidently regards ἐx as a much more trusty ally than ἀπὀ. While he places much confidence in "going *up from*" to prove an immersion, he regards "going *up out*" *of* as demonstration.

Let us gratify the Doctor by associating "out of" and "Jordan," and see what is the result. We have the materials in this v. 19: "And the people went *up out of* the Jordan." Here is the "going up," the "out of," and "the Jordan;" where is *the immersion?* It is quite evident, that "going up," "out of," and "Jordan" have no power to save this imperiled error.

Eἰς.

Joshua 4 : 5. "Pass over before the ark of the Lord your God (εἰς μέσον τοῦ 'Iορδάνου) into the midst of the Jordan."

The association of the preposition εἰς with Jordan has been claimed to be decisive of a dipping into *water.* We have, here, that form presented in the strongest possible manner, εἰς μέσον τοῦ 'Iορδάνου, and yet there is nothing but dry ground. Certainly if Jordan and water were equivalent terms we should have here an immersion of the profoundest sort; but these chosen men march "into the midst of Jordan" and do not wet the soles of their feet.

We have now examined the word "river" and the "names of rivers" (Cherith, Kedron, Kishon, Euphrates, Jordan) with a view to determine their necessary equivalence with *water;* and we find that there is no such thing known to the writings of Jews or Gentiles.

We have, also, passed in review passages presenting the prepositions ἐν, διὰ, ἐx, εἰς, in relation with "rivers," and the "names of rivers," to see whether they could lend any power to convert such terms into *water;* but we have found them powerless to effect any such result.

We have followed διa βαινω, ἐx βαινω, ἀνa βαινω, "*through* the river," "*out of* the river," "*up from* the river," and instead of being thoroughly immersed in water, we have not so much as wet the soles of our feet.

We have seen the first Elias, John's great Prototype, "dwelling in a brook" for days, and weeks, and months, and having no other contact with its waters than that of his lips as he quenched his thirst.

We have seen an army of some hundreds of thousands "hiding in a brook" without any water hurting their weapons of war.

We have seen an army defeated "in a brook" without victors or vanquished being troubled by water.

We have seen an idol "burned in a brook" without water quenching the fires.

And we have seen, outside of the Scriptures, a forlorn wanderer "lodging all night in a river" without either being drowned or having his raiment uncomfortably damp when he awoke in the morning.

And, now, when we return to the second Elias, still (to use the language of Justin) " dwelling upon the river Jordan," shall we be saluted with that argumentative refrain— " baptizing in the Jordan, therefore (ex necessitate rei), *dipping in the water ?* "

Possibly, after this exposition, some apologist for the theory may say : " While we have repelled the claim, that Jordan was a locality, by replying, ' if it is a locality that locality is a river; ' and while we have repelled the claim, that ἐν may mean *at* (Gesenius), and may *include the country around* (Harrison), by declaring such suggestions to be ' perversions of the word of God; ' and while we have introduced the river and the preposition, in order to introduce the water, still we did not believe, that there was any water in the river, or in the preposition, but only in our most trusty and well-beloved βαπτίζω."

Very well; then, having emptied the water out of " river" and " Jordan," we must follow the receding waters into the recesses of βαπτίζω.

'Εβαπτίζοντο ἐν τῷ 'Ιορδάνῃ.

It is claimed, that the presence and power of βαπτίζω in the phrase, " Were baptized in the Jordan," determines "Jordan" to be used only as another term for *water*.

Before giving reasons why this position cannot be accepted, a word may be said as to the translation, "*in* the Jordan."

Gesenius says, the Hebrew preposition and the Greek preposition with the name of a river, or with "river"— ἐν 'Ιορδάνῃ, ἐν πόταμῳ, is properly expressed by "*ad* fluvium," *at* the Jordan, *at* the river. Matthies, Rosenmuller, Alexander, Harrison, and almost every one else, give the same decision. Now, suppose, under the shadow of such authority, we translate, " Were baptized *at* the Jordan," what becomes of the Baptist argument from the passage? Such translation is not only vindicated by the approval of these scholars, but by the argumentation of Dr. Carson himself. He says, John's baptizing *in* Bethany, means that he was baptizing *in the neighborhood* of Bethany. Thus, while he retains the form of the word, he breathes into it another life, just such as the scholarship of the world designates by the changed form, *at, near, in the valley, region, neighborhood, contiguous.*

Such translation, on general principles, is beyond impeachment.

But it is urged, "Any such translation is arrested by the presence of the Greek verb." Then, let the examination proceed in this grave presence and with this claimed translation.

1. We observe first : Under the translation, " baptize *in* water," and " baptize *in* Jordan," it is possible that there may be essential difference in these phrases. It is in the most absolute proof that ἐν 'Ιορδάνῃ does not, of necessity, express *in water*, but may express in the channel on dry ground, or, within the banks on dry ground. And it is in equally absolute proof, that βαπτίζω does not necessitate a physical baptism whether in water or in any other substance.

The translation then being granted, there can be no baptism *in water* without the double assumption, 1, Jordan represents *water* and not locality; 2, that the Greek verb does, here, call for physical envelopment contrary to its more frequent use where it calls for no such envelopment.

It is quite possible that these assumptions are not well-grounded.

2. I observe secondly: There is a probability that ἐν Ἰορδάνῃ denotes locality. This position is founded not merely in the admitted fact, that Jordan is sometimes used as a locality without reference to water; but on the equally admitted fact, that other localities in which baptism took place are denoted by the same preposition and in connection with the same verb. Thus John was baptizing *in the wilderness*, βαπτίζων ἐν τῇ ἐρήμῳ; baptizing in Bethany, ἐν Βηθανίᾳ βαπτίζων; baptizing in Ænon, βαπτίζων ἐν Αἰνών; and under the same form we have, " were baptized in Jordan ἐβαπτίζοντο ἐν τῷ Ἰορδάνῃ." The same identical form of the verb is used here, and in the baptizing at Ænon: "John, also, was baptizing in Ænon, and the people came and were baptized (ἐβαπτίζοντο) in Ænon," as expressed in the former part of the sentence.

Now, inasmuch as Jordan is a locality, and the precisely same phraseology is used to express the baptizing here, as in the case of all other localities, we say, it is probable that "Jordan" represents locality where the baptizing took place.

3. We observe thirdly: The presence of βαπτίζω has no power, under the circumstances of the case, to determine the meaning of Jordan to be *water* rather than locality, nor yet to beget a probability of such a meaning; no, nor even to raise the possibility of any such meaning.

It is cheerfully admitted that the phrase ἐβαπτίζοντο ἐν τῷ Ἰορδάνῃ stripped of the specialties of its use, and regarded merely in the possible force of its terms, may express a mersion in the Jordan. For example: If we regard Gennesaret as a simple expansion of the Jordan, as is sometimes done and as it in fact is, then, the vessels and their crews of which Josephus (Antiq., III, 10—Jud. Bapt., p. 63) speaks, " ἐβαπτίζοντο ἐν τῷ Ἰορδάνῃ *were baptized* IN *the Jordan*," at its lake expansion. And there, *at the bottom of those Jordan waters vessels and crews lie until this day*. The form of the verb which Josephus employs to express this Jordan baptism is (ἐβαπτιζόντο) the same, letter for letter, as that which is used by Matthew and Mark in the passage under consideration. Such and such only is the baptism which can be got out of these words interpreted in the literal, physical, enveloping sense claimed for them by the theory.

We say, that such is the baptism not which may, under hard pressure, be extracted from the words, but that which actual usage demands; and that not in exceptional, nor in ordinary cases, merely, but in every case without exception.

And here is the proof:

CLASSIC WRITERS.

1. Βαπτιζόμενοι ἐν τοῖς τέλμασιν . . . . . . Polybius, V, 47, 2.
2. Βεβαπτισμένη ἐν τῷ σώματι . . . . Plotinus, I, 8, 13.
3. Βεβαπτισμένην ἐν τῷ βάθει τοῦ σώματος . Alex. Aphrod., II, 38.

1. "Baptized in the pools" = death by drowning.
2. "Baptized in the body" = death of the soul by corruption.
3. "Baptized in the depth of body" = death of the perceptive power.

ECCLESIASTICAL WRITERS.

1. Βαπτισθέν ἐν βάμματι τὸ ἔριον . . . . . . Basil M., On Baptism.
2. Βαπτιζόμενος ἐν τῷ πυρὶ ὁ σίδηρος . . . .   "   "

1. "Wool baptized in dye" = remaining in.
2. "Iron baptized in fire" = remaining in.

JEWISH WRITERS.

1. Βαπτιζόμενος ἐν κολυμβήθρα, τελευτᾷ . . Josephus, Jew. War, I, 22.

1. "Baptized in a pool, he died" = death by drowning.

These are all the cases of this particular form (the verb with ἐν and a physical element) now within my knowledge. And it will be seen at a glance, that in every case, without exception, the baptized object is not taken out of the baptizing element, but remains within it. We say then, that the phrase ἐβαπτιζόντο ἐν τῷ Ἰορδάνη is competent to effect a baptism in the waters of Jordan, *but it must be such a baptism as will place its object* WITHIN THE WATERS WITHOUT REMOVAL.

The baptism of John was not designed to deposit penitent

Jews in the depths of the Jordan. It is richly ludicrous to see the theorist running his head against Greek philology, and Greek syntax, and Greek usage, and saying, "All these must perish that our theory may live. We do not mean to drown, therefore (under our abuse of words), the Greek language must be changed to suit our self-created necessities, and βαπτίζω must be converted into βάπτω."

4. We observe fourthly: The presence of βαπτίζω does not preclude the interpretation of ἐν 'Ιορδάνῃ as a locality. It is possible that the baptism is not physical. While the usage of the Greek word is so nearly equally divided between baptisms physical and non-physical, that no one has a right to assume a physical baptism in any disputed case. That it is possible for these words to express a baptism which is without any water covering, whether by dipping or by honest immersion, is not difficult to prove.

Let us suppose that the river in which Dr. Carson says Ulysses found refuge was the Jordan. As it was "a rueful night" we may suppose, that if he, and any companions that might chance to be with him, had any of that wine with which they baptized the Cyclops, that they would make free use of it; in which case one passing early in the morning would be likely to say of them—ἐβαπτίζοντο ἐν τῷ 'Ιορδάνῃ—phraseology which Jew and Greek well understood as expressive of an excessive use of wine. We might complete this pregnant form of speech by adding to it the words of Josephus, and say: ἐβαπτίζοντο ἐν τῷ 'Ιορδάνῃ, οἴνῳ πόλλῳ, εἰς ἀναισθησίαν καὶ ὕπνον, "they were baptized in the Jordan, by much wine, into insensibility and sleep."

In such a baptism we have an exhibition of the possible force of terms. The meaning of the verb is classical, Jordan is local, wine is the instrumental means, and insensibility and sleep form the ideal element. While, however, it is a baptism quite possible to the terms, it is a baptism quite impossible to the circumstances; yet, not more impossible than that baptism which must result under the notion of the theory, that men and women are to be deposited ἐν 'Ιορδάνῃ.

5. We observe fifthly: That the true interpretation of this

24

passage will treat it as elliptical; the ellipsis to be supplied
being found in Matt. 3 : 11, and in parallel passages. Thus :

$$'E\beta a\pi\tau\iota\zeta\acute{o}\nu\tau o \;\;\dot{\epsilon}\nu\; \tau\tilde{\omega}\; 'Io\rho\delta\acute{a}\nu\eta \left\{ \begin{array}{l} \dot{\epsilon}\nu\; \ddot{v}\delta a\tau\iota \;(\text{Matt., John}) \\ \ddot{v}\delta a\tau\iota \;(\text{Mark, Luke}) \end{array} \right\} \;\epsilon\dot{\iota}\varsigma\; \mu\epsilon\tau a\nu o\acute{\iota} a\nu.$$

" They were baptized in the Jordan, with water, into repentance."

1. In vindication of this interpretation it may be observed :
Whenever baptizing is spoken of at any other locality, the
form of expression is elliptical. Thus we are told, John
was " baptizing in the wilderness," " baptizing in Bethany,"
" baptizing in Ænon," all which expressions are incomplete,
and need the addition of an essential element in order to
complete the idea. Now, when it is said of another locality
in the same form—John was baptizing " in the Jordan "—
the inference is irresistible, that the expression is elliptical
as in the case of all other localities, and the same supplement
is needed in order to the completion of the idea. If to this
it should be answered : The ellipsis is not necessary in this
last case, because it is contained in " Jordan." I reply : All
that can, possibly, be taken out of " Jordan " is *water*, and
this is inadequate to supply the ellipsis. If the baptism
were such as that of the Classics, or of Josephus (in his account of the boats with their crews baptized in the waters
of Jordan Gennesaret), this would answer; the putting of
men and women in the depths of Jordan's waters would be
the alpha and the omega of the affair; but this is no such
murderous baptism. It belongs to another class of baptisms;
a class of baptisms which, to say the least, is as fully represented in the Classics as are death baptisms by water envelopment. It is " John's baptism ;" not " *John's* baptism " as
distinguishing him as a man from Alcibiades or Timon, but
as distinguishing his *baptism* from their drowning water-
envelopment baptism. It is " John's baptism ;" not as distinguishing him, personally, from Thebe or Ishmael, but as
distinguishing their baptisms; his baptism *with water* from
their baptism *with wine;* his baptism *into* REPENTANCE from
their baptism *into* DRUNKENNESS.

It is manifest, therefore, that no ellipsis which merely

supplies *water* can meet the case. "John was baptizing in the wilderness, in Bethany, in Ænon, in Jordan, *in water*," has no other Greekly meaning than death by drowning.

2. We have already seen, in previously commenting on Luke 3 : 16, *'Εγὼ μὲν ὕδατι βαπτίζω ὑμᾶς*, that the passage was elliptical, requiring the supply of *εἰς μετανοίαν*. Now, we are not at liberty to make or to complete an ellipsis at our own pleasure. It must be made and supplied by something more reliable than our imagination. Dr. Carson (p. 329) well says, " Words which are introduced to supply an ellipsis must be taken from some other passage where they are literally expressed. It is a strange ellipsis that supplies to a word or phrase an idea never elsewhere expressed." We must, then, find the ellipsis which we would introduce into this passage literally expressed elsewhere in Scripture. This reasonable demand is promptly and fully met for us by Matt. 3 : 11, *'Εγὼ μὲν βαπτίζω ὑμας ἐν ὕδατι εἰς μετάνοιαν*. This declaration is entirely disjoined from and wholly independent of locality. It states the essential elements which distinguish John's baptism, namely, pure water as the symbol instrument and repentance as the verbal element. No baptism of John can, possibly, be complete without these elements expressed or understood. It follows therefore as a necessity, that where there is a statement of baptism administered, and the place where it took place, we must supply by ellipsis the symbol instrument and the verbal element. Thus *βαπτίζων ἐν ἐρημῳ, ἐν Βεθηνια, ἐν 'Αινῶν, ἐν 'Ιορδάνη—ἐν ὕδατι εἰς μετάνοιαν*. To each place where the baptism was administered must be added, "WITH *water* INTO *repentance*." This was John's baptism. The reference to this peculiarity, in diverse forms, as "the baptism of John," "the baptism of repentance," "baptized the baptism of repentance," abounds in Scripture.

It is obvious then, that if Jordan be taken as the equivalent and representative of *water*, we still have an ellipsis to supply, as in Luke 3 : 16, which ellipsis can only be *εἰς μετάνοιαν*; which at once and forever determines that the baptism (as we had before on philological and grammatical principles proved) cannot be a baptism into water. To refuse to accept this elliptical εἰς μετάνοιαν, and to insist on the exclusive ἐν ὕδατι, is not merely to refuse the express statement of the word of God, but to seize the sword and divide in twain the living testimony of the Holy Spirit, and set up man's dead theory for God's living truth.

3. The passage, as thus completed, leaves nothing to be desired for the most definite and complete knowledge of the baptism of John. We have not only *the place* where he baptized (Jordan), but we have *the symbol instrument* of baptism (water), and farther, *the verbal element* (repentance) into which the soul is baptized.

What is lacking? Does some friend of the theory sadly say, "A great deal is lacking; there is nothing said of the mode in which the water is used?" It must be acknowledged that such information is lacking. And the only comfort which I can extend to those who are distressed by the deficiency is this: *Never since the Greek language had existence did a baptism depend upon, or have the remotest concern with, a modal use of the* AGENCY *by which it was accomplished.*

This important passage has now been examined in its separate elements, and in their relations to each other. My conviction of the truth of the conclusions reached could hardly be more profound. Yet if the Angel Gabriel were to differ from me, I should not be disposed with the great friend of the theory to "order him to school." Nor would I dare to say with him (omitting the negative), "If John did (not) immerse his disciples the narrative of the evangelist is false" (p. 336). Nor yet would I say to any human being questioning these conclusions, "To deny this is to give the lie to the inspired narrator" (p. 450). And, until some higher power than an Œcumenical council shall invest me with the attribute of infallibility, I will not betray the folly and incur the guilt of saying, that a denial of my judgment is "to give the lie to the Holy Spirit" (p. 453). Before such things shall be written or uttered by me, "may my right hand forget her cunning and my tongue cleave to the roof of my mouth." It is enough for me to hold my convictions with respectful firmness, justly subject to the criticisms of friend or foe, and open to the corrections of a higher wisdom and a truer learning.

Especially in every conclusion as to the teaching of inspiration would I lay down every result at the feet of the Only Wise, subject to correction and reversal in every thought, and word, and letter, by Him who cannot err.

It only remains, before leaving these "places of John's baptism," to show by historical evidence, that there was every facility for John's baptizing "in the Jordan," without his being incommoded by the water.

Dr. Carson gives no proof from the facts of the case, that Ulysses could lodge all night "in the river" and yet lodge on dry ground. He thinks that $\dot{\varepsilon}\nu$ $\pi\dot{o}\tau\alpha\mu\omega$ means *within the banks*, and concludes, that in such case there must have been dry ground enough for him to sleep on "in the river, which includes all within the banks."

Now, we will ask no one to accept of our reasoning when in the dark as to the facts; but will show to those who insist on cutting to the quick in translating $\dot{\varepsilon}\nu$ $'I\!o\rho\delta\dot{\alpha}\nu\eta$, that historical facts relieve of all difficulty even in such a case.

Maundrell, in his travels through the Holy Land, thus speaks of the Jordan: "After having descended the outermost bank, you go *about a furlong* on a level strand, before you come to the immediate bank of the river. This second bank is so beset with bushes and trees, such as tamarisks, willows, oleanders, &c., that you can see no water till you have made your way through them."

Here we have "in the river" (within the outer and inner banks) one-eighth of a mile of "level strand," wherein thousands, tens of thousands, or hundreds of thousands could be accommodated, and all be "baptized in the Jordan," without being troubled by the water.

We can also understand, by this statement which encompasses John "in the river" with "bushes, trees, tamarisks, willows, oleanders, &c.," how closely identical were the baptisms "in the wilderness," and "in the Jordan."

BAPTISM OF JESUS.

ITS PLACE—UPON THE JORDAN.

MATTHEW 3 : 13.

Τότε παραγίνεται ὁ Ἰησοῦς ἀπὸ τῆς Γαλιλαίας ἐπι τὸν Ἰορδάνην πρὸς τὸν Ἰωαννην, τοῦ βαπτισθῆναι ὑπ' αὐτοῦ.

"Then cometh Jesus from Galilee to John, upon the Jordan, to be baptized by him."

JORDAN—LOCALITY AND NOT WATER.

Ἐπὶ τὸν Ἰορδάνην.

THERE is no possible room for doubt as to the sense in which Jordan is used in this passage. It expresses locality and not water. It indicates that feature in the complex term which has in it dry land and not fluidity. The passage locates John on this dry ground, and to this standing-place it brings Jesus to be baptized by him. And here, without change of position (if our judgment is controlled by the inspired narrative), he was baptized. But this will not answer for the theory. For how could Jesus be dipped in water if he was baptized " upon the Jordan ?" But it is no novelty for the theory to be dissatisfied with the language of inspiration. The cases are quite exceptional where it can take the word of God at its real value and just as it stands.

So little sympathy has ἐπὶ with water that it not only will not carry into water when water is not mentioned, but when construed with water it constrains us to step aside lest we should come in contact with the naked element. This is exemplified in *Exodus* 7 : 15, *αὐτὸς ἐκπορεύεται ἐπὶ τὸ ὕδωρ*—" He goeth out upon the water." Pharaoh did not go into the water, nor did he walk upon *the water* of the Nile. But, as we have heretofore seen the name of a river, embracing all of its constituent elements, employed when one only of those constituents was involved, so, here, we have one of the elements employed when the river, as a whole, is intended. That "the water" represents the Nile generally, and not the water of it specifically, is shown by the words immediately following—καὶ, ἔσῃ συναντῶν αὐτῷ ἐπὶ τὸ χεῖλος τοῦ ποταμοῦ—" And thou shalt meet him upon the bank of the river." Here, another particular (the bank) entering into the idea of a river, and that which is specifically indicated by " upon the water" is brought into view. Such passages show how unsafe it is to press the phrases "into the river," "in the river," " upon the river," as certainly synonymous with *water*, when " upon the water" must be interpreted as meaning not water, specifically, but " upon *the bank* of the river."

A parallel passage may be found in Tobit 6 : 1, ἦλθον ἐπὶ τὸν Τίγριν ποταμὸν καὶ ηὐλίζοντο ἐκεῖ, "they came upon the river Tigris and lodged there." Now, whether the Angel and Tobias " lodged within the bank," or without the bank, or on the top of the bank, I am quite unable to say; this only is certain, they did not lodge *in the water*, although they " lodged upon the river."

While certain parties proclaim "Jordan" to be only another method for spelling *water*, the number is small who will venture to assert that Jesus came to John " upon the *water*" to be baptized by him. Dr. Conant, in the New Version, translates as a locality, " Then comes Jesus from Galilee *to the Jordan*, to John, to be immersed by him." And Dr. Carson's inimitable courage would hardly allow him to say, " If Jesus came from Galilee upon the Jordan, as a locality, still that locality was a river, and, therefore, he came upon the *water*, and, necessarily, *in* the water, as is evident from his object in coming, namely, ' to be *immersed* by him;' and no great scholar in Europe will deny that Jesus was immersed *in* the Jordan, and it is only the confidence of ignorance which will venture the extravagance to

deny it." Dr. Carson, however, might as well build up
such an argument on this passage of Matthew (cementing it
with his usual anathemas), as to present unnumbered other
equally "unanswerable" arguments for dipping into water.

Justin Martyr uses this preposition with marked persist-
ency. He says (588), "John came before crying unto men,
Repent! and Christ, while he yet dwelt (ἐπὶ) upon the river
Jordan, came" .... (685). "And Jesus having come (ἐπὶ)
upon the river Jordan (ἔνθα), where John baptized, Jesus
going down to (ἐπὶ) the water, fire was kindled in the Jordan, and he retiring (ἀπὸ) from the water, the Holy Ghost
like a dove descended upon him." The language of Justin
will suit the theory as little as that of Scripture. He places
John *upon* the Jordan, brings Jesus *upon* the Jordan, con-
ducts him down *to* the water, leads him back *from* the water;
everything but "*in* the water." And, again (688), "John
dwelling upon (ἐπὶ) the Jordan and preaching the baptism
of repentance (κηρύσσοντος βάπτισμα μετανοίας), Jesus having
come upon (ἐπὶ) the Jordan" .... I do not know that we
can mend the language of Justin and of Scripture. I presume it must stand as written. John was upon the Jordan
as his abiding-place; "there" he baptized; thither Jesus
came; he went down to (ἐπὶ) the water; he came back from
(ἀπὸ) the water; and was baptized without (Justin being witness) being in the water.

It may be well, in passing, to call attention to the fact
that Justin says, "John cried unto men, Repent," and, also,
says, that "he preached the baptism of repentance." Now,
I wish to say, that between these statements of Justin as to
the subject-matter of John's "crying" and "preaching"
there is just the same difference that there is between *six*
and *half a dozen*, a difference of form without a particle of
difference in substance. There is just as much water in
μετανοεῖτε as there is in βάπτισμα μετανοίας, and there is no more
of ritual ordinance in preaching βάπτισμα μετανοίας than there
is in crying μετανοεῖτε. The imperative verb makes demand
for true and profound repentance; and the phrase, with its
substantive and defining genitive, requires a condition of

soul marked by the influence of a controlling repentance, and has as little water in it as the desert of Zahara.

Justin and the Bible bear one testimony as to the subject-matter of John's preaching and baptism.

As to the nature of the baptism which Jesus came to receive from John I shall, at present, say nothing directly. It may be well, however, to remember these two things, 1. Baptisms, in contradiction of all the conceptions of the theory, are of endless variety; 2. Baptism might be received from John without receiving the technical "baptism of John."

According to the theory, as stated by Carson (p. 55), "My position is, THAT IT ALWAYS SIGNIFIES TO DIP; NEVER EXPRESSING ANYTHING BUT MODE;" there can by no possibility be any other than one baptism, whether heathen or Christian. But we have had abounding evidence to prove, that no statement could be more utterly at war with the facts of heathenism and the declarations of Christianity than is this statement. I repeat therefore, that the baptism of John was only one of a possible thousand, and whatever baptism he may have preached or ritually administered to Pharisee or Sadducee, to the soldier or the publican, there was no necessity whatever, either from the nature of a baptism or from any other cause, that the same baptism should be preached and ritually administered to the Lord Jesus Christ.

When John's great announcement, "Behold! the Lamb of God that taketh away the sin of the world," shall be proved to be all a mistake, then, may we hear of the Forerunner preaching to the Mightier One, "Repent!" and expect to witness his ritual baptism "with water into repentance;" but until then, we say, with shuddering at all such conception, *Procul, procul abesto!*

MARK 1:9.

—ἦλθεν Ἰησοῦς ἀπὸ Ναζαρὲτ τῆς Γαλιλαίας, καὶ ἐβαπτίσθη ὑπὸ Ἰωάννου εἰς τὸν Ἰορδάνην.

"Jesus came from Nazareth of Galilee to the Jordan, and was baptized by John."

Εἰς τὸν Ἰορδάνην.

There is no passage in the New Testament which has so much of the appearance of meeting the construction demanded by the Classics in order to secure the introduction of an object within water as the passage now claiming consideration.

It is not only right, but it is the dictate of true wisdom to make prompt and cheerful concession of all that is true, or of what has the honest semblance of truth, in the views of an opponent.

The sentiments and practices of all Christian men should be recognized as held by them for reasons which seem to them to be adequate and true, however inadequate and untrue they may seem to be to us, or may be in reality.

The man who has found a bit of gold and some gold-like particles on his farm, and has erroneously concluded that this precious metal underlies all his broad acres, will not have his delusion best dispelled by a dissertation on geological formations as excluding his farm from the sphere of gold deposits, for he will still shake his head and say, " No matter for all you say; I have found what none can deny is gold, and something which, certainly, looks like gold." It will be better to admit the " looks like gold," and in the laboratory show him by inexorable tests, that " appearances are deceitful;" and, also, to make full admission that his " bit of gold" is, in very deed, gold, pointing out to him the evidence that it is not *virgin* gold, that it has already passed through the crucible, and is not native to the soil. Thus he is satisfied. His *amour propre* is conserved by the acknowledgment, that there was, really, a bit of gold and something like gold; while the mistaken gold-dream grounded on these things is, although not without a sigh, yielded up.

Now, although we, the rejectors of " the theory," are pronounced to be absurdly destitute of all truth, and to lack moral honesty, far more than we lack intellectual light, still, I would accord to the friends of the theory whatever bit of truth, or whatever " looks like" truth, may be discoverable in their views, assured, that the logical laboratory will both strip off the mask of a false appearance, and will show that what is real truth is not virgin to the soil of the theory. Thus, the way will be prepared for Christian men to abandon, with self-respect, error which had been incautiously received.

I do, then, cheerfully admit the truth, that βαπτίζω εἰς is the Classic form indicative of an object being introduced within a fluid element; and I do farther admit with equal cheerfulness, that 'Ιορδάνην has such a "looks like" *water*, that it might, right honestly, be taken for genuine water. And, having made this twofold admission, I have no difficulty in the farther admission, that any one who wished very much to find out a dipping into water, might, with all honesty of purpose, as he stumbled on ἐβαπτίσθη εἰς τὸν 'Ιορδάνην, cry out, "I have found it!" And, in fact, this passage has awakened a joyous outbursting cry from the hardly-pressed friends of the theory. It is our business to inquire into the grounds of this good cheer.

Dr. Carson.

Carson (pp. 302, 303) says, "Mark 1:9, then, itself decides the controversy. It is *into* Jordan; and nothing but *into* Jordan can it be. I venture to assert that there is not an illustrious name among grammarians that will sanction the use of their doctrine that is made of it by this writer. There is not in Europe, there never was in existence a great scholar who would deny that Jesus Christ was immersed in the Jordan. Nothing but the confidence of ignorance could ever venture such extravagance."

This is sufficiently explicit; an excellence seldom lacking in Dr. Carson's downright style of speaking. He regards the passage as of such pre-eminent value to the theory as to be able, single handed, to win the controversial battle.

In venturing to confront this universal challenger I make no claim to be enrolled "among the great scholars of Europe," nor yet of America. And it may be, that it is only "the confidence of ignorance" which prompts to such "extravagance" as the questioning of a decision made by Dr.

Carson; but I will "venture" to do so even under the frown of such a foreannounced verdict. It may be well, however, for the blow to fall first on one who has worthier claim to be entitled a scholar, even " a European scholar."

Dr. R. Wilson, Professor of Sacred Literature, Royal College, Belfast, thus writes:

" The preposition εἰς, with a word *supposed* to signify the baptizing element, forms the regimen of βαπτίζω, in one solitary occurrence. The unique exception to which we refer is found in Mark 1 : 9, ' He was baptized of John in Jordan.' On this construction great stress has been laid, as if it necessarily affirmed that our blessed Lord was dipped into the river of Israel. . . .

" We are not disposed, however, to surrender to our opponents the preposition εἰς in this important testimony. Supported by the authority of New Testament usage, we maintain that in numerous constructions, several of them closely parallel to the example before us, εἰς is employed where motion is not indicated by the verb with which it stands connected, and where, therefore, the rendering *into* is totally incompatible with the existing syntax. Bruder, in his Concordance to the Greek Testament, enumerates not fewer than *sixty-five* instances of this construction, and among them he includes the text under discussion. . . .

" We see little ground for dissatisfaction with Dr. Carson's mode of explaining instances of this class, particularly as it serves rather to confirm than invalidate the conclusion which we believe to be founded in truth. . . . ' My doctrine is,' says Dr. Carson, ' that the motion is implied in a verb which is understood, and is not properly communicated to a verb which has no motion in itself. It is absurd to suppose that the same verb can designate both rest and motion. It is impossible to stand and move at the same time. What I say is, that when εἰς is construed with a verb in which there is no motion, there is always a verb of motion understood, and which is not expressed because it is necessarily suggested.'

" Though the writer styles this *his* doctrine, and introduces it as a novelty, yet we find the knowledge of it to be, happily, not uncommon among Greek scholars whose works have been for a considerable time before the learned world. Hemsterhusius stated it in a note on the Plutus of Aristophanes, v. 1169, and illustrated his meaning by a parallel example from another Greek writer. Krebs not only applied the principle to the interpretation of Mark 1 : 9, but classed this particular use of εἰς, instead of ἐν, among the more elegant constructions of the language. It is, also, found in some of the best lexicons; and among other critical authorities, Winer in his Idioms of the New Testament, and Fritsche in his Commentary on Mark, employ it in expounding the passage under consideration. . . .

" The bearing of the principle on Mark 1 : 9 now solicits our attention.

" We have seen that some of the most learned interpreters, such as Krebs, Winer, and Fritsche, consider the text to be a case in point. Whether Dr. Carson's view entirely coincides with theirs appears somewhat doubtful, as he has advanced two views, which are not particularly consistent with each other. ' Jesus,' he says, ' was baptized into Jordan. This shows, not only that the action of the verb was performed in the water, but that the performance of it was a putting of the baptized person *into* the water.' Again, he says, ' The account of the Evangelist not merely asserts that Jesus went *into* the water, but that, when in the water, he was baptized, or immersed *into* it.' Of these statements the former connects the preposition *into* with baptized; the latter supplies a *verb of motion* before baptized, and joins the preposition successively with both, thus compelling it to do double duty. Against this flagrant error in syntax we enter our protest. The author palpably violates the principle which he had imposingly laid down as *his* doctrine, and illustrated at some length. According to this doctrine the preposition belongs to a previous verb of motion understood; and Dr. Carson so employs it when he represents the Evangelist as asserting that ' Jesus went into the water.' Thus, the preposition εἰς, separated from ἐβαπτίσθη and joined to a preceding verb, is finally disposed of. But our author, as if he had effected no such separation, again very complacently construes the same preposition with ἐβαπτίσθη in order to prove that the baptism was *into* Jordan !

" The simple record of such philology proves its exposure and refutation. With either verb the preposition may be legitimately connected; but to use it with both, especially in the teeth of Carson's own doctrine, is preposterous and indefensible. Fritsche's construction is obnoxious to censure on the same ground, and hence it does not call for a separate exposure. The conclusion, then, is irresistible, that in Mark 1 : 9 the introduction of a verb of motion, immediately connected with the preposition, has the inevitable effect of eliminating from the diction of the New Testament the only instance it contains of βαπτίζω followed by εἰς and the accusative of the term denoting the baptizing element.

"Admit Dr. Carson's principle, and baptism *into* Jordan is neither Scriptural nor practicable. Admit it, and Mark 1 : 9, as a boasted testimony to immersion, is silenced forever." (*Mode of Baptism*, pp. 235–40.)

It would appear then, that unless the names of Bruder, Krebs, Winer, Fritsche, Wilson, and not a few others, are to be stricken from the list of scholars, "great scholars," "European scholars," it is possible that something else than the "confidence of ignorance" may lead to question a conclusion of Dr. Carson; and even to doubt whether there is any self-evident proof in the language of Mark, that the Lord Jesus was dipped "into the Jordan."

Carson's Argument Extended.

Dr. Carson, while digging a pit in εἰς for the "boldly ignorant" to fall into, may find that he has opened an abyss sufficiently profound to swallow up himself, and friends, and theory, together.

He says (p. 298), " This syntax is not confined to *one* instance in the New Testament; it is found in many instances. *Εἰς* is connected with βαπτίζω in the commission. Now, though water is not the regimen, yet, it is the meaning of the preposition in reference to the performance of the rite that must regulate its meaning in all cases."

While Dr. Carson says, There are many instances of the syntax which unites βαπτίζω and εἰς (although not involving a physical element), and that in all cases the translation of the preposition must be the same, namely, *into*, yet, he specifies but one case, that of the commission. Why did he not adduce those other cases, and draw out their emphatic indorsement of Mark 1 : 9 by spreading out the translation "into?" Was there a reason for this failure? Perhaps we can find an answer to this question by doing what he has failed to do. Let us try it in those two passages which have come under our notice—"I baptize you *into* REPENTANCE;" "Preaching the baptism of repentance *into* THE REMISSION OF SINS."

In these passages we have βαπτίζω εἰς *but not with* WATER *as the regimen*, which, however, we are told, makes no difference, the force of the preposition is just the same and must in all cases be translated "into." But, how will this doctrine affect Conant, and Hackett, and the New Version translators, who do not "in all cases" translate this syntax by "into?" Are they, therefore, to be placed by their friend among the no scholars, and the "confidently ignorant?"

We have had occasion to complain both of error and inconsistency in the translation of εἰς μετανοίαν "*unto*" repentance instead of *into* REPENTANCE, and εἰς ἄφεσιν ἁμαρτιων " *for*" the remission of sins, instead of *into* THE REMISSION OF SINS; but I never thought of charging these translators with "presumptuous ignorance," or of erasing their names from the list of scholars. But it may be an exclusive privilege belonging to the friends of the theory to treat this syntax as a waxy mass to be moulded at their pleasure into the varying forms "into," "unto," "in," "for," while to others it must have an adamantine inflexibility.

If Dr. Carson's axiom, " βαπτίζω εἰς = baptize *into*, in all cases," be carried out, the theory is at once buried out of sight by a baptism "into" REPENTANCE, not into *water*, and by a baptism "into" REMISSION OF SINS, not into *Jordan*.

We are willing to subscribe to and abide by this proposition : Whenever βαπτίζω, in truth, has for its complement a word (physical or meta-physical) in regimen with εἰς, the translation must, "in all cases," be *into*.

In applying this proposition to Mark 1 : 9, the vital point which arises for determination is this: Is "'Ιορδάνην," in truth, complementary of βαπτίζω? And before this can be determined we must reopen that snap judgment which Baptist interpreters have taken on this passage, and bring into the light a number of points which they have left in the dark.

Does Juxtaposition make Words Complementary?

The statement in John 3 : 22 might have been ἦλθεν ὁ Ἰησοῦς καὶ ἐβάπτιζεν εἰς τὴν Ἰουδαίαν γῆν; would such juxtaposition of words have necessitated a dipping "into the land of Judea?"

It has been assumed by Baptist writers, on the mere ground of the juxtaposition of words, that "Jesus was dipped into the Jordan." This assumption cannot be made without making a handful of other assumptions: 1. The assumption, that εἰς, here, means "into," while, elsewhere, it means *unto*. 2. The assumption, that "Jordan," here, means *water*, while, elsewhere, it means *locality*. 3. The assumption, that the phrase εἰς Ἰορδάνην is complementary to βαπτίζω, which assumption is based on a previous assumption, that the phrase denotes *water*, and which assumption rests on the antecedent assumption, that proximity makes complement. 4. The assumption, that βαπτίζω is, here, used in a primary and literal sense, while, elsewhere, it is used in a secondary and figurative sense. 5. The assumption, that βαπτίζω here means *dip*, while, elsewhere, and everywhere, it has no such meaning. 6. The assumption, that Mark in relating the same transaction which is related by Matthew, gives an entirely different representation from his fellow Evangelist, while his language is capable of the most absolute unity of interpretation.

These points have been *assumed* as though so vulgar a thing as proof was quite unnecessary. And to call in question such assumptions, we are told, is to display an overweening ignorance.

To those whose "ignorance" makes them sufficiently courageous to enter upon an examination of these assumptions the following considerations are submitted:

First Assumption. The assumption that εἰς, here, means "into" (water) has no adequate ground in the radical idea of that preposition. Harrison (p. 210) says, "The proper signification of εἰς is *within, in*, with the idea of being within a space having boundaries." He adds, " This proper meaning is seen in derivatives and in compounds: To confine within, to hedge within, to be arrived within, to seat oneself within, to lie within, to dwell within. Comparing these compounds with those in which εἰς is joined with words expressing action or motion, as to come into, to run into, to collect into, to cast into, it is plain that ' into' is not the simple sense of εἰς, but arises from combining it with the notion of reaching some object."

Now if we give to the preposition, here, its radical meaning, " within," it is made harmonious with the use of other prepositions, ἐν Ἰορδάνη, ἐπὶ Ἰορδάνην, which place John and the baptized *in, within*, " a space having boundaries," to wit, the banks of the river. If we take in the special features of this case, which is found in the presence of a verb of motion (ἦλθεν), the assumption that the preposition originates with, and gives an exclusive interpretation to ἐβαπτίσθη, is, again, dissipated. When a preposition stands related to two verbs of diverse character, it must either be understood in a sense adapted to both, or it must be assigned to the word to which its form is obviously due, and out of it, or out of the obvious circumstances of the case, provision be made for the associate word.

In the present case the radical meaning of the preposition (" within ") is adapted to both verbs: " Jesus came from Nazareth of Galilee within the Jordan, and was baptized within the Jordan by John." Thus, the place whence he came, and the place whither he came, are distinctly indicated.

In any case the statement requires, that the preposition be referred primarily to the verb of motion as the leading word, and whose idea is incomplete without it. The translation may be *to*, or *unto*, but, however translated, the exigency of the passage demands, that the coming of Jesus from one locality shall terminate on some other locality. Thus εἰς is precluded from becoming exponential of βαπτίζω except as to the place where the baptism took place, and the assumption

25

of the translation "into" as indicative of a receptive element is proved to be nothing but assumption.

Second Assumption. The assumption, that "Jordan," here, means *water* is no less gratuitous. It is in admission by friends of the theory, that Jordan does, primarily, denote locality and not the element water. There is not a particle of proof, that this term is used in a single instance, in connection with John's baptism, to denote the simple element water. The assumption that it is so used in this passage is assumption and nothing but assumption.

The case requires locality; "Jordan" furnishes locality; and locality it must remain until something more efficacious than assumption shall work a change.

If an attempt be made to sustain this assumption of water and a dipping into water by the presence of εἰς, it will be found that confidence is placed in a reed which, leaned upon, will break and pierce instead of giving support. "The venerable Booth" (I, 507) says, "Εἰς, when connected with ὕδωρ, Ἰορδάνης, or ποταμός, never, if I mistake not, has any other meaning than *into*." This opinion of Booth is undoubtedly erroneous; but it is advanced with so much just reserve as to claim the gentlest correction.

R. Ingham (Handbook on Baptism, London, 1866, p. 324) utters the same sentiment with less reserve. Having charged Professor Stuart with asserting what was "clearly fallacious and unjust," he attempts to support the charge by the flaunting challenge: "Let any person adduce any Greek writer of any period in the world's history, who has used the words κατέβησαν εἰς τὸ ὕδωρ with any other meaning than 'they went down into the water.'" The assertion involved in this utterance is as little worthy of our reliance as would be the proffer of the back of a sleeping whale for a dining-table. Both would be likely to go under on the first attempt to make use of them. There is absolutely nothing in the phrase of Mr. Ingham which, of necessity, would carry any one "into the water."

It is an easy task to find passages, which by their number

and their facility of access, make the statements of these writers as surprising as they are erroneous.

3 Kings 2 : 8. *Κατέβη εἰς ἀπαντήν μου, εἰς τὸν Ἰορδάνην*—"He came down unto the Jordan to meet me."

This passage contains the identical words (if Jordan means water) by which, according to Ingham, every Greek writer, of every period in the world's history, is to put men into the water, and by which Moses Stuart is to be proved "fallacious and unjust," and yet nobody is wet even by so much as the soles of their feet. David was not in the waters of the Jordan, that it should be necessary for Shimei to go down into them to meet him there. The passage, also, proves, that *εἰς Ἰορδάνην* is not the equivalent of "into water." Shimei went down *εἰς Ἰορδάνην*, although he did not go to the water's edge; he may have stopped at the outer bank, and the water have been "a furlong" distant. Facts are annoyances to theories.

2 Kings 2 : 6. *Κύριος ἀπέσταλκε με εἰς τὸν Ἰορδάνην*—"The Lord hath sent me unto the Jordan."

Here we have *εἰς* with Jordan, and yet no entrance "into" its waters. Elijah was not sent into the water although he was sent *εἰς Ἰορδάνην*. The conjunction of this preposition, then, cannot turn "Jordan" into water.

2 Kings 6 : 4. *Καὶ ἦλθον εἰς τὸν Ἰορδάνην*—"And they came unto the Jordan."

Again, we have the same lesson taught us. Elisha and the sons of the prophets did not go "into" the running stream to fell trees, although they did go for this purpose *εἰς Ἰορδάνην*. When you remember, that after "going down the first bank," and advancing "a furlong along a level strand," you come to "the second bank which is beset with bushes and trees, such as tamarisks, willows, oleanders, &c.," and that it was to this second bank Elisha and his company came (for in cutting wood the axe fell into the water), we can fully understand how *εἰς Ἰορδάνην* may be sharply translated "*into* the Jordan," and yet all be outside of the water;

for, as Carson says, "all within the banks" is the Jordan.
Is it not, then, the boldest assumption to affirm, that when
the Lord Jesus came from Nazareth εἰς Ἰορδάνην, he came
into the *water?*

2 Kings 2 : 21. *Καὶ ἐξῆλθεν Ἐλεσαιὲ εἰς διέξοδον τῶν ὑδάτων*—"And
Elisha went out unto the gushing forth of the waters."

Elisha did not go *into* the gushing waters, although he did
cast some salt into them. And, again, we are reminded not
to trust too fondly to prepositions to get within the water.

Judges 4 : 7. *Καὶ ἐπάξω πρός σὲ εἰς τὸν χειμάρρουν Κισῶν*—"And I
will draw to thee unto the brook Kison."

Sisera and his army were not to be drawn *into* the waters
of the river Kison that they might be drowned; but they
were to be drawn unto that river as a battle-ground. Thus
the notion of Booth, that "εἰς with Jordan, water, river, can
have no other meaning than *into*," is corrected; and the
challenge of Ingham to show a case in which καταβαινω, in
such combination, does not "carry down into the water," is
disposed of; and the assumption, that εἰς has a magic power
to convert "Jordan" into *water* is effectually arrested.

Third Assumption. The assumption, that the phrase εἰς τὸν
Ἰορδάνην owes its form to ἐβαπτίσθη, is complementary of it, and
therefore filled to repletion with water, is equally groundless.

This phrase has a common relation to ἦλθεν and ἐβαπτίσθη.
It is not necessary that this relation should be the same in
all respects; nor, that it should be exhibited in the elements
of the phrase separately considered. The form of the phrase
may be due to one verb rather than to the other, while under
that form may be embraced, and out of it may be deduced,
all that is suitable and required by the other.

There is, obviously, one aspect in which this phrase may
stand in a common relation to these diverse verbs; it is
the relation of locality. The verb ἦλθεν demands a locality
on which its movement may terminate, which is furnished
by "Jordan;" and ἐβαπτίσθη demands a locality where its
requirement may be executed, and this, too, is found in

"Jordan." But one of these verbs is a verb of motion, while the other is not; if, therefore, the locality which both call for be but once expressed, there must be a choice as to the form of the preposition especially adapted to the character of the one or the other. The choice has fallen on εἰς, satellitic to verbs of motion, and we must regard the form in which "Jordan" (embodying the common requirement of locality) is presented, as due to ἦλθεν, the verb of motion.

This is the usual course pursued under like circumstances. The reason for it is not established to universal satisfaction. Some (Halley) regard it as a corruption of language. Some (Krebs) regard it as an elegance. Some (Matthies) suppose that εἰς reflects its power back upon the verb imparting to it motion. While others (Carson) think that a verb of motion should be understood.

Dr. Carson remarks: "This phraseology is exemplified by Xenophon, 'Cyrus commanded an officer to stand *into* the front.' Now, there must here be motion before standing. We ourselves exemplify this every day. A soldier not in straight line is commanded to stand *into* his rank."

"Stand into rank" is an abbreviation of the fuller form, "Go, from the place in which you now stand, into rank, and stand there, in rank." The form "*into* rank" is due to the verb of motion, and "*in* rank" is involved in "standing" after reaching "into rank." So, the form εἰς 'Ιορδάνην, place whither, is due to the movement from Nazareth, while in that phrase (the baptism taking place subsequent to the reaching that point) is necessarily involved ἐν 'Ιορδάνην, place where.

The following are some, of many, illustrative passages:

Acts 8 : 40. Φίλιππος δὲ εὑρηθη εἰς Ἄζωτον—"Philip was found at (literally unto) Azotus."

In this passage we have a form abbreviated beyond that of Mark 1 : 9 by reason of the omission of the verb of motion.

The translation of the passage as given above is taken from the Commentary on Acts by Dr. Hackett, Professor of Biblical Literature for many years in Newton (Baptist)

Theological Seminary, and recently transferred to the Baptist Theological Seminary at Rochester, N. Y. The personal character and accomplished scholarship of Professor Hackett needs indorsement from no one; but recollections of personal association in student days prompt me in passing to pay heart homage to them both. This eminent scholar, in explanation of his translation, "Philip was found at (literally unto) Azotus," adds, "*i. e.*, was next heard of there, after the transaction in the desert; εἰς arises from the idea of the journey thither." Thus, in the absence of a verb of motion in the text, Professor Hackett supplies one in order to meet the exigency of the syntax.

He, also, approves the translation "at" (which meaning Carson says this preposition never has), while he regards "unto" as more literal.

Although, then, εἰς Ἄζωτον stands in immediate juxtaposition with εὑρέθη, it does not derive its form from that verb, but from one which must be supplied. It is also obvious, that under the foreign form "was found *unto* Azotus" is necessarily involved "*in* or at Azotus," the form which is specifically demanded by εὑρέθη. Professor Hackett, very properly, abandons in his translation the Greek form which identifies the preposition with the verb of motion understood, and brings it into conformity with that which is expressed, "was *found at* Azotus," making it much more intelligible to the English reader. He thus justifies the principle (although he might not accept the application) which refuses to translate Mark 1 : 9, "He came from Nazareth of Galilee and was baptized *unto* Jordan," but translates, more intelligibly, "He came from Nazareth of Galilee and was baptized *at* Jordan." This syntax and this translation are entirely identical with that of Professor Hackett's—"Philip came from the desert and was found (εἰς Ἄζωτον) *at* Azotus." To whichever verb the preposition is made conformable, another preposition suitable to the nature of the second verb must be understood. Philip came *unto*, and was found *at*, Azotus. Jesus came *unto*, and was baptized *at*, Jordan. And this is just what Matthew says (3 : 13).

John 20:19. ἦλθεν ὁ Ἰησοῦς, καὶ ἔστη, εἰς τὸ μέσον—"Jesus came, and stood, into (unto, within) the midst."

Under no possible view can εἰς τὸ μέσον derive its form from ἔστη with which it is in juxtaposition. We must expound this form by the remoter ἦλθεν. We may either retain the form and relation of the preposition, translating, "Jesus came *into* the midst and stood there;" or, change the form and relation of the preposition, translating, "Jesus came and stood *within* the midst." Either translation has adequate foundation. But a translation which would disrupt the relation of εἰς with ἦλθεν, and form a relation with ἔστη, under a conception peculiar to that word and exclusive of its associate verb, is a translation wholly without reason. The striking harmony between the structure of this passage and that in Mark will be seen at a glance when placed side by side:

Mark 1:9.	ἦλθεν Ἰησοῦς	καὶ ἐβαπτίσθη	εἰς τὸν Ἰορδάνην.
John 20:19.	ἦλθεν Ἰησοῦς	καὶ ἔστη	εἰς τὸ μέσον.

If εἰς τὸν Ἰορδάνην is made to depend on ἐβαπτίσθη, and to signify dipping into water, then, all relation with ἦλθεν is dissolved, contrary to the construction, which shows a common interest on the part of those verbs in this phrase, and which can only be met by community of place—the place whither he came, and the place where he was baptized.

But if it be possible as a matter of syntax, thus to account for the form of this phrase, then, an impassable barrier has been established against the conclusion "Mark 1:9 itself decides the controversy. It is *into* Jordan; and nothing but *into* Jordan can it be." I say, an impassable barrier is established against this conclusion if it be *possible* to account for this syntax in any other way, for Dr. Carson unhesitatingly admits, that while possibility cannot prove, yet, it may very effectively object. We expect to do something more than indicate a possible explanation, but at this stage of the argument against any dipping into water being contained in this passage, we content ourselves with showing, that it is quite possible to account for εἰς τὸν Ἰορδάνην without making it dependent for its life on ἐβαπτίσθη.

Matt. 2 : 23. ἐλθὼν, κατώκησεν, εἰς πόλιν λεγομένην Ναζαρέτ—'' Came into a city called Nazareth, and dwelt there.''

How εἰς πόλιν can be made to depend for its form on the verb of rest, with which it is associated by immediate position, I do not know. It is precisely that form which is demanded by the remoter verb of motion.

The New Version translates, " came and dwelt *in*," conforming the preposition to the verb of rest; as, also, in Acts 8 : 40, " was found *at* Azotus (εἰς Ἄζωτον"). That version, however, is not satisfied with " was baptized *at* Jordan (εἰς Ἰορδάνην").

Acts 12 : 19. κατελθὼν ἀπὸ τῆς Ἰουδαίας εἰς τὴν Καισάριαν, διέτριβεν —"Went down from Judea unto Cæsarea, and abode there."

The collocation of the preposition and its regimen is different, here, from the preceding quotations. Does any one feel, on that account, any more assured of their logical relation to κατελθὼν, rather than to διέτριβεν? Certainly no one would think, now, of making the form of the preposition and its case to depend upon the verb of rest. But every one will take *place* out of the point on which the verb of motion terminates, and attach it, verbally or mentally, to the verb of motion. This is done, in the New Version, by supplying the adverb of place—" and *there* abode." And this is just what must be done under the other arrangement of words. In the sentence, " The ball was shot *into* the wood and remained," we supplement, in word or thought, the verb of rest, by " there," or " in the wood." And if the sentence should be, " The ball was shot, and remained, into the wood," we could only, on any rational interpretation, attach "into the wood," logically, to the verb of motion, and treat " and remained" as an interjected addendum which secures to itself position (in the wood) from the associate words.

Luke 21 : 37. ἐξερχόμενος ηὐλίζετο εἰς τὸ ὄρος τὸ καλούμενον ἐλαιῶν— " Went out unto the mount called of Olives, and lodged."

Matt. 21 : 17. ἐξῆλθεν ἔξω τῆς πόλεως εἰς Βηθανίαν, καὶ ηὐλίσθη ἐκεῖ— " He went out of the city unto Bethany, and lodged there."

These two passages are placed together both because of agreement and difference. They agree in having the same verbs both of motion and of rest. They differ in the collocation of the preposition and its regimen. In the first passage, it is in juxtaposition with the verb of rest; and in the second, it is placed in relation with the verb of motion. In the second passage we have expressed, what must in all other cases be supplied, or its equivalent (ἐκεῖ) the adverb of place, which attaches to the verb of rest.

Such usage appears to establish, very conclusively, that it is a matter of indifference whether the preposition and its regimen precede or follow the verb of rest.

John 9 : 7. ῞Υπαγε, νίψαι, εἰς τὴν κολυμβήθραν τοῦ Σιλωάμ—"Go, wash at the pool of Siloam."

John 9 : 11. ῞Υπαγε εἰς τὴν κολυμβήθραν τοῦ Σιλωάμ καὶ νίψαι—"Go unto the pool of Siloam, and wash."

These two passages refer to the same transaction and claim to make report of the same command. Both contain the same identical words, and differ only in their arrangement. Does this difference in the verbal arrangement work any change in the logical relations of the words?

No two passages could more perfectly embrace within themselves the elements of self-interpretation. Nor could passages be more kindred in their elements than these passages and that in Mark 1 : 9.

They all have verbs of motion and of rest; they all declare motion unto a water locality; they all contemplate the use of the water in application to the person; and they all make use of the preposition εἰς, now, in juxtaposition with the verb of motion and, now, in immediate sequence of the verb of rest, employing but one preposition for the two verbs.

Translation.

The translation of these passages, as given by the New Version, is as follows: John 9 : 7, " Go, wash thyself *at* the pool of Siloam." This translation modifies the preposition in accommodation with the verb of rest. With the avowal

of such purpose no exception can be justly made to it. **This**
is the translation of the Quarto, Greek; but the later revised
English translates, " Go wash *in* the pool of Siloam." This
translation seems to proceed on the interchangeableness of
εἰς and ἐν, and the assumption by the former of the meaning
in, and by the latter of the meaning *into*. This idea Rosenmüller refers to in the interpretation of Mark 1 : 9, " Quidam
εἰς hic positum esse pro ἐν enallage Scriptoribus cum Sacris,
tum profanis usitatissima, existimant."

The idea of such interchange and exchange of meaning
is not approved by the best writers.

Harrison (p. 213) says:

" The accusative with εἰς, when used with verbs not containing the idea of motion, has more obviously the sense ' as to,' ' as
regards,' and marks within what limits the preceding statement
of which it is the qualification is to be taken." He adds, " Otherwise the verb of rest might be considered as used in a pregnant
sense, as, Od., XX, 96, ἐς μέγαρον κατέθηκεν ἐπὶ θρόνου, he came into
the house and deposited them ; this would not materially affect
the meaning of either the accusative or the preposition. So, Il ,
XV, 275, ἐφάνη λῖς εἰς ὁδόν ; here εφανη may be considered as having
a pregnant sense, ' the lion came into the path and so appeared.' "

In reference to the preposition ἐν being rendered by *into*, he
says (p. 254), " In quite a number of cases ἐν with its case is used
with verbs of action or motion, where εἰς with the accusative
and having the sense ' into ' might have been expected : Xen.
Hell., IV, 5, 5, οἱ δ' ἐν τῷ ῾Ηραίῳ καταπεφευγότες, not those ' who
had fled for refuge *into* the Heræum,' but ' those who had fled
for refuge, and, as such, were *in* the Heræum.' A little before,
in the same paragraph, the expression used with reference to
the same persons and the same occurrence is, ἐς δὲ τὸ ῾Ηραιον
κατέφυγον. In this place, the writer speaks of persons who fled
for refuge *into* the Heræum ; in the former, of the same persons
who were *in* the temple, having fled thither for refuge."

These passages are entirely parallel with John 9 : 7, 11,
except that the latter retain εἰς in both. But the same principle of interpretation applies, whether in the case of ἐν with
a verb of motion, or of εἰς with a verb of rest. In neither
case are the meanings to be confounded together.

That the Baptist version is made on this idea of confusion in these prepositions would appear from the fact, that they translate John 9 : 7, " Go, wash (εἰς) *in* the pool," and John 5 : 4, " Went down (ἐν) *into* the pool."

Winer objects to this idea. He says (p. 412, 4):

"It was formerly supposed, that in the New Testament ἐν was employed agreeably to the Hebrew idiom with verbs of motion or direction to denote *into*, as John 5 : 4, ἄγγελος κατέβαινεν ἐν τῇ κολυμβήθρᾳ. The latter, it was imagined, was used with verbs of rest to signify *in*, as John 9 : 7, νίψαι εἰς τὴν κολυβήθραν. Homer uses ἐν with verbs of motion to indicate at the same time the result of the motion, that is, *rest*. This they do from a love of terseness peculiar to the Greek race.

"More surprising still are the passages adduced in support of the assertion, that εἰς is used for ἐν. Even in Greek authors εἰς is not unfrequently construed with verbs of rest; and then the idea of motion (preceding or accompanying) was originally included, agreeably to the principle of *breviloquentia* mentioned above. In this way is to be explained Acts 8 : 40, 'Philip was found (εἰς) conducted *to* Azotus.' In John 9 : 7, εἰς τὴν κολυμβήθραν is, as respects sense, to be connected with ὕπαγε, cf. v. 11. So Luke 21 : 37. Still more easy of explanation is Mark 1 : 9."

Thus, these high authorities take away, on naked grammatical principles, from the theory the passage which, of itself, was to settle the controversy by converting a locality into water, robbing a verb of motion of its preposition, and revolutionizing the character of βαπτίζω!

The New Version translates John 9 : 11, " Go *to* (εἰς) the pool of Siloam and wash." In a note it is said: "It is generally supposed that he was not required to wash his entire body. Perhaps he understood the direction to mean simply, 'wash thine eyes.'" This is all very well; but it shows how greatly these prepositions εἰς and ἐν are controlled by the conception of the translator. The angel is sent down *into* the pool under no better authority than ἐν; while the blind man is arrested *at* the pool, although he carries εἰς as his passport. Dr. Carson however insists, that " he was to go *into* the pool that he might wash; literally ' wash *into* the

pool.' The blind man might as well have sent to the pool
for water to wash at home, as to take the water out of the
pool and wash" (p. 300). This is the old argument for
going *into* the Jordan, "What else would they go to the
river for?" "Judith might as well have sprinkled herself
in her tent. What would she go to the fountain for but to
go *into* it?"

This argumentation however does not, here, commend
itself to the translators of the Baptist Bible, as they allow a
man to go " to" a pool and take water out of it to wash,
without sending him *into* the pool. Carson is consistently
wrong, and the translators are inconsistently right. We (I
think both consistently and truly) say, that the blind man
went to the pool (εἰς κολυμβήθραν) without going *into* it; and
that Jesus went to the Jordan (εἰς 'Ιορδάνην) without going
into it.

Campbell (John 5 : 2) thinks, that " κολυμβήθρα signifies
more than the *water collected*, and includes the covered walks,
and all that had been built for the accommodation of those
that came thither. In this extent the word *bath* is familiarly
used by ourselves." It seems to be so used by Epiphanius
(I, 445), who says of the Apostle John, ἦλθεν εἰς τὸ λουτρόν, indicating only his coming to the place where the bath was
without his entering into the water. So it would seem that
Siloam, like Jordan, included more than *water*. In Luke
13 : 4, we read of the tower ἐν Σιλωάμ falling. This tower
certainly was not in the *water*. Stier (V, 41) says, "The
description ἐν τῷ Σιλωάμ is highly obscure in consequence of
the ἐν, but probably refers to a district or field, so-called
from the brook."

These passages are sufficient to establish the position, that
where εἰς and its case immediately follow a verb of rest preceded by and connected with a verb of motion, both verbs
have an interest in the phrase; in the one case indicated by
the form, and in the other case by necessary consequence.

They also disprove the assumption, that such phrase is
dependent on the verb of rest, and is to be expounded by it,
to the disregard of the verb of motion.

Fourth Assumption. The assumption, that βαπτίζω is here used in a primary and literal sense (while elsewhere it is used in a secondary and figurative sense) is without any adequate support.

It is in proof, both by Classic and inspired writings, that βαπτίζω is largely used in cases where there is no physical envelopment. Such use, therefore, may be legitimately adduced in any particular case as a possible use, and must be an effectual barrier against the assumption of a physical use. Such physical use must be proved. But no proof has been adduced in the present case. The word cannot prove it. "Jordan" cannot prove it. Εἰς ᾿Ιορδάνην cannot prove it. There is no evidence from any other passage of the primary, physical, use of this verb in a single instance in connection with John's baptism. There is no such language to be met with as baptism " into water." There is not a particle of reliable evidence adduced to disprove the position, that water in ritual baptism is a symbol agency, not an enveloping element. I repeat it then, that it is the sheerest assumption which attributes to βαπτίζω in this passage a primary, physical, meaning.

Fifth Assumption. The assumption, that βαπτίζω here means *dip*, while elsewhere and everywhere it has no such meaning, is pre-eminently baseless.

There is no word in the Greek language whose meaning rests on evidence more clear or more overwhelming than that meaning assigned to βαπτίζω which makes it the essential opposite of " dip." The very life element of " dip" consists in the performance of an evanescent act, putting an object within and, without resting in, withdrawing it out of a fluid element. Now, βαπτίζω makes demand for a condition of intusposition without regard to the manner of its accomplishment and without reference to any removal out of it; and no designed momentary introduction and removal is possible without destroying the life of the word. Proof of all these points has been abundantly given in Classic and Judaic Baptism. It is unnecessary to repeat it here. I only call attention to the fact, that the secondary use of the word is as clearly, as it is exclusively, based on an indefinitely prolonged continuance of condition, in contradistinction from one which is momentary and evanescent. Thus we have a baptism εἰς ἀναισθησίαν without removal; εἰς ὕπνον without removal; εἰς πορνείαν without removal. I call attention to this usage because it is that which characterizes the baptism of John. The baptism preached by John is a baptism εἰς μετανοίαν without removal; εἰς ἄφεσιν ἁμαρτιων without removal. These baptisms are intensely real; thorough and abiding changes in the condition of the soul, the work of the Holy Ghost. The baptism ritually administered was this same twain-óne baptism symbolized, as to essential nature, by pure water applied to the body. With the manner or extent of applying this symbol βαπτίζω has no more to do than has the lost Greek koppa.

As Dr. Carson says of Mark 1 : 9, "It decides the controversy;" so Dr. Fuller (p. 38) says of 2 Kings 5 : 14, "Does not this establish the meaning of the word? Can a candid man longer doubt what he means? Naaman went down and *dipped* himself seven times in the Jordan. This is admitted to mean Naaman *dipped* himself in the Jordan. Naaman went down and *dipped.* It was in this very river John baptized. Jesus uses the same word, and thus commands the very same act." *To dip,* then, is the claimed meaning. But to prove this meaning neither Carson nor Fuller gives one syllable of real evidence. They assume and assert, that is all. How their views, as to the meaning of the word, comports with that of an old Greek writer, may be judged from a passage relating to this baptism.

Didymus Alexandrinus (700), having spoken of the purging of the world from sin by the deluge, and the deliverance of the Israelites from Egyptian bondage through the waters of the Red Sea, and the new character given to the fountain by salt thrown into its waters by the prophet, as types of the blessing and salvation secured by Christian baptism, he speaks of the healing of Naaman of the leprosy as a type of the cleansing of the soul, as, also, the healing of Bethesda; these being images and not the real baptism, because they only healed diseases of the body and not the sins of the soul. The power to do this last was not imparted to the water until after the coming of the Son and of the Spirit.

He, especially, thinks, that the sevenfold use of the water was a shadowing forth, by the perfect number, of the Holy Spirit.

By the whole passage, preceding and succeeding the reference to Naaman's baptism, there is a constant, and clear, and exclusive reference to the *power* of baptism, and not to the mode in which water is used. Indeed, the mode in which the water was used was different in almost every case to which he refers. In them all there was the presence of a powerful influence. Of Naaman's baptism he uses this language:

εἰς τὸν Ἰορδάνην ἐπτάκις καταβαπτισθῆναι ἔπεμψεν.

"He sent to the Jordan to be baptized seven times, Naaman, the Syrian leper, a foreigner, asking to be healed by him; that by the voice of the Lord upon the waters his disease might be removed: he become a resemblance of the cleansed and sanctified soul."

The first point to which I would call attention is the fact, that εἰς τὸν Ἰορδάνην has nothing to do, as to its form, with καταβαπτισθῆναι. Whatever question may be raised as to Mark, none can be raised here; it is due to ἔπεμψεν.

The second remark which I would make is this: The verb is in a compound form; but as I have succeeded but poorly in impressing Baptists with the impropriety of translating, in critical writing, a simple form of a verb (entering into composition with a variety of prepositions) by a compound form, and they insist on translating the simple βαπτίζω by "*im*-merse, *im*-**merge**, *im*-bathe, *sub*-merge, *over*-whelm," I suppose it is not **worth** while to refer to this compound character.

If they are satisfied with it as it stands, I will raise no objections, but will be well content to allow this form of the word to speak for itself and see what it has to say about a "dipping."

Chrysostom (Hom., XIII) uses this word thus: "As a ship filled with water is quickly (καταβαπτίζεται) baptized beneath the billows." Does this sound like a "dipping?"

Eustathius (Hysmenias and Hysmene, VII) uses it thus: "Neptune pours down upon the sea all his fury, and seeks (καταβαπτίσαι) to baptize all the ship by the waves." Is this a "dipping?"

Alex. Aphrodisias (I, 16) furnishes the following example: "The physical force flows excessively with the blood deep into the body, and (καταβαπτίζει) baptizes the natural and vital heat." This is a case of death from fright. Does it look like a "dipping?"

And again (I, 17): "The quantity of the wine (καταβαπτίζει) baptizes the physical and vital power." This is a case of death from excessive wine-drinking. Is it a "dipping?"

These are all the instances, of a physical character, of the use of this word, which are now before me.

Some one may be tempted to ask, in view of the character of these quotations, "Do you believe, or do you imagine that Didymus believed, that Naaman was sunk to the bottom of the Jordan and lies there to this day, like those ships sunk to the bottom of the sea? or, Do you believe that he was killed at the Jordan like those wretches who died baptized by blood, and by wine?" To such inquiries I answer very promptly in the negative. If any one should think it worth while to ask, "Do you think καταβαπτίζω means *to dip?*" I answer, No; nor do I expect to make much progress toward such faith until my ears shall have attained a very sensible elongation. If it should be farther asked, "What is to be done in the case? Didymus applies a word, which by its usage expresses utter destruction, to a case in which there is no such destruction. What is to be done with the word?" I answer, Whatever is done with it, we must not attach to it any such meaning as will be so absurdly variant from its established character as to make us a laughing-stock throughout the world of letters.

Let us inquire for a secondary use of the word in which features more in harmony with the case in hand may be found.

Try the following passages:

Origen (John 11:45) speaks of certain persons "who (*κατα-βεβαπτισμένων*) were thoroughly baptized by wickedness." He speaks of those who are in a condition most profoundly displaying the influence of sin, even as a mass of putrid death.

Basil (XIV, 7): "Wine (*καταβαπτίζει*) thoroughly baptizes the reason and the understanding." He represents the drunkard as under an influence which places him in a condition of greater peril than a ship at sea without a pilot.

Alciphron (II, 3): "Life to me (*καταβαπτισθήσεται*) will be thoroughly baptized." He is speaking of a condition of things the influence from which will issue in the loss of life.

Eustathius (VI): "My whole mind (*καταβαπτισθείς*) was thoroughly baptized by the woe." Here is a condition of profound influence inducing anguish of soul.

Again (Book VII): "My soul (*κατεβάπτισας*) thou didst thoroughly baptize with seas of wailings." A condition resultant from the profoundest influence.

Achilles Tatius (I, 3): "Astounds the soul, befalling it suddenly, and (*κατεβάπτισε*) thoroughly baptizes it." A case of powerful and controlling influence.

Again (Book II, 31): "Whom, with the same drug (*καταβαπτίσας*), having thoroughly baptized." Here is a condition resultant from an all-controlling opiate influence.

In all of these cases the preposition (*κατά*), in composition, gives intensity to the meaning of the verb.

These passages present a usage which, I will not say with Carson "any child can understand," but which I submit to men of culture and ask, Whether there is not both a wide difference between these two classes of passages and, at the same time, an obvious and inseparable connection? Do they not differ, in that the former passages exhibit an encompassing physical element, while in the latter there is none? Do they not agree, in that both exhibit a condition of influence of the profoundest character; the one effected

26

through envelopment unlimitedly prolonged, the other by controlling influence not operating through envelopment? This exemplifies the ordinary development of language.

It should be noted, that the influences operative in these *κατα*-baptisms are varied in their character, while all have, in common, intense and controlling power over condition.

And now the question comes up, Does this new usage throw any light upon the word, in the passage under consideration, which was so impracticable under the usage first developed? And this leads us to inquire, Is there any powerful influence operating in the case of Naaman? And the answer comes promptly, That is the very feature of the case. There is influence operating as powerful as that of Jehovah, "whose voice," says Didymus, "is upon the waters." Is there any change of condition, not evanescent but abiding, effected by that influence? Leprous flesh is made as fresh and healthful as that of a little child; and that changed condition lasts through all after life.

What now becomes of the "dipping" (absurdly contradictory to the meaning of the word) so vauntingly introduced by Fuller as the result of demonstration? And what becomes of the assumption asserted into Mark 1 : 9 ?

If any one should stumble at the Hebrew word used to denote what was done by Naaman at the Jordan, they stumble at a shadow. This word (טָבַל), which expresses what was done, differs as much from the Hebrew word (רָחַץ), used by the prophet in commanding what was to be done, as the Greek word differs from it. And if the Septuagint translators saw proper to represent in their translation what the prophet commanded to be done, rather than that which Naaman did, is such freedom unpardonable or extraordinary? Is it not precisely that freedom which the inspired writer himself has exercised?

In view of the whole usage of *βαπτίζω* primary and secondary, and in view of this special, double usage of *κατα-βαπτίζω*, we adopt, with a single variation, the language of Dr. Conant: "The idea of a total submergence lies at the basis of these metaphorical uses. Anything short of this, such as the mere *dipping* of an object, viewed as the ground of these metaphorical senses, would be simply absurd."

The assumption of a dipping in Mark 1 : 9 must be dismissed. A dipping has no more mastery over the usage of βαπτίζω than has sprinkling or pouring. And while dipping and pouring may effect, as agencies, baptisms of influence and of symbol, all who take *a dipping* FOR a baptism *have no baptism*. They have clutched at a shadow and have lost the reality.

Sixth Assumption. The assumption, that Mark makes an essentially different statement from that made by Matthew respecting this same transaction, is without just foundation.

That one Evangelist may add to or take from the narrative of the same transaction, as given by another Evangelist, is undoubtedly true. Addition or subtraction may affect the completeness of a narrative, but does not necessarily work any change in the facts themselves. Our objection is, that the interpretation of the theory makes Mark state a fact which Matthew confessedly does not state, and in doing so converts "Jordan" into *water*, while Matthew confessedly uses that term to denote not water but locality; and, still farther, makes this change to give water as the regimen of εἰς, which, by confession, it has not in Matthew, or anywhere else, in the whole history of John's baptism, nor can have (with Classic usage) without destruction of life.

And all this is done, when the language of Mark may be fairly interpreted without deviating in the least degree from the statement of Matthew. Matthew states with a distinctness which admits of no denial, that Jesus came from Galilee and arrived *at* (upon ἐπὶ) the Jordan. He does not set before us the journey, but exhibits its termination by the arrival *at* Jordan. Mark exhibits the journey more *in transitu*, as setting out from Galilee and tending toward the Jordan, *to* which point it attains. More than this the language of Mark does not, by any necessity, express; while the relation of terms claimed by the theory gives an impossible, destructive meaning. This sixth assumption must perish.

While it may be true, that "Mark 1 : 9 does itself decide the controversy," that decision is a lightning stroke which smites the theory and leaves it a monumental wreck.

Patristic Writers.

Jerome in translating Matt. 3 : 13 adopts rather the form of Mark than of Matthew : "Tunc venit Jesus a Galilæa *in* Jordam ad Joannem."

Gregory Th., "παραγίνεται ἀπὸ τῆς Γαλαλαίας εἰς τὸν Ἰορδάνην πρός τὸν Ἰωάννην, 'Jesus comes *unto* the Jordan' to John."

If we take this language of Greg. Thaum. in connection with Mark 1 : 9, we have the same varied form of expression as is exhibited in John 9 : 7 and 11 : "Jesus *comes* (εἰς) *unto* the Jordan to be baptized"—and "Jesus comes to be *baptized* (εἰς) *at* the Jordan;" "The blind man *goes* (εἰς) *unto* the pool to wash"—and "The blind man goes to *wash* (εἰς) *at* the pool." Both Jerome and Gregory dissolve the imagined relation between εἰς Ἰορδάνην and βαπτίζω.

Mode of Baptism.

While the Scriptures preserve an absolute silence in relation to any forms of action entering into the administration of ritual baptism, there are statements made by Patristic writers in referring to the baptism of the Lord Jesus which, while without authority, are not without interest.

Hippolytus (X, 856) says, ἔκλινεν τὴν κεφαλὴν αυτοῦ βαπτισθῆναι ὑπὸ Ἰωάννου, "he bowed his head to be baptized by John."

The bowing of the head to receive the symbol water of baptism is the universal practice of all persons except among Baptists. Hippolytus says, the manner in which Jesus was baptized has no counterpart in the theory. Jesus "bowed his head" himself; it was not pressed down nor dipped by John.

Gregory Thaumaturgus (X, 1184–8) gives quite an extended description of the interview between John and Jesus and the subsequent baptism. John is represented as saying:

"How shall I touch thy undefiled head? How shall I stretch out my right hand over thee who hast stretched out the heavens as a curtain and established the earth upon the waters? How shall I stretch out my servile fingers over thy divine head? How shall I wash the spotless and the sinless? How shall I enlighten the light? How shall I offer prayer for thee who dost receive the prayers of those who know thee not?

"In baptizing others I baptize into thy name that they may believe upon thee coming with glory; baptizing thee of whom shall I make mention? Into whose name shall I baptize thee? Into the name of the Father? But thou hast all the Father in thyself, and thou art all in the Father. Or, into the name of the Son? But there is no other beside thee, by nature, the Son of God. Or, into the name of the Holy Ghost? But he is in everything united with thee, as of the same nature with thee, and of the same will, and of the same mind, and of the same power, and of the same honor, and with thee receives worship from all. Baptize, therefore, if thou wilt, O Lord, baptize me the Baptist. Make me, whom thou hast caused to be born, to be born again. Stretch out thy dread right hand which thou hast prepared for thyself, and crown by thy touch my head, that forerunner of thy kingdom, and crowned like a forerunner, I may preach to sinners, crying unto them: 'Behold the Lamb of God which taketh away the sins of the world.'" . . . .

Jesus is represented as answering:

"It is necessary that I should, now, be baptized with this baptism, and, hereafter, confer upon all men the baptism of the Trinity. Lend me thy right hand, O Baptist, for the present administration . . . . Take hold of my head which the Seraphim worship. Baptize me, who am about to baptize them that believe (δι' ὕδατος, καὶ Πνεύματος, καὶ πυρὸς) by water, and Spirit, and fire; (ὕδατι) by water, which is able to wash away the filth of sin; (Πνεύματι) by Spirit, which is able to make the earthy spiritual; (πυρὶ) by fire, consuming, by nature, the thorns of transgressions. The Baptist having heard these things, stretching out his trembling right hand, baptized the Lord."

This account of the baptism of the Lord Jesus Christ shows a baptism administered after a very different fashion from the baptism by Baptists of the present day. They never baptize by stretching out the right hand over the head of the baptized. All others do, always, thus baptize.

We have heard a great deal of "the act of baptism," "the act commanded." Was the act performed by John's out-stretched, trembling right hand, "the act commanded?" If so, what was the act?

But again, this narrative bears throughout evidence that the baptism did not consist in the manner of using the water, but in the effect produced by it as an instrumental means. This is confirmed by the language of the Saviour, who declares that his baptism is δι᾽ ὕδατος, καὶ Πνεύματος, καὶ πυρός, where agency is unmistakable. That John did not regard dipping into WATER baptism is shown by his inquiry, "*Into whose* NAME shall I baptize thee?" Gregory seems to have thought that John baptized into the name of the Lord Jesus, in which he was mistaken, for John "baptized into repentance," but it shows that this writer did not regard *water dipping* as baptism.

We may also learn, that baptism into repentance, &c., imported a thorough change in the condition of the baptized person in accordance with the nature of repentance, &c., from John's objection to the result of a baptism "into the name of the Father, or of the Son, or of the Holy Ghost;" he was ALREADY *in a condition perfectly conformed to these divine Persons*, and, therefore, a baptism "into them" was an un-meaning and supererogatory service. The Lord Jesus Christ is ἐν Πνεύματι Ἁγίῳ, "of the same nature, will, mind, power," and so baptizes ἐν Πνεύματι Ἁγίῳ, by the Holy Ghost.

From whatever standpoint we look at the theory all sub-stance of truth is lacking.

We have now considered the baptism of our Lord in re-lation to the place of its occurrence and the phraseology in which it is expressed. Few I think will hesitate to acknowl-edge, that the idea of Mark 1 : 9 "settling the controversy and determining a *dipping* into Jordan," is but a pleasant dream of the theorists dispelled by a stricter investigation.

The baptism received by Christ and the execution of its amazing responsibilities constitute the groundwork of CHRISTIAN baptism. This will form the subject-matter of additional inquiry, and conclude our investigation.

SUMMARY.

THE BAPTISM PREACHED AND THE BAPTISM ADMINISTERED.

THE Baptism which John preached and the Baptism which John administered were one and the same baptism. John preached the imperative necessity for a thorough change in the condition of the soul manifested by godly repentance and issuing in the full remission of sin through "the Lamb of God that taketh away the sin of the world;" which changed condition of the soul was the work of the Holy Ghost. This baptism of the soul which was *set forth by* WORDS in the preaching was identically the same baptism which was *set forth by* WATER in the rite. The purification of the soul was always effected, as a fact, by the Holy Ghost; and the purification of the soul was always exhibited, as a necessity, by the pure symbol. The AGENCIES differed infinitely; the BAPTISM was one absolutely—*effected* in the one case, *symbolized* in the other.

Matthew's "REPENT!" and Mark's and Luke's "*Baptism of* REPENTANCE *into* THE REMISSION OF SINS," and John's "Behold! the Lamb of God that taketh away the sin of the world," have all alike the same amount of water in them; that is to say, just as much as may be found in the burned out craters of the moon. The verb βαπτίζω and the noun βάπτισμα, as used in the history of John's baptism, have no more to do with the quantity or the manner of using the water employed in his symbol rite, than has the multiplication table to do with the amount or the manner of using Rothschild's wealth. Let these words mean what they may, they have no more control, in the relations in which they stand, over the use of the water, than a sleeping infant has over the earth's diurnal revolution.

Βαπτιστὴς.

There is not a particle of evidence conjoining *ὁ βαπτιστὴς* with a physical complementary element. The related term *ὁ βάπτης* presents no evidence, in its usage, of meaning "the dipper." *Merger*, the corresponding derivative from *mergo* (through merge), presents in its usage the most absolute evidence of divorce from physical relations. In evidence see the following: WHARTON'S LAW LEXICON, London; Article Merger: "MERGER (Latin *mergo*, to drown). The doctrine of *Merger* is simply this: that if two estates in realty vest in the same person in the same right, and without any other estate intermediate between them, the lesser is SUNK or DESTROYED in the greater. . . . . Thus if an estate for life, and a greater estate immediately expectant on it, meet in the same person, the first estate is *merged*. . . . . If the wife be tenant for life, and the reversion in fee be conveyed to husband and wife, the estate for life is *merged;* yet the wife surviving may revive it by expressing her dissent to the conveyance. . . . . Where any person having an estate capable of *merger*. . . . . Owners of both lands and tithes, even tenants for life, are empowered *to merge* tithes in the land. . . . . If the lessee make the freeholder his executor the term will not *merge.* . . . . It is doubtful when the second term is in remainder, whether a *merger* will take place. . . . . If a trust and legal estate unite in the same person, the former generally speaking becomes *merged* or *extinguished*. Equity will in certain cases relieve against a legal *merger*. The title of extinguishment differs from that of *merger* in being applicable to a charge or right instead of a preceding estate."

BURRILL'S LAW DICTIONARY, New York: Article "Merger (from French merger, *to drown;* from Latin mergere, *to plunge*). The drowning, sinking, absorption, or extinguishment of one estate in another. The *extinguishment* by act of law of one estate in another. The less is immediately *annihilated*, or in the law phrase is said to be MERGED, that is, SUNK or DROWNED in the greater. The term of years is merged in the inheritance, and shall never exist any more. . . . . An engagement by simple contract is MERGED in a deed contract (the engagement and the parties being the same), and becomes TOTALLY EXTINGUISHED."

This reference to the use of "Merger," as a law term, is in accordance with the counsel of Burke (Preface to Sublime and

Beautiful): "We ought to compare our subject with things of a similar nature, and even with things of a contrary nature; for discoveries may be, and often are, made by the contrast, which would escape us on the single view. The greater number of comparisons we make, the more general and the more certain our knowledge is likely to prove, as built upon a more perfect and extensive induction."

Nothing could more fully vindicate the view of βαπτίζω and *mergo* as prescribed in Classic and Judaic Baptism, or more absolutely extinguish the view of the theory, than this law usage of MERGER. It has been shown by a force of evidence which has not been attempted to be gainsaid, that this Greek and this Latin word are as nearly correspondent in radical and derived meanings as any two words in different languages could well be. And both these words have been shown to be the very opposites, in point of power, to βάπτω, *tingo*, DIP; because these latter words do not allow their object to abide within the enveloping element, while the former never makes provision for its withdrawal. Both the London and the New York lexicographers recognize this distinction when they derive "merger" from the Latin "mergo *to drown*," and from the French "merger *to drown*." Did any one ever define *tingo*, or dip, by *drown?* Would it be possible to substitute *dipper* for "merger" and make anything but nonsense? Try it on the definition as given by Burrill— "(Merger =) DIPPER: The *drowning, sinking, absorption*, or *extinguishment* of one estate in another." Could definition be the more absolute opposite of a defined word than in this case?

But in farther contrast, observe the usage in connection with this matter of estates of the word *dip*:

> " Put out the principal in trusty hands,
> Live on the use; and never *dip* thy lands."—*Dryden.*

" Lord T—— had *dipped* so deeply into his property."—*Mrs. Sherwood.*

By a "merger" an estate has an addition made to it, and it becomes enhanced in value by the new element incorporated in it; while by a *dipper* (= "a mortgage"), something is subtracted from an estate and by this loss it becomes diminished in value. Now, what would be thought of any one that should insist upon confounding and interchanging these words, substituting at will dipping for "merger" and "merger" for dipping? Would the judges of any court tolerate such lawlessness in any plea that might be made before them? Is it any more tolerable out of the court-room and in interpreting the word and law of God?

But this is what the friends of the theory insist upon. They insist in the name of a mistaken philology, that ὁ βαπτιστὴς shall mean "Dipper," and then to cover up their error, they farther insist upon spelling "Dipper" after the remarkable fashion, I-m-m-e-r-s-e-r! And when they are pressed with the undeniable point, that immerse does not take out what it puts in, they reply, "that they are excusable for an utter reversal of the meaning of the word used by the Holy Spirit on the ground, that God did not mean to drown the disciples;" quietly assuming the absolute error, that God meant that the disciples should be put into the water.

This law usage of "merger" farther claims attention because it exhibits an appropriated use of the word, and that outside of any physical application. As "merger" in law has nothing to do with liquids or physics of any kind, so βαπτιστὴς in religion has nothing to do with water in any form or measure. Let not ὁ βαπτιστὴς have his "long coat" trimmed down to the "short coat" of ὁ βάπτης until the use of the shears can claim "by authority" from some accredited quarter. Let not ὁ βαπτιστὴς be eviscerated of all power and life in order to save a hopelessly imperilled theory. Let not a union between ὁ βαπτιστὴς and water be attempted while the laws of language and the words of the Holy Ghost unitedly cry—*We forbid!*

Usage shows a strict and exclusive appropriation growing out of religious ceremonial purifications, and the teaching of a higher spiritual purification. And therefore it is, that John ὁ βαπτιστὴς is and can only be, John THE PURIFIER.

The only use of this term, ὁ βαπτιστὴς, as applied to any other than to John, confirms the position that it has no usage with physical adjuncts. The passage referred to is in Ambrose, II, 1227, "Ergo veniet Baptista Magnus." No one ever imagined that the title, "the Great Baptist," as applied to the Lord Jesus Christ, carried any water with it. And any one who imagines that the title, "the Baptist," as applied to John, carries water with it, indulges his imagination without warrant from one syllable of Scripture. If the Lord Jesus Christ was "the Great Purifier," his Forerunner was the preacher of that great purification and ritually a symbol "Purifier." This word as applied to John, is always used absolutely, and so indicates a Jewish origin; as in distinctively Jewish usage the Greek verb and its derivatives are always used absolutely, indicating long and common usage.

Βάπτισμα.

In the history of John's baptism the words βαπτισμός and βάπτισις, which were in Jewish use and expressive of the act of the verb, were rejected, and a new word, βάπτισμα, expressive of state or condition, is introduced. The new word has never any complementary relation with water. The following are the only relations in which it occurs by which its nature may be determined: 1. βάπτισμα ἀυτου. 2. βάπτισμα ᾿Ιωαννου. 3. βάπτισμα ἐκηρυσσε. 4. βάπτισμα μετανοίας ἐκηρυσσε. 5. βάπτισμα μετανοίας ἐβαπτισε. 6. βάπτισμα μετανοίας εἰς ἄφεσιν ἁμαρτιων κηρύσσων. In all these limiting and explanatory adjuncts water fails to make an appearance. And so long as the prophecies of Isaiah, and of Malachi, and of Zacharias, shall remain; and so long as the histories of Matthew, and Mark, and Luke, and John, shall live; and so long as repentance and the remission of sins shall find their motive and their end in the Lamb of God; so long must water be rejected as a receiving element in the βάπτισμα of John.

᾿Εν and Εἰς.

The New Testament usage of ἐν and εἰς on the subject of baptism is sufficient to extinguish the theory of a water dipping. The theory in its interpretation of these prepositions does nothing but confound what the Holy Spirit has made discriminatingly diverse. It rejects in inspired writings laws of language which had been accepted and respected in the writings of Judaism and Heathenism. The only apology for this must be found in the fact, that otherwise the theory would perish to be remembered only by its remarkable expletive vocabulary, and its historic errors as to the communion of saints and the constitution of the church of God. The following quotations will show, at a glance, the nature of this discriminating difference:

Place in which.

βαπτίζων $\begin{cases} ἐν ἐρημῷ \text{ in the Wilderness.} \\ ἐν ᾿Ιορδάνῃ \text{ in the Jordan.} \end{cases}$

Means by which.

$\beta\alpha\pi\tau\ell\zeta$ $\upsilon\nu$ $\begin{cases} \dot\epsilon\nu \ \Pi\nu\epsilon\acute\nu\mu\alpha\tau\iota \ {}^\epsilon A\gamma\ell\omega \text{ by the Holy Ghost (really).} \\ \dot\epsilon\nu \ \ddot\upsilon\delta\alpha\tau\iota \text{ (Matt.)}, \ \ddot\upsilon\delta\alpha\tau\iota \text{ (Luke), by water (symbolly).} \end{cases}$

Verbal element into which.

$\beta\alpha\pi\tau\ell\zeta\omega\nu$ $\begin{cases} \epsilon\dot\iota\varsigma \ \mu\epsilon\tau\alpha\nu o\ell\alpha\nu \text{ into repentance.} \\ \epsilon\dot\iota\varsigma \ \check\alpha\varphi\epsilon\sigma\iota\nu \ \dot\alpha\mu\alpha\rho\tau\iota\tilde\omega\nu \text{ into the remission of sins.} \end{cases}$

All outside of the theory will, I think, concur in the judgment, that the usage of the prepositions relating to John's baptism is sufficient of itself to determine this long-pending controversy, and to exclude forever the idea of a dipping *into* WATER.

John preached a baptism into the remission of sins ($=$ thorough purification and pardon), effected by faith in the Coming One "the Lamb of God that taketh away the sin of the world," through repentance wrought in the soul by the Holy Ghost. And John ritually administered this same baptism in the Wilderness, in the Jordan (locally), by water (symbolly), into repentance, into the remission of sins (verbal element expressive of thorough repentance required, and thorough remission promised). In the statement of this preaching and of this administration there never was a more absolute conformity to the Classic usage of $\beta\alpha\pi\tau\ell\zeta\omega$ as a word of power and making demand for condition thorough and indefinitely prolonged; there never was a more absolute conformity to the nature and power of $\dot\epsilon\nu$ (Classic and Hellenistic) *within*, 1. As within a bounded space, *e. g.*, of the Wilderness, of the banks of the Jordan; 2. As invested with power (power of influence being concomitant on withinness), *e. g.*, of the Holy Ghost, of symbol water; there never was a more absolute conformity to the nature and power of $\epsilon\dot\iota\varsigma$ *passing into*, as expressive of a thorough change of condition, *e. g.*, out of impenitence into penitence, out of the pollution of sin into the thorough remission of sin; and there never was a more just or a more perfect discrimination in the associate use of these prepositions exhibited in any writings Heathen or Christian. And on the other hand, never was the nature and power of a word more utterly misrepresented than by the theory in making $\beta\alpha\pi\tau\ell\zeta\omega$ demand a dipping or a temporary covering; and never was a phrase more essentially misinterpreted than when $\beta\alpha\pi\tau\ell\zeta\omega$ $\dot\epsilon\nu$ is made to carry men and women out of one

element into another; and never was there a more complete in-
version and perversion of language than that which makes
βαπτίζω ἐν dip into and arrests βαπτίζω εἰς on the outside of its
complementary adjunct by "unto."

If the theory can live after pulling down upon its head rocks
like these, it must have a hold on life even beyond that which
common fame attributes to ordinary error.

Βαπτίζω.

The theory has grown venerable with the years of a second
or third century in the assumption and assertion, that βαπτίζω
is a modal verb expressive of a definite act. This position has
been proclaimed to be its peculiar glory. All rejecters of it
were declared to be unfaithful to God. We insist on this definition being sustained by proof or being abandoned with confession of error and wrong done to the people of God. We will
again present the view of the theory as derived from a new
source; showing that we have given a true representation of it.
We quote from Alexander Campbell, President of Bethany College, as contained in his work on Christian Baptism (Bethany,
Virginia, 1823), pp. 116–130: "Argument 1.—*Bapto*, the root
of *Baptizo*, whence the adopted words *baptize* and *baptism*, like
all other radical words denoting specific action, never loses *its
specific sense* in its derivatives. The word *baptizo* is restricted,
circumscribed, a word of specification. It indicates an outward
and formal action. Baptism is a positive ordinance. Positive
precepts indicate some exact and well-defined action. Circumcision was a positive institution. It enjoined a specific act.
Baptism must have the specific action to be performed, implied,
and expressed in it. Jesus Christ must have intended some
particular action to be performed by his ministers, and it follows
that he did select such a word, or that he could not or would
not do it. . . . . Follows it not, then, that he *could*, that he *would*,
find such a word, and that he *has done it*—and that *baptizo* is
that specific word? In the common version *bapto* is translated,
both in its simple and compound form, always by the word *dip*.
Baptizo indicates a specification, and consequently, as such, can
have but one meaning. It is a word indicating specific action
and specific action only. *Baptizo*, confessedly a derivative from
bapto, derives its specific meaning, as well as its radical and im-
mutable form, from that word. *Baptismos, baptisma, baptisis*,

baptistees, baptomai, baptisomai, baptos, baptisteerion, bapha, baphi-kos, bapheis, through their two thousand flexions and modifica-tions, retain the *bap* and as uniformly the *dip* represented by it. All the learned admit that its primary, proper, and unfigurative meaning is *to dip*. All allow that *dip* is the primary and proper meaning of *bapto;* and as it is incontrovertibly certain that *bap-tizo* is derived from *bapto*, and therefore inherits the proper meaning of *bap*, which is *dip*, then is it not irresistibly evident that *baptizo* can never authorize or sanction any other action than dipping or immersion. No word in the Greek language has been more rigidly canvassed and more accurately traced than *baptizo*, and none more satisfactorily established. Since Messrs. Carson and Stuart's essays on this subject, it is agreed among the learned of all parties that *bapto* and *baptizo* do differ only in one point, not formerly observed by the lexicographers themselves; and that point is, that BAPTO IS NEVER USED TO DE-NOTE THE ORDINANCE OF BAPTISM, AND BAPTIZO NEVER SIGNIFIES TO DYE. In the radical and proper import, it is abundantly evident that they are *isodunai*, exactly the same as to significa-tion."

Such is a condensed statement, in his own words, of Alexander Campbell's view as to the meaning of βαπτίζω. It is the absolute *ditto* of that of Alexander Carson. It is the same as that pre-sented by all Baptist writers in theory. It is a view of the word which no writer in argument has even made an attempt to sus-tain. There is not the shadow of support for it in the full facts of usage. There is not a Greek lexicographer that ever lived who defined βαπτίζω as expressing "specific action and specific action only." And if it be true, as Campbell says, that " it is agreed among the learned that βάπτο and βαπτίζω differ only in one point (dyeing), and that in all other respects they are ex-actly the same as to signification," then, it is high time that some of the unlearned should step in and call attention to the facts in the usage of these words. No soberminded man can look at these facts and say, that they indicate these words to be " exactly the same as to signification."

Jewish and Johannic Usage.

The Jewish usage of this Greek verb, together with its deriv-atives, presents a very marked difference when compared with the usage of John. Thus we meet with such phrases as these:

βαπτιζόμενος ἀπὸ νεκροῦ, ἐβαπτίζετο ἐν τῇ παρεμβολῇ, βαπτίσαντες τῆς τέφρας, βαπτίσωνται ἀπὸ ἀγορὰς, ὃυ ἐβαπτίσθη πρὸ τοῦ ἀρίστου, βαπτισμῷ συνιέναι, βάπτισιν ἀποδεκτήν, βαπτισμοὺς κλινῶν, βαπτισμοῖς διαφόροις. These phrases show an absolute use of the word which in the absence of a defining adjunct requires special knowledge of Jewish thought and practice for its interpretation. To a Classic Greek ignorant of Judaism the darkness of Egypt would not be less penetrable than the thought in such phrases as—" baptized from the dead," " baptized in the camp," " baptized by ashes," " baptized from the market," " baptized before dinner," "come for baptizing," " acceptable baptizing," " baptizings of couches," " diverse baptizings;" but to the Jew there was no darkness in these phrases; *ceremonial purification* flashed out through them all. This thought had been thus expressed among them for a hundred years, and in no other terms. Long use had worn away explanatory adjuncts and the word alone expressed the absorbed meaning. But the facts are far otherwise with John's baptism. The phraseology which announced this baptism had no century of usage to fall back upon. It was a new baptism. An absolute use of words could not express it. Explanatory adjuncts were imperative. John, therefore, does not say, ʼΕγω βαπτίζω simply, but ʼΕγω βαπτίζω ε ἰ ς μ ε τ α ν ο ί α ν; he does not preach a βάπτισμα simply, but a βάπτισμα μ ε τ α ν ο ί α ς; he is not satisfied with teaching the nature of the baptism by tracing it to the source whence it proceeds, but gives the last degree of explicitness which language allows by tracing it into the verbal element within which it terminates, thus, βάπτισμα μετανοίας ε ἰ ς ἄ φ ε σ ι ν ἁ μ α ρ τ ι ῶ ν. Such phraseology would be just as intelligible to the Classic Greek as to the Jew. And the Jew needed such explanatory adjuncts to divorce his mind from his old baptism and to apprehend the new, just as much as the Classic Greek. And I trust the friends of the theory will not long stand aloof from those who accept this most explicit and divinely authoritative definition of John's baptism, frankly confessing their unhappy error.

Inasmuch as John cannot possibly use the Greek verb and noun in their acquired Jewish sense, he must fall back on the original force of these words (and even form a new word) developing a specific meaning by new combinations of words. John protects himself against misinterpretation by constructing a barrier of limiting and defining words, which can never be broken down or rejected without trampling under foot words spoken by inspired men "as they were moved by the Holy Ghost."

Classic, Judaic, and Johannic Usage.

The underlying force and language development of βαπτίζω is identically the same, in principle, with Greeks, and Jews, and John. The Greeks use the word first in physical relations, then in ideal relations, and finally absolutely, as expressive directly of a new idea—*to make drunk*. The Jews (Josephus and Philo) exhibit a like physical, ideal, and absolute use with that of the Greeks. While Jewish religious writings, inspired and uninspired, show a national appropriated use with the new signification—*religious ceremonial purification*. John never uses the word for the development of its force in any physical application; nor does he use it in the national appropriated meaning, for he did not deal with "ceremonial purifications;" but he shows a perfect mastery of the radical idea of the word by its use in new and ideal relations, thereby developing the truth announced in his mission with the greatest possible clearness and power. While in the application of this word there is the broadest diversity, and as a consequence the outgrowth of a diversity in the directly expressed meaning, yet, as to principle in the use and development of this word there is not the shadow of a difference whether under Heathenism, Judaism, or Inspiration

John and the Theory.

The theory proffers to John *a dipping into water* as his baptism. The son of Zacharias will not own it. He declares that the preaching of a water dipping illy becomes "the prophet of the Highest, preparing the ways of the Lord, giving knowledge of salvation unto his people by the remission of their sins" (Luke 1 : 76, 77). He refuses to recognize "baptism of repentance" and "baptism into the remission of sins," in the offspring of the theory—"*a dipping into* WATER *unto repentance, unto the remission of sins.*" He declares himself to be an utter stranger to any baptism made up of a momentary introduction into and extraduction out of water; while he is ready to administer a symbol ritual baptism by applying pure water to those who have received by the Holy Ghost that soul baptism which is symbolized in its purifying nature by the ritual water.

Whether the friends of the theory will receive John's teaching with any greater docility than that of the Angel Gabriel, or will "order them" both "to school," I do not know; but one thing is patent, that so long as they substitute a dipping into water for the divinely appointed symbolization of "baptism into REPENTANCE," "into the REMISSION OF SINS," they have blotted out from their ritual practice the handwriting and superscription of the skies. "Doctrine of man" has taken the place of the teaching of God. A human service has usurped the office of a divine ordinance. While grasping in the water after a shadowed substance, letting go their hold on the reality, they have both lost the substance and missed the shadow, and so find themselves without any baptism. No heathen Greek will recognize a dipping as a baptism; and neither John nor any other inspired writer ever taught a *dipping into* WATER. The theory has sold its birthright for a dip into the water.

CONCLUSION.

JOHANNIC BAPTISM is a spiritual condition of the soul, a *ΒΑΠΤΙΣΜΑ* "into repentance," "into the remission of sins;" which condition of repentance and of remission (like every other baptism) has no self-termination, and is the work of the Holy Ghost. This is Johannic Baptism in its reality.

This same *ΒΑΠΤΙΣΜΑ* is declared by word and exhibited in symbol, by the application of pure water to the person, in a ritual ordinance. This is Johannic Baptism in its shadow.

The manner of using the water in John's ritual baptism is not stated by any word. The word $\beta\alpha\pi\tau i\zeta\omega$, as used in Scripture, has no more control over or connection with the manner of using this water, than a broken arm has control over or connection with the movement of the solar system.

Dipping or mersing "into water" is phraseology utterly unknown to John's baptism. "Baptism into *repentance*" and "baptism into *water*" are, as to their nature, as far removed from each other as is pole from pole. The first of these is the baptism of John; the second (changed to a dipping, and therefore nullified as a baptism) is the baptism of the theory.

The theory has nothing to stand upon. In whatever aspect we look at it, it is "in the air." It is a contradiction of Classio usage. It is without support in Lexical definition. It is the antipodes of Patristic sentiment. It is not a "New Version," but it is an adding unto and a taking away from the Word of God which is utterly destructive to the most express teachings of the Holy Ghost.

Errors of the Theory.

1. *The theory* ERRS *as to the meaning of βαπτίζω*. It transforms this word into *βάπτω* *to dip*, and so introduces into baptism a conception entirely unknown to the language and utterly alien from the thought of inspiration.

2. *The theory* ERRS *as to the meaning of βαπτιστής*. It derives this word from the Classic *βαπτίζω* under a meaning erroneously attributed to it, instead of from the Jewish *βαπτίζω* and the meaning attached to it by national usage; thus converting a religious "Purifier" into a water *Dipper*.

3. *The theory* ERRS *as to the meaning of βάπτισμα*. Divine inspiration has constructed this word in order to meet its own exigency of thought, namely, a condition of soul thoroughly pervaded with spiritual emotion; but the theory has subverted all such purpose by fastening *a dipping* upon the word.

4. *The theory* ERRS *as to the meaning of the phrase βάπτισμα μετανοίας*. A condition of the soul proceeding from repentance is converted into a water dipping; as unscripturally associated with repentance as iron and clay are unprofitably commingled.

5. *The theory* ERRS *as to the meaning of the phrase βάπτισμα μετανοίας εἰς ἄφεσιν ἁμαρτιων*. It substitutes an unscriptural interpretation by which dipping into water is connected with the remission of sins, instead of the inspired declaration of remitted sins to the truly penitent through the Lamb of God.

6. *The theory* ERRS *as to the meaning of the phrase ἐν ὕδατι*. It misunderstands the logical relation of the phrase to the baptism, transforming the symbol agency into the receptive element; and therefore mistranslates the preposition, making it demand *within-ness*, while it represents instrumentality.

7. *The theory* ERRS *as to the meaning of the phrase βαπτίζω ἐν ὕδατι εἰς μετανοίαν*. Having mistranslated ἐν, and misinterpreted ὕδατι (investing both with the borrowed without leave rights of εἰς μετανοίαν), it only remained to cover the wrong by a fresh mis-translation of εἰς, and the excision of μετανοίαν from the baptism altogether. And this work of destruction the theory has done.

ΠΡΩΤΟΝ ΨΕΥΔΟΣ

Dr. Halley says, " Let us agree to find out the truth, adhering closely to Scripture, carefully endeavoring to detect the cause of the error, on whichever side it be, the πρῶτον ψεῦδος, which vitiates all the subsequent reasoning, and then it cannot be difficult for an unprejudiced mind to ascertain the truth." This wise counsel I have endeavored to follow. Under it I have been led to this conclusion : *The ΠΡΩΤΟΝ ΨΕΥΔΟΣ of the theory is the erroneous meaning attached to BAΠTIZΩ = a definite act,* TO DIP. *Hence,* the rejection of ἐν ὕδατι from its divinely appointed relation to baptism as the symbol agency, and its unscriptural conversion into the receptive element. *Hence,* the mistranslation of ἐν. *Hence,* the destructive excision from the divinely announced baptism—εἰς μετανοίαν, εἰς ἄφεσιν ἁμαρτιῶν—of the verbal element. *Hence,* the mistranslation of εἰς. *And hence,* the sad aphoristic error against the Head of the church as well as against his people—" No DIPPING, NO BAPTISM." The truth in the case being—Accept *a dipping* and you reject *a baptism.*

The friends of the theory, deceived by a most remarkable delusion, have bartered the priceless baptism of inspiration for a worthless dipping of human imagination. Whenever they shall awake to a realization of their impoverished condition as without any baptism, they will find, unlike Esau, " the baptism of repentance" graciously awaiting their acceptance.

In the endeavor now made to exhibit the usage of βαπτίζω in John's baptism, I have sought to place myself, in a spirit of the most absolute dependence, under the guidance of the *ipsissima verba* of inspiration. If I have at any time spoken with positiveness, it was only because of a profound conviction that God's word was positive. But I indulge in no such folly as would substitute my conviction for God's truth. The ground of the conclusions reached is distinctly stated. It is deferentially submitted for examination. If it cannot abide the most searching scrutiny it will, and will most justly, fail. But if the foundation cannot be broken up, then *baptism of the soul* BY THE HOLY GHOST *and its ritual exhibition* BY SYMBOL WATER *applied to the body* will abide as the heritage of God's people ; while this unhappy theory leaves its too confiding votaries with *a dipping into water,* but, I am truly sorry to say it—with No BAPTISM.

In the Lord's Supper Bread and Wine are the elements divinely appointed to be used "*to show forth*" by their life-giving nature what is the life-giving nature of "THE LORD'S DEATH." In ritual Baptism Water is the element divinely appointed to be used "*to show forth*" by its physically purifying nature, what is the spiritually purifying nature of "BAPTISM BY THE HOLY GHOST." The sacrificial death of Christ *is not effected* by the ritual use of Bread and Wine; it is only "shown forth" by these appropriate life symbols. The Baptism of the Holy Ghost *is not effected* by the ritual use of Water; it is only "shown forth" by this appropriate purifying symbol.

The theory does not profess to "show forth" that divine baptism which is effected by the Holy Ghost, but claims to effect another and utterly diverse baptism of its own by dipping into the water. Now, if a dipping could be converted into a baptism, this baptism, thus effected by the theory, would be quite another thing from the baptism of the Bible. But a dipping is not a baptism; therefore the theory not only abandons the purpose for which ritual baptism was established, but substitutes a wholly different thing for the Baptism which is divinely enjoined.

Rome claims in her Mass *to effect* a sacrifice, not "to show forth" the sacrifice divinely accomplished. The theory claims in its ritual service *to effect* a baptism, not "to show forth" the baptism divinely accomplished. The Mass of Rome is not God's sacrifice. THE DIPPING OF THE THEORY IS NOT GOD'S BAPTISM.

INDEX.

JOHANNIC BAPTISM.

(401)

AMBROSE:

the Saviour is "the Great Baptizer" (Purifier), 203; ὕδατα πολλά many springs ("12"), 315; "these 12 springs the Church has in the 12 patriarchs and in the 12 apostles. By these fountains we must be sprinkled," 316–317.

AMERICAN CHRISTIAN REVIEW: criticism of Judaic Baptism, complaint that βαπτίζω not received as a word of specific modal action, 18; criticisms answered, 19.

APOCRYPHA:

βαπτίζω is used more than a hundred years before John, but never in the primary, physical sense, 91; ceremonially purifying cleansings, by sprinkling or pouring, extend from Sirach, 31: 30,* to Mark 7: 4; some two hundred years, 105; the ground by which ἐν is qualified to express agency, 162–166.

ARNOLD, PROF. A. N.:

admits Greek, Nestorian, and Armenian baptisms are by

* There is no evidence of λουτρόν, in religious use, requiring a general physical bath for bodily cleansing, or for ceremonial cleansing, or for symbol cleansing; its religious use is limited to express *complete cleansing* irrespective of mode or extent of using the cleansing agency. Sprinkling blood, (Heb. 10: 22), washes the heart (compare Rev. 1: 5), and sprinkling "pure water," (Heb. 10: 23) washes the body; also, regeneration (Titus 3: 5) is a washing (= complete cleansing). The complete ceremonial defilement of which Sirach speaks was effected by a *touch*, and complete ceremonial purification was restored by the touch of "the water of purification." In classic religious use λουτρά ceased to express washing in any way (see Cremer, s. v. λουτρόν).

effusion, standing or seated in the water, 37; failure to cover, a punctilio, remedied by the effusion (!), 38; "βαπτίζω means literally and perpetually *to plunge;*" pity de Stourdza without the light of Dr. Dale's volumes, 39; Gale, Cox, Booth, Carson, Fuller, and Conant repudiate this "plunge," 40; "See all the lexicons," 42; Baptists never gave one definition with attempt to sustain it, 43; teaching of the theory, inconsistency and contradiction, 44–50; Conant, 50–58.

ARRIAN:

use of παραβαπτιστής, 135.

AUGUSTIN:

water in baptism instrumental 234.

Βάπτίζω:

expresses, Jewishly, a thorough change of condition from ceremonial impurity to ceremonial purity, "dip," a feeble word, could not be so used, 106; classic fable illustrating change of condition without covering, 106; blood, ashes, water, baptized (without covering) by divine power, in order that they might baptize, (see note, Lightfoot, v. 37), 106; essential difference between βάπτω and βαπτίζω, 108; contact with βάπτω to dye, in which no modal act, 109; has the meaning to purify (Origen), 136; has not the meaning, to dip, 137; Conant's XV propositions sustaining "a particular act," with answers, 179–183; mean-

Βαπτισμός :
the usual word for Jewish "baptizings" (ceremonial purifyings) expresses the *action* of the verb, Mark 7 : 4, 92, 107, 113 ; Josephus, 125. The rejection by John of βαπτισμός and βάπτισις, words used by Jews for their baptizings (ceremonial purifyings), must have been for good and decided reasons ; perhaps, 1. To impress upon the Jews the essential distinction between their " baptizings " to change the ceremonial condition of the body, and his " baptism" to change the spiritual condition of the soul. This, no doubt, was the theme of discussion between the Jews and the disciples of John in John 3 : 25, and the ground of the *caveat* entered by Josephus against the confounding of bodily and soul purification (125), as also of the protest of John himself (Matt. 3 : 7–12), against them who came unbaptized (unpurified) in soul to receive his symbol baptism, as though it belonged to the same species with their ceremonial purifyings. 2. Because of the essential difference in the terms ; the one based in an *act* often changing the condition of the body, the other in an *effect* once accomplished and changing forever the condition of the soul. Jewish "baptizing" (ceremonially cleansing the body) might be twenty times a day ; John's "baptism," spiritually cleansing the soul by repent-

ance and remission of **sin,** was once for all, therefore its symbol was never repeated. 3. Because neither βαπτισμός, nor βάπτισις, would have allowed John to proclaim his message in those terms (the profoundest of which human language is capable) κηρυσσων βάπτισμα μετανοίας, βάπτισμα εἰς μετανοιαν βάπτισμα μετανοίας εἰς ἀφεσιν ἁμαρτιων — "the baptism " (the effect, result, the thoroughly changed condition, accomplished *not by water,* but) " by repentance " —" the baptism " (the thoroughly changed condition of the soul by passing without limit of time *not into water.* but) " INTO repentance "— " the baptism " (the thoroughly changed condition effected *not by water,* but) by repentance (introducing the soul not into a waterpool, but, without limit of time) " INTO the remission of sins." These appear to be adequate and necessitating reasons for rejecting the Jewish terms and introducing another. The fact that four derivatives from one word—βαπτισμός, βάπτισιν, βαπτιστὴς, βάπτισμα—are added to the Greek language by the Jews and John, and placed in novel and distinctive relations, would seem to indicate competent knowledge on their part, and a right to claim an interpretation within their chosen sphere.

BAPTISM :
"is a modal, specific act," therefore, "baptism in one

large for a dipping, yet baptized, 110 ; *purifyings* established as the meaning and shown by absolute use through centuries, 118–125 ; all Jewish baptizings examined, the result, 125 ; Cremer (Bib. Theo. Lexicon, s. v., βαπτίζω) says, "The New Testament use of βαπτίζω may be pretty clearly traced back to the Levitical washings, Hebrew רָחַץ. For according to Mark 7 : 4, Luke 11 : 38, βαπτίζειν appears to have been at that time the technical term for these washings ; cf. Matt. 15 : 2, νίπτεσθαι, for which Mark 7 : 4 has βαπτίζεσθαι." "Out of these washings certainly arose also the baptism of proselytes, which (according to the testimonies as to its age) cannot have suggested the New Testament βαπτίζειν." Accepting these views of Cremer the ground is taken from under those who search heathendom to learn the New Testament use of βαπτίζω, inasmuch as there is neither a dipping nor an immersing in the Hebrew word; certainly "rahats" was never used "*to dip* the tip of the finger in water," nor "*to immerse* the ship of Josephus in the Adriatic Sea."

BAPTISMS, SPECIFIC :
must have specific evidences, 197.

BAPTISM, JOHN'S :
βαπτίζω first used, under inspiration, by John, βαπτιστής, and βάπτισμα, first appear in Greek in connection with his minis-

try, 71 ; in what mode did John use water ? a question never asked for more than one thousand years after John was baptized by his own blood, under the ministry of Herod's headsman, 72. Patrists never discussed the mode of using water, or ashes, or blood, in baptizing, never imagined such an element entered into effecting a baptism ; they believed Jewish baptism, John's baptism, and Christian baptism, to be each diverse from the other, in nature ; Romanists and Tractarians adopt patristic views as to John's baptism ; in relation to Christian baptism, Reformers and modern writers exhibit diversity of views, 73 ; views of Baptist writers, Stovel, Carson, etc., 74 ; neither John's nor Christian baptism had anything to do with modal use of water, 75 ; John's baptism had neither actual nor possible application to "cups," "pots," "couches," as subjects of its baptism, nor to "ships," "armor," "axeheads." Judaism might purify household utensils, and heathenism might destructively baptize hostile ships in the depths of the sea, but how could the Forerunner preach the βάπτισμα μετανοίας to pots, and cups, and couches, to ships, and helmets, and iron axeheads ? How could he administer the water, symbolizing the purifying power in the soul of "repentance" and the "remission of sins,"

27, 28; Luke 11 : 20) ; these passages, both in grammatical construction and in principles of interpretation, accord with βαπτίσει ἐν Πνεύματι Ἁγίῳ (Matt. 3 : 11). The Baptist Bible version translates these passages thus : "He casts out *through* (ἐν) Beelzebub," "He casts out *through* (ἐν) the Prince of the devils," "If I cast out *through* (ἐν) Beelzebub," "If I cast out through (ἐν) the Spirit of God," "If I cast out *by* (ἐν) the finger of God." This translation of ἐν (*through, by*), is thus vindicated: " Ἐν (with dative of person) denotes the one in whom resides the power or authority by which a thing is done ; hence *by* or *through*." This doctrine destroys the translation "He shall baptize you *in* the Holy Ghost," except by denying the personality of the Holy Ghost while affirming the personality of the devil. The doctrine justly applied to the passage proves that the Holy Ghost is not a *quiescent medium within which* it is the office of Christ to put the souls of men, but that he being *in* the Holy Ghost is thereby invested with power to baptize *through* the Holy Ghost, 192-196.

BENGEL :

discriminating character of John's baptism, 76 ; use of parenthesis in John's Gospel, 310 ; Rom. 9 : 1, conscience "in"(therefore acting through the influence of) the Holy Ghost, 188.

BOOTH :

baptize denotes an *action* re quired by divine law ; it is a specific term; " dip ?' is a specific term, 44.

CALVIN :

meaning, power, and nature of John's baptism, the same as Christian, viz., the outward representation of repentance for the forgiveness of sins, 73: long-established opinion not law, judge the matter as it stands, 90 ; Rom. 9 : 1, ἐν Πνεύματι Ἁγίῳ, 188.

CAMPBELL, ALEXANDER (BETH ANY) :

βαπτίζω signifies specific act ; if it once so means can never mean any other act ; means *dip* by consent of the whole world ; error and inconsistency, 59 ;. translation of εἰς, 253, 256 ; "design of baptism," 263-266.

CAMPBELL, PRINCIPAL G. (SCOTLAND) :

ἐν means *with*, 158 ; quoted by Conant against the common version without effect, 344–346 ; on John 5 : 2," pool " includes more than water, 396.

CARSON, ALEXANDER, LL.D. (IRELAND) :

admits all lexicographers against him, as to *secondary* meaning of βαπτίζω ; no less true as to his limitation of *primary* meaning to modal act, 61–63; the theory — " βαπτίζω is formed from primary meaning, modal act *to dip*, and means nothing more or less," an error, 64, 65; "could be no difference in mode between

28

sistency, therefore, in translating ἐν in the one case *with*
(water), and in the other *in*
(the Holy Ghost). Water is
the measure of John's power
because he is " *in* the spirit
and power of Elias," and the
Holy Ghost is the measure of
the Saviour's power because
he is " *in* the Holy Ghost."
In the one case the symbol instrument is stated, and the
spiritual condition of the baptizer is left to be inferred ; in
the other the spiritual condition of the baptizer is stated,
and the divine efficacy of his
baptism is left to be inferred.
This interpretation is made
certain, because βαπτίζω ἐν
never expresses the passing of
a baptized object into water
or anything else. In consid-
ering the office of water and
the relation of John to it, it
should be remembered that
water is not used in religious
rites to wash dirty hands, or
dirty feet, or dirty bodies, but
that though these should have
been washed in " snow-water
and made never so clean,"
still water in religious rites is
demanded in its symbol power,
representing a higher than
physical purity. The idea of
water being used as a grave
in a religious rite is a thing as
irrational in itself as it is destitute of all warrant in the
Scriptures. Blood, as used in
religious rites, is not used for
any natural qualities belonging to it, and when "*washing*" by blood is spoken of all
feel that it is irrational to

suppose reference is made to
the application of blood to the
body as a washing element, as
this could only defile and de-
form. The blood of Christ
" washes " without touching
the body or the soul. Water
washes no more than blood.
Water in Christianity represents that blood in its washing, without touching, power.
Water is applied to the body
mainly to individualize and
to emphasize personal need.
When water is so used as to
wet the clothing all over, it is
an error worse than Petrine
(for he only asked this for
his uncovered " hands and
head "), and for which the
Scriptures have no responsibility. The reasoning back-
ward which claims a covering
of the body in water, or with
water, because " washing " is
used of the religious symbol
water, is remarkable. " Washing " cannot get into the
Christian religion without first
dropping on the threshold
mode, extent, and quantity,
retaining only the idea of
cleansing; while this reasoning (after admission within
the religious sphere on these
terms) claims that its presence proves that the inter-
dicted elements necessarily
inhere in its being, and must
be observed. Let such rea-
soners begin with their mode,
and extent, and quantity with
the blood of Christ, then come
to practice on the symbol of
that " which cleanseth from
all sin." But if it be allowed

that mode, extent, and quantity in the blood-washing are swallowed up by *faith* (which, under the Holy Spirit, applies this blood), then cease to look in the symbol for that which has no existence in the reality. The office of the Lamb of God was to effect an atoning purification through his blood "poured out" upon the cross and "sprinkled" upon the hearts of his people. The office of John was to preach this purification, to call to repentance in order to its reception, and to symbolize the purifying power of this blood declared to be "poured out" and "sprinkled" by *pouring out* or *sprinkling* pure water upon the penitent, 229–231.

JOHN, THE FORERUNNER PREACHER :

Wickliffe was the "Forerunner of the Reformation," because he preached its doctrines. John was the Forerunner of his Lord, because he preached his doctrines. John preached a "baptism" (Acts 10 : 37) = a thorough change of condition ; but this expresses an incomplete idea. He preached further (Acts 13 : 24), ("βάπτισμα μετανοίας), the baptism of *repentance ;*" here the idea is completed by the appended genitive, which makes particular an otherwise very general term ; it is a *repentance* baptism, such a thoroughly changed spiritual condition as repentance effects. But this does not exhaust the doctrinal preaching of the Fore-

runner. He preaches (Luke 3 : 3) an ulterior baptism, one beyond that of repentance, and of which repentance is the forerunner (as John of Christ), namely, "βάπτισμα μετανοίας εἰς ἀφεσιν ἁμαρτιων, the baptism effected by repentance *into* the remission of sins" —that thoroughly changed condition of the soul by the pardon of sin into which the repenting pass, through the grace of the Lamb of God which taketh away the sin of the world. This completed the limited but grandly sufficient preaching of the Forerunner. This preaching was embodied, in its purifying character, in a visible symbol applied to those who received the preaching, 248–267 ; John was no more sent to preach a ritual baptism than was Paul, 250–253 ; Baptist Bible translation of Mark 1 : 4, 253, 4 ; the baptism which John preached and the baptism which John administered was one and the same baptism ; in the one case requiring by words a thorough change in the condition of the soul by repentance securing the full remission of sins, and in the other case exhibiting the purity thus preached in a visible symbol the bearing of which was declared in a brief formula of words, 407.

JOHN, ὁ βαπτιστής :

= ὁ βαπτίζων, 252 ; his knowledge of βαπτίζω and its sources, 91 ; organized nothing, left Jewish economy and family

cidate but fails in analogy. "Inclosed," "swallowed up," carry with them the idea of consequent harm, oppression, destruction, and will apply to a limited use of βαπτίζω, as when applied to objects baptized in the sea, etc. The Egyptians, horses and chariots, were inclosed, "swallowed up," in the sea; Jerusalem is spoken of as being "swallowed up" in a yawning gulf; such cases present adequate resemblance to cases of ships and their crews baptized and perishing in the depths of the sea. Some resemblance might be claimed between cases where "priest and prophet" are said to be "swallowed up by wine" (Isaiah 28 : 7), and men "baptized by wine," but the cases differ. "Priest and prophet" are represented as *harmed, ruined*, in moral character by wine, this is a just analogical use of "swallowed up;" but it is not the use of baptized; this word does not represent the wine-drinker as harmed, ruined, but simply as thoroughly under the influence of wine in its physical characteristic. And this is the just analogical use of βαπτίζω. The difference between these forms of expression will be more strikingly seen by reference to their New Testament use. "The Egyptians essaying to pass through the sea *were swallowed up* (καταπίνω)," Heb. 11 : 29. "The devil, as a roaring lion, seeketh whom he may

swallow up" (1 Peter 5 : 8). here in literal use harm, destruction, stand out in bold relief; "Death is *swallowed up* into victory" (1 Cor. 15 : 54), "That mortality might be *swallowed up* by life" (2 Cor. 5 : 4), "Lest such an one *should be swallowed up* by overmuch sorrow" (2 Cor. 2 : 7): here the use beyond literal application justifies itself by alliance with the element of *harm, destruction*. But "harm and destruction" do not constitute the fundamental ideas of βαπτίζω in literal use, but a full development of the characteristic of the element and the communication of such characteristic to the objects placed within such element or in such other relation to it as will secure the same result. Therefore the Scriptures represent the soul as baptized "*into repentance,*" "into *the remission of sins,*" "into *Christ,*" "into *his death,*" always with the farthest possible remove from the idea of "harm," "destruction," and always vindicating a just analogical use, by developing and communicating the characteristic of its adjunct. Βαπτίζω εἰς in the New Testament does always express a thorough change of condition, the passing into a new state of life or experience; but *swallowed up* into repentance, *swallowed up* into the remission of sins, will only express the passing into a new life of repentance and